CW01501193

TOTAL
UNDERSEA
WAR

TOTAL
UNDERSEA
WAR

THE EVOLUTIONARY ROLE OF THE SNORKEL
IN DÖNITZ'S U-BOAT FLEET, 1944–1945

Aaron S. Hamilton

Seaforth
PUBLISHING

For submariners the world over.
They all face the same enemy … the unyielding pressure of the ocean's depths.

Frontispiece: The German snorkel device revolutionised undersea warfare. The once surface-bound submersible was turned into a 'true' submarine capable of remaining submerged almost indefinitely. This late-war innovation frustrated Allied intelligence and anti-submarine search technology, well into the age of nuclear power. After World War II the snorkel was introduced by all navies around the world, most notably in the ever-expanding Soviet submarine force. In this photograph, Engineer Emil Hymowitz, Chief of the US Navy's Search Radar Unit, pilots a captured German snorkel mounted on a sub-simulator around the Chesapeake Bay, in 1956. The German snorkel was used to test out new radar search systems designed to locate a snorkeling submarine during the Cold War. *(Official US Navy Photo, Author's Collection)*

Copyright © Aaron S Hamilton 2020
First published in Great Britain in 2020 by
Seaforth Publishing,
A division of Pen & Sword Books Ltd,
47 Church Street,
Barnsley S70 2AS
www.seaforthpublishing.com

British Library Cataloguing in Publication Data
A catalogue record for this book is available from the British Library

ISBN 978 1 5267 7880 2 (hardback)
ISBN 978 1 5267 7881 9 (epub)
ISBN 978 1 5267 7882 6 (kindle)

Pen & Sword Books Limited incorporates the imprints of Atlas, Archaeology, Aviation, Discovery, Family History, Fiction, History, Maritime, Military, Military Classics, Politics, Select, Transport, True Crime, Air World, Frontline Publishing, Leo Cooper, Remember When, Seaforth Publishing, The Praetorian Press, Wharncliffe Local History, Wharncliffe Transport, Wharncliffe True Crime and White Owl

Maps by Peter Wilkinson
Designed and typeset by Stephen Dent

Printed and bound in Great Britain by TJ International Ltd, Padstow

Contents

Part III A Case Study in U-Boat History and Maritime Archaeology
305

Acknowledgements

This book was a six-year research project that spanned two continents, four countries, nearly a dozen libraries, as well as public and private archives. I read every surviving U-boat war diary, known as Kriegstachbuch (KTB), of all snorkel-equipped U-boats that conducted a wartime patrol. All available German wartime technical documents that could be located were consulted. Allied Ultra intercepts for each snorkel-equipped U-boat were examined, as well as every available intelligence assessment of late war U-boat operations and technical development. More than a dozen interviews were conducted with maritime archaeologists, members of the dive community, researchers and even one of the few remaining members of the U-boat veteran community. I personally dived several snorkel-equipped U-boat wrecks. Yet, this book would never have been published without the support and encouragement of many individuals.

Chief among them is US Navy (Rtd) Captain Jerry Mason, who operates the online U-boat research website, www.uboatarchive.net. Jerry supported my work with enthusiasm from the very start and helped review hundreds of U-boat KTBs to identify snorkel installations and their configurations. Jerry selflessly provided primary documents from his extensive collection and offered his expertise to any questions I had. Without exception, Jerry's website is the single best source for primary documents about the Battle of the Atlantic on the internet. Royal Air Force Air Commodore Derek Waller (Rtd) contributed significantly by sharing his years of dogged archival investigation into late war U-boat dispositions. Derek also identified significant sources of primary documents from the Public Records Office and Gosport Archives that were critical to this study. Dr Axel Niestlé, a noted U-boat authority, graciously reviewed several early chapters and offered important corrections. Maritime archeologist Dr Innes McCartney surveyed more snorkel-equipped U-boat wreck sites than perhaps anyone in the world. He provided details about the configuration of various U-boat wrecks he investigated over his career. Despite *U-869* being a well-worn topic, John Chatterton answered a series of nuanced questions about the wreck site. His answers revealed previously unpublished details that helped to place this U-boat's demise into historical context. Retired US Navy diver Brian O'Connor provided insight on the evaluation of internal explosions on wreck sites gained from years of surveying the USS *Arizona* that were useful in constructing the *U-869* case study. Fred Engle, a former US Navy submariner with first-hand experience of post-war snorkel operations, provided critical feedback and advice while reading many of the early chapter drafts.

My trip to the Deutsches U-boot Museum and Archive in Cuxhaven served to finalise research for this book. This trip's success was due to the gracious support of Frau Annemarie Bredow, Peter Schulz, and especially Rainer Stührenberg, who located a trove of relevant snorkel documents that my research required.

Many others contributed research and assistance along the way, including Kai Steenbuck, Arthur O. Bauer, Fritz Deters, Dr Zdzisław J Kapera, Michael LoCicero, Ed Gosling, Paul Meriam, the late Raul Diepeveen, and Trevor Yorke, who provided the technical sketches for this book. My editor, Julian Mannering, receives special mention as he embraced this project when others did not, and ultimately is responsible for bringing it to print. Most importantly, I must thank my family who has endured another book, and unending research trips.

Preface

The literature of the Battle of the Atlantic is dominated by histories of German U-boats that ravaged the US East Coast and fought the convoy battles in the mid-Atlantic, leading up to what is often characterised as their defeat during 'Black May' of 1943. Yet, the war against the U-boat continued for two more years. Histories that survey the final year of the war are universally dismissive of the U-boat's continued effort in the North Atlantic. They often focus instead on the threat of the Type XXI 'wonder weapon' U-boat that never conducted a single combat patrol. Despite the distorted historiography of the last year of the Battle of the Atlantic, the U-boat survived and continued to pose a real threat against all German and Allied expectations.

The once surface-bound diesel-electric U-boat, guided by the vision of a few pioneering German naval engineers, ushered in the age of 'Total Undersea War' with the introduction of an air mast – or 'snorkel' – as it became known among the men who served in Admiral Karl Dönitz's submarine fleet. These U-boats no longer surfaced to charge their batteries or refresh their air. They rarely communicated back to their command, operating silently and alone. These U-boats and their crews remained submerged continuously for a few days at first, then a few weeks, and finally for months at a time. German U-boats became the living embodiment of Jules Verne's vision of Nemo's *Nautilus*. The snorkel-equipped U-boat foreshadowed the untrackable weapon and instrument of intelligence the submarine became in the post-war world.

By the autumn of 1944 the sinking of Allied ships was up and the loss of U-boats down to the lowest point at any time in the prior eighteen months. U-boats rarely sent wireless messages as they remained submerged almost their entire patrol. Their silence diminished Ultra's value. Allied intelligence grew concerned and struggled to meet this new threat as U-boat operations shifted from the deep water of the mid-Atlantic to the shallow waters of the English and Irish coasts. Soon, an entire second wave of U-boats was sent against North America for the first time in more than two years.

The snorkel was universally accepted by German U-boat crews, contrary to the inaccurate depictions of the device in post-war histories. The snorkel dominated all subsequent technical and tactical innovation in the German U-boat fleet when it was introduced in the autumn of 1943. It alone drove the shift in operations from the mid-Atlantic to Allied coasts that fundamentally evolved U-boat tactics and procedures. Its importance was greater to submarine development than the new Type XXI electro-boat that proved operationally irrelevant without a snorkel – a fact recognised by the Kriegsmarine. After the war Allied naval leadership conceded that the snorkel was more successful than anyone predicted. This German wartime innovation was copied immediately and remains a critical feature on every submarine produced the world over.

Much of the archival data used in this book is new. Some was declassified in the last several decades, while other material was in misidentified files, or simply not catalogued. The result is that *Total Undersea War* is more than a chronological history of the final year of the Battle of the Atlantic.

This book serves as a reference guide to the snorkel-equipped U-boats that operated near the coasts of the United Kingdom and North America. Every snorkel configuration is exhaustively detailed. How U-boat commanders employed new technology and evolved submerged tactics is revealed for the first time in print. This operational and technical data offers a new perspective for maritime archeologists as to why many snorkel-equipped U-boats met their fate the way the way they did in the age of Total Undersea War.

Aaron S. Hamilton
Fairfax, Virginia
2020

Introduction

The combination of Allied cryptologists breaking the Kriegsmarine Enigma cipher known generally as Ultra, microwave radar detection, and escort carrier-based Allied air power, rendered surface-bound German U-boats and their Wolfpack tactics ineffective by 1943. Dönitz needed to evolve his U-boats and their tactics if he intended to continue to carry on the Battle of the Atlantic in any form.

Up to this point in the war U-boat survivability was predicated on depth. This had worked well when U-boats were primarily engaged by Allied surface forces and could dive deeper than the settings of depth charges. By 1943, however, U-boats were predominantly being located and sunk on the surface by escort carriers and land-based Allied aircraft. This was because U-boats had to operate on the surface to obtain the air needed to run their diesel engines and recharge their batteries, send wireless signals to co-ordinate during convoy attacks, and to be able to manoeuvre quickly when convoys were located. Dönitz needed a way to overcome the challenge of Allied airpower, otherwise his U-boats were no longer viable operationally. If no solution was found, any hope of continuing the Battle of the Atlantic was over.

Salvation came in the form of a letter from a private U-boat engineer, Dr Hellmuth Walter, who served as Dönitz's chief innovator, at the height of U-boat destruction known as the 'Black May' of 1943. He proposed a novel concept to equip U-boats with an 'air mast' designed to allow them to recharge their batteries without surfacing and proceed on full diesels while submerged, thereby limiting their time exposed to Allied radar and aircraft. While U-Boat Command, known as *Befehlshaber der U-Boote* (BdU), was not aware that the Allies had broken their Enigma cipher, U-boats that employed the 'air mast' would no longer send regular, frequent wireless signals back to Germany. This 'air mast', soon to be termed *Schnorchel* (hereafter referred to as snorkel), also had the secondary, though unintended, effect of limiting the effectiveness of Allied decryption efforts in the last year of war.[1]

While not part of the May 1943 proposal, it was the 'air mast' that drove two additional initiatives. Months after the introduction of the snorkel it was realised that something had to be done to coat the exposed portion of the upper snorkel mast and intake to obscure it from Allied radar. This initiative was known as *Schornsteinfeger* (Chimney Sweep).[2] As operations developed based on the use of the snorkel, tactics evolved, and U-boats no longer utilised depth as a means of survivability as they once did. U-boats now returned to the shallows off Allied coasts and cruised with near impunity offshore. The requirement to surface was now gone and with it the fear of detection by Allied aircraft. Once detected by Allied surface anti-submarine vessels (ASV) in the shallows, U-boat captains learned to hide below thermal layers and bottom among the uneven features of rocky coastal sea floors in order to throw off Allied sonar, known as ASDIC. In order to help U-boats in this regard, the snorkel gave new life to an older initiative to coat U-boats in rubber, thereby reducing their sonar return against ASDIC. This initiative was known as Alberich.[3] These two initiatives were designed to provide an enhanced form of stealth to the new snorkel-retrofitted U-boat fleet, though only *Schornsteinfeger* entered widespread operational use.[4]

These developments were part of Walter's singular vision to enable submarines to range the oceans undetected. It was his *Ortungskampf* concept – 'battle of location' – he championed during the war. If a U-boat could not be located, then it could never be attacked. This concept remains the basis of all submarine operations to this day.

The introduction of the snorkel proved an unqualified success. The phrase 'Total Undersea War' was in regular use by Dönitz and BdU by November 1944, just a few short months after the snorkel's introduction. During a meeting with his senior operations staff in Berlin on 24 February 1945, Dönitz articulated the transformative role of the snorkel while recounting the various operational shifts of the U-boat war up to that point. Prior to the introduction of the snorkel the U-boat 'was weaker than the enemy' Dönitz noted. However, he concluded that:

These conditions have now changed fundamentally. The snorkel has almost completely made even the old submarine type to an *underwater vessel* [emphasis added]. Its weakness [on the surface] is no longer relevant, it no longer needs to surface. Weeks' long patrols are carried out with no or only a few hours on the surface. The U-boat can again fight and be successful in the most strongly monitored areas, where for years it could not even survive. It can again bring all its beneficial properties into force, features against which the formidable naval power of the Anglo-Saxons is essentially powerless because they rule on the [surface] and in the air above the water, but not under the water.

With the perfect underwater vessel a turning point in naval warfare [has occurred].[5]

Even at war's end the British Royal Navy and US Navy officers alike continued to struggle with their inability to effectively track, locate and destroy U-boats in the age of Dönitz's 'Total Undersea War'.

The last year of the Battle of Atlantic was very different than the first five years due to the introduction of the snorkel. Gone were the days when U-boats massed in Wolfpack formations during the convoy battles that raged across the North Atlantic. Now single U-boats stalked quietly close to shore as lone wolves. Their hunting grounds were no longer the deep blue ocean over the mid-Atlantic ridge, but the ports of embarkation and debarkation used by ships before or after the convoys formed. U-boats cruised the narrow choke points around the United Kingdom from the English Channel to the Irish Sea for the first time since 1940; they returned to Canada's St Lawrence River for the first time in two years; and in a final act of desperation U-boat Command sent nearly twenty U-boats to operate off the US East Coast in 1945. This latter group prowled the approaches off Boston, New York City, the entrance to the Delaware River, Cape Hatteras and all points in between. Each individual U-boat captain was now authorised to search out and find their own hunting grounds as operational considerations dictated. Not since the spring of 1942 – nearly three years earlier – did so many U-boats cruise the North American coast from Newfoundland to the Florida Straits. This renewed offensive against North America sparked a wave of fear from Boston to Washington DC over the possibility that these U-boats were being sent to launch modified V1 rockets against American cities in a final wave of terror that foreshadowed the future threat of the ballistic missile submarine.[6]

The single greatest difference in the period of 1944–45 from that of 1939–43 was that by using a retrofitted snorkel, U-boats remained submerged for fifty to seventy days, setting human endurance records that surprised Dönitz and the Allies alike.[7] These records were not surpassed until the introduction of nuclear-powered submarines decades later. The physiological strain under which U-boat crews operated, despite the increasingly technical skills required to function in an underwater environment where sound dictated each tactical decision, has gone largely ignored in post-war histories. By remaining underwater they did not send wireless signals as transmissions from a snorkelling U-boat proved problematic. This reduced the effectiveness of Ultra, which was the single greatest Allied asset in the war against U-boats. The Allies might know where BdU directed a U-boat to operate, but there was often no radio confirmation from the U-boats that they were there. In the last twelve months of war the Allies were increasingly unable to fix U-boat locations as they ran silent. Patrick Beesly, who served as the Deputy Chief of the Admiralty's Submarine Plotting Room during the Second World War and who was responsible for exploiting the decrypted U-boat signals through Ultra, wrote after the war:

> A new situation arose in the second half of 1944. There was then a reversion to individual operations with considerable latitude left to the U-boat commanding officer. This called for far less signalling, and as this phase coincided with the almost universal fitting of the Snorkel, aircraft sightings and attacks also fell almost to zero. Information from cryptanalysis, direction-finding, and aircraft decreased alarmingly ...[8]

It is not surprising that in the last year of war many U-boats went completely undetected by the Allies, causing significant confusion in post-war loss assessments. Staying submerged also meant the effectiveness of Allied airpower lost its status as the primary U-boat killer it had enjoyed just a year earlier.

Often operating in depths of less than 40m when hunted by Allied ASVs, U-boat captains no longer needed to run for deep water as in the past. New tactical guidelines were issued that directed U-boats to move even closer inshore when hunted, where they 'bottomed out' and waited for their pursuers to tire of the chase and end the hunt. Even experienced Allied U-boat hunters found it difficult to locate their prey in shallow coastal waters where uneven bottoms, varying thermoclines and density layers significantly reduced the effectiveness of sonar. To paraphrase, 'do the opposite of what the pursuer expected', was the guidance issued by BdU and it worked. The outdated diesel U-boat fleet had not only survived in the wake of 'Black May', but they had resumed the offensive despite all expectations.

In June 1943, a few months after Dönitz authorised the development of the snorkel as a defensive means of survivability for his diesel U-boats, he authorised priority production of a new electric-powered Type XXI U-boat design that he believed would allow his U-boat fleet to resume Wolfpack tactics in the mid-Atlantic with devastating effect. This design offered high-underwater speed to allow the new Type XXI to close with convoys under-water, thus reducing their detectability on the surface by aircraft.

High-underwater speed had been pursued by Walter since the early 1930s but remained elusive until the latter half of the war. However, the

Electro-boat was defeated before its design even left the drawing table. The Electro-boat suffered from the same critical vulnerability of its diesel predecessor, namely that it needed to remain surfaced to recharge its batteries. For the Electro-boat, this was an even more acute concern given the significant increase in the size of its battery banks that were the key to its high underwater speed and endurance.

The original design plans for the Electro-boats included no snorkel, because the snorkel was not invented yet. Once the snorkel was operationalised in the diesel U-boat fleet, Dönitz decided not to redesign the Electro-boats with an integrated snorkel, but rather to retrofit it after assembly in order to avoid production delays. This was an inevitable, yet problematic, decision made under the wartime circumstances.

The snorkel design, retrofitted into the existing prefabricated hull sections, proved to be the technical Achilles heel in the Electro-boat during the war. Allied intelligence recognised that the Electro-boat inherently was not a concern, but an Electro-boat equipped with a snorkel was. US Navy Captain Kenneth Knowles served as Head, Atlantic Section, Combat Intelligence on the Staff of Commander-in-Chief, US Navy during the war. He was solely responsible for analysing the intercepted and decoded German U-boat wireless traffic decrypted through Ultra. He concluded after the war:

> Historians generally consider the turning point in the Battle of the Atlantic came after the summer of 1943, following the sinking of some 90 U-boats … After that period we certainly had the distinct edge, especially since the Germans had lost so many of their experienced U-boat captains. However, in the background was emerging a whole new ball game: a fleet developing of highly sophisticated Type XXI 1,600-tonners and smaller Type XXIII U-boats, with new snorkels, permitting underwater speeds exceeding most of our escorts. Once these boats became operational, it would be touch-and-go all over again …
>
> It was providential that the periscope/snorkel vibration problem of the new U-boats so delayed their development that but one Type XXI 1,600-tonner became operational by the German surrender.[9]

Even with the introduction of a new revolutionary streamlined U-boat design with increased battery capacity that set the stage for all submarine development in the post-war era, it was the snorkel that was required to operationalise the design, and ultimately the snorkel that delayed its deployment before war's end.

Post-war myth-making has trumped historical reality in some cases, especially regarding the prowess of the new Electro-boat concept. The Type XXI is often lauded as a 'war-winning U-boat design' by authors who claim that if it had just entered service in large numbers earlier in the war it could have changed Germany's fortunes.[10] While the Type XXI was revolutionary in its streamlining and increased underwater endurance and performance, it suffered from critical design flaws and troublesome craftsmanship, specifically with its snorkel apparatus. This forced U-boat Command to plan on a complete redesign of its superstructure to replace the telescoping mast with a folding one. The operational impact of a Type XXI Wolfpack unleashed into the North Atlantic is pure conjecture given the technical struggles the new design faced and the reality that submerged communication was not yet operationally possible. Without frequent wireless communication, there could be no Wolfpack, a fact too often neglected by historians of the period. In the final analysis it was the snorkel more than any other invention of the U-boat war that evolved what was a surface-based submersible into an underwater submarine and guided post-war development in navies worldwide.

As many wrecks of snorkel-equipped U-boats and their victims from the 1944–45 period can be located in relatively shallow water, it is through the understanding of the snorkel's technical development and the evolving operations and tactics in U-boat warfare that many questions of post-war maritime history can be answered. If a thorough understanding of snorkel operations existed twenty or even thirty years ago, there would be no question why *U-853* (IXC/40) was operating in shallow water off Rhode Island in May 1945. It was not because this U-boat's captain was looking for an 'Iron Cross' as so many in the dive community still opine given what they view as an audacious, near suicidal attack on the SS *Black Point*, so close to the coast in the last days of the war. *U-853* was simply following the new standard operating procedures. It was also not the last U-boat to fire the final torpedo of the war off the US East Coast. The identity of *U-869* (IXC/40), found off New Jersey and originally dubbed *U-Who?*, should have been identified almost immediately and its potential demise might still not be under debate. Despite its status as a National Marine Protected Area, the story of the *U-1105* 'Black Panther' is far from accurate or complete. As one of the best-preserved representations of technical evolution of 'Total Undersea War' embodied in its snorkel and rubberised anti-acoustic coating known as Alberich, *U-1105*'s brief wartime career has often been lauded as confirmation of its stealth properties embodied in Alberich. However, a careful review of the historical record suggests it was its snorkel and new underwater tactics that were more important.[11] The introduction of the snorkel operationalised Alberich, and even this latter technical develop-

U-995 (VIIC/41) in Laboe, Germany, 2017. Unfortunately, this U-boat inaccurately depicts a late-war snorkel-equipped VIIC. The starboard-side snorkel trunking and the GHG Balkon are missing, as both were removed when it was turned into a museum display in the 1970s. The piston and snorkel mast are not original. The snorkel locking mechanism on the port side of the conning tower as well as its protective cladding was also removed. The inaccurate *U-995* combined with the fictitious 'Type VIIC 1944' plan published in numerous U-boat histories have sowed confusion among historians, maritime archeologists and model makers alike as to how a snorkel-equipped Type VIIC was actually configured. *(Author's collection)*

ment remains obscured. For example, *U-480* (VIIC) is often cited as the first 'operational' Alberich-covered U-boat, a claim that does not stand up against the documented historical record.

This book was written with the primary purpose of providing a long-overdue context to the technical and tactical evolution that shaped late-war U-boat operations through a comprehensive review of all related primary documents. This evolution is extended into the post-war period to show the impact it had on modern submarine warfare the world over. Additionally, this work is intended to be an empirical guide to snorkel-equipped U-boats that can be used by maritime archeologists to assist in the identification of yet-to-be discovered wrecks of Dönitz's U-boats in European and North American coastal waters without the surprise, confusion, or speculation that often comes with such a discovery. There is no greater discriminator of a U-boat wreck identification than the snorkel. It can be used to identify a U-boat's classification and assist in placing it in an operational time and place.[12]

Chapter 1

The U-Boat War in 1939–1944

Germany possessed few U-boats when war broke out in September 1939 following the Wehrmacht's invasion of Poland. There was a total of thirty Type II (250-ton) 'Coastal Boats', eighteen Type VII (500-ton) and eight Type I and IX (750-ton) 'Atlantic Boats' that were either commissioned or would be commissioned within weeks. There were only a few trained crews with limited operational experience. This low level of readiness was a by-product of the Treaty of Versailles. The first German U-boat constructed since the First World War was launched in 1933.

The Anglo-German Naval Agreement of 1935 authorised the construction of 'submarines' equal in tonnage to that of Great Britain, without surpassing the ratio of 35:100 in terms of actual vessels. The U-boat arm was not ready for war in 1939. Yet, by the war's end German U-boats operated in nearly every ocean of the world. In the waters off the United Kingdom and the United States they could be found conducting what they termed 'Total Undersea Warfare'. New technology and tactics employed in the last twelve months of the war set the evolutionary direction of submarine warfare followed by all post-war navies.

At the start of the Second World War U-boats deployed around the British Isles and its western approaches, just as they had in the First World War. Unlike that conflict, Dönitz planned to pursue a tonnage war that sought to mass U-boats against convoys, rejecting the guerre de course (commerce raiding) pursued by the Imperial German Navy. What became known as Wolfpack tactics were tried towards the end of the naval war of 1914–18, but they had proved ineffective due to inadequate communication equipment that did not allow for centralised U-boat co-ordination. This situation changed with the development of high-powered shortwave radios in the 1930s that permitted long-distance wireless communication between U-boats and BdU. U-Boats could now effectively co-ordinate their actions when a convoy was engaged and receive real-time orders from BdU.[1] While the use of wireless communication to control U-boats was a main enabler of the Wolfpack, it also served as a critical component of its demise. High-frequency direction finding (HF/DF) by fixed, shored-based stations, and mounted on Allied vessels afloat, allowed for general fixing of U-boat positions when they sent communications. British and US cryptologists eventually cracked the Enigma cipher and read much – but not all – of the two-way communications through the Ultra programme. This latter capability, considered Top Secret by the Allies, allowed the British to defensively redirect convoys around screening lines while the US tended to use the information offensively to vector anti-submarine warfare (ASW) assets to attack the U-boats. Dönitz never suspected that the code was broken during the war and his U-boats and their operational effectiveness suffered accordingly.

U-boat combat operations began almost immediately in October 1939 with the deployment of five U-boats in the western approaches to the British Isles. The application of BdU's tonnage warfare concept was interrupted by the campaign for Norway that brought U-boats into coastal areas for defensive operations against the Royal Navy during April 1940. The ability of U-boats to operate in coastal conditions was lost on U-boat Command as they managed a crisis in torpedo misfiring that shook the U-boat arm's confidence. This crisis highlighted a side of Dönitz repeated at every crisis during the war – resilience and perseverance in the face of adversity. He pushed his men and machines beyond what many would consider acceptable today. Dönitz had a choice. He could recall his U-boats to port until the issue of faulty torpedo firings was resolved or he could send them out to sea and work the problem in parallel. He always chose to take the fight to the enemy and maintain offensive pressure. His overriding belief that U-boats could affect the course of war overrode all concerns voiced by his subordinates. 'I cannot leave the boats idle,' he stated, 'without causing incalculable harm to the U-boat arm. As long as there is the smallest prospect of hits, operations must continue …'.[2] Dönitz's perseverance paid off as technical issues with the torpedoes' depth setting and pistol mechanisms were fixed and his U-boats began to prove their worth.

At the outbreak of war, the U-boat arm operated under the Prize Regulations that allowed only certain military classes of vessels to be sunk without warning, while others had to be stopped and warned first. There were several reasons for this, the primary one being that Hitler did not want to bring the US into the war as Germany's unrestricted submarine warfare had done during the First World War. By early 1940 zones were established around the British Isles. After an announcement to neutral countries of the

German intention to allow U-boats to attack without warning in May 1940, the first step towards unrestricted submarine warfare was taken. After the US entered the war in 1941 it was practised by all nations that operated submarines.

Operations so close to the coast became problematic, especially with the increased use of British air power that often spotted and attacked surfaced U-boats. With the fall of France the prospect of conducting a war in the Atlantic Ocean beyond the reach of land-based Allied aircraft become a reality. U-boats could now operate from Atlantic bases on the French coast and launch directly into the North Atlantic, where it was possible to remain on station for more than a month. The Wolfpack tactics envisioned by Dönitz finally manifested themselves with deadly effect in the North Atlantic between the second half of 1940 until the end of 1941. It was during this period that U-boats enjoyed what became known as the first 'Happy Time' as Allied merchant losses were exponential compared with U-boat losses. The tonnage war Dönitz envisioned since his days as a U-boat commander in the First World War went into full swing.

Allied countermeasures, and by 'Allied' it is meant British and Canadian, from 1939 to the end of 1941, became increasingly more sophisticated. The convoy system was introduced in 1940. The number of frigates increased, and aircraft protection was organised close to the coast. President Roosevelt, with approval of Congress, provided the Royal Navy with fifty First World War-era destroyers in March 1941 and the US Navy began to take over escort duties west of Greenland, allowing the Royal Navy to deploy more escorts into the convoy routes, especially around the danger areas along the western approaches. On 9 May 1941 the British boarded *U-110* after bringing the boat to the surface during a depth charge attack and captured an intact three-rotor Enigma machine as well as associated code books. This helped enable British cryptologists to break the Kriegsmarine's naval codes under the code name Ultra. Also, in May the Type 271 search radar was fitted onto Royal Navy ships, allowing for the detection of a surfaced U-boat at 3,500 yards and a periscope at 900 yards. This was the first operational microwave radar set. Operating on a 10cm wavelength, it proved deadly effective at finding U-boats in all weather conditions, day or night. In July 1941 high-frequency detection-finding equipment known as 'Huff Duff' (HF/DF) was used to triangulate on the wireless communications coming from the spotter U-boat that first detected a convoy and began its shadowing duties to direct the rest of the Wolfpack. This enabled the British to attack the U-boat, thereby breaking its contact with the convoy as it changed direction to evade the Allied destroyer. By the end of 1940 Royal Air Force (RAF) Coastal Command aircraft began being equipped with the

ASV II (Air-to-Surface Vessel) radar that could detect a surfaced U-boat at ranges of up to 58km. It could not detect a U-boat accurately at a range of less than 1.6km, its only drawback. The introduction of new Allied countermeasures and tactics in the spring of 1941 brought the end of what the U-boat crews came to call the first 'Happy Time'.

The U-boat's greatest nemesis since the start of the war was an Allied destroyer equipped with Allied Submarine Detection Investigation Committee devices (ASDIC) and depth charges. Introduced in the First World War, ASDIC used audible and ultrasonic sound waves to detect underwater contacts. ASDIC transmitted sound energy, a so-called ping, from a hull-mounted transducer and received an echo or a return from a submerged object. In order to defeat this Allied capability U-boats adopted the tactic of night surface attacks, because ASDIC could not detect a submarine operating on the surface. Prior to August 1941, U-boats also had standing orders to avoid attacking convoy escorts. They were to focus instead on merchant shipping.

The early technical response of the Kriegsmarine to the growing threat of ASDIC was to pursue two early forms of stealth development that had the potential to obfuscate a submerged U-boat's location to Allied ASVs, thereby giving it time to escape. These two initiatives were known as Alberich and Bold. Alberich was a 4mm thick layer of rubber that initially was attuned to reduce Allied ASDIC returns at depths greater than 120m. Initial experiments were difficult to evaluate, in part because of the impact of salinity content and temperature. *U-67* (IXC) received a coating in April 1941, but the failure to master the adhesive process caused the project to be abandoned temporarily.[3] Bold was a 10cm container with positive buoyancy filled with calcium hydride. It was launched from the torpedo tube of a submerged U-boat and floated to a depth of 30m, producing hydrogen bubbles intended to provide a false target for ASDIC. This simple innovation went into production and was fitted to U-boats starting in 1942.

The Kriegsmarine also pursued the increase of a U-boat's diving depth to increase survivability. In 1941 a U-boat's main killer was the pressure wave sent by exploding depth charges that could lead to a catastrophic hull breech. The Royal Navy understood that U-boats could only dive to a certain depth and they set their depth charges accordingly. The German thinking was that if a U-boat could dive deeper than the maximum setting of a depth charge it would be likely to survive an attack and escape. More importantly, deeper-diving U-boats did not need Alberich. The decision was made to modify the pressure hull of the VIIC, which had become the workhorse of the U-boat fleet, without interfering with its serial production.[4]

German naval engineers believed that a U-boat's diving depth could be increased by 20 per cent without compromising the boat's stability. Advances in electronics since the mid-1930s allowed the U-boat builders to scale down the electrical and radio equipment in the vessel, reducing its weight by 115 tons. They replaced the extra saved weight with a thicker, thus heavier, pressure hull. The thickness of the standard pressure hull was increased by 2.5mm, from 18.5 to 21mm. This added 10 tons without a significant impact to the ballast. The diving depth of a Type VIIC increased from 100 to 120m, the test diving depth from 150 to 180m, and the calculated destruction depth from 250 to 300m. A side benefit was that a thicker pressure hull offered added protection from a possible catastrophic rupture.[5] This allowed a VIIC to dive to a maximum depth of 300m, effectively below what was believed to be the maximum depth of an Allied depth charge. This modification to the Type VIIC became known as the VIIC/41 due to the first contracts being issued in October 1941, the year the design was approved.

The VIIC/41, however, never realised the benefits of its modification. By the time this design entered service in large numbers the convoy battles of the mid-Atlantic were over. The VIIC/41s were employed primarily in the shallow coastal waters around England, mitigating the main benefit of a deep-diving U-boat. It is also a fact that outside any technical design documents of the Kriegsmarine, the operational records of the BdU, as well as post-war assessments of the Royal and US Navies, made no distinction in terms of nomenclature between the VIIC and VIIC/41. The VIIC/41 was simply called a VIIC, which also confirms how technically alike these two U-boat variants were. As the post-war assessment of U-boat design models by the US Navy Technical Mission Europe concluded: 'This class was identical with the VIIC except that it was given a pressure hull of heavier steel …'.[6] There is nothing outwardly unique in appearance that distinguishes a VIIC/41 from the VIIC.

Operation *Paukenschlag* (Drumbeat) began on 12 January 1942 and lasted until 19 July of that same year.[7] The density in traffic between New York and Cape Hatteras was immense, with between 120 and 130 vessels requiring escort protection each day. Most of these vessels were oil tankers transiting from the refineries in the Caribbean to their destinations along the US East Coast and Europe. Known also as the 'Tanker War', *Paukenschlag* was an important, but temporary excursion for Dönitz from the main theatre of the North Atlantic. Dönitz saw this as a component to his overall campaign. He referred to this operation later in the war as the way that U-boats defended Germany on 'America's shores'.[8] The first five U-boats that came across the Atlantic opened what became the second 'Happy Time' due to the ill-prepared defences along the US East Coast and

Canada. Once the US convoy system was introduced and the US Coast Guard and Navy assets became more proficient in hunting U-boats, BdU ended operations off America with the caveat that '… henceforth it was our intention to send only single boats there occasionally, and perhaps to lay mines off the ports.'[9]

The battle in the North Atlantic continued unabated during 1942. As U-boat losses slowly mounted, Kriegsmarine engineers sought new ways to improve U-boat survivability. In the summer of 1942 existing U-boats were starting to receive Metox receivers. This was an acknowledgement by the Germans that the Allies were finding their U-boats on the surface by radar with increased efficiency. Both the Type VIIC/41 and Metox were incremental steps applied to an already outdated submarine design. Dönitz believed that the Wolfpack tactics would continue for some time and decided to modify the VIIC design yet again in pursuit of an even deeper diving capability. Unlike the interim-VIIC/41, this was going to be a true evolutionary step. The decision to increase a U-boat's diving depth was again driven by the fact that depth charges were the U-boats' primary killer.[10] Unlike the interim VIIC/41, which saw no external modifications, the next VIIC was longer and wider. It had to be to accommodate the increased weight of the pressure hull in order to effectively double the diving depth to a proposed destruction depth of 500m and allowing for standard operations at around 300m. The length was planned to increase to 68.73m and the beam to 6.7m. With a pressure hull of 28mm, the normal steel (St 52 KM) could not be used and a new tempered steel (armour plating) had to be employed. The pressure hull was increased by 5mm.[11] The VIIC/42 used the same engines, with the exception that they were supercharged to get the performance of the larger ocean-going Type IX U-boats. Along with its size, its cruising range was increased as the operational area now spanned the whole of the North and South Atlantic with U-boats operating into the Caribbean, the Gulf of Mexico and off the coasts of South America and Africa. This new design was called the Type VIIC/42 after the year the design was approved. Keels were laid, but unlike the VIIC/41, none were ever commissioned. The contracts for these boats were cancelled in July 1943 in favour of the forthcoming Type XXI Electro-boat design.

Increased diving depth was a defensive solution to a single Allied capability. A U-boat's primary weakness was that it still spent most of its time surfaced. A U-boat could only run its diesels while surfaced. It also ran on the surface in order to charge its batteries or gain the speed required to penetrate a convoy. Submerged, it could only use its batteries for a limited time and move at a significantly slower speed. A U-boat was also required to surface in order to send wireless signals to other members of the

Wolfpack or BdU. A U-boat had to be on or near the surface to observe Allied vessels, calculate a firing solution, and then launch a torpedo. The U-boat's required time on the surface in the mid-Atlantic thus began to prove its ultimate weakness.

As the war moved from the winter of 1942 into the spring of 1943 U-boats were still employing the same surfaced night-time offensive tactics against convoys as they had been for the past three years. The Allies, however, recognised this weakness and exploited it to a great extent through the introduction of the escort carrier that operationalised airborne radar and Ultra with devastating effect.

One of the most effective Allied innovations was the introduction of the S-Band airborne radar. Based on the magnetron transmitter tube, which entered operational service early in 1943, the British Mark III series, and the US SCR-717 and ASG, both proved capable of detecting surfaced U-boats at increased ranges. They also had the added benefit of immunity from the German radar detection device known as Metox that was deployed in mid-1942, eliminating any warning to U-boat crews. U-boats were now tracked by Ultra intercepts, and Allied ASW air assets vectored in from escort carriers to their radar returns and subsequently attacked. The North Atlantic was no longer the U-boat hunting ground it once was as losses increased with the start of 1943.

In response to increasing losses, Dönitz turned to his chief innovator, Dr Walter, and requested options to mitigate the various Allied threats to his U-boats, particularly air power. Dr Walter started Walter Werke in 1935 as a small engineering firm with an attached workshop. The focus of this firm was to continue the development of a hydrogen peroxide (H_2O_2) U-boat conceived by Walter in 1933 that could produce a high underwater speed. The hydrogen peroxide was to be produced in a stabilised form called Perhydrol and used in a closed-cycle engine.

The firm started with a single engineer. An initial proposal for a high-speed underwater U-boat was rejected by the Kriegsmarine in 1934. Walter was not deterred and expanded the firm in 1936. In 1937 he showed his plans to then Kapitän zur See Karl Dönitz, who commanded a U-boat training flotilla at that time. Dönitz was intrigued and ensured a development contract was issued. Walter was a visionary who impressed Dönitz. The connection between the two men was critical to Walter's designs becoming operational. As in most great endeavours, personal and professional relationships often drive innovation. Walter and Dönitz were neighbours during the interwar years, as Dönitz had lived in a house owned by the parents of Walter's wife. Their relationship continued to grow with the outbreak of war.

Shortly after the start of the war in 1939 Walter received an order from the Kriegsmarine to produce a single non-operational prototype U-boat that could achieve his claim of 25 knots submerged while still being controllable. The design also extended the underwater range on paper of any submarine operating at that time in any navy. More than just high speed, this was an evolutionary step from submersible to submarine. The hull was streamlined from the start and designed purely for underwater use. Dr Walter handpicked the staff to be employed in his firm. They were, what we might term today, 'out-of-the-box' thinkers. They were not stereotyped in their views. As an example, Herr Poschen who was assigned the task of designing hull resistance and the submerged control, was 'previously a designer of printing machines'.

The initial project was the V.80, termed for its displacement in tons. The next version was the V.300. Whereas the V.80 design was completely under the control of Walter Werke, the V.300 was designed in conjunction with Germaniawerft (GW) and the High Command of the German Navy. This distressed Walter, as his designers were forced to work with 'short-sighted' naval officers rooted in the 'old conceptions' of submarine design. This brought down the intended underwater speed of 26 knots to 19. So distressed was Walter that he approached Großadmiral Erich Raeder, who was chief of the Kriegsmarine at that time, and announced the project a failure.

Subsequently a new project began with the originally intended Walter Turbine. Two parallel programmes were established, the Wa201 (*U-792*) developed by Blohm & Voss and Wa201 (*U-793*) by Germaniawerft. The Blohm & Voss design proved better due to a longer hull and less beam. Both U-boats were designated Type XVII and deployed as school boats without torpedo tubes. Based on the assessment from the trials, Blohm & Voss received an order to produce six such U-boats but only three were completed: *U-1405*, *U-1406*, and *U-1407*. Two others, *U-1408* and *U-1409*, were badly damaged in air raids. A final one, *U-1410*, was transferred to Germaniawerft for closed-cycle engine testing. It was the Type XVII, which developed into the Type XXIII Electro-boat. As the Type XVII progressed, a larger version, the Type XVIII, was developed. This design was to have two 7,500hp turbines giving a shaft horsepower of 12,000. Originally the XVII was to have had two screws but Walter argued for just one, believing that the power could be maintained while saving space. Walter also thought the design was too big, while Admiral Dönitz believed it was required for Atlantic operations. The design never left the drawing board, but it became the basis for the Type XXI Electro-boat and the later Type XXVI. It was from Walter's work on these advanced designs for pure underwater submarines that many of his future technical solutions presented to Dönitz in the wake of 'Black May' were derived.

Walter had other supporters in the Kriegsmarine besides Dönitz. This included Vizeadmiral Hans-Georg von Friedeburg, who succeeded Dönitz as Commander U-boats in February 1943, and Chief of Engineering, Konteradmiral Otto 'Papa' Thedsen, who led the technical department on Dönitz's staff.[12] These were key relationships that ensured Walter not only had access to Dönitz, but could ensure compliance across the U-boat command of non-traditional ideas. It was not until 1943, when Dönitz was promoted to Großadmiral over the Kriegsmarine during the height of the Battle of the Atlantic, that military necessity trumped the traditionalists and was able to secure the required funding and priority for Walter to move his design ideas forward.

On 24 May, 1943 Dönitz suspended all offensive operations against North Atlantic convoys after losing thirty-one U-boats in the previous thirty days.[13] The percentage of kills that could be directly related to Allied aircraft reached over 60 per cent. It was an upward trend that had grown exponentially over the previous three months. Dönitz summarised the situation to Hitler on 31 May 1943 at the Berghof in Bavaria:

> The substantial increase of the enemy air force is the cause of the present crisis in submarine warfare … However, the simmering crisis would not have come about solely as a result of an increase in enemy aircraft. The determining factor is a new location device evidently also used by surface vessels, by means of which planes are now in a position to locate submarines … We must conserve our strength, otherwise we *will* play into the hands of the enemy.[14]

In the meeting Dönitz went on to explain to Hitler that he withdrew his U-boats from the North Atlantic to an area west of the Azores in the hope of encountering less air resistance. He outlined the steps he intended to take to re-equip his U-boats with weapon systems that could allow them to be effective again in the North Atlantic. Dönitz proposed the creation of a new radar interception set that would show the frequency used by the radar-equipped plane and would warn a U-boat of an impending attack. He spoke about how U-boats would be equipped at the beginning of June with the so-called 'Aphrodite' radar-jamming system. He also discussed the use of a new rubber coating around a U-boat's conning tower to absorb Allied radar waves. He did not use the term *Schornsteinfeger* in this discussion, but he did point out that the anti-radar reflection could reduce the conning tower's detectability by about 30 per cent or 'an enemy who was formerly able to detect the U-boat from a distance of 9,000m can now do so only from a distance of 3,000m'. Not one to offer only defensive solutions, Dönitz outlined how the U-boats' anti-aircraft armament was to be increased in calibre and a second aft gun deck would be added that became known as a '*Wintergarden*'. This is indicative of his thinking at that moment that his U-boats would still operate primarily surfaced. Two new torpedoes were also proposed. The LUT acoustic homing torpedo was effective against Allied merchant vessels operating at less than 12 knots, and the Zaunkönig torpedo could strike at Allied combat vessels manoeuvring at speeds of 18 knots.

Characteristically, Dönitz stated to Hitler: 'I am convinced that submarine warfare must be carried on, even if great successes are no longer possible. The forces tied up through submarine warfare were considerable, even during the world war.' Hitler interjected: 'there can be no talk of the let-up in submarine warfare. The Atlantic is my first line of defence in the West, and even if I have to fight a defensive battle there, that is preferable to waiting to defend myself on the coast of Europe. The enemy forces tied up by our summary warfare are tremendous, even though the actual losses inflicted by us are no longer great. I cannot afford to release these forces by discontinuing submarine warfare.'[15] Hitler and Dönitz shared the same perspective. As he noted several months later in August, 'whoever thinks he can do better than the Führer is a madman'.[16] The U-boat maintained this strategic purpose through to the end of the war, despite the operational and tactical hardships faced by the U-boat men.

Dönitz believed his U-boats could play a critical role in adversely affecting the Allied plans to invade the European continent. The BdU assessed in May 1943 that the Allies had only replaced about 50 per cent of the 30 million tons lost. Maintaining pressure on the North Atlantic was still paramount as an OKW assessment in August 1943 argued that while the Allies could land small forces with its transportation assets as they did during the amphibious invasion in North Africa, they did not possess enough for a large-scale invasion of mainland Europe. Once that was overcome, and a landing was made, then this put victory within the Allies 'grasp', making the need to continue U-boat operations 'essential' to deny the Allies their strategic naval operational capability.[17] The U-boat had to survive and had to take the fight back to the Allies.

Dönitz tackled the technical and tactical problems he faced in May 1943 with the same steadfastness he did during the torpedo crisis in the Norway campaign. Walter's innovations were critical to his effort and he did not disappoint Dönitz with his ideas.

Part I:

TECHNICAL INNOVATIONS

Chapter 2

The Snorkel

No other Kriegsmarine technical development during the Second World War had a greater impact on U-boat operations than the introduction of the 'air mast'. Termed Schnorchel by the Germans, 'snort' by the British, and just 'snorkel' by the Americans, this device allowed the diesel-powered U-boat fleet to resume the offensive in the wake of the 1943 'Black May' defeat and operationalise the new Electro-boat designs. It was the snorkel that introduced the evolutionary next step in submarine warfare that transformed submersibles into submarines. Even today the snorkel remains a prominent feature on modern nuclear-powered submarines.

The idea of an extensible air intake and exhaust system to facilitate the charging of a U-boat's batteries while keeping it submerged circulated among U-boat officers long before the start of the Second World War.[1] The post-war US Navy assessment of the snorkel remarked how it was suggested during the First World War.[2] The first serious effort to develop an extensible air mast was included by Professor Hellmuth Walter in his October 1933 proposal to the then Reichsmarine Construction Office for a high-speed U-boat powered by hydrogen peroxide (H_2O_2). Originally, an air mast was required for what was later called the 'Walter boat' because his design called for a low-silhouetted profile without a significant conning tower. Such a design caused the U-boat to be awash with sea water and his air mast allowed the vessel to pull in fresh air for the crew when required without the threat of being swamped. The original U-boat proposal, which employed the hydrodynamic properties of a fish shape, led to several concepts that evolved into the Types XVII and XVIII. These early design plans, however, omitted the air mast. The air mast was only reintroduced after the successor Types XXI and XXIII Electro-boat designs were approved in July 1943.[3]

Professor Walter was not the only marine engineer looking at ways to maintain a submarine submerged through an air mast. American Quaker, mechanical engineer and naval architect Simon Lake, who competed with John Philip Holland to build the first submarines for the US Navy, successfully patented an intake and exhaust mechanism with an automatic shut-off valve in 1905.[4] In Europe, Italian naval engineer Major Pericle Ferretti conducted trials with a snorkel on submarine *H3* in 1923 and patented the device in 1923.[5] The Dutch experimented with submarine ventilation through two fixed pipes during the First World War. Lieutenant J J Wickers of the Royal Netherlands Navy (RNeN) submitted a design to the RNeN in 1937 for an extensible intake air mast.[6]

Wicker's proposal was primarily based on the requirement to provide Dutch submarines with an advantage against the numerically superior Imperial Japanese Navy surface fleet, which was viewed as their likely opponent in the Pacific.[7] This device implemented on *O19* and *O20* in 1939 had an automatic head valve and a motor-driven lift system for the intake. The exhaust pipe was a rigid mount. It allowed the submarines to run their diesels underwater. *O21–O27* also received the air masts. Further development was ongoing when the Netherlands was occupied by the Germans in 1940.

All Dutch Royal Navy submarines with extensible air masts were turned over to the Royal Navy or captured in their dry docks by the German Army in May 1940. Only *O19* remained in Dutch service, though its air mast was removed while in dry dock in Grangemouth, Scotland, from February 1943 to February 1944.[8] The British Royal Navy saw no interest in the air masts and dismantled them.

The U-boot Acceptance Commission (Ubootabnahmekommando/UAK) tested the air mast in the captured *O26*, which was redesignated *UD-4* during 1941.[9] German testing confirmed a series of technical and tactical problems inherent in the Dutch design that prevented its employment in actual combat operations. The RNeN had identified these issues themselves, but installed the system on six of their submarines regardless. Among the problems were significant vibrations inside the boat when running the diesel engines underwater that caused the periscopes to become unusable; oil fumes were not vented properly and diffused throughout the boat; the intake mast was too large and created a wake of 300–600m that was highly visible at night and in phosphorescent seas; the exhaust mast was too short and had to be extended; and the Dutch system did not allow simultaneous charging of batteries while running the diesels.[10] One aspect of the Dutch design that was of positive note was the automatic head valve on the intake pipe that closed when submerged.[11] The UAK noted real concern about U-boat crew health and safety given the significant pressure generated within the Dutch submarines by their design when the intake valve was inadvertently shut due to waves or tactical manoeuvres while in use.[12] The UAK subsequently ordered further testing cancelled in early 1941 and the snorkel systems removed from all captured *O25–O27* Dutch submarines.[13] The Dutch snorkel, while innovative, was not operationally useable as designed.

Walter provided an update to Dönitz in May 1943 on a discussion he had on 2 March regarding the technical feasibility of an air mast. The result of the theoretical tests undertaken was deemed positive, as Walter explained to Dönitz in a letter:

May 19th, 1943

>   Secret
>   Registered!
>   Nr. 1149/43

To the Supreme Commander of the Navy
   Großadmiral Dönitz, Berlin

Sir,

When during my visit of March 2nd, 1943, I asked for Baudirektor (Director of Construction) Dr Fischer, who, incidentally has undertaken his tasks with visible success, I mentioned that it would be possible to run the diesels when a submarine is submerged to the periscope depth, by obtaining the induction through a pipe. Meanwhile I have submitted this proposal to the K-Amt. Fresh air and exhaust pipes would be raised and lowered similar to the operation of a periscope. When flooded, the pipes would be automatically shut and opened again. At a speed of 7 knots the diesel could suck the air from the engine room for a period of up to 60 secs. The spray water which might be entrained would be separated in a special water separator.

The increasing threat to the U-boat's warfare from the air, led me to consider this idea, which is certainly not a new one. The following would result:

1. The outward and homeward voyage of the boat would be made almost without danger. The location of the periscope and air pipe by R.D.F. is exact only at a short distance, and in sea-going conditions practically impossible. Also, it seemed feasible to eliminate the reflection property (capacity) of this pipe without any great difficulty. Visual location by aircraft is very difficult in normal sea condition and in any case it is only possible from such a distance that the U-boat would have been for same time beforehand, aware of the presence of the enemy.

An unidentified Royal Netherlands Navy submarine (*O19* or *O20*) with its original two-mast snorkel installation. The forward pipe (left) is the intake and the rear pipe (right) is the exhaust. This system was not capable of employment in the rough North Atlantic and lacked tactical efficiency for combat operations. The intake mast had to be raised while surfaced. German engineers drew little inspiration from the innovative but inefficient Dutch system. *(Author's collection)*

2. The exact position of the U-boat in the combat area could not be determined by the enemy. I assume that the enemy is now in a position to locate most of the U-boats by using the R.D.F. (Radio Direction Finder) not of its own air reconnaissance. Even though the U-boat would be forced to proceed on the surface at top speed, she could afterwards change her position to the appreciable degree when submerged and at the same time the batteries for electric drive could be charged.

The air pipe is of particular value for the fast submarines. From a technical point of view they do not need to proceed at all on the surface. For tactical reasons it is, of course, still necessary in order to locate the enemy. However, the duration of travelling on the surface can be still further reduced by using the radio and acoustic locator. The type XVIII fitted with air pipe and corresponding (Direction Finder) detecting apparatus resembles very nearly the ideal U-boat.

The value of the gunnery armament for submarines of such a type is, in my opinion, problematical, since as a result of its installation, the resistance of the submarine increases by 20–25% and by using it the boat exposes itself to greater danger than by using it at all.

For carrying out of the trials, I propose:

A [Type] IIB boat should be fitted with air pipe in lieu of a dismantled periscope.
A Type XVII submarine should be equipped in the same way, on completion of satisfactory trials of (1).

If the trials prove a successful, all types of submarines should be fitted with air pipes.

In this short statement I have certainly have not introduced some of the disadvantages which may give rise to criticism from the Naval point of view. I look upon the Problem as an Engineer who is 'consciously one-sided'. I ask you, Sir, to make allowance for this fact.

   With kindest regards and Heil Hitler
     (Signed) Walter[14]

This proposal came at the time when U-boats were increasingly being located and destroyed on the surface. It offered Dönitz an option that could counter that threat. Interestingly, he dismissed the idea of up-arming the U-boat, as this would add drag to its underwater characteristics, a design factor Walter continued to fight against with the traditionalists in the Kriegsmarine right through until the end of the war. We also see recognition that the new Type XVII 'Walter boat' design did not then have an integrated air mast. Walter proposed its addition in order to increase its operational effectiveness. This fact contributes to the evidence that the early design for the Electro-boat also did not have an air mast integrated in the original proposal presented at the Paris Conference in late 1942. This proved problematic, as discussed in the section of this chapter below on snorkel installations in the Electro-boats. Dönitz was encouraged by Walter's letter and replied on 27 May that the trials would commence immediately.[15]

Walter offered Dönitz a solution to the main threat confronting his U-boats – detection and destruction from air attack. It must be stressed that the original intent of the snorkel was simply to provide a means for U-boats to quickly transit an area threatened by Allied aircraft. Specifically, this meant running submerged on diesels across the Bay of Biscay. As the snorkel became operational, U-boat captains found new ways to employ it and tactics evolved accordingly.

Walter moved forward with the design, which now received the German name *Schnorchel*. The term was a rather vulgar German term for a nose, but it was kept. Responsibility for developing the snorkel was given to his lead engineers, Dipl. Ing. Ulrich Gabler and Dipl. Ing. Heinrich Heep.

When Gabler and Heep began work on the snorkel system they pursued a uniquely German theoretical design. What made the system successful was Gabler's principle of using the entire interior of the U-boat as an 'air cushion' that the diesel engines could use to freely suck in air, thus reducing the significant pressure experienced when the air intake was submerged due to heavy seas or during a tactical manoeuvre. This concept was combined with Heep's idea of a double-seated pressure-release valve to take in air, but keep water out of the intake during rough seas.[16] Heep did use the Dutch head valve spherical shape as an initial model, but that is where any reuse of the system ended.[17] From this point forward Gaber and Heep followed a uniquely German engineering trajectory in submarine snorkel design. In the spring of 1943, three of the leading U-boat shipyards were asked to submit proposed snorkel construction plans.[18]

Deutsche Werke Kiel AG (DWK) produced the most workable design. The company received a contract for the initial design with a floating head valve in June 1943. The training boats *U-57* and *U-58*, both Type IICs, were fitted with temporary prototype snorkel masts. Initial tests were carried out with *U-58* by running from Kiel to the entrance to the Flensburg Fjord and back. This test proved that the diesels could be run on full while the U-boat was submerged using the snorkel mast to take in air and expel the exhaust gases. The next trials were carried out at Gotenhafen on the Baltic and they reduced the concern for crew health during extended snorkel use, though at that time there was not a single person in the Kriegsmarine who thought that crews would remain submerged for thirty days or more. In August, Baltic tests proved the practical nature of the device, provided that an even depth was maintained.[19] Gabler and Heep presented Konteradmiral (ING) Thedsen with a design for the first Type VIIC snorkel. Thedsen developed all the future standing orders for snorkel operation once the device was adopted across the U-boat fleet.

The three Type VIIC repair boats *U-235*, *U-236* and *U-237* were selected for the next snorkel trials. *U-236* received the first installation. Its mast consisted of a double tube with a mounted float valve and an underwater exhaust that rested on the deck and was raised and lowered manually by a pulley while the boat was surfaced. This first trial was conducted successfully by the 5th U-Flotilla on 29 September during a transfer cruise of *U-236* from Kiel to Sonderburg. While at Sonderburg *U-236* received a hydraulic piston lifting mechanism and an early experimental ring float, before it conducted the next trial cruise on 11 October.[20] During this next cruise the order was given to dive to a depth of 18m at short notice. The ring float valve failed, however, preventing fresh air from passing into the boat and generating a negative pressure of 200mbar. The recommendation to blow ballast and surface was countermanded by the head of training onboard the U-boat. This decision was compounded by a machinist in the diesel room who failed to turn off the mechanical blower, which led to such a vacuum that the crew passed out completely. Only the quick action of a single crew member prevented a catastrophe as the inflow valves were manually opened with his final breath, and fresh air flowed into the boat once again. The current ring float design adopted for this trial was quickly scrapped.

When *U-236* returned to Kiel in November, a British air raid temporarily shut down the DWK yards. A scale model (1:2) of what was to become the new production ball float model was salvaged undamaged from the collapsed design hall along the wharf after the raid and given to Germaniawerft (GW) to copy and produce immediately. In early November 1943, *U-236* received its third snorkel system to include Heep's new ball float design, a recessed snorkel well on deck, improved oil pressure controls for the piston and other enhancements.

One important test undertaken by *U-236* in late November was infrared (IR) testing against its snorkel exhaust gas. There was concern in the Kriegsmarine at that time that the Allies were ranging U-boats through IR. An IR device was set up 2km away from *U-236* on Aabenraa Fjord in Denmark and three separate tests were conducted against snorkel exhaust.

One of the first experimental snorkel installations occurred on *U-235* (VIIC) in autumn 1943. A Type I (flange) snorkel mast sits at rest in the snorkel well. The snorkel well was deepened in later installations, so the mast was completely recessed below the deck line. The original lifting mechanism was a pulley, as noted by the wheels and cable in the foreground, powered by a high-pressure oil. The next feature is the air intake flange, followed by the metal bracket where the locking pin was inserted once the mast was raised. Further up the mast can be seen the exhaust vent. Its placement underwater was based on testing against an infrared sensor to determine the best position from which to vent exhaust gases. Note the bifurcation of the exhaust line around the flange. *(Bundesarchiv-Militärarchiv, W04/17145)*

A close-up of the original pulley lifting mechanism on *U-235*. This lifting system was later replaced with a piston. *(Bundesarchiv-Militärarchiv, W04/17145)*

The port-side air intake trunking on *U-235*. The air intake connected into the normal diesel intake that ran into the engine compartment. In later installations the intake trunking was raised and the slight upward angle eliminated. Note the long piston locking rod to the left. *(Bundesarchiv-Militärarchiv, W04/17145)*

The Type I snorkel mast on *U-235* being raised into position. The flange on the snorkel mast and port-side trunking had to have a flush seat to prevent seawater from entering into the diesel engines. This proved problematic and was eventually replaced with a Type II non-flange snorkel mast in 1944. Also note the locking pin and snorkel clamp. The locking pin was operated from the control room. One can see the pin's operating rod run down the face of the conning tower in front of the wave guard. A protective cladding was later added in 1944 and the locking rod was run flush against the conning tower. *(Bundesarchiv-Militärarchiv, W04/17145)*

The first test was with exhaust gas expelled over water, the second with exhaust gas expelled on the waterline, and the third with exhaust gas expelled about 30cm below the waterline. The test proved that the snorkel exhaust gas could be identified by IR in the first two scenarios, but not the third. This finding ensured that future snorkel mast production would include an underwater exhaust port.[21] Additional trials with all three Type VIICs continued into the autumn, but the decision had already been made to equip the U-boat fleet with a snorkel. There was great anticipation of this and Dönitz even conducted his first and only snorkel cruise that lasted a few minutes onboard *U-235* in May 1944.[22]

The KII U department in the Kriegsmarine was responsible for the development of the snorkel. They received an initial order for twenty snorkels for the Type VIIC on 9 September 1943. A further 100 were ordered on 24 September based on the design of Deutsche Werke Kiel with installation to occur in Kiel and Wilhelmshaven. While the first three snorkels were intended for *U-235–237*, the next four were destined for the 29th U-Flotilla in Toulon for Mediterranean boats. Nine of the original deck-rested pulley versions employed on *U-235*, and two piston-driven masts employed by *U-237*, were destined for FdU West to be installed on U-boats at French

The snorkel mast on *U-235* now fully raised and seated. The Type I mast had two pipes. The exhaust trunking that bifurcated around the flange and expelled the gases through the exhaust port below the snorkel head. The other pipe brought in fresh air from the snorkel head into the U-boat through the port-side trunking. When the Type II mast was introduced the intake and exhaust lines were run through a single pipe. *(Bundesarchiv-Militärarchiv, W04/17145)*

ports.[23] Another forty snorkels were ordered for the Type IXC and IXD U-boats.[24]

Concern remained within conservative circles in the Kriegsmarine, who were unconvinced of the viability of what was a very complicated

The starboard-side exhaust trunking on *U-235* during its installation. Every single snorkel-equipped Type VIIC had above-deck exhaust trunking. The shut-off valve for the exhaust line pictured in the centre was operated in the control room (see next image), directly below. The exhaust valve proved to be the most important feature of the entire snorkel system. If the shut-off valve failed or did not work properly, back pressure, or even seawater, could force exhaust gases into the engine room during emergency manoeuvres, raising the potential of carbon monoxide poisoning or oxyhydrogen explosions. *(Bundesarchiv-Militärarchiv, W04/17145)*

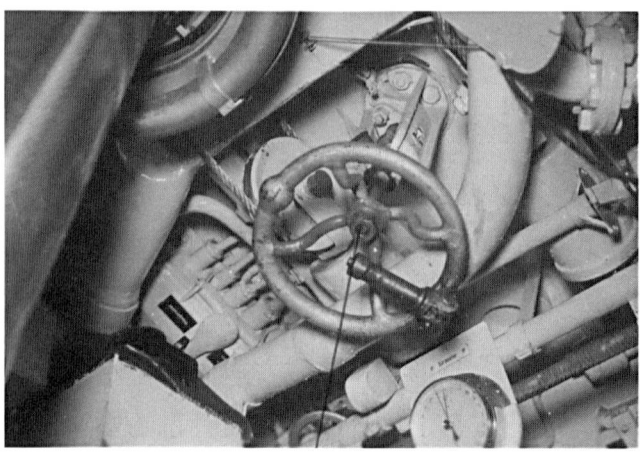

The snorkel exhaust shut-off valve in the control room was installed to the right of the air observation scope housing (when looking forward). *(Bundesarchiv-Militärarchiv, W04/17145)*

mechanism that if employed incorrectly could jeopardise a crew's safety. Despite misgivings, installation proceeded slowly through the winter months of 1943–44 under a veil of secrecy.

Part A
Technical Characteristics of the Snorkel

Part A describes the technical aspects of the snorkel design and its variations across different U-boat types. While this section is not intended to be a comprehensive operational history of the snorkel-equipped U-boats, the technical evolution of the snorkel was shaped by its employment and thus aspects of its early operational use are described below.

All diesel-powered U-boats required air to run their diesel engines. The crew required fresh air to breathe. If a U-boat attempted to run its diesel engines submerged without a continual source of fresh air, the available air inside the U-boat would be sucked into the engines. The crew would experience excruciating pain due to the vacuum, followed by death through asphyxiation. Using a snorkel apparatus, a U-boat could suck in fresh air while running the diesel engines during a submerged cruise. The boat could be ventilated and the high-pressure air flasks charged. The snorkel as designed allowed for a U-boat to maintain a submerged speed of 6 knots, though some U-boats reached as high as 8 knots. One of the main achievements with the snorkel was that the batteries could be charged while submerged, typically over the course of three to five hours at night (significant variations in time occurred for many reasons). Most importantly, the U-boat never needed to surface.

Originally the German term for this device was the *Klappschnorchel* (folding snort), noted Fregattenkapitän Günter Hessler, a former U-boat captain and BdU operations officer.[25] Other Allied and German documents used the term *Klappmast* to define the new apparatus. The term represented the original folding design employed on the Type VII and Type IX U-boats as there was not enough room in the conning tower to allow for an extensible version.[26] An extensible version was adopted for the Type XXI and XXIII boats only.[27]

Each diesel U-boat type required a slightly different snorkel configuration as outlined below, but the main characteristics were similar. On diesel boats the snorkel apparatus was a streamlined cylindrical mast that measured 9m (29ft x 6ft) in length. It contained two air conduits. One brought air into the engine compartment of the U-boat through a float valve at the top of the mast designed to stop water from entering the system if submerged. The other line vented the carbon dioxide and monoxide exhaust, oxyhydrogen from the batteries, and other internal gases from the diesel engines at a point 1m below the top of the snorkel float valve at a 90° angle. The design expelled the gas underwater while snorkelling to minimise not only detection, but interference with periscope vision. The snorkel was raised at a depth of about 25m from either a stationary or moving position using either a pulley or piston. Once raised, the snorkel was held in place by a staying rod that locked on the mast by a mechanism in the control room. When lowered, the mast was locked in a recessed well on the deck on diesel boats. This was the basic configuration of the snorkel. How it was installed onto each U-boat type was different.

Snorkel Building and Installation Process
Due to the pressure to field operational U-boats under a wartime production footing, the decision was made not to interrupt the current diesel U-boat building process simply to add a snorkel apparatus. Instead, the snorkel was produced separately and sent to the shipyard or bunker, where the completed U-boat was retrofitted with the new apparatus. This was true for all diesel U-boats and some Type XIII Electro-boats. Unfortunately, many sub-contractors were not up to the task of manufacturing the complicated parts, including the pressure-tight casting at the foot of the snorkel.[28]

Research reveals that nearly all snorkel installations were retrofitted into diesel U-boats after commissioning, often during their final overhaul at the end of training.[29] There were exceptions, such as U-boats that were equipped with Alberich that were commissioned with their acoustic camouflage and snorkel already applied. All Type XXI Electro-boats received a snorkel during their construction process, after the assembly of the prefabricated hulls. Only the last eighteen Type XXIIIs built before the end of the war had the extensible snorkel mast integrated during construction due to a bottleneck in production with GWK. The earlier Type XXIIIs had their snorkels added at the end of the production process or during their final overhaul.[30] By the end of 1943 every U-boat type design included an integrated snorkel installation.

No single primary document exists to detail all U-boats that received a snorkel, where it was installed, or under what circumstances. A detailed review of each KTB was conducted for every U-boat commissioned or operational after February 1944 for any of the following official snorkel installation or related terms:

Schnorcheleinbau – snorkel installation
Schnorchelerprobung – snorkel testing
Schnorchelabnahme – snorkel acceptance (usually in regards to testing)
Schnorchelbeanstandungen – snorkel complaints (technical issues)

Schnorchelausbildung – snorkel training
Schnorchelrestpunkte – snorkel 'completion/discharge' (remaining issues to
   be fixed or worked out/practised)
Schnorchelbeklebung – snorkel adhesive/radar covering applied
Schnorcheltarnung – snorkel camouflage/anti-radar covering applied

In some cases, U-boat captains did not record any of these terms in their KTBs, even when they received a snorkel retrofit.

Further analysis of available U-boat photographs was conducted that included wartime, post-war and, in some cases, images of underwater wreck sites. First-person accounts, both published and unpublished, were also reviewed for any mention of a snorkel as well as to develop a comprehensive understanding of snorkel installation and operations.

This comprehensive analysis revealed that some 353 diesel U-boats received a snorkel retrofit during the period 1944–45.[31] This includes approximately eighty-six installations on training and transport U-boats, former Italian U-boats, and U-boats that never saw a single operational patrol due to damage incurred in port by Allied air raids, or the inevitable end of the war. Of the 267 diesel U-boats that conducted an operational patrol, approximately 46 per cent received their installation after at least one patrol. Nearly all the other 54 per cent received their snorkel after being commissioned as part of their final overhaul that occurred before release to an operational command. Retrofits were completed after acceptance testing and training. At least fifty-eight snorkel installations took place at U-bases along the Bay of Biscay in France, twenty-six at various Norwegian bases, and eleven at remote locations such as Toulon, Bordeaux, Salamis and Penang. Most installation occurred in German ports from Hamburg to Königsberg. The U-boat installations identified by type are as follows:

IID	4
VIIC	202
VIIC/41	73
VIID	2
VIIF	2
IXB	1
IXC	4
IXC/40	48
IXD1	2
IXD2	12
XB	2
XIV	1

The priority of snorkel retrofits was shaped by operational needs. The first order for twenty snorkels for Type VIICs was issued on 12 August 1943. Just over a month later, on 24 September, both the Naval Arsenal at Kiel and the Kriegsmarinewerft Wilhelmshaven (KMW) were ordered to urgently produce a further 100 snorkels for the Type VIICs in service and forty for the Type IXC and Type IXD U-boats. The first priority for the snorkel retrofits was operational U-boats currently employed in the North Atlantic and based in France. Following these orders, new U-boats were also to be retrofitted as a second priority. In the latter case, Atlantic-bound U-boats were at the top of the list while those operating in other theatres, such as the Arctic, were at the bottom. So concerned was the BdU about U-boat losses due to air attack that the operationally untested snorkel received significant priority in the already stressed Kriegsmarine building programme during the autumn of 1943. As noted in the 15 November 1943 letter from Ministerial Counsellor Bröking, the head of KII U, to the two main suppliers Germaniawerft and AG Weser 'The completion of these snorkel installations for operational boats and new boats is to be accelerated by every means. In the discussions at Supreme Naval Command, it has been expressly stated that no delays must occur in the delivery programme through efforts to bring about improvements in the first installations.'[32] Despite the fact that snorkel retrofits were given top priority by the Kriegsmarine, the problem was that there was a shortage of experienced workers. The decision was made to pull workers from the current building programme, reducing the building rate of new U-boats, so that the older ones could receive a retrofit and have experienced technical staff on-hand to troubleshoot issues and make repairs.[33]

Surviving German documentation on the installation process is unfortunately limited. However, a set of documents located in the Bundesarchiv-Militärarchiv detail the snorkel order and installation process of *U-249* (VIIC) that took place at Kiel in early 1945. *U-249* was commissioned on 20 November 1943. The original order for the snorkel was placed on 26 April 1944. All the components were produced, packaged and shipped on 24 November 1944. The packing list for Order No. 9426 issued on 24 November from Germaniawerft Kiel contained all the parts for this retrofit. *U-249* received the 'G53' snorkel, which meant it was the fifty-third snorkel produced by Germaniawerft Kiel in its production run. There was a total of fifteen large loose items, one banded, and one crate weighing a total of 3,571.60kg (3.93 tons). The first seven major 'loose' components that made up the shipment consisted of:

1 x *Klappmast* (folding mast)

1 x *Drucközylinder* (hydraulic cylinder)
2 x *Lagerbeck* (bearing block)
1 x *Ausblaseventil* (exhaust valve)
1 x *Sperrvorrichtung* (locking device for tower)
1 x *Keil mit Spindel* (wedge with spindle or mast)

The crate contained hundreds of the smaller components for the snorkel installations. All the piping, both steel and copper, came banded together. Finally, the last eight unpacked items consisted of the hydraulic piston components.[34]

Surviving documents reveal three production series for diesel U-boats.[35] First production run issued 4 October 1943:

Arb. Nr. 85023 SS4931–7435/3693
  Sangerhausen: S40–75

The records do not indicate the order details for S1–39, if that production run existed.

Second production run issued 15 January 1944:

Arb. Nr. 85320 SS4931–2439/42601
  Germaniawerft: G1–110
  Sangerhausen:[36] S76–199

It appears that within the S76–199 production run Deutschewerft was responsible for the following:

S87–96
S121–130
S151–165
S185–199

Third production run issued 20 April 1944. This production consisted of snorkel masts without a flange for the intake:

Arb. Nr. 85944 SS4931–7439/4851
S200–220

It should be noted that the total of 330 snorkel masts referenced in the above production lines is approximately twenty fewer than the total number of retrofitted diesel U-boats identified in this current research.

The standard retrofit installation process took twenty-eight days.[37] Documentation reveals a complex process was required to conduct an installation that required co-ordination between shipbuilders, machinists, and welders. One of the first items installed was 'a depth gauge (25m) and an aneroid barometer in the diesel room'. However, operational considerations altered the length of time considerably. For example, *U-437* (VIIC) received a snorkel installation in ten days during August 1944 while in its Bordeaux bunker. Obviously, a shorter installation time introduced the possibility of technical problems. Some of the U-boats in French bunkers received installations that eliminated the lifting mechanism in order to shorten the time taken to get the craft operational and out to sea. These U-boats were equipped with a rigid snorkel mast locked in the upright position. This was done to get U-boats out to sea and back to Norwegian or German ports as quickly as possible after the Allied breakout from Normandy occurred in August 1944. The U-boats identified with rigid installations were as follows: in Bordeaux were *U-857* (IXC40) and *U-534* (IXC40); in Brest was *U-256* (VIIC); and in St Nazaire were *U-255* (VIIC) and *U-267* (VIIC). These U-boats were expected to receive a fully operational folding snorkel once they reached their final destinations.

The KTB of *U-534* (IXC/40) reveals the technical issues with such a makeshift installation during its trip back to Norway from France in August. Kapitänleutnant Herbert Nollau noted in his KTB how shipyard time was dramatically reduced by eliminating any mechanism to raise the snorkel: 'Boat departed for Norway after a short time spent in the shipyard undergoing a makeshift repair and installation of a fixed snorkel. Technical defects affected the crew the entire trip. To recharge the battery, long surface marches were ordered.'[38] More importantly, the installation was faulty due to the shortened time and posed major problems for Nollau.

On the night of 26 August, Nollau ordered the U-boat to initiate a snorkel run at 11.50pm. No sooner had it begun when the engine room began to fill with smoke due to a leak in the snorkel exhaust line. The U-boat was immediately ordered to surface and the crewmembers in the engine room opened the battery hatch to ventilate the boat. That same evening a Vickers Wellington of 172 Squadron (NB798) was heading towards the Bay of Biscay. At a quarter past midnight on the 27th the Wellington, piloted by Flying Officer G E Whiteley, found Nollau's *U-534* surfaced after receiving a bearing on its radar. This radar return was most likely due to *U-534*'s permanently raised snorkel mast that increased its radar profile dramatically while cruising surfaced. Whiteley dropped his depth charges wide. This was probably due to accurate flak fire from Nollau's alert crew. The Wellington was hit and went down in flames with the loss of one crew member, the rest being rescued.[39] After the incident Nollau continued to run on the surface at night during its long journey due to continued technical failures with its snorkel. Only through continuous work by the crew's machinists while surfaced was the snorkel's exhaust fixed during the final leg of the trip.

This case study represents an example of how faulty snorkel installations could be the direct cause of a U-boat loss. Forced to surface in order to ventilate the boat, a U-boat operating in coastal waters quickly became an easy target for Allied aircraft equipped with radar.

Technical Operation

Precise snorkel orders were introduced over time as U-boat captains gained operational experience. These orders fell under sections titled: Stand by to proceed snorkel; Change from proceed submerged to proceed snorkel; Battery charging; Change from proceed snorkel to proceed submerged; and Action stations when proceeding on snorkel.[40] The basic operation of a snorkel was clearly technical, but not impossible to manage by a well-trained crew.

There were a set of technical terms used exclusively by snorkel-equipped U-boats in their KTB to note what phase of operation was being undertaken. They were:

Schnorcheln – snorkelling
Schnorchelte – snorkelled
Schnorchelfahrt – snorkelling
Schnorcheln beendet or *Schnorchelfahrt beendet* – snorkelling ended
Müllschuss – refuse shot
Schnorchelfahrt, Boot durchlüften or alternatively *geschnorchelt Boot belüftet* –
   to ventilate boat
Schnorchelbetrieb – operation
Schnorchelanlage – snorkel equipment

Four snorkelling operations were generally conducted:

1. Snorkelling while running both engines on charge and propelling the U-boat with silent motors from the battery.
2. Running one engine and using its associated main motor (as a generator) to carry a float current through the control board that was used to power the other shaft. This was known as an 'electric drive' by the crew and saved diesel fuel and battery charge.
3. Straight propulsion in the normal manner for surface operation except

that air intake and exhaust was by snorkel. This allowed maximum speed while submerged.

4. Charging with one engine and direct propulsion with the other engine.

The U-boat submerged if surfaced or came to an even depth if submerged in order to snorkel following standard operating procedures. The order 'stand by to snorkel' was issued verbally by the captain. The U-boat then proceeded to a depth of 25m and was stopped or slowed. Under no circumstances was the snorkel mast to be exposed to the force of the sea during its raising. Once the mast was raised and secured in its arm bracket, the U-boat proceeded to periscope depth so that the snorkel float valve was positioned above the water while the exhaust return was underwater. The water in the flooded snorkel mast was drained into the boat and expelled through the bilges.

Proceeding on diesels underwater while snorkelling occurred the same way as it did while surfaced. The exception was that the mechanical blower (either the Germaniawerft box blower or Maschinenfabrik Augsburg-Nürnberg (MAN) motor's Turboblower) was not turned on during a snorkel cruise as there was a specific danger of air shortage and overpressure that brought immediate pain, and in severe cases, lasting health issues. Assuming perfect depth-keeping by the chief engineer and that the snorkel head was not submerged accidentally, there was a slight, but noticeable back pressure of about 0.15–0.2 atmospheres above normal and a constant sub-normal pressure of 50 millibars. It was not uncommon for a U-boat to utilise the snorkel for as much as nine to ten consecutive hours per day when running the diesels in order to transit quickly a dangerous area such as the Bay of Biscay or the south of Iceland.[41]

Charging batteries while submerged was no different than while on the surface, though the technical expulsion of gases was. U-boats typically charged their batteries while snorkelling over the course of three to five hours, stopping every twenty minutes for an all-around listen for enemy vessels or aircraft as any direction finding was impossible during snorkel operation. Typically, running one diesel engine and charging with the other while snorkelling for three hours produced enough battery charge to last the U-boat for one day of operations.[42] Before battery charging began the battery ventilation and exhaust was turned on first. The exhaust fan drew the battery waste gases out of the battery as usual, but while submerged it forced the gases to the front of the diesel engine, where they joined with the diesel gases and exited from the diesel exhaust that led to the snorkel mast. While submerged, the ventilation and exhaust for the battery had no direct connection with the atmosphere. The battery charge was not to exceed 145 volts.

The onset of gas formation while cruising submerged was to be avoided at all costs as it could be dangerous to the crew. When the charging was finished it became necessary to vent the battery for fifteen minutes with the diesel engine running and the charge turned off to expel excess gases. If the charging was interrupted due to a tactical manoeuvre that resulted in the diesel engines being stopped, and all cut-offs closed, and the snorkel mast flooded, then the batteries had to be slowly vented for ten to fifteen minutes at subnormal pressure. The gases had to be dispersed within the U-boat in order to avoid a concentration in any one place, which could result in an explosion of oxyhydrogen gas. According to one report, it was noted that 'it is in the interest of the U-boat's safety to continue airing the battery for a quarter of an hour at periscope depth with the diesel engine running after the charge has been turned off.'[43]

The fact that a build-up of gases could cause an internal explosion may have been among several causes, including carbon-based poisoning, that contributed to the mysterious loss of several snorkel-equipped U-boats. Konteradmiral Thedsen issued specific battery charging guidance in February 1944 that was to be followed with 'strict discipline'.

When the diesel engines were running and charging of the batteries was required, the chief engineer announced 'Set Battery Charging with snorkel'. The diesel machinist would have to respond 'Snorkel ventilation is running'. The diesel engine watch then had the responsibility of battery ventilation through the loading diesel engine. If the batteries had to charge and the diesel engines were not running yet, the chief engineer ordered 'Start battery charging with recirculation ventilation'. As soon as the diesel engines started running, when the U-boat came to snorkel depth and raised the snorkel mast, the diesel engine watch then switched from recirculation to ventilation through the snorkel. The chief engineer had to be notified immediately of the switch. If the U-boat stopped the charge due to a crash dive, the diesel engines were stopped immediately and the battery ventilation switched to recirculation by the diesel engine watch. If either of these two steps failed to occur in quick succession, then a catastrophic situation could develop. There is no doubt that U-boats were lost this way.[44]

The outer muffler valves formed the only cut off of the exhaust pipes against outboard pressure. They were required to be completely airtight as a prerequisite for secure snorkelling. If they burst the boat could flood through the exhaust system.

Snorkel Questionnaire
There was no time to conduct proper operational testing of this new device. BdU issued a multi-page mandatory questionnaire to be complet-

ed by all returning snorkel-equipped U-boats.[45] This series of questions was required to be answered in order to better understand the technical and operational limitations of snorkel use. BdU wanted to standardise the feedback from U-boats in order to improve the technical innovation technically and form better operational guidance for the fleet. Once complete, the questionnaire was filed with BdU or FdU, along with the U-boat's KTB. This was a standard form, however, if there were special situations or snorkel failures then the U-boat commander could elaborate at the end. These questions reveal how much effort was put into improving the snorkel's function, given the wartime pressure that the U-boat fleet was under.

Battery Explosions

As noted above, improper outgasing of oxyhydrogen after a snorkel run could result in a catastrophic explosion that might significantly damage or destroy the U-boat. Even when a snorkel was not in use, if the diesel engine exhaust head valve was closed for even the shortest amount of time while the batteries were running, oxyhydrogen could build up to dangerous levels and ignite by a simple spark, as occurred on the *U-490* (XIV), causing an explosion.[46] In the case of *U-490*, even a few battery cells exploding could cause major damage and require extensive repairs.

It was stated by the chief engineer of *U-1229* (IXC/40) that because batteries generated gas when charged at 149 volts or higher, they were never charged at more than 145 volts. Ventilating lines were installed in each battery compartment to lead off the gas. These lines were connected with the main air exhaust line and were fitted with barometers that indicated the pressure in the compartments. A change of pressure of 14 millibars or more indicated a dangerous concentration of gas. The gas was passed through the ventilating lines and into the main air exhaust line. It was then conducted through special leads to the diesel air intake. The oxyhydrogen was then sucked by the superchargers into the diesels and expelled through the diesel exhaust system.[47]

The Royal Navy quickly became familiar with this issue during post-war U-boat testing. British Naval officer Lieutenant S S Brooks documented his first-hand experience with such an explosion onboard the ex-German *U-3017* (XXI) in August 1945, which was docked in port at the time. The British crew was taking samples of the hydrogen content coming from the German batteries as they 'gave off more Hydrogen than ours', according to Brooks. The measured level was 4 per cent, which was considered dangerous. All batteries were overcharged except for No. 5, which was slightly lower. An order was given to equalise the charge and bring up the No. 5 battery bank to equal the others. When the battery fan switch was thrown, a near catastrophic explosion resulted as the electric current sparked against the oxyhydrogen. While the explosion did not rupture the hull in this case, it wounded nine British sailors, several seriously, who were in the control and engine rooms.[48] This raised immediate concern with the Royal Navy personnel in charge of testing ex-German U-boats. Testing of hydrogen content in U-boats, especially after snorkelling, was immediately directed. On 22 October 1945 a report was issued that 'found that a hydrogen content of 3.5 per cent was reached after four hours on open circuit. It is, therefore, considered that the interval between the operation of battery ventilation fans should not exceed this period.'[49]

This recommendation suggested that improper venting after snorkelling, or a faulty exhaust pipe when snorkelling, could cause dangerous levels of oxyhydrogen to build up within the U-boat. The Captain of Submarines in Loch Ryan conducted an interview with German engineer officer Oberleutnant Rossa regarding the possibilities of battery explosions. Rossa, a prisoner-of-war, was assigned to assist the British in the management of ex-German U-boats. He provided the Captain of Submarines with seven specific reasons that the battery banks could explode based on his wartime experiences with the Type XXIs and XXIIIs, but these could easily be applied to the older Type VIICs or IXs. These reasons included: shorts caused by poorly insulated main cables that interacted with bilge water; faulty battery plugs or blockages that could 'give rise to a large concentration of gas inside that particular cell'; connection tubes between cells were known to deteriorate and crack suddenly; overtopping of distilled water; insufficient observation of nanometers; bad contacts, loose terminals and wires, or straps left in the battery tank during construction caused arcing; and exceeding 137 volts in a Type XXI during a normal charge. It was noted by Rossa that he knew of four Type XXIs that experienced battery explosions during the war.[50] Battery explosions on a U-boat operating at depth could be catastrophic. Unless there was a survivor, no one would have known the cause of the U-boat's demise.

Snorkel Training
A normal training routine began with the UAK, where normal pressure tests on the hull were carried out. These were followed by technical trials at Gotenhafen with the UAG (one of the six U-boot Acceptance Groups subordinated to the UAC) in the Baltic, where actual dive tests were performed. The U-boat then proceeded to a training flotilla for three weeks, followed by the Argu-front where combat trials were conducted. Time was spent at the torpedo testing section, then the U-boat finally left the Baltic and

returned to Kiel. Here the boat typically received a final overhaul, live ammunition, then departed on its patrol. Snorkel training was added to the end of this typical routine.

Snorkel training followed a similar procedure throughout the war. Crews of U-boats that received a retrofit in Germany received basic familiarisation before departing for Norway. Once the U-boat arrived at Horten, full training and technical adjustments were made while with a section of the Argu-Front.[51] If a U-boat received a retrofit in Norway, it conducted its full training there before departing on the first patrol. U-boats that received a retrofit in French ports had limited opportunity, if any, to conduct training. In most cases, such U-boats deployed straight into combat after receiving their retrofit in their bunker berths.

Horten developed into the final pre-operational evaluation port of call for most outbound Atlantic U-boats from Germany starting in the autumn of 1944. Technical specialists and engineers were assigned to Horten as well as the Werkstattschiff *Huascaran*.[52] U-boats that arrived in Horten conducted snorkel training over the course of three to five days. Because of the depth of the Norwegian fjords, U-boats were also required to conduct a deep diving test to check the pressure hull. Any issues were identified and corrected by the on-hand specialists. Trondheim also served as a secondary location for snorkel testing and repairs in 1945.[53]

Admiral Thedsen began to issue training guidance out to the fleet in February 1944. However, these 'Special Orders' and 'Snorkel Special Experience Messages' were not generally informed by combat experience, but through testing. It would be the commanders' experiences in the crucible of combat that evolved snorkel operations, not theory.

Snorkel instruction and training was often just enough to make the crew familiar with the strange new mechanism. Each crew had to master the apparatus on its own, often under the extremes of weather and combat. If it failed to do so, death and destruction of the U-boat could occur, as in the example of *U-997* (VIIC/41). *U-997*'s snorkel was installed in February 1945 at Trondheim. One of the crew's first training exercises with the new device almost became its last:

> The boat was outfitted with a new snorkel and the crew was given brief training with it into Trondheim harbour before they set out for Harstad – in extremely rough weather. 'About 5 o'clock in the morning we were ordered to go to snorkel drive, in spite of a very heavy sea astern. Sometimes we cut under and were submerged for minute. When the snorkel mast went below water, all the air was sucked out of the boat, and the crew had to quickly cut off the diesels.' On one occasion the starboard diesel suddenly conked out,

and 10 to 15 tons of water poured into the diesel room through the open air intake and exhaust valves in the snorkel mast. 'We tried to drain the water out of the diesel into the bilge, then we tried to clear the port diesel, but it would not start either.' Meanwhile, carbon dioxide from and exhaust smoke started to fill the boat, and almost every crewman, unable to grab his breathing device, started gasping and choking. Commander Lehman brought the sub back to the surface as fast as possible, trying to overcome the problems of sick crewmen who could hardly function and 15 tons of water in the diesel room bilge.

Once more on the surface, the water was pumped out, engines start again, and *U-997* began to recharge its batteries. The fuse box caught fire, the black smoke billowed out, and to top things off, the Gyro and magnetic compass failed. During this bedlam, the bells screamed, and *U-997* dived, pitching forward at a sharp angle, and Bootsmaat Sachse fell overboard. When Lehman surfaced again, he was unable to find his crewman.'[54]

Additional training was simply not possible under wartime operational pressures.

Vision and Vibration
The introduction of the snorkel altered basic periscope use on the Type VIICs, but not the Type IXs. It also introduced a vibration effect that was not universally experienced on diesel boats but became a critical flaw on the Electro-boats, as discussed later in this chapter.

When snorkelling in a Type VIIC, only the attack periscope could be used at snorkel depth as the attack periscope could be raised 20cm higher that the top of the snorkel. However, the forward air observation periscope was, at 12.2m, too short to be used while at snorkel depth. On the VIIC the snorkel exhaust produced only a small blind spot on infrequent occasions when using the attack periscope. The attack periscope had two powers, 1.5 and 6, giving a field of view from +30° to −10°. The line of sight could not be elevated. Standard practice when snorkelling was to sweep once on magnification 1.5, and then a second time on magnification 6 to check for Allied surface vessels or aircraft. Snorkelling reports were received that varied from slight shuddering in the periscope during periods of waves that did not impact operation, such as in the case of *U-971* (VIIC), to serious vibrations that were sufficient to cause some blurring when cruising at 7 knots, as experienced by *U-672* (VIIC).[55]

On Type IX U-boats, either periscope could be used at snorkel depth. If both were raised together, the aft attack periscope suffered severely from vibration, but the forward one remained completely rigid at all speeds and

U-826 (VIIC) in the foreground with a ring float. A comparison of a raised snorkel mast ring with the raised air observation scope (forward) and attack periscope (aft). The air observation scope was too short to be used when snorkelling on the VIICs. Only the attack scope could be employed during a snorkel run. The exhaust gases and spray often interfered with the periscope vision on Type VIICs. *(Author's collection)*

in all seas. Either periscope could be used separately satisfactorily, without vibration. In practice the forward air observation periscope was always used on the Type IXs.[56]

Lifting Mechanism for Diesel Boats

The first snorkel installations completed in French U-boat bases were achieved with the use of a wheel and pulley mechanism powered by high-pressure oil. The only U-boats identified as having this system come from

U-889 (IXC/40) after its surrender with snorkel mast and air scope fully raised. On the Type IXs either scopes could be used while snorkelling. *(Courtesy of NARA)*

photographs and wreck surveys. So far the only documented installations are on *U-235* (VIIC), *U-269* (VIIC), *U-275* (VIIC), *U-441* (VIIC), *U-953* (VIIC), and *U-984* (VIIC).[57] The pulley system was replaced by a hydraulic piston starting in April 1944.[58]

The standard equipment for a folding snorkel was a cylinder and piston located in the superstructure and driven by oil pressure from the periscope hydraulic system. The gear was designed to operate with 40 atmospheres of pressure and to safely withstand a pressure of 80 atmospheres. A double packing in the piston rod stuffing box, with a drain onto the hull between the two sets of packing, was intended to prevent oil from leaking outboard, and sea water from leaking into the oil. This and all other drains were generally led into an open funnel in the control room so that operators could observe any excessive leaking. It operated satisfactorily as far as the snorkel was concerned but, in spite of special precautions, it still leaked excessive amounts of oil.[59]

Intake System

There were two induction systems on diesel boats. The first was known as the Type I snorkel mast with a flange seat. The second, which was introduced later, was known as the Type II snorkel mast without a flange. All Type VII U-boats regardless of design variation, were equipped with either Type I or Type II snorkel masts throughout the war. Type IX U-boats were predominately equipped with the Type I masts, however, at least four, but as many as eight, were equipped with the Type II.[60] Type XB U-boats received Type II installations. Type XIV U-boats received a Type I installation.

During operation of the Type I induction system, air was sucked in through the float valve, down the air induction tube to a point halfway down the mast. There it passed through a flange seated joint into the horizontal trunking system that ran alongside the conning tower to the diesel engine. The flange intake system was the original design. A metal flange on the snorkel mast bedded onto the beaded rubber seat on the snorkel intake mounted on the conning tower. The flange seat was at a height of 1.385m above the deck line on a Type VII U-boat and 2.850m on a Type IXD2 U-boat as per general specifications. It sat slightly slower on the Type IXCs.[61] However, in practice the height varied due to individual yard specifications and decisions made under the pressures of war. The trunking contained a valve used to flood the snorkel mast when diving deep or when lowering the snorkel into the seated position within the deck well. This was a required design feature as the snorkel system was not designed to be pressurised. Any air left inside the system when diving deep could cause a structural failure. Once through the flange valve the air passed through the intermediate induction trunking along the conning tower (27.43cm in diameter), at the foot of which was a water trap fitted with both main and auxiliary drain valves. The main valve served to drain rapidly into the bilges. When the snorkel mast was first raised, approximately 1 ton of water resided in the intake system and had to be drained prior to operation through this mechanism. The auxiliary valve was kept permanently open when snorkelling to drain any water that might make its way into the system. From here the air passed through the lower horizontal induction trunking either into the normal diesel air induction trunking, and hence through the main pressure hull induction valve into the diesels, or through the valve into the boat's ventilation system.[62] The snorkel mast flange valve was problematic and in the summer of 1944 an improved Type II design was introduced. This eliminated both the flange valve and the trunking along the port side of the conning tower. The air intake was routed through the snorkel mast's pivot joint, also known as the 'boot heel', just under the decking.

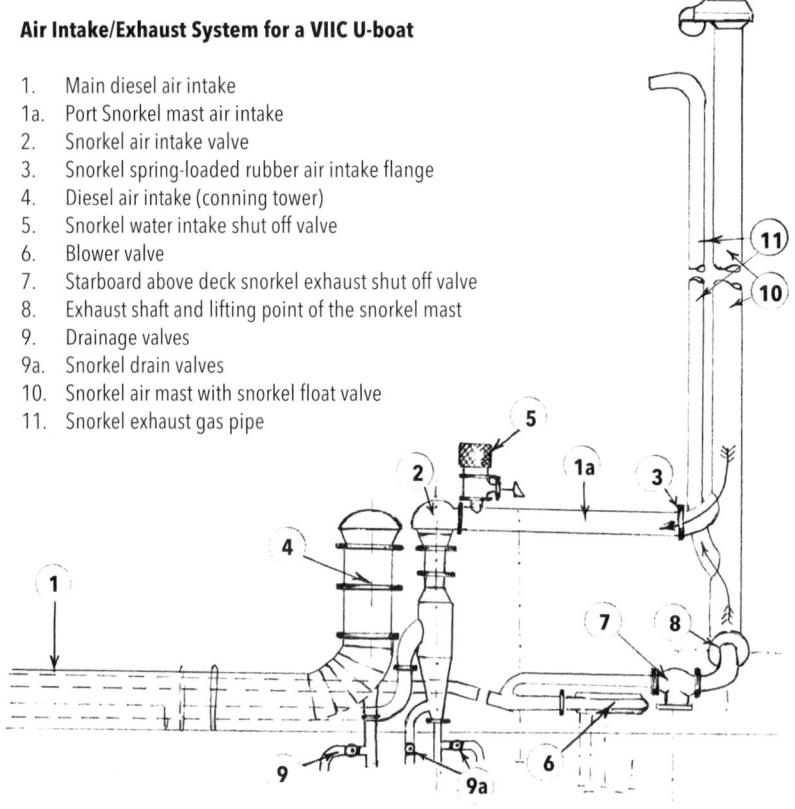

Air Intake/Exhaust System for a VIIC U-boat

1.   Main diesel air intake
1a.   Port Snorkel mast air intake
2.   Snorkel air intake valve
3.   Snorkel spring-loaded rubber air intake flange
4.   Diesel air intake (conning tower)
5.   Snorkel water intake shut off valve
6.   Blower valve
7.   Starboard above deck snorkel exhaust shut off valve
8.   Exhaust shaft and lifting point of the snorkel mast
9.   Drainage valves
9a.   Snorkel drain valves
10.   Snorkel air mast with snorkel float valve
11.   Snorkel exhaust gas pipe

Air intake and exhaust system for a Type VIIC U-boat with a Type I flange snorkel mast. *(Author's collection)*

Interestingly, only the Type VII U-boats received the Type II as a priority, while all other U-boat types primarily continued to employ the Type I flange mast until the end of the war. The Type II was delivered in late spring/early summer based on a memorandum sent to all U-boat bases from Germanienwerft, Kiel, on 30 May 1944 that detailed the technical modifications.[63]

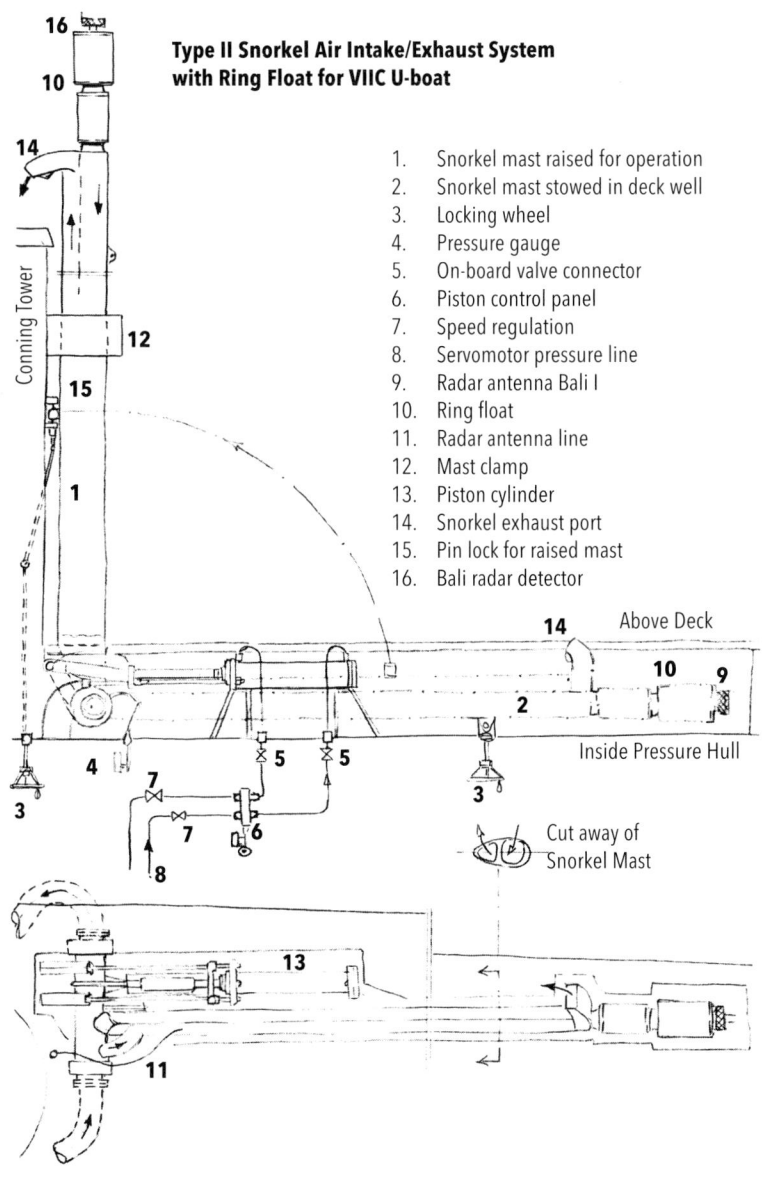

Type II Snorkel Air Intake/Exhaust System with Ring Float for VIIC U-boat

1. Snorkel mast raised for operation
2. Snorkel mast stowed in deck well
3. Locking wheel
4. Pressure gauge
5. On-board valve connector
6. Piston control panel
7. Speed regulation
8. Servomotor pressure line
9. Radar antenna Bali I
10. Ring float
11. Radar antenna line
12. Mast clamp
13. Piston cylinder
14. Snorkel exhaust port
15. Pin lock for raised mast
16. Bali radar detector

Air intake for a Type VIIC Type II non-flange snorkel mast. *(Author's collection)*

A central lubrication point for the snorkel system was added, as well as a third filter in the battery exhaust line safety system. There was definite concern over the process of venting battery gas as 'when the new blower spring coupling is being installed, the battery exhaust line is to be moved to the suction nozzle of the blower when [the] snorkel is used'.[64]

The first confirmed Type II installation on a Type VIIC occurred on *U-998* (VIIC) in May 1944, followed by *U-313* (VIIC) in July. Most Type II retrofits on Type VIICs occurred in 1945.

Exhaust System

The exhaust gases departed the boat through the normal exhaust group valve located in the pressure hull and into the exhaust trunking. Then it passed through a branch just short of the normal tank blowing system valves and through the main snorkel exhaust shut off valve, through the horizontal trunking to the heel at the base of the mast, then up the snorkel mast and out through the exhaust outlet bend below the snorkel head to be expelled into the water. The blowing of gases into the water reduced any smoke discharge that could be detected visually by Allied aircraft or ships. The fact that the sea water could circulate around the exhaust pipes as they ran from the engine to the mast reduced the heat effect proportionally. Thus, the heat signature was reduced to an undetectable level by infrared sensors. Unfortunately, the exhaust could impede the tactical employment of the periscope due to the position of the snorkel mast.

The initial trial version Type I snorkel masts on the VIIC had the exhaust pipe split at the flange, exit the main snorkel mast, then re-join after routing around the flange as it worked its way up the mast as a separate pipe connected to the intake by brackets. This design was certainly not hydrodynamic and added some complexity to the exhaust system. The production version of the Type I flange mast kept the exhaust bifurcation at the flange but encased both the intake and exhaust tubes within a single mast that improved both form and function. The Type II mast routed both lines internally as well, within a teardrop-shaped tube.

In the installations on the Type VII and Type IX U-boats the snorkel mast was forward of the periscopes. Even though when raised the top of the snorkel head was slightly lower than the extended periscope, the exhaust gases adversely affected vision ahead. On all other U-boat types, the installation was placed abaft the periscope to avoid this issue. This is specifically true on the Electro-boats.

The overall snorkel system was not pressurised and had to be flooded when diving. In U-boats equipped with Germaniawerft engines it was found advisable to blow the water out of the snorkel exhaust lines before starting the diesels. A pressure of about 8 atmospheres was used for this purpose. In MAN engines the air connection was not considered necessary, although in each case it was necessary to guard against flooding of the engines through the exhaust line when starting them.[65]

The outer exhaust valve formed the only barrier against outside water pressure. The tightness of the outer exhaust valve was a prerequisite for 'perfect snorkelling'.[66] This valve can be seen on all Type VIICs along the starboard side external trunking at the point when it drops beneath the decking at the forward base on the conning tower.

The Type VIIC exhaust trunking was routed above deck as there was probably no space below deck to incorporate the required shut-off valve that was operated from the control room. Early testing proved that the GW motor onboard this U-boat type was not strong enough to counter high back pressure in the line, especially when an operating snorkel was submerged.[67] Significant design changes were introduced specifically in the

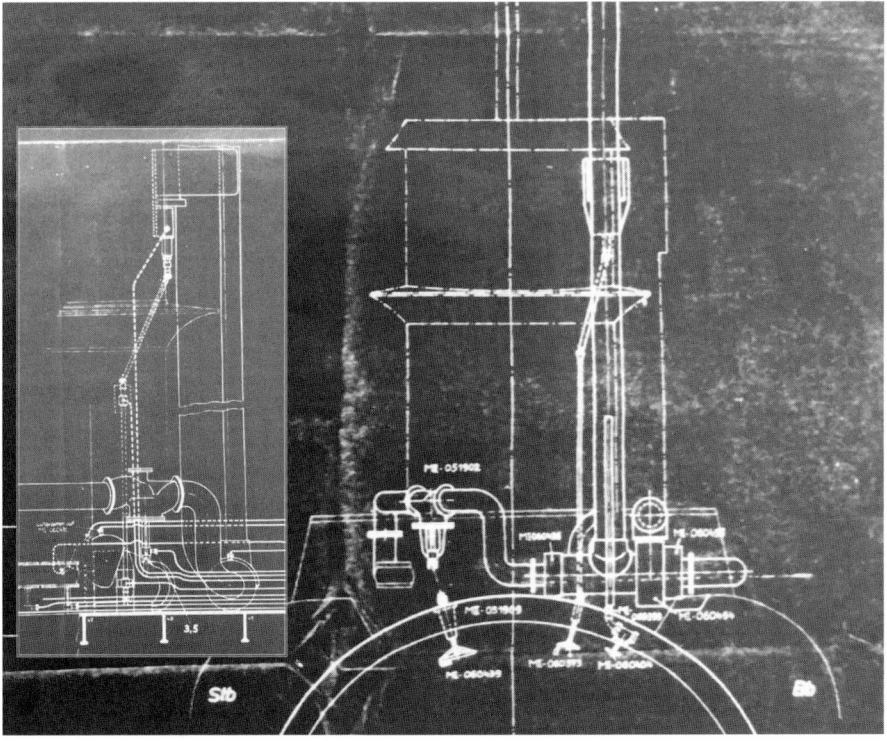

Original Kriegsmarine construction diagram showing the starboard-side snorkel exhaust system on a Type VIIC. Note that the exhaust trunking exited the deck near the engine room, then ran above deck, before turning slightly to port at the front of the conning tower, and routing below deck into the snorkel mast boot heel. This configuration was without exception on all Type VIICs and VIIC/41s. Three hand controls were installed in the control rom. The left handle operated the snorkel exhaust shut-off valve, the middle handle operated the mast locking mechanism and the right handle operated the hydraulic piston. *(Author's collection)*

U-929 (VIIC/41) autumn 1944. Lt.z.S. Joachim Hardam, the first watch officer, is seen sitting on the free-standing compass housing that replaced the attached housing that U-boat crews used to call 'the compass nose'. To the left of Hardam is the exhaust trunking and shut-off valve for the snorkel system. To the right is the piston mechanism. This U-boat had a Type II snorkel mast. Behind Hardam's left shoulder is the metal cladding that housed the snorkel mast's locking mechanism. *(Thomas Hass collection, courtesy of Axel Urbanke)*

Type VIICs that included new snorkel cams. The shut-off valve in the exhaust trunking, however, proved not to be watertight and leaked sea water into the exhaust system. This could prevent the diesel engines from starting and appears to have been an issue only on the Type VIIC U-boats. A fix was introduced by the crew of *U-671* (VIIC), whereby a connection into the exhaust system was arranged from the high-pressure airline to the exhaust manifold. This allowed the U-boat to economically blow all water out of the exhaust side of the diesels before starting up.[68]

These issues did not exist in the Type IXC and IXD2 equipped with MAN engines, thus the exhaust trunking remained below deck and was routed into the boot heel of the snorkel mast from the port side of the conning tower.

Exhaust gases were intended to be expelled underwater. However, the exhaust outlet could be exposed to the surface air if proper depth was not maintained for any reason. If there was a strong wind blowing from the aft of the U-boat it was found that the pressure could force the CO/CO_2 gases back down the exhaust trunking and into the boat. Snorkelling into the wind was therefore advised.[69]

Snorkel Heads on Diesel U-boats

Two snorkel heads were developed and employed across all on diesel U-boats. The first generation was the ball float (*Kugelschwimmer*) and the second generation was called the ring float (*Ringschwimmer*). They were opened by gravity and closed by the buoyant action of the float when the upper end of the snorkel mast was submerged. When the snorkel mast was not in use and locked in the deck well the float valve was forced open in order to flood the mast when housed, otherwise it could rupture during deep diving. The use of gravity to control the float valve opening was a simple yet brilliant feature. When the snorkel head was inadvertently submerged underwater by a wave, poor depth keeping, or an emergency manoeuvre, it closed automatically. While this function immediately, though temporarily, caused uncomfortable back pressure, it prevented flooding of the diesel engines and the boat. Experience showed that occasionally the float valve would stick in the open or closed position, especially on the second-generation float valves, and would force a U-boat to surface in order for the crew to service the valves. In early versions of the ball float design installed on both the Type VIIC and Type IX U-boats there was a slender hand-operated rod that extended from the control room to the float for the purposes of manually flooding the mast before it was returned to its housing in the deck well. This proved problematical and was discontinued, being replaced with the automatic flooding feature.

In all snorkel heads the floats were weighted to open at a constant air pressure of 400 millibars. Although the valve was balanced against static pressure differentials, there was an increase in air velocity (hence a decrease in pressure) directly under the seats where the valve first started to open under conditions of differential pressure. Without the weights the valve tended to stick in the partially opened position. After the modification of adding the weights, it was necessary to increase the size of the buoyancy chamber in order to recapture the previous standard of closing force.

Before installation, extensive shop tests of each individual valve were required to ensure that the ability to open the valve against 400 millibars existed, and that the other weight requirements were exactly correct. Later, another modification was made that included the addition of small vanes that were intended to utilise the dynamic action of the water flow when the head dipped, in order to speed up the valve closure. Then a fairing was added to the forward side of the valve support that reduced the wake of the head considerably.[70]

After months of practical experiences with the ball float a series of disadvantages were identified by the German engineers that raised concern.

Ball Float Snorkel Intake

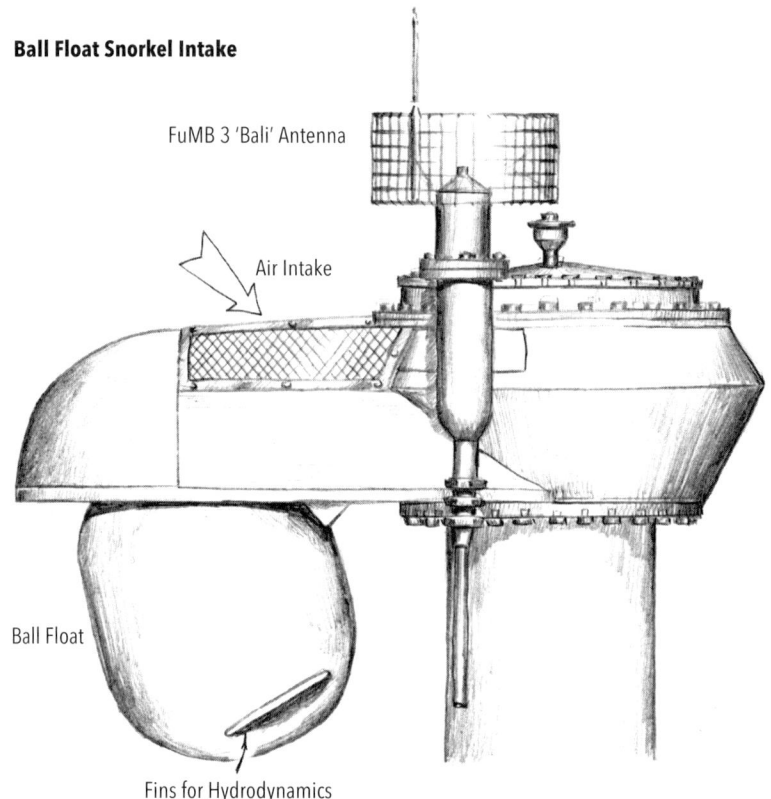

FuMB 3 'Bali' Antenna

Air Intake

Ball Float

Fins for Hydrodynamics

Standard ball float snorkel head. *(Author's collection)*

They were: the counterbalancing weights necessary to cause the valve to open under a continuous pressure differential reduced the closing force and proved unreliable; the shape of the ball float valve was such that it was difficult to cover with anti-radar material; pre-installed testing procedures were too extensive and time-consuming; and if a hole occurred in the float, the valve would remain open at all times.[71]

Due to these disadvantages the ring float became the standard float in the autumn of 1944. According to the snorkel production document, the last ball float order appears to have been G47 and S86, with the first ring floats appearing as early as G29 and S76. The ring float, as mentioned above, was introduced in October 1943, but the early design appeared too problematic and was abandoned in the spring of 1944 when it was improved. The basic concept was the same as the ball float design. This cylindrical shape proved more effective against radar, but practical experience proved that the ball float was technically more reliable. The ring float had too much surface area for its volume.[72] Being cylindrical in shape, this type lent itself readily to the application of the most successful anti-radar covering, but it was also sensi-

A comparison of ring floats on *U-278* (VIIC) top, and *U-975* (VIIC) bottom. Note that the Bali antenna wiring ran along the outside of the early ring floats that had an extra angled sheathing above the exhaust outlet. Later versions had the Bali antenna mounted on the top centre and the wiring ran down inside the snorkel mast, into the U-boat. *(Author's collection)*

tive in operation. The float had to bear its own weight and had no dynamic help from fins as on the ball float. In practice it required as much preassembly testing as the ball float. In operation the ring float valve also proved sluggish when closing due to a water cushion forming in the space between the float and the top of the valve housing. The ring float was made of thin aluminum as it is difficult to make the shape by means of welded construction. The aluminum proved easily distorted by sea water, which altered its shape and made it harder to seat properly.[73]

Based on the issues encountered with both the ball and ring floats, a new snorkel head with a pneumatic float valve was designed and tested successfully before the end of the war. Heinrich Heep was responsible for the development of the experimental electro-pneumatic design.[74]

The electro-pneumatic snorkel head proved highly successful during its four weeks of Baltic testing. Ten were initially ordered by the Kriegsmarine for wider operational testing.[75] However, only two U-boats are known to have received this installation before the end of the war.

The new valve was single-seated. It seated with sea pressure and was operated by an air piston. The air supply to this piston was controlled by electro-magnetic relays, which were in turn actuated by the sea water making or breaking the control circuit through contacts located at the head of the mast.[76] Stainless steel contacts protruded through the anti-radar covering. These were energised from a 24-volt AC circuit supplied through a small transformer from the U-boat's 220-volt AC circuit. This prevented inadvertent operation other than by immersion. If the snorkel hood dipped below the water, the contacts operated and closed the circuit, causing a relay to operate. The relay triggered a switch that completed a 110-volt DC circuit, triggering an indicator lamp in the control room. This energised a solenoid that operated a three-way valve, admitting air at 12 atmospheres from the line, which was then exhausted to the piston, preventing the painful drop in pressure felt when the earlier snorkel head valves became inadvertently submerged. If the snorkel head emerged above the surface, breaking contact between the two electric circuits, then the control valve dropped and air would flow into the U-boat as normal. A hand emergency valve was placed in the control room. At 12 atmospheres air could be supplied into the U-boat manually if the electric gear was out of action, and the snorkel valve closed by operating the piston. The first pneumatic heads were covered with ribbed anti-radar covering. Later they were to receive thicker mats.

Crewman Wolfgang Giebel served on *U-481* (VIIC), which received one of the first electro-pneumatic float valves. In a post-war letter he attested to its effectiveness.[77] The testing by *U-481* produced good results and the Kriegsmarine placed an order for 150 in order to refit all operational U-boats with the new electro-pneumatic head.[78] However, the war ended before this order was completed.

An entirely new electro-pneumatic snorkel system was designed before war's end that included support to the periscope in order to reduce the inherent vibrations felt in all U-boat types. It was patented by Oelfken. The

Late-war pneumatic snorkel head with protective anti-radar coating on *U-481* (VIIC). The pneumatic snorkel was significantly advanced and proved more effective than the ring or ball floats. It is not precisely known how many U-boats were retrofitted with this advanced design. It was decades ahead of any exiting snorkel systems or patents that existed at the time. *(Author's collection)*

Oelfken Snorkel

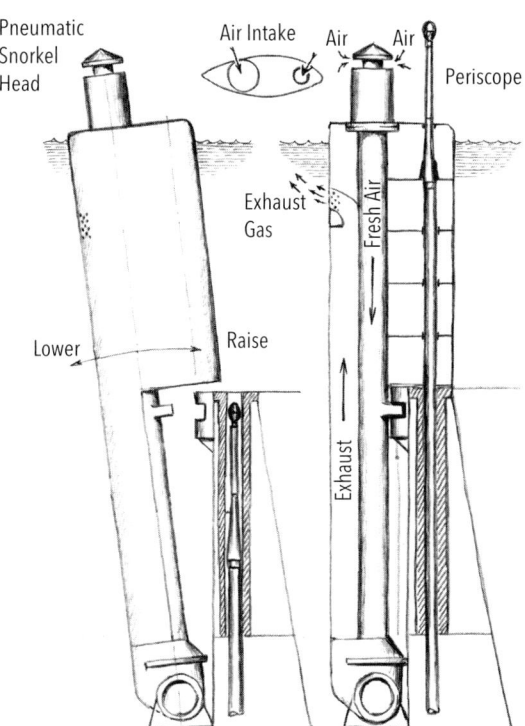

The Oelfken snorkel mast used an integrated housing for the pneumatic snorkel head, exhaust and attack periscope that eliminated all vision and vibration problems. This design never left the drawing board. *(Author's collection)*

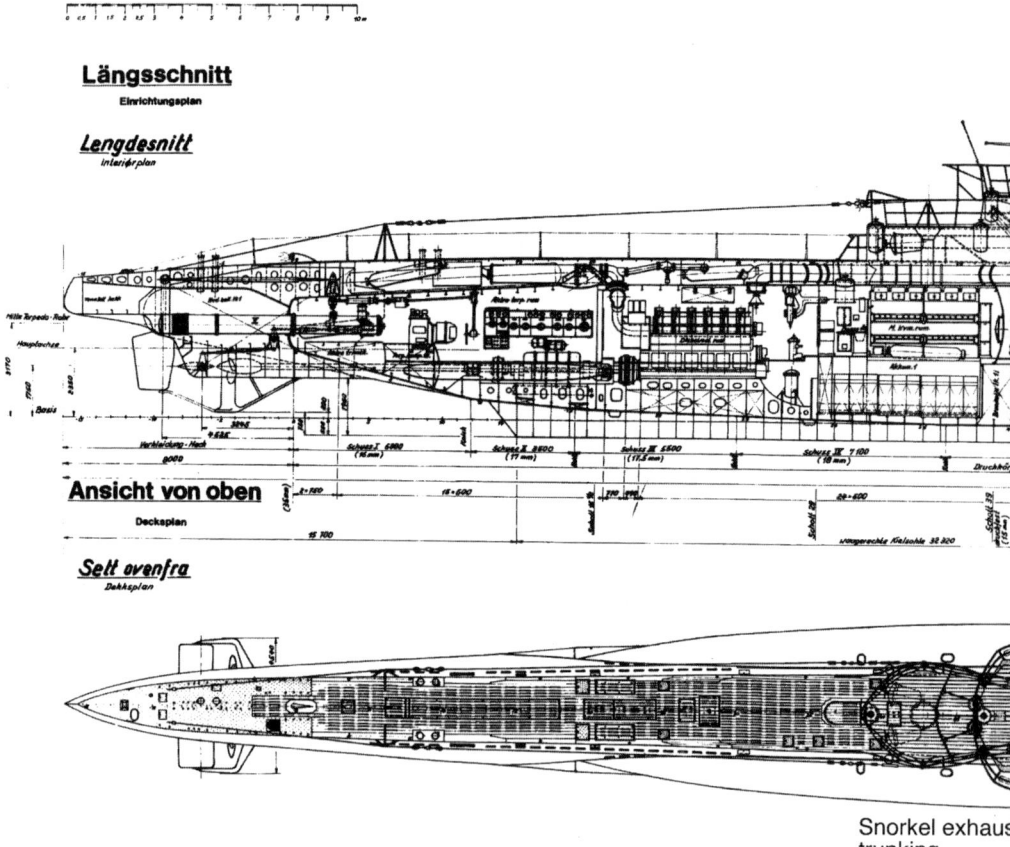

Längsschnitt
Einrichtungsplan

Lengdesnitt
interiørplan

Ansicht von oben
Deckplan

Selt ovenfra
Dekksplan

Snorkel exhaust
trunking

The correct technical diagram for a Type VIIC or VIIC/41 retrofitted with a Type I flange snorkel configuration. Note the starboard-side above-deck exhaust trunking left off the fictional Type VIIC (1944) deck plan. This trunking was present on all retrofitted VIIC and VIIC/41 U-boats. *(Author's collection)*

folding snorkel mast was raised when the periscope was down. When in the up position, the periscope was raised and lowered through a hole in a hydro-dynamically shaped hood covering connected to the snorkel. This reduced vibrations in the periscope shielding and provided significant stability when it was raised to the highest position. The Chief U-boat Engineer Admiral Thedsen believed that the Oelfken design was the best at the time and should be a standard fitting across all U-boats.[79]

Snorkel Configurations in U-boat Types VIIC, VIIC/41, VIID and VIIF
Installation of the snorkel retrofits was no different between any of the Type VIIC U-boat variants. In all such models the snorkel was situated on the port side of the conning tower, practically flush with its forward fairing.

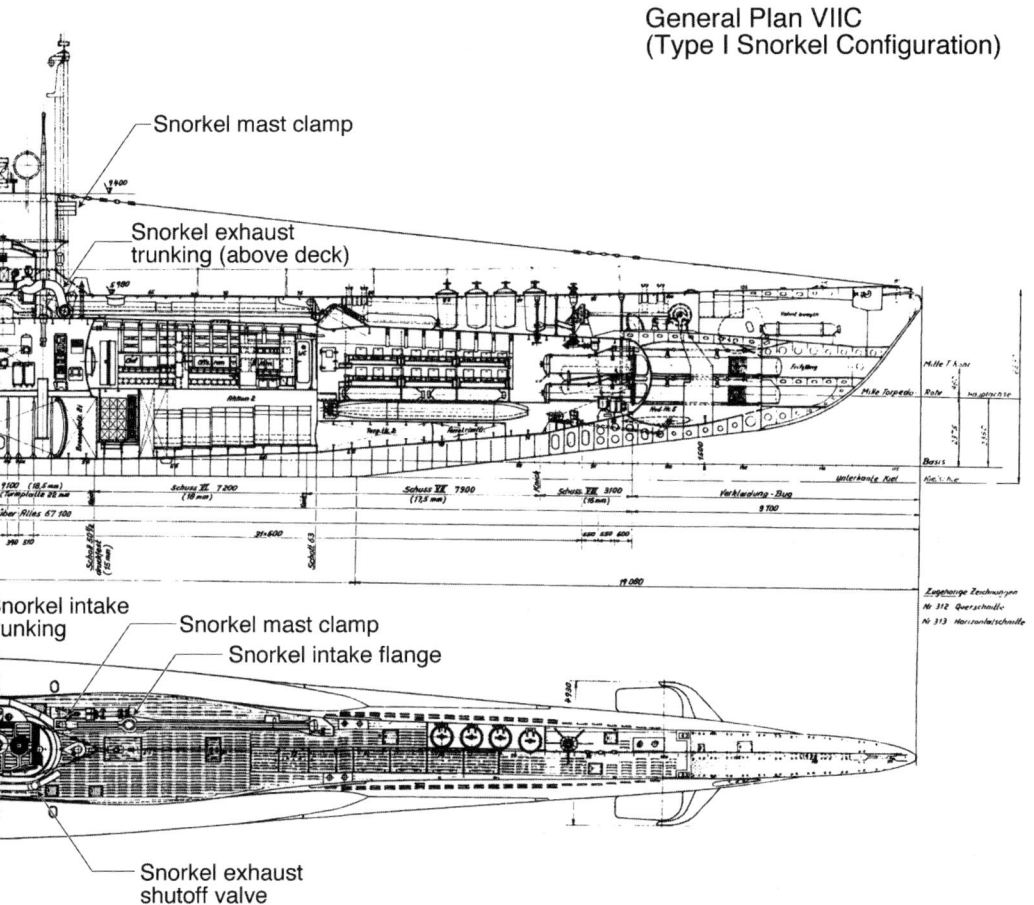

General Plan VIIC
(Type I Snorkel Configuration)

Snorkel mast clamp

Snorkel exhaust
trunking (above deck)

Snorkel intake
trunking

Snorkel mast clamp

Snorkel intake flange

Snorkel exhaust
shutoff valve

Two versions of the snorkel mast existed in the Type VIICs, as previously
noted. The initial version, known as the Type I, contained a flange midway
up the snorkel mast that mated with the intake piping that ran along the
port side of the conning tower as noted above.

Later, in the autumn of 1944, a Type II mast was introduced that eliminated the flange and routed the intake through the heel below deck. The
two tubes that made up the snorkel mast were attached to each other. The
intake was 230mm in diameter and the exhaust was slightly smaller at
180mm. The walls of the snorkel intake itself were 7.5mm, while the
exhaust line was 6mm. The possibility also existed for the intake/exhaust
tubes to be connected to the snorkel casing by fairings and not to each
other in some cases. The snorkel height from the upper deck to the top of
the air intake, but not including the upper half of the float valve mechanism, was 8.2m (26ft 11in) and the height from the upper deck to the centre of the exhaust outlet was 6.9m (22ft 7in). From the upper deck to

this point, the width of the snorkel mast was approximately 4.8m (15ft 9in).

The exhaust outlet on the Type VIIs was directed downward and aft. The exhaust line stopped at the exhaust outlet. On all Type VIIs the exhaust trunking emerged above deck on the starboard side, allowing access to the emergency shut-off valve before dropping below deck and running along the front of the conning tower to the enter the heel of the snorkel mast. It is not clear why the exhaust piping ran above decking on the Type VII U-boats, but not on the Type IXs, as there appears to have been enough room to run the piping below the decking. It is important to emphasise that every Type VIIC without exception had exhaust trunking that ran above deck along the starboard side of the conning tower without exception.

There has been post-war confusion about the late-war configuration of the Type VIIC. For example, a design plan of a Type VIIC (1944) published in a variety of otherwise superb technical U-boat histories, presents an integrated streamlined snorkel installation with the intake and exhaust trunk-

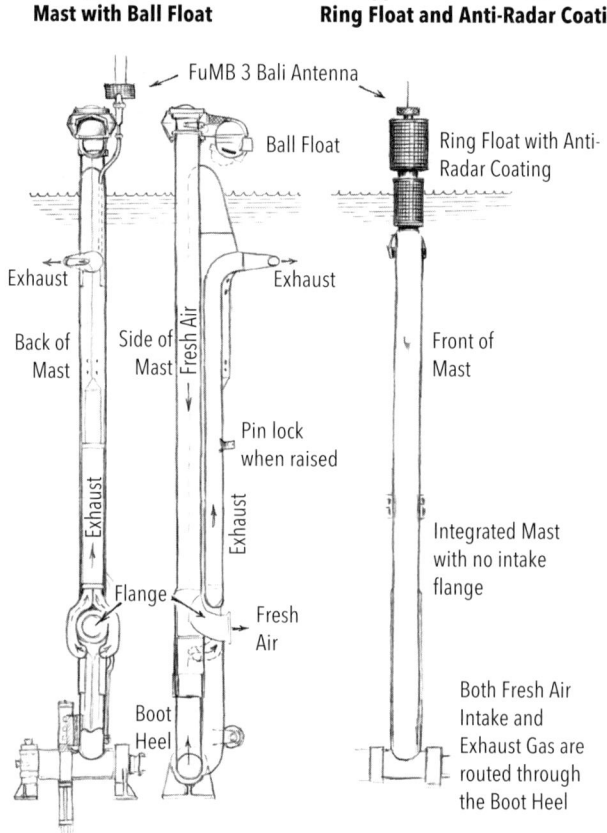

VIIC Type I Snorkel Mast with Ball Float

VIIC Type II Snorkel Mast with Ring Float and Anti-Radar Coating

FuMB 3 Bali Antenna

Ball Float

Ring Float with Anti-Radar Coating

Exhaust

Exhaust

Back of Mast

Side of Mast

Fresh Air

Front of Mast

Pin lock when raised

Exhaust

Exhaust

Integrated Mast with no intake flange

Flange

Fresh Air

Boot Heel

Both Fresh Air Intake and Exhaust Gas are routed through the Boot Heel

A comparison of Type I and Type II snorkel masts on a VIIC. *(Author's collection)*

A comparison of *U-1058* (VIIC) Type I snorkel mast (left) and *U-278* (VIIC) Type II snorkel mast (right). Note the differences in the upper portions of the mast. *U-1058*'s upper mast and snorkel head has an anti-radar coating applied. *(Left image author's collection and the right image Benson Collection, courtesy of Axel Urbanke).*

ing running from the snorkel mast boot heel under the decking of the outer hull.[80] While the intake did run under the deck on Type II masts, the exhaust trunking never did. A Type VIIC (1944) deck plan never existed in theory or practice during the war. This was a composite drawing rendered by German researcher Fritz Köhl in the late 1960s or early '70s to represent a VIIC with all possible snorkel modifications introduced before war's end. Unfortunately, this fictional rendering has been accepted as an actual wartime design.

This incorrect representation of a VIIC snorkel installation is compounded by *U-995* (VIIC/41) on display in Laboe, Germany. Period photos of *U-995* published in Eckard Wetzel's *U-995*, clearly show above deck exhaust trunking that was retrofitted onto this U-boat during the last days of the war.[81] When *U-995* was gifted back to Germany in the early 1970s by Norway to be turned into a museum exhibit, the German engineers responsible for its overhaul artificially removed the external exhaust trunking.[82]

This has given rise to an incorrect interpretation that Type VIIC/41 U-boats had no above-deck exhaust trunking, or that this was a Type VIIC (1944) version. Neither interpretation is historically correct.

The Type VIID was equipped with a Type I snorkel mast and the Type VIIF with a Type II.

Snorkel Configurations in U-boat Types IXB, IXC, IXC/40 IXD1, and IXD2

The snorkel in a Type IX U-boat was mounted on the starboard side only and was predominantly the Type I flange design with the intake trunking running along the conning tower. As many as eight out of fifty-three Type IXs were equipped with the Type II snorkel mast with the exhaust trunking routed below deck. In both cases the exhaust trunking ran entirely below the starboard-side decking. *U-1233* was the first Type IX to be fitted with a

A comparison of *U-953* (VIIC), a 'Landwirt' boat (left), and *U-1009* (VIIC/41) (right). Note that *U-953*'s magnetic compass is attached, the lifting mechanism is a pulley, and the flange system is an early retrofit, whereby the intake trunking is lower, and the flange on the snorkel mast is not fully recessed. In addition, the locking mechanism is exposed as it runs down the front of the conning tower into the control room. Oblt.z.S. Karl-Heinz Marbach is pictured on the conning tower. On *U-1009* the magnetic compass was detached. The intake trunking is positioned higher, which allowed the flange to be moved slightly higher on the mast and more easily recessed below deck. The locking mechanism is now streamlined and runs flush down the conning tower, protected behind a steel tube in this case. The lifting mechanism is a piston. *(Image on the left is courtesy Axel Urbanke, the image on the right is from the author's collection)*

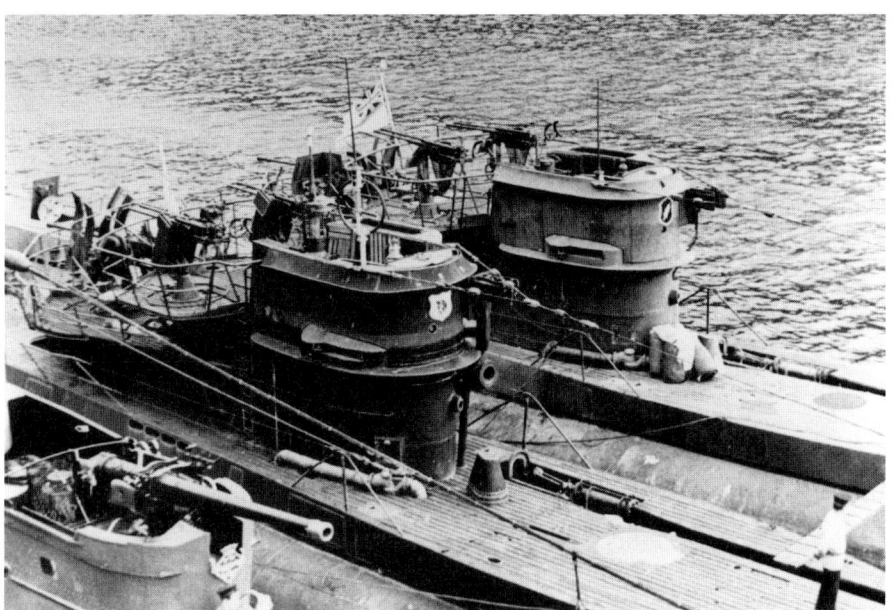

A comparison of *U-1105* (VIIC) (left) and *U-1171* (VIIC/41) (right). *U-1105* is coated with Alberich. Both show the starboard-side exhaust trunking, detached compass housings and piston lift mechanisms. *U-1105* is a Type I snorkel mast with the locking mechanism secured within a pipe as it runs into the control room. *U-1171*'s locking mechanism is slightly exposed, as it routes through the wave deflector into a cladding attached to the conning tower. *(Author's collection)*.

Type II snorkel mast. In this first installation the intake line was through the boot heel of the snorkel around the conning tower, then under the port-side decking. As a by-product of this configuration, the snorkel mast rested on the intake line when recessed back into the deck well. This could cause cracks in the intake line that resulted in leaks upon the next use. It is not certain if the intake trunking was rerouted aft of the snorkel mast boot heel on subsequent Type II installations.

The snorkel head was primarily of the ball float design, though a small number of Type IXs were equipped with a ring float, as in the case of *U-874* (IXD2).[83]

A slight difference between the VIIC and IX U-boats is that the snorkel was level with the aft periscope. Because the snorkel mast was positioned at the forward end of the conning tower, the snorkel outlet was directed downward aft and slightly to starboard to ensure the gases did not interfere with periscope operations. The exhaust line continued up to the base of the float valve. The shape of the snorkel mast in the Type IXs appeared to be pointed at the back, i.e. to have a teardrop shape.

Additional changes were ordered to the snorkel installations on Type IXC U-boats as late as 21 March 1945, and these include the elimination of the flood and emergency shut-off valves in certain circumstances.[84] The reasons for these changes are not entirely clear, and in any case they were never implemented.

Charging Procedures for a Type VIIC U-boat

Charging batteries while snorkelling was a standard U-boat practice. Normal operational practice was to run the diesel at 340/350rpm with the supercharger for charging batteries only, and the other diesel running 250rpm for propulsion, with its motor 'floating' across the bus bands and giving a small charge. This resulted in a speed of 5–6 knots and a charging rate of 1,000/1,200 amps. One diesel engine could also be run as a generator while the other was on propulsion, giving 6 knots and a charge of 1,000 amps. Another procedure was to run the diesel at 400/500rpm with the supercharger for generating only. The electric motor was run between 90/150rpm for propulsion. The rougher the sea, the higher the rpm. This procedure produced 1,600 amps. Another procedure was to run both diesels with the superchargers at 210rpm driving both propulsion and generators, thus producing a speed of about 6 knots and a charge of 1,300 amps. German crews believed this was the most economical method for proceeding to or returning from an operational area.[85]

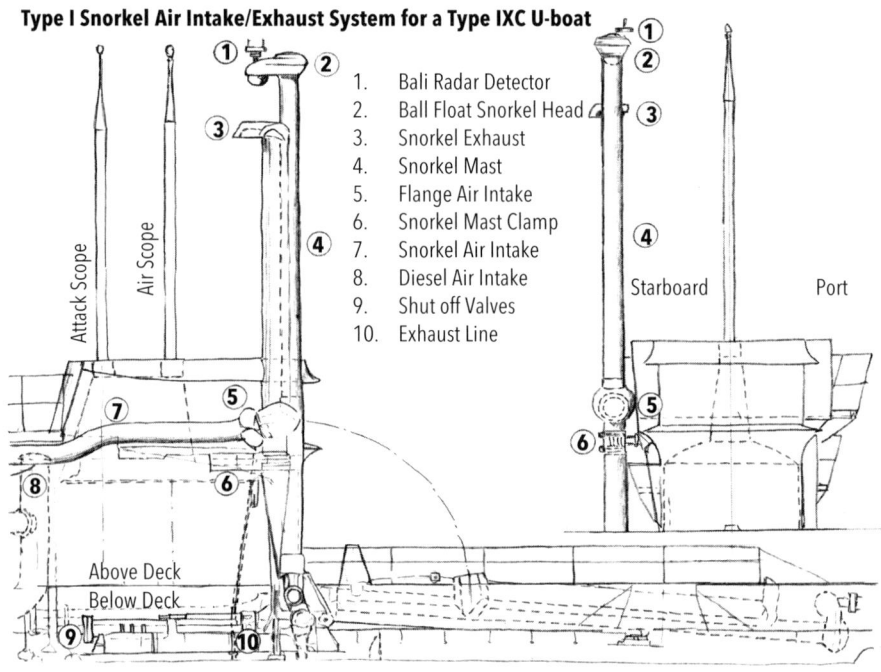

Type I Snorkel Air Intake/Exhaust System for a Type IXC U-boat

1. Bali Radar Detector
2. Ball Float Snorkel Head
3. Snorkel Exhaust
4. Snorkel Mast
5. Flange Air Intake
6. Snorkel Mast Clamp
7. Snorkel Air Intake
8. Diesel Air Intake
9. Shut off Valves
10. Exhaust Line

Attack Scope

Air Scope

Starboard   Port

Above Deck
Below Deck

The Type I snorkel configuration on a Type IXC and Type IXD2. Several Type IXCs were equipped with a Type II snorkel mast that ran their intake trunking below deck and a ring float. *(Author's collection)*

Charging Procedures for a Type IX U-boat
The most commonly used method was to snorkel in calm sea with both diesels running at 270rpm, resulting in a speed of 6.5 knots with one diesel at 200rpm, the other turning free giving a speed of 5.5 knots, or again, with one diesel at 250/260rpm charging and one electric motor at 140/150rpm,

A comparison of the Type I snorkel configurations on *U-1228* (IXC/40) (left) and *U-190* (IXC/40) (right). Note that *U-1228*'s mast is a single piece, while *U-190*'s upper mast is bolted to the main mast. Both upper masts have an anti-radar coating. The Bali antenna wiring is routed differently on both masts. Some snorkel masts, like *U-190*'s, were equipped with a welded wedge at the front to help with hydrodynamic performance during snorkel operation. *(Images on left courtesy of NARA, and image on right taken by John Taylor RCNVR and made available by his son Bill Taylor)*

giving a speed of about 5 knots. Another procedure that was considered more economical was to run one diesel at 250rpm for both propulsion and charging, thus producing a charge of about 400 amps. One U-boat commander stated that he frequently ran one diesel at 400rpm and charged the battery at 1,800 amps, whilst the other diesel was coupled to the propeller shaft at about 240rpm, producing exhaust temperatures of 480/500 degrees. This process resulted in the valves badly sooting up. Despite a warning from BdU not to use this method, this was a common procedure, according to crewmembers from other U-boats. Another procedure was to run one diesel at 250rpm for propulsion, producing a speed somewhat under 4 knots. The other diesel was used for charging at between 380/400rpm, giving a charge of 1,400/1,500 amps in batteries connected in series and supplying approximately 250 amps. Charging rates as high as 2,000 amps were obtained for short periods by overloading the generators. An alternative procedure for bad weather was to connect both diesels to the propeller shaft at 250rpm, producing a maximum speed of 6 knots whilst simultaneously charging the batteries at about 800 amps in a series, plus generating approximately 200 amps for the boat's supply.[86]

Aerials

By mid-to-late 1944 U-boats were routinely equipped with detectors capable of identifying a variety of Allied radar devices. These were known collectively by the Allies as German Search Receivers (GSR). There was the standard Funkmess-Beobachtung (FuMB) 7 Naxos receiver that was linked to an FuMB 24 'Cuba I' Fliege detection antenna in February 1944, which could provide bearings in the 8–12cm range and proved especially effective in the 10cm wavelength. In May 1944, a FuMB Mücke detection antenna was added that could detect along the 2–4cm wavelength. Both the Fliege and Mücke detectors were considered complementary and were combined into the FuMB 26 Tunis aerial later in the year. However, they were not watertight and had to be installed manually after a U-boat surfaced. The FuMB 7 Naxos 1 continued to be utilised independently, though its detection range was limited.

Starting in March 1944 U-boats were equipped with the Funkmess-Ortung (FuMO) 61 Hohentwiel U active detector (1m x 1.4m) carrying 4 x 6 dipoles that was installed on the port side and raised and lowered when the U-boat was surfaced. This device operated on a turntable. This passive detector could give early warning against early warning of about 8–10km for surfaced vessels and 1–25km for aircraft. This device only worked when a U-boat was surfaced. After the introduction of the snorkel they were rarely used as U-boats remained submerged for almost their

Ball float snorkel head on *U-516* (IXC). Note the waffle pattern of the anti-radar coating, the two-piece construction of the upper and main mast and that the Bali antenna wiring runs down along the snorkel mast. *(Author's collection)*

entire cruise, with only the snorkel head exposed above the surface for any length of time.

Initially, snorkels had no detectors mounted on the top of their mast, making a U-boat blind to approaching surface or aircraft when snorkelling. While this was a concern, the snorkel head's rather small size produced a significantly smaller radar target, as predicted by Walter when he first proposed the device to Dönitz. In addition, snorkel heads and upper portions of the exposed snorkel mast began to receive an anti-radar reflective coat-

The starboard-side air intake of *U-190* (IXC/40). The locking mechanism for the mast can be seen to the right of the raised mast running down along the conning tower and into the snorkel well. *(Image taken by John Taylor RCNVR and made available by his son Bill Taylor)*

ing known as *Schornsteinfeger* (Chapter 3). Nevertheless, a detection solution that could be mounted to a snorkel mast was devised.

Snorkel heads were soon fitted in mid-1944 with the watertight pressurised version of FuMB Ant. 3, known as the FuMB 29 Bali Runddipole basket-type aerial. The Bali passive radar detector covered metered wavelengths. It was also known as the 'round-dipole' or simply 'dipole' antenna. Sometimes it was called *Hächhen* (bunny), colloquially by its crews, when both polarised detection antennas were affixed to the basket, causing it to resemble a rabbit's ears. The FuMB 29 Bali did not have to be removed when diving and remained affixed to the snorkel head. The lead-in from the dipole passed from a pressure-proof housing through the inside of the intake mast via a water-tight conduit tube down into the U-boat's sound room. The conduit tube was permanently connected to the boat's internal wiring.

The FuMB 29 Bali could detect Allied millimetre radar waves at the short distance of 1,000m when snorkelling, which allowed sufficient time to dive before an effective attack could be undertaken by the detecting aircraft. A functioning snorkel round-dipole could give a snorkelling U-boat a fifteen-second advantage in diving when Allied active radar in the metered wavelength was detected. Centimetre wavelength detection from the dipole was not implemented on diesel boat dipoles before the end of the war, but was under development.[87]

The FuMO 65 Hohentwiel-Drauf was installed on the new Type XXIs,

The ring float of *U-875* (IXD2). The Bali antenna is integrated and the snorkel head on the IXD2 has a Wesch anti-radar coating. Note its size when compared to the Kriegsmarine U-boat man sitting on it. *(Author's collection)*

but like the version for the Type VIICs and IXs, it would rarely, if ever be used, given that U-boats now remained submerged for their entire patrol. The Germans also developed the new FuMB 35 Athos dipole early warning receiver system mounted on a mast that consisted of two circular array antennas mounted inside a pressurised structure and placed on top of a telescopic mast. The upper part covered the 'X' frequency band and the lower part the 'S' frequency band. The receiving electronic equipment was very sophisticated; it had four independent amplifiers and a cathode ray screen.

A close-up image of *U-1228*'s (IXC/40) ball float snorkel head. Note the mesh that allows the airflow into the mast during operation. *(Courtesy of NARA)*

The snorkel mast configuration of *U-234* (XB). The mast was a Type II (non-flange) equipped with a ball float. When raised the mast sat further back along the conning tower than on any other U-boat type. *(Author's collection)*

The antenna was watertight and this device displayed the output on a cathode ray tube.

Radio Communications and Snorkelling
Standard procedures during the height of the convoy battles in the North Atlantic included a constant flow of wireless radio transmissions to BdU and retransmission of orders back to the Wolfpacks. U-boats typically maintained long surface times through 1943, especially at night, which allowed them to co-ordinate their attacks against the convoys with BdU.[88] However, by the autumn of 1944 snorkel-equipped U-boats remained submerged, often for their entire patrol. This introduced three major problems that affected the previously normal communication.

First, submerged U-boats could receive very limited shortwave and VLF (very low frequency) signals through the round dipole mounted on the snorkel. However, signal reception degraded once a U-boat submerged and eventually was lost the deeper it went. BdU issued guidance in July 1944 that stated 'maximum diving depth for reception 20–22m with strongest very low frequency transmitters and good receiving conditions. Diving depths are reduced with increasing distance! In the North Atlantic diving depths of about 18 to 20m are anticipated!'[89]

Second, U-boats that stayed submerged and did not surface, did not transmit radio signals. Wireless transmissions through the round dipole proved problematic due to a lack of signal strength, though some boats were still equipped with rod antennas. U-boat commanders were initially often admonished by BdU for their lack of wireless transmissions. This was especially true for those U-boats operating between Norway and the eastern approaches to Great Britain, as well as those operating in the Channel and the Irish Sea. These operational areas were close to German U-boat bases and U-boats could remain submerged to and from their operational areas for almost the entire patrol. Type VII U-boats operating close to England often waited until they were a day away from returning to their Norwegian base before they sent a mission report, though this was due to their fear of being HF/DF'ed by Allied ship and shore stations. Many U-boats simply returned to base without transmitting a single signal. Instead, the commanders handed a written report into their 10th U-Flotilla once their boat was docked.

The Type IX snorkel U-boats sent to the North American coast often surfaced south of Iceland, where they had a brief opportunity to send passage and weather reports as required. However, it was found that atmospheric conditions caused havoc with transmissions in this area and many snorkel-equipped Type IXs sent across the North Atlantic experienced issues receiving transmissions from BdU. The problems increased as powerful transmitter stations in Europe, including 'Goliath', shut down with the Allied advance in 1945.

Third, long underwater cruises wrought havoc on the communications equipment outside and inside U-boats. Outside the U-boats, antennas and external connectors quickly became damaged due to the extended time spent near the surface, where components were subject to strong sea states while snorkelling. For example, *U-427* (VIIC) was on its first snorkel patrol in April 1945 and only a week out when its KTB recorded on 30 April that: 'In operational area nothing heard from round dipole. Wireless reception from round dipole while snorkelling up to a maximum sea state 4 possible; beyond that just received broken pieces since dipole flooded too often.'[90] Long exposure to sea water accelerated the rate that external components became corroded.

Snorkelling brought high humidity within the U-boat that caused everything to remain damp. Electronics began to short out within several weeks of the start of a patrol, including the radios. Even when a U-boat surfaced to transmit, the captain often found it impossible to do so. A few Type IX U-boats, as noted in later chapters, adopted a makeshift antenna system by attaching an antenna wire from the conning tower radio to an Aphrodite balloon that was sent aloft in order to establish a functioning receiver. This was an event that even *U-853* probably attempted before it was sunk off Rhode Island.

After sinking the SS *Black Point*, on 4 May 1945, witnesses onboard the SS *Karmen* reported seeing *U-853* surface. They observed several crew members emerge from the conning tower, head to the 'aft deck' and attempt 'to deploy a yellow inflatable raft'. Within moments, the crew scrambled back down below deck and submerged, likely after realising they were under observation by a steamer.[91] Given both the colour and texture of the observed item, *U-853*'s crew was attempting to send up an Aphrodite anti-radar balloon in order to improve radio reception with BdU. It is likely they heard a garbled transmission to surrender broadcast from Germany and attempted to get clarification.

U-boats that had trouble sending or receiving wireless messages attached a copper wire that was hooked up to the auxiliary radio in the conning tower and sent the balloon aloft to be able to improve transmission and reception back to BdU. Other Type IXs operating off the North American coast deployed this device, as in the case of *U-541* (IXC/40) operating off Canada in September 1944 and *U-1233* (IXC/40) operating off the US East Coast in January 1945.

These infrequent wireless communications impacted Allied Ultra intercepts in the last twelve months of war. The lack of U-boat signals meant a loss of situational awareness. In addition to the snorkel's impact, two other developments in radio communication emerged that alarmed the Allies. On 17 November 1944 U-boat traffic indicated a new policy of sending certain messages in a special individual cipher. These appeared to be of operational importance, containing the assignment of heading points and attack areas. At the same time the new short signal code 'Ursula' was introduced. By the end of April 1945, a relatively small number of special cipher messages were broken. Ursula was reconstructed by Allied cryptologists before the code book itself was captured by the British. While the use of the special cipher and Ursula interfered to some extent with Allied knowledge of U-boat movements, the continued reliance by BdU on their normal cipher for the bulk of their communications tended to negate the advantages of the new systems, not only in terms of following the U-boats' movements, but also in terms of security.[92]

Another capability introduced by the end of 1944 was called 'Kurier' and it alarmed the Allies. Kurier was a high-speed flash transmission system that sent 600 words per minute. The spacing was such as to make reading from film easy. Flash transmission was first tested in the spring of 1943. It compressed a communication, which could contain as many as seven letters in the Morse alphabet, into an elapsed time of 425 milliseconds. Previously the British had estimated the duration of one transmission to be a third of a second. This not only prevented the U-boat from being located through radio direction finding, but also prevented burst transmissions from being intercepted and read by Allied cryptologists. The system contained two parts. A Phillip CR-101-A Receiver and a 'Gerber' KZ G44/2 (Pulse Giver) transmitter. The only drawback was that it had limited range.[93]

Snorkel-equipped U-boats began to be equipped with the flash transmitting gear in the late autumn/early winter of 1944. Kurier was a standard fitting in the Type XXI and Type XXIII Electro-boats. U-boats were only to be equipped with the Gerber transmitting gear. It was noted that Kurier transmissions from a snorkel round dipole that was submerged to periscope depth were not successful. One submerged test was conducted at 9.15am on 13 December 1944 by *U-864* (IXD2). A transmission was sent from the U-boat's snorkel round dipole but receiving its submerged signal proved ineffective. The reply in response from BdU was 'radiation of snorkel round dipole very weak, and small hope of success. Radiated output is greater when wave is shorter. Therefore, the frequency is most favourable. Kurier received only in Bernau, although Kurier receiving set was turned to the greatest sensitivity for round-dipole signals.'[94] The number of diesel U-boats that received the new Kurier system is unknown, but available period documents suggest that it was widely introduced starting in mid-1944. U-boat crews threw them overboard with other sensitive gear when they surrendered.

Navigation

New navigational challenges were introduced with the snorkel. Technical difficulties were experienced with the fixed eyepiece periscope during long underwater cruises. The periscope housings were not airtight and the build-up of dust and oily air in snorkelling U-boats entered the mast and reduced visibility. Improvements were introduced that made the periscope housing more airtight and reduced the impact.[95]

By the autumn of 1944 U-boats were operating near Allied coasts and remaining completely underwater in most cases. This brought new challenges in navigation, especially with crews that were generally inexperienced compared to their counterparts of earlier years. U-boat crews had to develop specialised navigation skills that were simply non-existent in any other navy at that time. During tactical situations, for example, it might be required to turn off the gyrocompass and echo-sounder to reduce noise. After some hours of manoeuvring like this neither commander nor navigator had any idea of their position.[96] Navigation in coastal waters was a matter of concern because of costly accidents to U-boats that had been sustained when it had gone wrong. Accurate dead reckoning, terrestrial navigation and the utilisation of lines of sounding were recommended for their reliability; but the exercise of appropriate caution was urged as the basic principle in coastal navigation. One innovative method introduced by the end of 1944 was 'Elektra-Sonne'.[97]

Both Arctic and Atlantic U-boats were asked to make tests with Elektra-Sonne beacons that were already in use by the Luftwaffe as navigational aids starting in the spring of 1943. The use of beamed signals enabled U-boats to fix their position by employing only an ordinary radio receiver. A great deal of attention was given by BdU to amassing information on the adequacy of navigation by this means. The results of early experiments were not directly available to Allied intelligence through Ultra because they were included primarily in the written communications reports of the U-boats. However, there were several instances where successful navigation by Elektra-Sonne was confirmed through Ultra.

U-boat commanders found that Elektra-Sonne was highly useful in those that were making long submerged cruises, as the beam signals could be received over the snorkel round dipole. Experiments began in the spring of 1943 with both *U-456* (VIIC) and *U-566* (VIIC) using Sonne 6. Additional testing followed in June using Sonne 15. Special charts (Charts 882 for Sonne 6 and 883 for Sonne 15) were issued that were used to determine U-boat positions. Oberleutnant Max-Martin Teichert reported from *U-456*: 'observations from 28 April until 2 May between 10 and 18 W. Sig. Str. 5. As directional beacon maximum error 1° each side, as radio beacon maximum error up to 2° each side owing to a very broad minimum at times.'[98] Despite the early successes in testing, it was the introduction of the snorkel that operationalised the concept.

U-boat commanders were slow to transition to Elektra-Sonne navigation. On 22 March 1944, BdU encouraged Elektra-Sonne use: 'Recent experiences have shown that after repeated practice in navigating by Elektra-Sonne very good results were obtained. Work with it as often as possible, particularly in the North Atlantic.'[99] A few days later the U-boat crews were told: 'Navigation by Elektra-Sonne had not been tested fully enough in the past. U-boats have used the Sonnen almost exclusively just for taking bearings and thus have yielded insufficient results. The advantage of the Sonnen is that positions may be ascertained without D/F set.'[100]

Not until the autumn of 1944, when U-boats began month-long underwater cruises without surfacing, did Elektra-Sonne become all-important. BdU emphasised this in their Experience Message 181 sent out on 6 November: 'Commanders still pay too little attention to Elektra-Sonne navigation. Good navigation capabilities even when submerged, lots of favourable experience. Elektra-Sonne navigation is always to be used for training, even if other equipment is available. This allows comparison capabilities and experience in preparing intelligence reports. Commanders must justify not using it.'[101]

As noted, submerged U-boats were able to hear Elektra-Sonne signals over the snorkel round dipole when the snorkel mast was extended, while transmissions could be heard over the D/F loop if it was out of the water. By the end of November, BdU reinforced the use of this navigational aid: 'Avoid surfacing for astronomical fix as far as possible. Keep scrupulously exact dead reckoning, allowing for current. Use of sounding apparatus, Elektra-Sonne and radio beacons make a thoroughly exact determination of position possible, according to available experiences. Make use of every possibility for determining positions by landmarks when near our own and enemy coasts.'[102]

The extent to which navigation by Elektra-Sonne had been developed by the closing months of the war was indicated by a message stating: 'One U-boat returning from mid-Atlantic had a correction from estimated position of only 2 nautical miles on entering port after a 4-week passage without taking position by star sights. Navigation by Elektra-Sonnen only. In addition, a running fix outside the port of destination was taken from Sonne 8.'[103] Six stations were established across Europe before the end of the war.

Two other forms of navigation introduced were VLF direction finding in January 1944 within the North Atlantic, and sonar soundings. By the end of 1944 it became apparent that nearly all snorkel U-boats in the Atlantic were equipped with VLF direction finders mounted in the form of their round dipoles. While BdU considered this the secondary means of navigation after Sonne, it was still employed by U-boats in certain circumstances. VLF enabled U-boats to take as many bearings as possible on American and European transmitters, logging the results and comparing them with their own dead reckoning or astronomical fixes. They enabled the U-boats to determine whether or not it was possible to obtain cross bearings in mid-ocean, as well as the longitudinal limits at which sufficient accurate bearings could be taken on American and European transmitters.[104] Oberleutnant Hans-Joachim Förster in *U-480* (VIIC) reached his destination on his first patrol through an exact determination of position by the VLF procedure. Without any further navigational aid, he reached the escort pick-up point.

Sounding in the form of sonic telegraphy was also recommended based on the experiences of Oberleutnant Hartmuth Schimmelpfennig, who commanded *U-1004* (VIIC/41). He measured depths of over 1,000m by sending out sound by sonar and timing the interval before the return of the echo.[105] This experience was soon turned into guidance to all U-boats in the form of new navigational policy given the increase of collisions and overall difficulty in shallow water coastal navigation.

A message on 24 December 1944 summed up the desired navigational policy as follows: 'Since astronomical reckonings are not to be carried out in enemy coastal regions, the greatest value and extreme care must be put on very plentiful terrestrial navigation, painstaking dead reckoning with consideration of current according to current atlas, and utilisation of soundings (line of soundings).'[106] Soundings became a critical tool for U-boat navigation close to the coasts as they could identify variations in underwater terrain and use them defensively to hide or for accurate submerged navigation. Leutnant Ludwig-Ferdinand von Friedeburg in *U-155* (IXC) made his way into Flensburg through the Faroes Islands passage guided by the Elektra-Sonne, then reached the escort pick-up point without difficulty by means of soundings.[107]

Acoustic Detection

As early as mid-1942, engineers at Deschimag proposed a modification to the existing standard placement of the passive sonar array known as *Gruppenhorchgeräte* (GHG). They proposed to reduce its complexity and increase its effectiveness at shallower depth through the installation of twelve hydrophone receivers on each side of the keel. Installation and testing was conducted on *U-185* (IXC) in the summer of 1942. The new placement improved detection at shallower depths when running on electric motors as previously the sounds of waves interfered with the acoustic sensors. With the new device the U-boats gained improved listening close to the surface, but they had to maintain a depth of about 20m. Any shallower, the acoustic sensors simply did not work well. Later, when the snorkel was introduced, a U-boat had to occasionally stop its engines completely, turn off the snorkel, then quickly check the sonar to determine if any enemy vessels were approaching.

Further testing resulted in a new proposal to develop a 'Balkon' or semicircular 'Balcony' that would extend beyond the front of the keel and be equipped with 2 x 24 receivers. This was expected to increase the listening range even further. By September 1942 a version was installed on *U-194* (IXC) and *U-719* (VIIC). Tests with *U-194* were conducted on 25–27 February at a depth of 70m outside of Rönne, followed by *U-719* from 31 August to 1 September 1943.

The results were better than expected. Overall the Balkon increased the interception range by 70 per cent when compared to the near frontal placement of the original system. This increased the forward sensing capabilities of the GHG system, although it left a blind spot aft between 150° and 210°.

The first operational installations began in the autumn of 1943 with the IXC U-boats *U-66* and *U-505*. Neither of them received a snorkel retrofit. *U-66* was sunk on its patrol and *U-505* was captured by the US Navy, hence any operational experience from these two U-boats was lost. After the introduction of the snorkel it was determined that sound bearings while snorkelling and running the diesel engines caused considerable issues with the standard placement of the passive GHG sonar array. Snorkel operations

The GHG Balkon on *U-1105* (VIIC). This new array improved underwater sound detection by 70 per cent. It was the most advanced passive sonar array fielded by any navy during the war. It allowed U-boats to function submerged for weeks and months at a time. *(Courtesy of Royal Navy Submarine Museum)*

in the late spring and summer of 1944 proved that sonic information could not be received with accuracy, if at all, when a U-boat was submerged running the diesel engines while snorkelling. The GHG Balkon's placement overcame this problem to a great extent.

Only U-boats retrofitted with the snorkel received the GHG Balkon from mid-1944 through to the end of the war. The next U-boats that received it were the following IXCs: *U-539, U-882, U-877, U-881, U-889, U-890,* and *U-891*; IXDs *U-180,* and *U-195*; and the IXD2 *U-873*. One large XB, *U-234,* also received the Balkon. Note that *U-882, U-890* and *U-891* were destroyed or damaged in bombing raids and further construction stopped.

The first VIICs to receive the new GHG Balkon were *U-682* and *U-1172* in September and October 1944. They were soon followed by *U-1002, U-1019* and *U-1105,* as well as *U-1306–1308*. It became standard on the Electro-boats and Walter boats.[108] There may have been other Type VIIs that received the Balkon, but the historical record is not complete in this regard. Suffice to say, few U-boats operated with the device compared with the number that actually received a snorkel.

In practice the GHG Balkon proved highly effective near the surface but not near the bottom. One of the last patrols of the war was conducted by the GHG Balkon-equipped *U-1305* (VIIC/41). *U-1305* operated off Malin Head and the north of Ireland from 20 April to 1 May. When the U-boat was bottomed or operating near the bottom, the GHG Balkon proved useless due to the constant low-frequency ocean noise.

Oberleutnant Helmut Christiansen, the U-boat's commander, wrote in his KTB on 20 April that: 'Balkon GHG is of little use on the bottom, because with the low [frequency] sea state noise sounds drown everything.' However, when he was near the surface the new Balkon proved so sensitive that he could not use it effectively to judge the distance of any sound. While operating north-west of Tory Island on the 20th he recorded: 'Continuous propeller sounds at various volumes. Nothing seen in the periscope. Very good sound conditions. From previous experience, volume in the GHG gives no indication of range. Propeller sounds were heard shortly before yesterday's shot at range 7,500 metres at the same volume as with the current sound bearings with no visual observation.'[109] The problem was not the technology per se, it was training. Most sonar operators were young, had conducted few, if any, operational patrols, and received little training on new, highly sensitive equipment. Only experience and experimentation over time provided the necessary skills.

Further development of sonar based on underwater experiences continued. An even more advanced sonar array was developed before the end of the war. *U-889* (IXC/40) was the only U-boat to receive a specialised onion-shaped sonar dome mounted on the upper deck at the point of the bow, known as the *Zwiebel*. This innovation was another step in giving U-boats the maximum hydrophone coverage underwater.

Automatic Depth Keeping

The development of automatic depth keeping gear was pursued by Firm Askania for some time during the war, with the earliest trials beginning in 1935. With the introduction of the snorkel there was a desire to ease the burden on hydroplane operators by installing automatic hydroplane gear on snorkel-equipped U-boats. Extensive trials were carried out by *U-235* at the end of 1943 and into early 1944. The Type XXI *U-2511* also carried out tests in the Baltic during mid-1944. The results were promising as it turned out that the automatic gear 'enabled depth keeping to be more precise with a snorkel than when hand operation was used.'[110] Successful trials in sea states as high as 5 were achieved in the Baltic, which contributed to the decision to install the gear on all snorkel-equipped U-boats despite the fact that there had been no prior operational Atlantic experience with the device. 'When running on snorkel the sensitive membrane is used, whereas the coarser membrane control is used when running deep. The sensitive membrane involves the use of both the forward and after hydroplanes.'[111]

Operational employment of Askania gear proved that different U-boats had different requirements. Installations in the Type VIIC U-boats became defective from the first day 'owing to water entering the equipment when the splash-proof cover was off'. This, of course, could be rectified after a U-boat returned from patrol. Installations on the Type XXIII U-boats were considered low priority owing to the Type XIII's excellent depth control while snorkelling. It was also not a high priority for the Type XXI U-boat, but it proved of great advantage to the Type IXC.[112]

Automatic Stop Trimming Gear

The demands of maintaining a U-boat submerged for long periods of time required the installation of a stop trimming apparatus (Schwebe-Gerät) that could keep a stopped trim with a reduced electric battery expenditure compared with using the propeller at 'slow down one'. Experimental trials occurred with a Type VIIC, a Type IXD and a Type XXI U-boat (*U-2511*). Development began in 1943 in parallel with the snorkel. A German design was introduced, but it used too much electric power and its overall concept was considered problematic as it attempted to keep a set depth without any variation. An exchange of military designs with the Japanese in 1943 facilitated the introduction of Japanese gear that was employed successfully in the Type VIIC U-boats. The design was based on a rocking lever that was set by adjusting a spring by hand, once the U-boat was settled. Once contact was made between the rocking lever and either the right or left contact due to some disturbance in the water, a series of automatic adjustments were made that resulted in flooding or blowing the amidships tank. 'Not only is the electrical power requirement reduced by this type of apparatus, but also a reduced demand on blowing and flooding reduces the noise that it causes. Only a few litres of water are moved at a time until the vessel can be steadied somewhere near the depth required.'[113] The ability to maintain a consistent depth quietly, combined with overall sound dampening, allowed a U-boat to manoeuvre tactically in coastal water with a high degree of stealth.

IXC Hull Modification

The experiences and perspectives of Kapitän zur See Dobratz, who commanded *U-1232* (IXC/40) and later served as Chief of Staff to Admiral Friedberger, were unique given that he was a former Luftwaffe officer. He noted that when the IXC U-boat had a standard forward hull it was necessary to keep the horizontal bubble at about 1.5 degrees aft when snorkelling and to keep the U-boat heavy by 9 tons, especially when snorkelling in heavy seas. If the vessel had to dive deep in an emergency this 9 tons, together with another ton for the compression of the hull, had to be pumped out. However, when the superstructure was 'waisted' forward – cutaway into a narrow beam – the 9 tons was reduced to 1.5 tons and that gave a great advantage. The cutaway occurred between bow frames 89 and 124.5, except in a single case on *U-539* where it was wider, starting at frame 86. First, it improved the dryness of the bridge and, second, it allowed for a quicker recovery of the bow when plunging into a heavy sea. These were incidental to the main purpose of reducing the dive time by three to four seconds. Nevertheless, only a few Type IXs were modified in this way, as it turned out that larger holes in the superstructure produced the same result.[114]

Part B Inception to Implementation March 1943–June 1944
First Snorkel Installations

The first twenty Type VIIC snorkels kits were ordered as early as 12 August 1943. On 24 September the Naval Arsenal at Kiel and the Kriegsmarinewerft Wilhelmshaven were required to produce as a matter of urgency another 100 snorkels for the Type VIICs in service and forty for Type IXCs and Type IXDs. As previously noted, a letter to Germaniawerft and A G Weser from BdU dated 15 November 1943 set the priority for snorkel retrofits as operational U-boats, followed by newly commissioned U-boats. Production proceeded slowly due to bottlenecks in priority and work.[115] The first snorkel retrofit kits finally reached French U-boat bases by late December 1943.

A limited number of U-boats received their snorkel retrofit in early 1944 for the purpose of conducting secret operational trials. There were no procedures established yet for its use. BdU required experience reports from each captain to be sent both during and after each patrol in order to evalu-

U-190 (IXC/40) showing the cutaway hull that reduced diving time by three to four seconds. This modification occurred only on a few Type IXs and was introduced by a former Luftwaffe pilot turned U-boat commander. *(Image taken by John Taylor RCNVR and made available by his son Bill Taylor)*

ate the snorkel's potential. The first U-boat to receive the snorkel installation was *U-264* (VIIC) in January. *U-264* sailed on its fifth and last patrol from St Nazaire on 5 February 1944 under the command of Kapitänleutnant Hartwig Looks. *U-264* participated in a convoy operation with *Gruppe Hai* and was ordered by BdU to report its snorkel experiences on the 21st and 22nd and to give its position on the 24th, but no reply was received to any of these calls. *U-264* was then listed as 'probably lost during convoy operation, cause unknown' by BdU.[116] *U-264* was indeed sunk at 5.07pm on 19 February in the North Atlantic south-west of Ireland, by depth charges from the British sloops HMS *Woodpecker* and HMS *Starling*. The surviving members of the German crews were interrogated. The Royal Navy learned that '"U-264" was fitted with an extensible Diesel air intake and exhaust, referred to in the U-boat Arm as a "Snorkel." Its purpose was to permit the batteries to be charges while proceeding submerged.'[117] The crew willingly detailed their experience with the snorkel, which was concluded as being positive.

British intelligence now knew more about the first operational use of the snorkel than BdU! Yet that knowledge did not help the Royal Navy to develop effective countermeasures (see Chapter 8). *U-575* (VIIC) was the second U-boat to receive a snorkel installation. This was completed in February in the U-boat pen at St Nazaire. Oberleutnant Wolfgang Boehmer received a request from BdU about his snorkel experience during the patrol. He reported this by wireless as follows: 'In areas with strong patrols of search groups it is not possible to run on the Schnorchel as it is impossible to listen. It is also inadvisable because smoke is made. Periscope observation is perfectly feasible. When running on the Schnorchel "Wanze" location (radar) has been observed.'[118] Shortly after that transmission *U-575* was sunk north of the Azores on 13 March by depth charges and gun fire from a combined sea–air action.

The third snorkel U-boat that went out to sea was more successful. *U-667* (VIIC) received its snorkel installation at St Nazaire in February 1944. Under the command of Kapitänleutnant Heinrich-Andreas Schroeteler, *U-667* participated in the *Gruppe Preussen*, the last named Wolfpack of the war in the North Atlantic. Its cruise was successful in the fact that it returned back to St Nazaire on 19 May after a seventy-three-day patrol and reported having completed what was the longest underwater cruise to-date:

U-667 reported on putting in that she had a continuous submerged passage for 9 days from 150 W., using the 'Schnorchel' apparatus. The Commander was enthusiastic about the 'Schnorchel'. The boat still has the old unimproved system.[119]

It is not clear what was meant by 'unimproved system' other than it had the pulley wheel and not a piston. The improvements represented by the non-flange Type II and ring float were not introduced until autumn 1944.

Out of the first six Type IXs outfitted with a snorkel only two survived their first patrol. *U-107* departed on 12 June for a patrol off Nova Scotia and returned on 27 September, while *U-858* departed on the same date for a mid-Atlantic patrol and also returned on 27 September. *U-543* departed on 28 March and *U-1222* on 16 April for their patrols. Both were sunk by Allied aircraft on their return journey. *U-867* departed on 9 September but was lost due to heavy weather eleven days later.

U-859 was the first Type IXD2 U-boat and *Gruppe Monsun* boat to be fitted with a snorkel, but it was sunk on its first snorkel patrol on 23 September 1944 near Penang in the Straits of Malacca by torpedoes from the British submarine HMS *Trenchant*.

During the trial phase, a number of experiments were conducted with the purpose of evaluating the effects of snorkelling on the crew. There was specific interest in the reduction of the oxygen content within the U-boat. One of the more interesting experiments was the employment of 'Snorkel Pigs' (actual guinea pigs) onboard the *U-490*, the only Type XIV supply U-boat to be retrofitted with a snorkel. Commissioned on 27 March 1943, *U-490* went through nearly ten months of standard work-ups and training in the Baltic before arriving at Kiel at the end of March 1944. One year after commissioning it received its snorkel retrofit. The snorkel was installed on the port side, like the Type VIIC. Its first and only cruise began on 4 May 1944. On the order of its captain, Oberleutnant Wilhelm Gerlach, it remained submerged as often as possible during the outbound cruise. Once it reached the Azores, *U-490* did not use the snorkel that often. It was discovered that at a depth of 40m or greater it could not receive any wireless transmissions from BdU. The best reception was at about 18m or less. This was one of the first major side effects of the snorkel that BdU did not fully appreciate at that time. As U-boats remained submerged for long periods of time they were unable to pick up any wireless communications and often never responded to requests for reports by BdU. Both BdU and Allied intelligence discovered that wireless communication dropped off significantly with the introduction of the snorkel. *U-490* was sunk on 12 June north-west of the Azores by depth charges. The entire crew survived and all of them were taken aboard the escort carrier USS *Croatan*, where they were interrogated. The snorkel apparatus featured prominently during questioning. The interrogation report described an interesting procedure used to deal with the drop in pressure caused by the snorkel float's submergence during diesel operation:

U-490 was not able to use her Schnorchel when the sea was stronger than Force 4. When proceeding submerged with the Schnorchel, either one or both Diesels were used at speeds of from 200 to 300 rpm. The maximum submerged speed on both Diesels at 300 rpm was about 5½ knots.

Both Diesels were employed only in very calm weather as there was always danger of the nose of the Schnorchel undercutting a wave. When this occurred, the automatic shut-off valve in the nose was actuated, causing a rapid drop of pressure within the pressure hull. In order to prevent the change in pressure from becoming dangerous, a man was stationed at the Diesel controls. He constantly watched a barometer and when the pressure dropped from 1,020 millibars (normal) to 850 millibars, one Diesel was shut off. If the pressure dropped to 750 millibars, both engines were stopped.

Air bottles were occasionally charged when submerged, by using either the electric or the Junkers compressor. When the Junkers compressor was employed, the exhaust gas was caught in a cone-shaped tin funnel which reflected it towards the Diesel air intake. The gas was expelled through the Diesel exhaust. This funnel had been designed by the Engineer Officer of U-490 and was made by members of the engine room crew.

The latter procedure was a modification made by the crew. Being one of the first U-boats equipped with a snorkel, *U-490* did not attempt any long underwater cruises. The longest use of the snorkel was about eight to ten hours. One lesson learned by the crew was that 'the tremendous heat together with the constant changes in atmospheric pressure could be relieved by opening all pressure-tight doors throughout the entire U-boat. Thus, not only the diesel personnel but the entire crew suffered piercing ear-aches.' Other U-boats learned this fact and all pressure-tight doors remained open during snorkel cruises. This represented an obvious danger in the case of a breech in the pressure hull, as the U-boat could flood rather easily.

The ship's surgeon, Marinestabarzt Herbert Stubbendorff, was not inter-rogated. The interrogation report noted that 'he must have been a man of some intellectual curiosity since he had about two dozen guinea pigs onboard on which he conducted experiments. At least ten were kept in the diesel room. The intent was to test the effects of pressure on the ear drums. The effect on the pigs was to be recorded. They were known throughout the boat as the '*Schnorchel* pigs'. These pigs were killed during the attack for fear that their squeals might give away the U-boat's position.'[120]

Basic procedures were developed by BdU for snorkel use that were issued on 24 March 1944 based upon Baltic sea trials and the few operational patrols. One aspect noted in the report was critical: 'It is possible to use

Schnorchel up to sea state 3, at night only because of smoke.'[121] The 'smoke' referenced in the last sentence became an object of some debate in both German and Allied naval circles as apparently it was only present in the winter months. For the moment, snorkel heads and masts were not covered with anti-radar reflective coating, though that changed in the autumn with the results of the year-long *Schornsteinfeger* project (See Chapter 3).

These early experiences provided limited data to BdU by which an assessment of the snorkel's value could be made. The snorkel-equipped U-boats such as *U-264* and *U-575* employed in the last Wolfpack operations did not have an opportunity to exercise the attributes that the new device offered. A more controlled trial was organised by BdU in May.

Gruppe Dragoner

The US Navy's OP-20-G picked up traffic through Ultra that caught their attention in late May. They reported out in their weekly secret report that 'several U-boats recently were located patrolling north-east of Ushant. This is the first time that U-boats have entered the English Channel since the early days of the war.'[122] What Allied intelligence identified was the first test of snorkel-equipped U-boats in the English Channel. Aware that a cross-Channel invasion was highly likely in the coming month, BdU wanted to test the feasibility of operating in coastal waters with the snorkel, and how well their actions could be co-ordinated. An important aspect of this test was ensuring that U-boats could charge their batteries while snorkelling. This meant that a U-boat stayed submerged and did not have to surface for this procedure. The first U-boat involved was *U-764* (VIIC), which departed on 18 May on an eleven-day patrol, followed by *U-275* (VIIC) and *U-441* (VIIC) on 20 May for a four- and eight-day patrol respectfully, followed on 22 May by *U-984* (VIIC) for six days, *U-953* (VIIC) for seven days, and *U-269* (VIIC) for seven days. All departed from Brest, except for *U-269*, which departed from Lorient, although all returned to Brest at the end of their brief excursions.[123]

U-764 sailed as the first boat of the *Gruppe Dragoner*. One of its crewmembers, Heinz F K Guske, was not entirely impressed with the operation from his perspective. The boat had been retrofitted with a snorkel in April 1944 '… and was to be on a special hush-hush operation into the western Channel.' His colourful recollection of the enterprise highlights the secretive nature and special status of the operation by BdU:

> The objective of this mission was, in the first instance, to ascertain whether the snorkel would permit the boats to operate in shallow waters on the enemy's doorstep without being located. And secondly, to gather information

with regard to the enemy's air surveillance as well as guarding against a possible surprise landing or invasion attempt by giving warning of such moves.

We were sent hither and tither without making direct contact with surface vessels of any kind. On 23 May, however received orders to surface and were promptly attacked by aircraft.[124]

At the end of *U-764*'s KTB, BdU annotated that the first 'enterprise' into the western Channel of snorkel-equipped U-boats provided 'valuable, positive experiences and proved the boat is able to operate in areas where this would be inconceivable without a snorkel'.[125]

U-953 (VIIC) received its snorkel retrofit in La Pallice during March 1944. It then conducted an independent trial during a three-day redeployment from La Pallice to Brest in preparation for its participation in the upcoming secret operation in the western Channel. Oberleutnant Karl-Heinz Marbach's recorded that during his U-boat's participation in *Gruppe Dragoner*: 'The boat operated the snorkel during submerged transit covering about 100 nm in about 37 hours in Sea 1–3.' He noted that the main advantage was ventilation, that 'lifts the mental depression of the crew, a particularly evil of today's underwater war' and that 'the second positive factor comes from the possibility of simultaneous charging'. He believed that despite the requirements of ongoing trials, the snorkel proved a relative success.[126]

Marbach's thoughts about running one engine on electric and charging the battery with the other while snorkelling become a standard operating procedure for the snorkel-equipped U-boats. It was one of the many unintended consequences of the device. On 27 May BdU recorded the results of the operation in its KTB.[127]

OP-20-G tracked the progress of these U-boats accordingly and reported in their Top Secret Intelligence assessment on 3 June:

Six 500-ton U-boats from Brest were employed in maintaining a patrol of 3 U-boats off the French coast from Ushant to Cherbourg between 18–25 May. Small surface ships, possibly decoys, operated within the same area. Probably all these U-boats were equipped with schnorchel and, after the U-boats reported being continuously harassed by aircraft, [BdU] decided that the schnorchel funnel was being located by aircraft radar. On 24 May all *Dragoner* U-boats were told to return to Brest 'because of enemy situation, which at the moment promises no further successes'.

U-764 (Bremen), one of the *Dragoner* Group, is believed to have been sunk in the Channel area about 24 May by UK-based aircraft.[128]

We know that six U-boats participated in the experimental operation and that *U-764* was not sunk. The inaccurate information recorded by Ultra was the start of a systemic problem of reporting during the last year of the war based on incomplete radio traffic. Two-way wireless communication with submerged U-boats was a problem, as noted by Hessler:

> … during Group *Dragoner's* brief sortie into the Channel in May there had been many instances of boats missing important messages through having to Snorkel, despite careful timing of long-wave routines. It was most likely, therefore, that in the present circumstances the boats would have few opportunities to transmit, and that the command would have to rely entirely upon radio intercepts and the reports of returning commanders for a picture of the situation.[129]

While BdU and the Allies were not entirely sure how to gauge the success of *Gruppe Dragoner*, the fact remained that these U-boats had entered coastal waters under the nose of the Allies and operated submerged for nearly a week and survived. No one could predict how this foray into the western Channel foreshadowed extensive submerged U-boat coastal operations in the coming months, or the havoc they later wrought among Allied naval commands.

An Extraordinary Solution

The design and development of the snorkel under wartime pressure was an amazing feat of ingenuity that maintained the U-boat's survivability through to the end of the war and allowed it to shift operations back to the offensive, despite many of the inherent technical problems it introduced. By the end of the war it was assessed by US Naval intelligence that 'there is virtually unanimous opinion among German submarine designers and operating personnel that a snorkel or similar device is absolutely essential to modern submarines'.[130] This sentiment can be found in scores of experience reports located in U-boat KTBs. Experience reports from U-boats recently retrofitted with a snorkel were required by BdU, which was evaluating the new technology operationally and working on devising new tactical guidelines. Below are just some of the comments made by U-boat captains about their crew's first snorkel experience as noted in their KTBs or through wireless communications back to BdU:

> *U-441* (VIIC). May 1944. 'The technical operation of the snorkel has awakened confidence.'
> *U-763* (VIIC). July 1944. 'Snorkel essential when operating in an area of heavy [enemy] activity. The term 'Total Undersea War' gave a psychological boost to the crew.'

U-482 (VIIC). September 1944. 'Snorkelling has proven itself and is highly regarded by the crew.'

U-1003 (VIIC/41). November 1944. 'Today I am delighted with the snorkelling and my crew as well. We feel very secure while snorkelling …'

U-1199 (VIIC). November 1944. 'Felt unconditional superiority with snorkel-boat.'

U-483 (VIIC). November 1944. 'This first undertaking was the most thorough training for the entire crew. Snorkelling proved its worth. It was always possible to keep the battery well charged, and staying unnoticed was also done to the maximum.'

U-978 (VIIC). December 1944. 'The snorkel proved itself very well during the whole patrol. The crew grew accustomed to snorkel operations very quickly.'

U-1221 (IXC/40). December 1944. 'The new snorkel-related difficulties and conditions were soon overcome and mastered. The snorkel has proven itself excellent in all situations and allows for unnoticed operations …'

U-312 (VIIC). January 1945. 'Snorkelling practice was ordered as the crew did not have practical experience. Depth control was a problem at first, as the snorkel valve kept closing; but with increased experience the snorkelling proceeded satisfactorily. The attitude of the crew was good.'

U-427 (VIIC). April 1945. 'First snorkelling cruise. Crew has won full confidence in stability of the boat and recognised the great opportunity of snorkelling.'

Snorkelling proved possible in sea states of up to 5 or 6. Submerged snorkelling speeds averaged 6 knots for diesels boats when not charging batteries. Cruises of fifty to seventy days submerged became the norm and not the exception. Underwater endurance records were set that were not surpassed by the US Navy until the 1970s. Throughout the autumn of 1944 the snorkel was mastered, and tactical procedures codified by BdU. By January 1945 there was no reason for U-boats to ever surface once submerged on an operational patrol. The US Navy assessed that '… actual snorkel performance far exceeded the purpose for which the device was originally designed, namely in the charging of batteries while proceeding submerged at 2–3 knots'.[131] This assessment was an understatement. In a matter of months the diesel U-boats were given a new breath of life and brought back from the verge of defeat in the waters of the North Atlantic. While the U-boat never again achieved the level of Allied sinkings it enjoyed in the early days of the war during the 'Happy Times', it was never defeated as a weapon system. The Allies found their once-easy quarry increasingly harder to locate, even though U-boats were now hunting in shallow water within eyesight of the coast. The age of 'Total Undersea War' was at hand.

Chapter 3

Snorkel Protective Coating

Rubber coating was used to obscure the snorkel head and mast above water from Allied radar detection starting in the spring of 1944 through to the end of the war. This concept evolved from BdU's desire to protect the exposed portion of a surfaced U-boat, particularly the conning tower, in the wake of 'Black May'. In June 1943, shortly after the withdrawal of U-boats from the North Atlantic, a conference took place in Berlin at the initiation of Dönitz for the purpose of presenting the problem of protecting U-boats against Allied radar. The conference was attended by about 400 technical representatives from various organisations across Germany. The problem was described to the attendees by Konteradmiral Stummel, who was designated as the senior naval officer for the project code-named *Schornsteinfeger* (Chimney Sweep).[1]

The military aspects of the anti-radar problem were not clearly defined at the time of the June conference. Requirements with respect to wavelength coverage, weight and thickness of the coating, durability standards, etc., still needed definition. The desire to reduce the ability of the Allies to detect a surfaced U-boat during convoy battles through the application of radar camouflage for the conning tower and possibly for part of the upper hull that was exposed when surfaced drove the technical discussion. Top priority was assigned to the project by BdU. The conference attendees were asked to submit proposals immediately with the aim of solving the problem within three months. As the snorkel was being developed in parallel and was considered 'secret', the conference attendees knew nothing of the future apparatus. The few personnel that were involved with both projects did not envision at this time that a snorkel might require anti-radar protection. This opinion slowed the *Schornsteinfeger* programme until the autumn of 1944, when it was decided that anti-radar protection for the snorkel was required.

Four proposals were selected for further development out of a large number submitted at the conference. These were placed under the direction of a civilian technical director, Marineoberbaurat Kühnhold from BdU Wolfenbüttel, although a man named Prof. Kupfmüller was able to override Kühnhold's decisions beginning in about July 1944.[2] The four principal projects organised under *Schornsteinfeger* were Netzhemd, the Becker-Hellwege absorber, the Jaumann absorber, and the Wesch absorber. However, only the latter two saw operational employment.

Netzhemd was an attempt carried out by Dr Bachem of Konstanz to adapt the principle of the quarter wave plate by the use of conducting screens, for a wavelength of 1.5m. Although a model made by I G Farben at Hoechst was given an operational trial near Kiel, it was entirely unsuccessful because of mechanical failure. This type of device was deemed incapable of absorbing both S and X-bands and further development was halted by January 1944.

The Becker-Hellwege absorber was pursued by Deutsche Gold-und-Silber-Scheideanstalt (DEGUSSA), based near Frankfurt, under the direction of Dr Untermann. It consisted of several layers, alternately semi-conducting and non-conducting material, and employed a Buna-lampblack mixture and air for the alternate layers. This development originated from a theory of Professors Becker and Hellwege, who worked in Göttingen. However, it never reached a practical stage at DEGUSSA for various reasons, including wavelength selectivity and mechanical problems. Further investigation was halted in July 1944.

By the end of the summer of 1944 BdU decided that there was no longer a need to protect the conning tower of a U-boat with anti-radar absorber. U-boats were no longer remaining surfaced for any length of time thanks to the unexpected success of the snorkel. Now that the snorkel was the only portion of a U-boat exposed above the surface, it was determined that it required anti-radar protection. Only two absorbers remained in initial development that might provide the required protection.

Jaumann Absorber

Development of the Jaumann absorber commenced several months after the June conference. Its success in laboratory tests soon identified it as a potential answer to the new requirement to protect snorkel heads and the upper mast with an anti-radar absorber. Jaumann was the first absorber to be put into operational use around September 1944. While no precise record exists of which U-boat may have conducted the first operational patrol with the coating, *U-958* (VIIC) is a prime candidate as it conducted its first snorkel-equipped patrol in May 1944 after being retrofitted with snorkel order G47, which according to records was a ball float coated with an anti-radar absorber.

The line of initial theoretical development was pursued by Prof. Johannes Jaumann of Brünn. The actual development was centralised under contract with BdU at the I G Farben factory in Hoechst, near Frankfurt, where Prof. Jaumann acted in an advisory capacity. The I G Hoechst undertaking was organised under Dr Kiesskalt, who was responsible within I G Farben for the general project, and more directly under Dr Patat, who was in charge of the development, production and testing of the components. The development and control of the necessary materials were the responsibility of Dr Brennschede, a chemist. All electrical measurements were the responsibility of Dr Rathscheck, and Dr Kiesskalt provided the liaison between I G Hoechst and BdU.

The production form of this absorber consisted of a hollow cylinder that fitted over the snorkel. It had a wall thickness of about 7.5cm. The cylinder was made up of seven layers of thin, semi-conducting paper separated by layers of spacers that consisted of cellular igelit about 9mm thick.

The surface conductivity of the paper was graduated exponentially from layer to layer. The function of the cellular igelit, the electrical properties of which resemble those of air, is to maintain constant spacing between the paper layers, as well as to maintain the overall form of the absorber. The military requirements finally specified by BdU, in addition to broad waveband coverage, included the requirement that the performance of the absorber should not be hampered by submergence of the U-boat to a depth of 150m. The absorber could withstand a depth of nearly 200m. This represented approximately the limiting depth for the strength of the cellular igelit. Depth tests to determine this were conducted in a water pressure chamber at Kiel.

In spite of the efficiency of the Jaumann absorber, there appeared to have been a certain amount of pessimism about its viability due to the belief that the Allies could change operational wavelengths at will, and thus negate the entire *Schornsteinfeger* programme if a wavelength outside of the 3–30cm band was adopted. It was reported by German intelligence at the end of 1944 that the Allies were again using wavelengths in the 1.5m band. This caused an increased effort to further broaden the effective band width by introducing iron into the absorber spacers. Since it was thought at I G Hoechst that it was unfeasible to design an absorber that could be effective against the entire range of radar bands that the Allies could employ, a second initiative began involving the design a separate Jaumann absorber that could be effective over the 1–2m band. Since an absorber of this type, employing spacers of cellular igelit, would be very thick, the use of Buna, containing iron spacers in place of the igelit, was contemplated.

The Jaumann absorber proved effective operationally across a wide band of wavelengths. The absorber reduced detection to 15 per cent of an uncoated snorkel against 'Rotterdam' radar on 9.3cm wavelength under calm sea conditions. While the Jaumann absorber could be applied to a circular cylinder form by bending the igelit sheets before gluing, it proved too difficult to be applied to more complex surfaces such as elliptical cylinders used in the teardrop shape of the Type IX U-boat's snorkel mast or the ball float snorkel heads. This absorber was utilised primarily on heads. By early 1945 it was decided to employ the Jaumann absorber on ring float snorkel heads and cylindrical snorkel masts only. When applied to the snorkel masts that mounted a ball float, the snorkel head would utilise the Wesch absorber (described below).

The total number of Jaumann absorbers fabricated between November 1944, when production began, and March 1945, when production was disrupted by the Allied invasion of Germany, was estimated by German sources to be just less than 100. A monthly production rate of between thirty and sixty was attempted, but the total completed and shipped each month was about 50 per cent fewer less than the projection. For example, in March 1945 only twelve to fifteen absorbers were completed. The total number of U-boats fitted with the absorber was stated by D Kiesskalt to be about sixty. The average time interval between production and final testing after installation was said to be four to five weeks. The installation reject rate at Kiel averaged 30 per cent in October 1944, but only 2 per cent in March 1945. This latter percentage may have been driven by the fact that quality control checks were no longer being emphasised due to operational needs.

Wesch Absorber

The Wesch absorber, or 'Wesch-Mat', was developed under the leadership of Prof. Wesch of the Welt Post Institute (WPI) in Heidelberg. During the conference in June 1943 Wesch recalled Stummel stating that the entire U-boat was to be covered by an anti-radar coating. The wavelength, against which protection would be required, was not stated, however, in September 1943, Wesch was informed that the band to be covered was 100–200cm and that only the conning tower was to be coated.

In November 1943 the facilities of IG Oppau were placed at Wesch's disposal for development of suitable materials. Between November 1943 and January 1944, experiments were made on the 1–2m band using a single layer of 'lossy' (electrically conductive) material 2–4cm thick. These experiments did not result in reflection coefficients less than 30 per cent. In January 1944 Wesch produced an absorber for the 1–2m band using 'I-Gummi' with 80 per cent iron. The reflection co-efficient produced was as low as 15 per cent in the middle band, rising to 40 per cent at the ends. This absorber was rejected by BdU. Following this lack of success, Wesch concentrated his effort on improving the apparatus and measurement techniques used in his laboratory. In March he had available radiation in the 8–200cm band. Between March and September 1944 Wesch developed the essential features of the absorber that would bear his name.

Sometime between August and September 1944, Prof. Kupfmüller learned of Wesch's activities and advised him of the new operational requirements of protecting a new device known as the 'snorkel' against 9cm radar. Up to then, and given its 'secret' classification, Wesch had not heard of the snorkel. For test purposes a dummy snorkel made of wood and sheet metal was set up at Kohlhof, but Wesch did not consider such tests capable of yielding useful results. He used the mock snorkel only as a demonstration piece. In October 1944 Kupfmüller announced that the Wesch absorber was to be tested with the ball float valve. The tests were conducted at Kiel and the results were better than expected. It was reported that the range of detection by Allied Rotterdam radar equipment was reduced by 50 per cent. As a result of these tests an order was placed with I G Farben Ludwigshafen/Rhein to produce the new Wesch absorbers. Provisional instructions were issued in October that detailed how to affix the new absorber onto the snorkel heads.[3]

Nevertheless, it was late in December 1944 before the manufacturing difficulties had been overcome and the Wesch absorber began operational employment on the ball float valves. Among the first operational U-boats with the Wesch absorber was *U-286* (VIIC) – an Arctic boat.

In December a request was made for coverage in the 3cm band. Although the Wesch absorber was designed to have an absorption band around 9cm, it did in fact exhibit a further absorption band beyond the new band requirement. Consequently, the request for 3cm coverage was largely met even before the requirement was issued.

The production form of the Wesch absorber consisted of a rubber mat about 50cm square that contained a high percentage of iron powder. The mat was produced in 'waffle', or matrix form, with a thickness of about 4mm and with the height of the waffle ridges about 4mm above the mat surface. For operational use, or testing, this mat was glued to a sheet of rubber about 1mm thick, known as 'Oppanol-0'. This assembly was then glued to the metal surface.

Through operational use it was determined that the Wesch absorber was more suitable from an adhesive perspective for curved surfaces than the Jaumann absorber. Accordingly, the Wesch absorber was formally adopted by BdU as the covering for all ball floats. Good protection was provided in the S and X band frequencies, where the reflection coefficient for flat plates was said to be anywhere less than 10 per cent (amplitude), although there was a maximum between these two bands of about 30 per cent in the neighbourhood of 6cm. The total service production of Wesch mats, between January and March 1945, was stated by Dr Wesch to be enough for about 200 snorkels.[4] According to post-war analysis, it was believed that about 100 U-boats were equipped with the Wesch absorber.

Measurements of the anti-radar reflectivity of the new snorkel mats were conducted in November 1944 with *U-325* (VIIC/41), *U-682* and *U-1172*. The results were communicated by wireless and were thus intercepted by the Allies through Ultra. The intercepted report revealed that the radar reflection of a coated snorkel head that was 1m above the surface was measurably reduced.[5] This intercept revealed that detecting a snorkelling U-boat equipped with an absorber was difficult under normal circumstances, but even more so in high sea states. This message also demonstrated that the ball float proved more difficult to identify than the ring float, probably because of its rounded design that offered less of an angular surface area for detection.

The Allies became increasingly aware of the rubberised coating on U-boats' snorkel masts through prisoner-of-war interrogations conducted with the surviving German crewmen of sunken boats. They identified in the autumn of 1944 that *U-877* was fitted with a rubber coating over its snorkel in Kiel. The application was applied along the top 2m of the snorkel mast, which had been burnished. Three thick layers of smooth rubber were applied, one on top of the other, followed by a fourth layer of rubber 1½–2cm thick that was criss-crossed with ridges ½cm high and about 1cm apart. The ridges formed a series of hollow squares that were then lacquered.

On 28 November 1944 the U-boat base at St Nazaire sent a communiqué to BdU related to the application of camouflage mats on U-boat snorkel heads and masts. It stated:

> Camouflage mats prove quite satisfactory. U-773 has an air blister of 10cm diameter on the snorkel neck. U-722 small air blister in the centre of the snorkel mast. Probably due to hurried fitting. Welded rubber seems in order in both boats. In U-773 the varnish has been burnt at the level of the exhaust, causing a layer of rust 12cm high. U-722 has small patches of rust at the weld the rubber seats. Boats snorkel to sea state five – six. No damage.[6]

Both boats received snorkels in Kiel in August and were then sent to French bases. The snorkel reports related to the application of the mast absorbers.

As these were new, BdU wanted to know about their performance during the trip from Germany to France.[7]

The Wesch mats were considered extremely sensitive from a security point of view. BdU did not want them to fall into the hands of the Allies. It therefore ordered that any Wesch mats that could not be transported from French U-boat bases should be burned, if necessary, to prevent their capture by the Western Allies.[8]

Due to the length of time it took to produce the special mats, then to ship them to the various U-bunkers, and finally to apply them to the snorkel float valves and masts, some flotillas were attempting to apply other mate-

A close-up of the ball float snorkel head of *U-889* (IXC/40). This image provides excellent detail of the waffle-style Wesch anti-radar absorber. This view also shows the detail of the wedge and fins affixed to the actual ball float that improved hydrodynamics to allow the float to quickly shut when submerged. Few ball floats had this configuration. *(Courtesy of NARA)*

rial, most notably wood as reported in the case of *U-1209*.[9] BdU sent a message to all U-boat flotillas via 'Officer Cypher' in April 1945 to halt this practice.[10]

In December 1944 the Electro-pneumatic snorkel was planned to have Jaumann absorber applied on the cylindrical part of the mast and Wesch absorber on the hood. It was also proposed to cover the periscope with the absorber, though this does not appear to have occurred.

The US Navy post-war survey of anti-radar covering adopted a different naming convention for the two types of absorbers, referring to their composition instead of their project names as in the case of 'Tarnshalle' (Jaumann) and 'Tarnmatte' (Wesch).[11] They viewed the modification favourably and noted its protective qualities:

> The covering, which was in effect a limited application of Alberich, made it 'impossible' for radar on wavelengths of between 3–9 centimetres to detect snorkels. It could be picked up by longer wavelengths but they would be detected by the G.S.R. on the snorkel. The head of the snorkel was covered with a dark gray-brown checkered rubber all around.[12]

The application of Jaumann and Wesch absorbers offered a major benefit to snorkel-equipped U-boats. While the US Navy made the assertion that the anti-radar coating was akin to Alberich, the two developments were actually very different in form and function.

Chapter 4

Acoustic Camouflage

The coating of U-boats with rubber to reduce their sound signatures is one of the least understood wartime technical developments. In the way that the snorkel was conceived to counter Allied airpower and radar detection in 1943, acoustic camouflage through the use of a rubber coating, had been pursued since the start of the war to counter the sound waves emitted from Allied sonar. Allied sonar, otherwise known as ASDIC, was the single greatest threat to U-boats at that time. German technical research in the area of acoustic camouflage, also known as sound dampening, was ground breaking. The operational employment of acoustic camouflage was hampered through 1942 by a lack of suitable adhesive. By 1943 that was overcome practically, but was delayed again, only to be adopted for the shift in U-boat operations from deep water to shallow water with the introduction of the snorkel in 1944.

The Admiralty took note of this wartime development when captured U-boat crewmen divulged information about the existence of rubber absorbers for snorkel masts and then for an entire U-boat (understanding the difference in application between each). During the war the Allies knew very little about how advanced German technical development was in this area. Not until Germany's capitulation was the extent of the technological achievement in the application of acoustic camouflage revealed when two U-boats, *U-485* and *U-1105*, both Type VIICs, surrendered coated with the sound-absorbing material. Given the Royal Navy's experience in dealing with German U-boats during the two world wars they were keen to understand this technology and find ways to counter the masking effect of acoustic dampening material.

In 1946 the Admiralty brought together all the surviving German scientists that were engaged in this research into the British Zone of Occupation in order to write a paper on the topic. Led by Professor Erwin Meyer, Walter

Kuhl (PhD in Engineering), Hermann Oberst (PhD), Eugen Skudrzyk (PhD) and Konrad Tamm (PhD in Engineering), they all contributed to an unclassified scientific summary titled 'Sound Absorption and Sound Absorbers in Water: Dynamic Properties of Rubber and Rubberlike Substances in the Acoustic Frequency Region'. Interestingly, the US Navy was not involved in this action and remained largely uninterested in the topic until the 1980s.[1] However, an untranslated copy of the paper was given to the US Navy Bureau of Ships in 1947, which translated the document. In the translator's preface to the US Navy version written by Charles E Morgan, Jr, is a sentence that reads: 'The text relates the developments of underwater sound technology undertaken in Germany during the war years ... It is believed that none of the operational units was in combat.'[2] Morgan's statement runs counter to the fact that the US Navy had already inspected *U-485* at the time of the surrender and had already been allocated the rubber-coated *U-1105* for salvage testing. He likely was never made aware of the classified US Navy report on this topic prepared in September 1945, and discussed below. Details of the wartime service of both these U-boats were available on request to US Navy inspectors from their Royal Navy counterparts, but the opportunity was not taken up. Captured German U-boat crewmen provided very solid facts about the use of acoustic camouflage to their British counterparts during the war, including details of the successful patrol of the acoustically camouflaged *U-480* in the English Channel. The disconnect between historical fact and Morgan's statement clearly shows how little the US Navy understood the employment of acoustically camouflaged U-boats, despite their interest in the theoretical formulas that drove their development.

It was the acoustic department of the Heinrich-Hertz-Institute fur Schwingungsforschung (Vibration Research) at the Technical University in Berlin that investigated the scientific foundations of the absorption of underwater sound and was charged particularly with the development of sound absorbers that served 'as camouflage materials for submarines against ASDIC as well as absorption materials to deaden water tanks by a coating for measuring purposes'.[3] These investigations began long before the war and as a result of the requirement to conduct physical testing, led to the building of a large hall that was sound dampened for sound measurements. This followed the 'new principal of a gradual matching between air and sound materials'.[4] Professor Meyer struck at the heart of the wartime goal of this research: 'The main point of the investigation was the development of a resonant absorber which, in the range of 9–18 kilocycles (KC), has a reflection coefficient of a few per cent with respect to the sound pressure and which is fastened like a kind of sound-absorbing wall paper having a thickness of only 4 millimetres (mm) to the outer hull of submarines, improving considerably their protection against detection.[5] Below is the beginning of Professor Meyer's own introduction to the conference paper. It provides a historical overview of the steps taken to reach his stated goal:

> For certain applications in underwater sound techniques, absorbers which cover only a limited frequency band, but involve a minimum of expense, are required. Such a problem occurs in the camouflage of submarines against ASDIC detection, which comprises approximately the frequency band of 1 octave from 9 to 18kc … The solution can only be found in a sound-absorber which acts according to the resonance principle. For only in this case is it possible to use thicknesses of layers which amount to only a small fraction of the wavelength occurring, and still fulfil the other conditions of ship construction. We succeeded, in fact, in developing a high-quality reso-nance sound absorber for underwater sound whose entire thickness amount-ed to only 4mm, and which was 'carpeted' on the outside wall of the subma-rine like a rubber mat. This acoustic covering received the code word, 'Alberich'. The increase in weight of the submarine travelling underwater due to this coating was wholly negligible and it played no part in the underwater trips. The outer surface was completely smooth so that in spite of an addi-tional fastening of the absorbing material by strips at specifically loaded points, no noticeable increase of resistance and no noticeable losses occurred. The adhesive force of the cement (code word, 'Gummlfolle Bordwand,') [was] finally so increased that it withstood all the demands at sea.[6]

The name of this coating was actually 'Alberich Verfahren', which was an allusion to the Wagnerian 'Nibelung Saga' dwarf who could make himself invisible by means of a cap. In the end, the code name was shortened to just 'Alberich'.

Meyer made an astute follow-on observation in his introduction that holds the key to understanding Alberich's operational employment. He stat-ed that the value of acoustic camouflage was inherent in a submarine's abil-ity to 'remain uninterruptedly underwater' given the advanced state of radar. It was the introduction of the snorkel that provided this ability to U-boats in 1944, thus linking these two technical developments.

Two additional archival documents of importance to the historical understanding of Alberich's development are the *Submarine Acoustic Camouflage* produced by the Department of the Physical Research, Admiralty Office of the Royal Navy in June 1948,[7] and the US Navy Technical Mission in Europe's Report No. 352-45, *Rubber Covering of German Submarines Anti-ASDIC (German Code Name 'Alberich')* dated

20 September 1945.[8] Both the Admiralty and US Navy reports were marked 'Confidential'. The Admiralty report, whilst a summary of the German conference report written in 1946, contains their analytic comments, which are useful in corroborating the overall significance and relevance of Alberich to wartime U-boat operations. The US Navy report is essentially a detailed technical history of how the rubberised covering was produced and applied, together with some commentary on its overall effectiveness. All three above referenced documents were drawn upon to detail Alberich's development as described throughout this chapter.

Technical Development
From 1933 until the 'Black May' of 1943, BdU regarded ASDIC as the most dangerous threat to U-boat operations. In the early part of 1939, before the start of the war, the acoustic reduction of a U-boat signature from ASDIC was assigned to I G Farben (Hoechst) with a high priority. Professor Meyer, along with Oberst and Tamm, had already begun the theoretical research, but actual experimentation did not start in earnest until 1940.

One of the earliest approaches to acoustic camouflage was to discharge bubbles into the water around the U-boat, the idea being that the bubbles would mask the craft. This proved unfeasible due to the fact that bubble distribution could not be controlled adequately, particularly with a moving U-boat.[9] This investigation led to a side development called 'Bold'. Bold represented the release from a U-boat of an airtight container with positive buoyancy that included calcium hydride bubbles. When released it floated in the water at a depth of 30m and released hydrogen bubbles with the intent of presenting a false target to ASDIC, thus allowing the endangered U-boat to escape. This became standard equipment on U-boats from 1942 onwards with improvements made.[10] The inability to mask the U-boat by bubbles then led to the concept of fixing the distribution of bubbles in a viscoelastic layer attached to the U-boat itself.[11]

The initial attempt at a fixed coating was a plastic-like substance that consisted of three triangular rubber strips cemented together in cross sections, with the middle layer containing punched cylindrical air-filled holes. This was known as 'Fafnir' (a dragon from Norse mythology). It showed excellent prospects for absorbing sound waves, but over time it absorbed water, which degraded its absorption properties.[12] Fafnir was applied to *U-11* (IIB) and *U-95* (VIIC), but discounted as impractical for lining anything other than laboratory tanks because it was easily damaged by waves. The decision was made to adopt the rubber coating known as Alberich. Alberich consisted of two 2mm thick rubber sheets, with the inner perforated and the outer not perforated. It could absorb sound waves between 9 and 20kc.

The laboratory development of Alberich resulted in a two-ply rubber sheet 4mm thick cemented onto the hull and superstructure of the U-boat. The inner sheet was perforated with 2mm and 5mm diameter holes that determined the resonant nature of the coating. The two sheets were energised by passing an electric current through the plating and measured against the principal parameters of hull plate thickness and whether the backing was air or water (as in the case of the ballast tanks). The working pressure for the initial experiments was 15 atmospheres (150m) with a working temperature of 10° Celsius. The result was that on a standard 6mm outer hull, the number of perforations required per each 20 sq cm piece of Alberich was 53 x 2mm and 11.6 x 5mm holes. The thicker the hull plating, the more 2mm holes and the fewer 5mm holes were required. The thinner the hull plating, the exact opposite was required. The below table provides the exact configuration for each piece of 20cm Alberich according to the thickness of the steel plating and operating environment (water/air):

Thickness of Iron Plating (mm)	Backing	No. of perforations per 20 sq cm of Alberich	
		2mm diameter holes	5mm diameter holes
3	water	64	7.9
4	water	80	8
5	water	64	10.5
6	water	53	11.6
7 to 9	water	30	14
10 to 13	water	4.5	18
6	air	64	13.5
18	air	None	19

The initial sea tests were conducted in the Skagerrak against a coated U-boat, by a surface vessel travelling at 7 knots. These tests resulted in an inability to verifiably locate the boat, whilst an uncoated U-boat was detected at a range of 1.6km. Testing was done down to a depth of 150m as per the theoretical model. This test was used to effectively calculate the reduction in ASDIC effectiveness. Knowing that the limitation was the noise of the coated U-boat, whether it was running on electric or diesel engines, the tests proved that a reduction in reflectivity of 20 per cent would reduce the range of ASDIC detection anywhere between 20 and 60 per cent. It was also found that the reflectivity did not exceed 10 per cent in +/– 4 atmospheres of the target, allowing for effective sound absorption within a depth variance that allowed for tactical manoeuvring. The detection device used by the German engineers during this test was the 'S-Gerät' hydrophone system. It was noted that in shallow water natural reverberations off the surrounding ocean floor made the coating even more effective. However, Alberich did not have consistent performance at varying depths, and it therefore had to be 'tuned' accordingly.

The overall performance of Alberich was dependent upon both pressure and temperature. This necessitated the preparation of designs to meet varying operational requirements. As the pressure (depth) increased, the numbers of both large and small holes had to increase in order to maintain optimal conditions. When the depth decreased, the opposite was required. What this meant was that if a U-boat was configured with an Alberich coating to function at a depth of 40m or less, but found itself in an evasive tactical situation at a depth of 150m, the reflective reduction of its coating would be greatly diminished, making it more visible to ASDIC detection. Temperature, however, had an opposite effect, so that the reflection loss factor decreased with increased temperature, requiring a smaller number of holes to meet the operational conditions. Pressure and temperature thus had opposite effects, with an increase of pressure from 0.6 to 1 atmosphere compensating for a temperature increase of 1° Celsius.

Oberst stated that the initial operational requirement from BdU was to tune Alberich to function at a depth of 150m. The original thinking was that if under attack by a surface vessel, the U-boat would attempt to depart the area by diving deep. In theory the Alberich coating was expected to reduce its signature and prevent the surface vessel from zeroing on the U-boat as it made its escape. However, this requirement changed in 1944.

Walter's pursuit of a high-speed submarine generated early thinking that it might be tactically useful to coat such a U-boat with Alberich to mask its approach to a target at a more moderate depth.[13] This was clearly an offensive-minded application for camouflage and theoretical models were developed. By 1944 the operational requirement for acoustic camouflage shifted decisively with the employment of snorkel-equipped U-boats almost exclusively in shallow coastal waters. Given that snorkelling occurred close to the surface, Alberich would aid in masking a U-boat. In addition, it would give the U-boat an advantage in its approach to a target. Alberich was subsequently tuned to be effective at 40m or less and applied to snorkel-equipped Type VIIC and Type XXIII U-boats.[14]

Application Process
Synthetic rubber was ultimately selected as the material to form the Alberich coating. Natural rubber was found to be satisfactory during testing, but quickly became scarce as the war progressed and, more importantly, it proved less capable of withstanding the deteriorating effects of harbour

waters covered with grease and oil. The expectation was that a piece of synthetic rubber had a lifespan of two years if properly maintained. Several of the first U-boats to be covered had their Alberich painted over to make it less noticeable. Unfortunately, the paint caused a chemical reaction that produced conspicuous colours. Because of the visual discolouration, and the fact that the new operational procedures employed by U-boats in the latter years of the war meant they would surface only at night, the practice of painting Alberich was halted.

The final rubber compound used was jointly developed by Continental Rubber Co. of Hanover and I G Farben of Hoechst. Smaller quantities were produced by Phoenix Gummiwerken of Harburg and Semperit Rubber Co. of Vienna. Buna S, which was 100 per cent plasticity, was combined with a number of other synthetic ingredients in a vulcaniser. Before the war ended there was a plan known as 'Auma' that consisted of a design for a large vulcanising machine in a new plant located outside Hanover in order to produce the sheets in large quantities. Once synthetic rubber sheets were produced, they were sent to I G Farben in Offenbach, where they were ground by machine, similar to wood.

One side was ground at a time and the process helped to achieve better adhesive qualities. After grinding, the sheets were perforated by hand using a template and a revolving cutting tool attached to a motor-driven flexible shaft. The work was transferred to Sorst at Hanover in early 1945, where a perforating punch was designed. The large holes were punched first, then the smaller ones. However, the results were unsatisfactory as proper sheet alignment could not be maintained when it was fed through the machine. Shortly before the end of the war the machines were redesigned to allow for simultaneous punching of both the 5mm and 2mm holes, thus avoiding issues with hole placement. Once the holes were made, the sheets were transferred back again to I G Farben at Offenbach, where the rolls were received in 20m lengths.

The sheets were then fed through a cleaning machine, once for each side. Now both of the sheets were cemented together by hand as they sat on three rows of two 10ft tables. The non-perforated sheet sat on one row with the perforated sheet on the other. Two coats of cement were applied by paint brush. It could take from five hours to two days for a single sheet to be glued, dried and ready for rolling. Once rolled, the sheets sat for an additional two days while drying at room temperature before they were wrapped and shipped to the shipyard. The bonding agent used for the application of the rubber was extremely complex. The work of covering U-boats with this rubber was undertaken primarily at Kiel, but also at Hamburg, Flensberg and Bremerhaven.

The U-boat was placed in dry dock and allowed to dry thoroughly, after which it was sand- or grit-blasted completely. All paint, rust, barnacles, etc., were completely removed. From this point on great care was taken to see that no dust, oil or moisture settled onto the clean surface. The surface of the U-boat was then marked off with chalk to show where the different patterns were to be used.

The first coat of cement to be applied to the hull was the thinner grade. The other three coats were of the regular consistency and all were applied with brushes. Each coat was applied over the whole U-boat at one time. The drying time for the various coats of cement varied according to atmospheric conditions of temperature, air circulation, etc. Total drying time took as long as four months.

The rubber was cut to size with square edges. Templates were used. When large sheets were applied they were rolled in cotton cloth to keep out moisture. The sheets were carefully positioned, butting edge to edge, and rolled. If for any reason it was found necessary to remove a sheet once applied, the whole steel surface had to cleansed with a wire brush and all old cement removed, then the work started again by reapplying the cement coats. Where there were openings in the outside shell of the U-boat the rubber was cut back about 20mm from the edge of this space and filled with a putty mixture.

In the relation to the propellers and areas where there would be a great water turbulence, steel bands about 20cm wide and 4mm thick were added to the metal to protect the edge of the rubber from being torn loose. The same practice was followed around openings where heated exhaust pipes were located.

After the sheets had been in place on the whole U-boat for least twenty-four hours, a strip about ¼in wide was cut around the periphery of each one and filled in with a putty mixture. The reason for this was due to the difficulty of making a good butt joint without leaving openings to the steel. The putty mixture was a modification of Buna S. The bottom of the keel was not covered. Under good atmospheric conditions a U-boat could be covered in three to four weeks. A gang of thirty to forty men worked on each U-boat, including five or six supervisors.

Due to variations in the amount of liquid in ballast tanks, it was found necessary to line part of the inside of these with rubber. For this purpose a rubber lining that consisted of a perforated rubber sheet 6mm thick were applied to the steel. Then two perforated sheets, each 1mm thick, were applied on top, with a final 1mm unperforated sheet applied. The holes in all perforated sheets were 3mm in diameter with staggered rows. There was about 1mm between edges. There was no attempt to align the holes on these perforated sheets. All sheets were cemented together and attached to the steel in the same manner as described for the rubber covering on the outside of the U-boat.[15]

After the U-boat was completely covered it was allowed to stand in dry dock for a week. Then it was floated out and submerged to a depth of 40m for eight hours so the pressure could ensure a strong bond between the rubber and steel. It also removed air bubbles to ensure that, acoustically, no air was trapped in the bond. A separate account cites a slightly different process whereby the U-boat was dived to 25m for three to four hours, and then surfaced. After a quick inspection it was dived again to 100m for twenty-four hours.[16]

Around the waterline wood blocks were fastened to protect the rubber covering when the U-boat came alongside a dock. At first these blocks were covered with rubber, but it was then deemed unnecessary.

Once completely coated in Alberich the U-boat had to be navigated with great care to avoid scraping off any portions of the covering. Admiral Thedsen commented that such U-boats 'had to be treated like an egg'.[17] By the spring of 1944 all Alberich was applied to select U-boats before they were launched.

Alberich on U-boats
The first trials with Fafnir began in 1940 on *U-11*. These confirmed that Alberich could reduce the effectiveness of ASDIC in the 10–18KHz range by approximately 15 per cent, but not consistently through varying depths.[18] This led to the concept of tuning the acoustic camouflage by adjusting the number of 2mm and 5mm perforated holes applied to any given 20cm sheet, as noted above. The most significant problem proved to be finding a suitable adhesive to ensure the rubber sheets remained attached to the hull of a U-boat during actual sea conditions. The first U-boat covered with Alberich was the Type VIIC *U-67* in April 1941.[19] The coating was applied to the conning tower and side of the hull. Testing followed in the Baltic against ASDIC during June, and further trials occurred in July. All Alberich was reportedly removed prior to its final cruise into the North Atlantic, possibly due to adhesive issues.[20] A second set of trials were made that year on the former Dutch submarine *O26* (UD-4), which resulted in similar issues of adhesion as those probably experienced on *U-67*.[21] Shortly after this, the decision was made by BdU to forego further development of Alberich for acoustic camouflage. Instead, they pursued greater depth as means of protection against ASDIC, an initiative embodied in the future designs of the Type VIIC/41 and Type VIIC/42 as noted in Chapter 1.[22] Despite BdU's shift in emphasis to depth, Meyer's staff continued to work on developing an effective adhesive.

It was not until almost two years later that Alberich was again applied to a U-boat and tested operationally in the summer of 1943. The next U-boat coated was *U-470* (VIIC) during a two-month period while at Kiel from 15 June to 17 August 1943. After the application, *U-470* finished its regular training in the Baltic, then departed for Bergen, where it arrived on 12 September. *U-470* conducted three days of Alberich testing with the uncoated *U-958* (VIIC) as directed by Dönitz in the memorandum Kom.Adm.U-Boote g.Kdos. 3393 A 2 von 20.6.[23] The Alberich was probably tuned to be effective at the original planned depth of 150m (as noted below). Under the command of Oberleutnant Günther-Paul Grave, *U-470* then departed Bergen on 28 September for a deployment in the North Atlantic, but was sunk on 16 October south-east of Cape Farewell by depth charges from three RAF Liberator aircraft, one coded 'C' of 59 Sqn, and 'E' and 'Z' of 120 Sqn. Alberich's effectiveness was thus not fully realised due to *U-470*'s sinking by aircraft. It should be highlighted that *U-470* was not snorkel equipped. It was probably caught on the surface where its acoustic coating offered no protection from radar detection. An interrogation of the two U-boat survivors revealed the following information to the Allies for the first time:

> This was described by one prisoner as consisting of two thin layers of rubber, the under layer being perforated. ('Nothing but thousands of holes,' as a prisoner said.) The total thickness was not more than a fraction of an inch. ('A few millimetres thick' was the prisoner's description.) It was laid on in long strips about a yard wide.
>
> After the deep diving tests, the rubber became so firmly attached to the hull that it was impossible to pick it off. Neither survivor could offer any explanation as to the possible purpose of this rubber covering.[24]

While BdU believed they had identified a suitable material and appropriate adhesive, the cost and time to coat a boat appeared too prohibitive. The planned use of Alberich was again dropped.[25] Only once the snorkel was introduced in 1944 and operations shifted to shallow coastal waters did Alberich emerge again as a consideration for U-boat survivability against ASDIC.[26] An Alberich-coated U-boat that had to surface rendered the covering useless because a U-boat's greatest asset was its ability to remain hidden. The snorkel enabled a U-boat to do just that by removing its need to surface and recharge batteries.

The second operational U-boat coated with Alberich was *U-480* in the early summer of 1944, one year after *U-470*. During its testing in the Skagerrak '… it could not be detected by the German echo ranging gear …'[27]

U-480 reported positive operational results during the shallow Channel operations at the height of the Allied invasion of Normandy. At the same time, BdU decided on 11 July 1944 to coat some of the new Type XXIII coastal U-boats with Alberich at a rate of two to three a month. It was hoped that perhaps a rate of two per month could be reached by the end of 1944.[28]

The Allies still knew little of the Alberich in 1944, other than the information they received from captured German U-boat crewmen rescued at sea. One item gleaned from such an interrogation was the physical difference of the Alberich coatings between *U-470* and *U-480*. One report produced in early 1945 identified the thickness of the covering on *U-480* as being only a few millimetres, whereas *U-470* supposedly 'had quite a thick covering'.[29] If this was indeed true, then the difference might be attributed to *U-470*'s acoustic camouflage being tuned to a depth of 150m while the latter was tuned to a depth of a shallower 40m.

Given that the early testing by Meyer showed a tolerable variance of +/– 40m, the tuning application of a 40m operating depth would effectively protect a U-boat from periscope depth down to 80m. This was the operating depth of the English Channel, which was *U-480*'s assigned operational area.

British intelligence struggled with understanding the reasons for a U-boat to be covered with rubber. An internal Admiralty report dated 21 November 1944 stated that finally:

> Intelligence has clearly established that the enemy is expending considerable effort in endeavours to cover U-boats with rubber, and from recent Prisoner of War reports it appears that it is, in all, probability, an attempt to reduce the range of detection by ASDICs. There have also been indications recently that the Schnorkel is being covered with some material to render it undetectable by Radar, but it is not yet clear what material is being used for the purpose.[30]

British intelligence had investigated a number of theories as to Alberich's application before settling on ASDIC protection, believing at one point that the rubber coating was designed to reduce the effect of depth charge explosions or even to streamline the hull against underwater resistance.

The first Type XXIII U-boat coated with Alberich was *U-4709*. This example was not completed until February 1945 and it did not become operational before the end of the war. *U-4704* (XIII), *U-4708* (XXIII) and *U-4709* (XXIII) were also coated with Alberich. All three were scuttled in Operation *Regenbogen* without ever conducting an operational patrol.[31] There was also a proposal by BdU to apply Alberich to the new Walter Type XXVI medium U-boats, but delays occurred and the effort was cancelled given the required 5,000 to 6,000 man hours required to produce each boat.[32] With regards to this latter point, there was never any consideration given during the war to cover the Type XXIs with Alberich.

Late in 1944, it was thought that Dönitz had ordered all U-boats covered with Alberich. While one could believe that Dönitz might want this, there were immense logistical challenges in converting such a desire a reality.[33] Plans were drawn up to develop a large plant outside Hannover where the rubber sheets could be processed in large quantities, but this never occurred before the war's end.

After September 1944 the decision was made to apply Alberich to Type VIIC U-boats.[34] U-485 (VIIC) and U-486 (VIIC) were coated in Alberich during a month-long stay at Kiel in October–November 1943. Both U-boats then departed for Horten in 7 November, where they conducted their final snorkel and deep diving testing from 9 to 17 November. U-485's first patrol was the last to the English Channel conducted that year, and almost proved disastrous as its snorkel exhaust trunking malfunctioned and caused cases of carbon monoxide poisoning among the crew. Despite the snorkel mishap, Kapitänleutnant Friedrich Lutz lauded his snorkel's capabilities in his final report to BdU on 31 January 1945.[35]

U-485 went on to successfully complete two more war patrols. It surrendered at sea on 11 May, and arrived in Gibraltar on 12 May 1945 under Operation Black Flag. Its captain stated during his interrogation at the time of internment that: 'Rubber covering was against [Allied] ASDIC. His was one of the first boats to be so fitted, and he personally had insufficient experience to be able to assess its value.'[36]

U-486 conducted two patrols. During the first in the English Channel it sank four vessels, including the SS Leopoldville carrying the US 66th Infantry Division to Cherbourg as reinforcements during the Battle of the Bulge. U-486 was subsequently sunk on 12 April 1945 in the North Sea, north-west of Bergen, Norway, by a torpedo from the British submarine HMS Tapir after it aborted its second patrol due to snorkel trouble. It was caught on the surface when it was sunk.

No other Alberich-covered U-boats saw combat patrols in 1944, but the following Type VIICs were coated with Alberich and were active in 1945. U-1105 (VIIC) carried out a single operational patrol and surrendered under Operation Black Flag. U-1106 (VIIC) was sunk on its first patrol, nine days out, on 29 March 1945 in the Norwegian Sea north of the Shetland Islands by depth charges from a British Liberator aircraft (224 Sqn RAF/O). U-1107 (VIIC/41) conducted one patrol, sinking the British SS Empire Gold. U-1107 was subsequently sunk after thirty-three days at sea on 30 April 1945 in the Bay of Biscay west of Brest by a homing torpedo

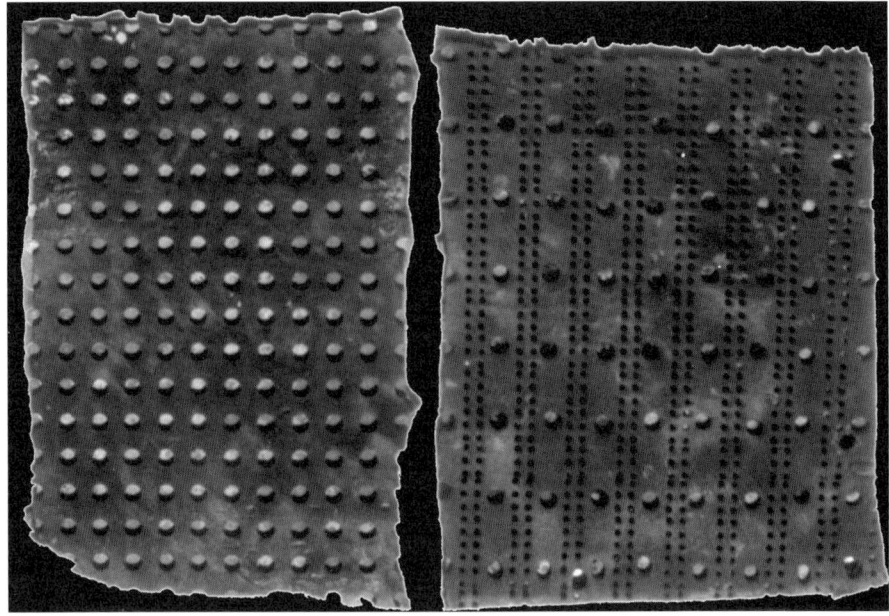

Two-piece Alberich coating from *U-1105* (VIIC). The right layer had a series of 2mm and 5mm holes, while the left layer just had 5mm. The spacing and density of the holes had to be configured for the type of operational depth, as well as whether the rubber coating was fitted on sections of the hull that were filled with air (like the conning tower) or fluid (like the ballast tanks) to be most effective. Alberich decreased Allied ASDIC by as much as 20 per cent. *(Courtesy of Maryland Historical Trust)*

from a US Liberator aircraft (VP-103 USN/K). *U-1304* (VIIC/41) and *U-1306* (VIIC/41) were covered with Alberich but conducted no operational patrols. Both were scuttled by their crews in Operation *Regenbogen*.

A total of thirteen U-boats, to include a Dutch submarine, were covered with Alberich during the war. Only two surrendered intact to the Allies, *U-1105* and *U-485*. *U-1105* was thoroughly inspected and tested by the Royal Navy. *U-485* was inspected but not evaluated operationally by the Allies. Instead, the US Navy inspection team, armed with the reports on Alberich development, inspected *U-485* in July–August 1945. *U-485*'s actual covering was found to be at 'variance' with available German documentation: 'It was also observed that there were two places where the pattern of the holes was different than those reported to have been used at the end of the war.'[37]

These variances caused the US Navy inspectors to incorrectly conclude that *U-485* was one of the first Alberich-covered U-boats. It *was* the second U-boat covered with an application that was probably tuned for 40m, after *U-480*, but what the inspectors did not realise at the time was that *U-485* had conducted more combat patrols and amassed more days at sea than any

Alberich covering on *U-1304* (VIIC/41) at the time of its launch in August 1944. This U-boat never conducted a wartime patrol. Note the unique seawater vent pattern on the forward portion of the hull. This can be seen on other Alberich U-boats such as *U-1105*, but it is not known if this pattern was unique to them or not. *(Courtesy of the U-Boot Archive)*

other Alberich-coated U-boat during the war. This length of operational service seemed to have revealed previously unanticipated problems with the Alberich, causing it to require ad hoc servicing between combat patrols. It also appears that substitute rubber covering was probably applied in several places while *U-485* spent March 1945 in Trondheim.

Alberich proved effective as acoustic camouflage during the war given the fact that no U-boat covered with the rubber was identified by ASDIC or sunk by surface ASW assets. The acoustic camouflage was initially conceived as a defensive system for deep-water operations, but was ultimately employed offensively in shallow, coastal waters. By itself, however, Alberich was limited in its usefulness. A U-boat that had to surface for long periods to recharge its batteries or communicate with BdU risked identification by Allied radar. Once identified, Allied ASW assets could be vectored to the area, and the U-boat would be forced into a desperate defensive struggle that could last days, even when coated by Alberich. Alberich's inherent benefit of stealth worked due to the introduction of the snorkel, whereby a U-boat no longer needed to surface to recharge its batteries and rarely sent any communications to BdU. By remaining submerged, it avoided Allied radar, except when deploying a snorkel, and through Alberich could effec-

Alberich covering of *U-4709* (XXIII). The Alberich covering on *U-4709* was very different from on VIICs due to the spherical hull design. *(Courtesy of the U-Boot Archive)*

tively obfuscate its sound signature against Allied ASDIC. Allied sonar men, who often had no idea that a U-boat was even in the area, might easily overlook a diminished return, thinking it to be a false echo or a school of fish. For acoustic camouflage to be effective, as its innovator Erwin Meyer perceptively concluded, a submarine 'must remain uninterruptedly underwater', thus without the innovation of the snorkel, Alberich may never have been employed operationally with such success after it was applied to *U-470* in 1943.

Chapter 5

Electro/Hydrogen Peroxide-Powered U-boats (Type XXI, Type XXIII, Type XXVIW)

The Type XXI and Type XXIII Electro-boats were wartime interim solutions in a line of H_2O_2-powered Kriegsmarine submarine designs. Both Electro-boat designs were approved before the development of the snorkel. Once the snorkel became necessary, both types required an extensible snorkel retrofit into already approved technical drawing and prefabrication production. The smaller Type XXIII's hull shape proved better at accepting the extensible snorkel, primarily due to its lower submerged speed. However, the extensible snorkel mast proved problematic on the larger Type XXI, especially at high speeds. The snorkel integration delayed the Type XXI's deployment to the point that it did not become a factor in the Battle of the Atlantic. Before war's end the Kriegsmarine made the design decision to forego the Type XXI and move forward with the smaller, more efficient H_2O_2-powered Type XXVI. Equipped with an integrated advanced pneumatic snorkel design, the Type XXVI – not the Type XXI – was considered the next evolution in U-boat design.

The early design for the closed-cycle Walter boats pursued in the early 1930s called for an air mast to inject air into the submarine without the need to surface. The air mast design, however, never left the drawing board. It remained an untested theoretical concept, while Walter's focus remained innovative propulsion and hull form. An air mast was simply a supporting design element. The Pr476 design, which was the follow-on from the original Wa201 boat, had no air mast in its final version. This is important to note, as this design was presented to the Kriegsmarine in October 1942 and became the basis of the Type XVIII U-boat that also had no integrated air mast planned at that time.[1]

In November 1942 Walter met with Dönitz in Paris during a conference on high-speed U-boat design. He proposed the new Types XVIIB and XVIII to Dönitz, who authorised the production of twenty-four of the former and two of the latter. It was recognised at the conference that a larger U-boat was required for Atlantic operations, but that the Walter turbine was not ready for mass production on that scale. There were also supply issues with the required H_2O_2, also known as 'Aurol' to the Germans and 'Ingolin' to the British. Dönitz ordered that additional designs for the larger Type XVIII be presented in several months' time. Deutsche-Werke Kiel was given the responsibility for the development of the larger Walter U-boat. However, its size meant several modifications were needed to meet the desired submerged speed of 24 knots.

In March 1943 the electric battery installation was reduced, because of the large H_2O_2 supply required onboard. This meant that when the Aurol ran out its submerged performance would be poor, and it needed to remain surfaced most of the time.[2] It was suggested by Heep that they could alter the shape of the U-boat into an '8' with the lower cross section extended a third of the way of the U-boat's length. In this space battery capacity was added that resulted in increased submerged speed and endurance.

Two months later, under the pressures of 'Black May', it was acknowledged that diesel U-boats were operating under a significant risk of Allied air attack and that a solution in the form of a high-submerged speed U-boat must be decided upon. Dönitz was presented with the plan for the Type XVIII and the new '8' design on 19 June. Dönitz expressed concerns about the size of the new Electro-boat embodied in the '8', but ultimately decided to pursue a combined design utilising the streamlined hull of the Type XVIII and the increased electric capacity '8'. He saw this as a replacement for the Type IX. Its new designation was the Type XXI. The final design for the Type XXI was approved on 29 July.[3]

Neither the Type XXI, nor the later Type XXIII, had an air mast in their respective designs prior to their proposal to Dönitz in March.[4] This is further confirmed in a direct statement by Dr Fischer, one of the chief Type XXI design engineers, who informed the post-war British technical survey team that 'at the time quick diving was the requirement since [the] snorkel was not then operational, nor did they think it would be as successful as it later proved to be.'[5] A final assessment of snorkel masts produced by the Kriegsmarine on 17 April 1945 stated that for the Type XXI, XXIII, IID, and XVII, '… the snorkel system had to be added later as a finished concept.'[6]

The snorkel design history completed by the US Navy in October 1945 is also clear that the decision to equip the Type XXI and Type XXIII U-boats with a snorkel was taken after its initial design was completed. German engineers debated the impact the already approved and ordered snorkel folding mast kits for diesel U-boats had on the overall underwater properties of the Type XXI and Type XXIII. Several factors that concerned the German engineers about adding a folding snorkel onto these new U-boats were that the prefabricated hulls could not accommodate the snorkel mast recess, the superstructures could not be enlarged enough for the required mast bracket, and regarding the Type XXI, a raised snorkel mast at the front of the conning tower reduced the firing arc of its ant-aircraft cannon.[7] Further, German engineers had to figure out the most efficient way to run the intake and exhaust trunking below deck in order to maintain the hull's streamlining.[8]

Based on these concerns it was determined that the folding mast was not acceptable. Instead they adopted an extensible mast for the new prefabricated hulls at some point in the late spring of 1944. The first operational snorkel tests in a Type XXI were conducted with *U-3005* on 26 September 1944.[9]

The introduction of the extensible snorkel into the Type XXI and Type XXIII represented a significant modification to an already approved design. Like their diesel counterparts, serial production of the U-boats was not to be interrupted in order to integrate the extensible snorkels, and they were produced as separate kits that were sent to the shipyards to be installed after assembly of the prefabricated hull sections. This was essentially a retrofit in design, if not in actual practice.[10] When the extensible snorkel was introduced into the Electro-boats there was no existing testing that could be called upon to inform the snorkel placement and overall characteristics in a high-speed submarine design. This decision introduced several flaws into the Type XXI.

All Type XXI and Type XXIII U-boats were fitted with a ball float. One novel feature introduced in the extensible masts was a small hole inserted in the lowest part of the float. When the U-boat submerged to a depth of 30m the water pressure compressed the air in the float to the extent that its remaining buoyancy was overcome by the weight, and the valve opened and flooded the mast.[11]

It was determined through operational employment of the folding mast design on diesel boats that expelling exhaust gases downward and out underwater through a central port to avoid interference with the periscope and reduce possible detection was not needed. While the retrofit snorkel kits for diesel boats were not modified, the design for the Electro-boats introduced several holes into the side of the extensible mast that allowed the exhaust gases to simply expel underwater.[12]

The extensible mast drive (also referred to as 'telescoping') was accomplished by means of an air motor located in the control room. By means of reduction gearing and shafting through the pressure hull, force was applied to a rack on the induction tube of the mast by a pinion fixed in a recess in the hull casting. The motor was intended to operate on 4 atmospheres, but attempts to make the mast packing tight introduced so much friction that 6 atmospheres were generally required.

The induction system was designed differently compared with the diesel boats. A water separator was placed between the mast and the quick-closing clapper valve. It consisted of an arrangement for changing the direction of the air flow, with appropriate drains into the hull. A flooding valve for the mast was also provided in this assembly. The quick-closing valve was power operated (air) and had a manual emergency closing feature. It was also equipped with a drain that had a pocket to catch water. There was a hull valve that could direct the air either into the boat's diesel system or the regular ventilation system's supply fan. The valve was operated manually. The boat's ventilation exhaust fan could be arranged to exhaust outboard through a standpipe when on the surface or inboard to the engine room when on batteries and using the snorkel. Only the starboard induction line was served by the snorkel.

All valves in the exhaust gas line were the metal-seated clapper type of the self-grinding variety (*Entachleifbar*). The grinding feature consisted of a means for rotating the disc against the seat by hand from within the vessel and was intended only to remove the carbon deposit. If the metal seat became scored it was necessary to disassemble the valve and reseat it in the usual manner.

The six-cylinder engine on the Type XXI was originally fitted with a 'Buchi' exhaust-driven supercharger. After some operational experience it was determined that the supercharger had to be removed, accepting a lowered engine output in order to snorkel. While the Type XXI could attain underwater speeds of up to 13 knots while snorkelling, it became inadvisable to do so because of the unacceptable vibrations that occurred in both the extensible mast and the periscope. This problem forced underwater speed to drop to 8 knots for anything but emergency tactical considerations. This speed was only 2 knots better than a snorkel-equipped diesel U-boat. In order to partially overcome these disadvantages, a protective tube was designed to be placed around the periscope, which was rigidly secured to the forward surface of the intake mast along the centreline of the housed periscope.[13] By the end of the war consideration was given to the 'Root Type' impellor blower for use during normal surface cruising.

The Type XXI U-boat was designed with two to three times the normal battery supply of normal diesel U-boats in order to primarily operate submerged. To get the high power from a small lightweight package the Type XXI's diesels were designed with superchargers that were powered by exhaust gases. As it turned out, the superchargers couldn't work due to the high back pressure of snorkelling and had to be removed. This incompatibility was probably due to the snorkel being added after the already approved design of the Type XXI. This considerably extended the snorkelling time required to charge (four hours instead of one) and was a major operating limitation of the Type XXI.

The maximum continuous-operating diesel back pressure while snorkelling was limited by instruction to 0.4–0.5 atmospheres and the exhaust temperature to 400–450°.[14] Despite this instruction, it was not uncommon for engines to be kept in operation with 0.8 atmospheres back pressure. It was standard procedure to test the exhaust lines to 4 atm. With a smooth sea, which permitted the head valve to remain open continuously, the pressure in the U-boat under the above conditions was stated to be about 0.1 atmosphere below atmospheric. Although, again, the actual practice varied with individual commanding officers, a minimum pressure in the ship of 800 millibars absolute was specified. This represented a drop in the oxygen content of consumed air from a normal 20.9 per cent to approximately 16.4 per cent. In this connection, tests showed that if the diesels were permitted to draw air from the entire vessel, the Type XXI engine could be run for at least four minutes within a closed boat without adverse effects, if any, being present only when the fluctuations of pressure were repeated and rapid. In order to avoid excessive pressure fluctuations to the engine room, all compartments were kept open to the diesel intake when snorkelling, either through the boat's exhaust system or through the bulkhead doors.

Testing of *U-3517* and *U-2502* in early January 1945 demonstrated the extent of the vibration and oscillation problems with the periscope and snorkel during various underwater speeds.[15] Stability was a problem that caused a delay in the new U-boat's deployment until they were resolved. Many of these technical reports were intercepted by Allied intelligence through Ultra.

Korvettenkapitän Adalbert Schnee commanded *U-2511*, the first operational Type XXI U-boat, during its final trials and reported that 'observation with extended 9m periscope while snorkelling was impossible even at crawling speed because of oscillation'; an observation that was picked up in an Ultra intercept.[16] Schnee turned around immediately and headed back to Bergen with the request that periscope and snorkel installation specialists be sent from Germany on the 'very next boat'. Due to the reported extensive issues with the snorkel on *U-2511*, BdU responded to the 11th

Flotilla with two follow-up questions on 23 April that were also intercepted by Ultra:

1. Report whether water intake while snorkelling unmistakably took place through float valve or whether the snorkel mast caulking possibly had become leaky.
2. Report alterations made to float.[17]

The snorkel was not the only problem encountered by Schnee. Deep diving trials, which were carried out at Horten, had to be stopped at 175m because of '… noises [which] were clearly recognised as signs of the beginning of permanent distortion or destruction …'[18] When Schnee left Bergen on *U-2511*'s first war patrol on 17 April 1945 he was forced back to port three days later because of diesel trouble.

After all the teething problems, the extensible snorkel mast proved to be the Type XXI's Achilles heel. It was not practical to streamline this mast, and its round form tended to initiate significant vibrations. The most persistent problem was that of obtaining a tight seal in both the intake and exhaust sections. Numerous forms of packing were tried on the intake pipe without success, including a type with the lip backed up by a hollow, pneumatically inflated circular ring. When the packing was eventually made tight the friction was too great and resulted in an incomplete extension so that it became necessary to slacken off again. The cumulative effect of repeatedly travelling at high speeds, enough to cause the mast to cock aft appreciably, gave rise to significant packing difficulties. A reliable seal that would stand up under service conditions was never achieved by war's end. The extensible mast design applied to the intake was considered basically unsound in that the hoisting force was eccentric with respect to the centre of gravity. This resulted in a cocking that not only caused binding, but also made it virtually impossible to obtain tight metal-to-metal joint seal in the exhaust gas portion of the mast.[19] Due to the shortage of critical materials, particularly bronze, the design of the extensible mast was poor from a material point of view, and excessively complicated processes were forced upon the manufacturers. Due to the inherent problems with the extensible snorkel mast, designs were drawn up to replace it with the proven folding snorkel mast on the Type XXIs, but this required the elimination of the aft 37mm gun mount.[20]

The changes in the snorkel design for the Type XXI resulted in extensive rework of the hull. Dönitz and BdU informed the Japanese Naval Attaché about all the issues with the Type XXI, who in turn reported them back to Tokyo in a wireless report on 7 March that was intercepted by OP-20-G. The transmission stated:

Dönitz's staff officer for operations, Admiral Wagner, states that operations of Type XXI U-boats on a large scale have been postponed until May or June 'because this type has not been sufficiently tested and also requires repairs, remodelling and training of crews.' One of the defects concerns pressure tightness of the snort exhaust. All Type XXI U-boats were forbidden on 2 March to use snort pending the outcome of an examination ordered about 19 February. Already two Type XXIII U-boats have operated while a third is currently estimated arriving off the east coast of Britain.[21]

The use of the word 'remodelling' is critical in realising the extent of the required alterations to the Type XXI U-boat. BdU knew of the design flaw as early as January–February 1945, ordering an investigation and forbidding all Type XXIs from using the snorkel during sea trials. While no archival document has yet been located that reveals how long this remodelling was to take, it is clear that such an effort was to set back the operational use of the Type XXIs even further, making them virtually unviable during any point in the war, regardless of the production disruption caused by Allied bombing raids.

Hitler was interested in the potential of the Electro-boat deployments and this was a topic of discussion with Dönitz when they met in Berlin on 17 February. Dönitz informed Hitler that the two Type XXIIIs had already been operating off the east coast of the British Isles and that the first XXI would be ready to 'leave for operations along the American East Coast by the end of February or beginning of March'.[22] This was clearly an overstatement, but it is interesting that Dönitz expected to deploy the Type XXI as a lone wolf off the US East Coast, commensurate with current snorkel tactics.

Even OP-20-G assessed that the Type XXI was not likely to see operational use due to this design flaw. As recorded in an assessment on 3 April: 'There are still no indications that the Type XXI U-boats have begun operations. It appears likely that the delay in their appearance may be due to operational defects in their design.'[23] As previously cited in the introduction, Captain Knowles of OP-20-G correctly recounted after the war that the 'periscope/snorkel vibrations' of the Type XXIs were the primary factor in the delay of their operational employment.

The issues related to the Type XXI snorkel installation have not been raised to any great extent in post-war literature. Korvettenkapitän Peter-Erich 'Ali' Cremer commanded one of the first commissioned Type XXIs (*U-2519*). He later commanded Dönitz's personal bodyguard at the end of the war. After the war he published a book titled *U-Boat Commander* that provided a grim, determined picture of the U-boat service through to the end of the war. He described a supposed event that occurred in which

Adalbert Schnee commanded the Type XXI *U-2511* out to sea in the first days of May 1945. This was considered the first combat patrol of the new Electro-boat. Schnee made his way into the North Sea and approached a British hunter-killer squadron, penetrating its destroyer screen and reaching within 50m of the cruiser HMS *Norfolk*. He is said to have made a mock attack, but did not fire torpedoes given that the BdU had just ordered all U-boats to cease hostilities. Instead, he turned and headed back to Norway on 4 May. Reportedly, Schnee concluded that in his experience the 'boat was excellent in attack and defence, something quite new for U-boat men'.[24] This report itself can be sourced to a variety of early German publications, going back to the 1950s.[25]

Given the issues raised by Schnee just a week earlier, his post-war claim appears highly dubious and self-serving. Unfortunately, this experience has been recounted numerous times by historians and hobbyists who insist that the Type XXI would have been a 'war winner' if it had just entered service earlier. It was a revolutionary design that had an impact on post-war submarine development, but as described above, the struggles with the extensible snorkel installation required a complete reconfiguration of the conning tower. A Type XXI without a snorkel had to recharge its batteries while surfaced at a rate that was close to double that of a diesel U-boat. Even when using a snorkel, battery charging times could be two to three times that of a VIIC. Clearly this increased a Type XXI's exposure and vulnerability to an Allied attack due to its size.

The late Horst Bredow, former U-boat crewman and founder of the Deutsches U-Boot Museum in Cuxhaven, Germany, penned an online article about Schnee's account and the myth that the Electro-boats were 'war winners'. He concluded that, based on new research by U-boat historian Axel Niestlé, Schnee's account of a successful mock attack in his *U-2511* is questionable at best. There is no evidence in Admiralty records of any British task groups operating near the area where Schnee manoeuvred on 4 May. It must be pointed out that Schnee's wartime sinking claims were inflated by some 50 per cent, drawing into question his accuracy and motivation. Rear Admiral (Rtd.) Erich Topp joined the Kriegsmarine with Schnee and headed the Kriegsmarine U-boat Test and Evaluation Command that oversaw the entire Electro-boat development programme. According to Bredow's research, Topp raised doubts about some of 'Schnee's memories on the details of the simulated attack, and he negated any last moment "turning point" in the war at sea through the introduction of the Type XXIs'.[26]

While the Type XXI's snorkel issues might have temporarily rendered the design incapable of conducting the high-speed manoeuvres intended by

BdU in the open ocean, there was one incident that offered some early assurance that many of its design innovations held value. Schnee was entering the fjord that led to Bergen on 8 April when he encountered what he suspected was an Allied submarine. Several days later he radioed a short report back to BdU:

1) U 2511 (Schnee) reports that when entering Bergen near the Korsfjord underwater, it met a submarine and stayed away. The submarine was kept under observation the entire night with no problems without the presence of a friendly boat being noted. The situation was under control because of the advantages of our boat type. OT shooting opportunities were good. No shots fired because of the possibility of confusion.
2) Because friendly boats are not used at night, it was definitely an enemy submarine.
3) The repeated clear danger of submarines near entry fjords is thus again confirmed.[27]

This chance encounter was probably the closest Schnee came to a real engagement during the war.

Concerns were raised that the Type XXI was just too large for convoy warfare in the North Atlantic, and that it was too costly to manufacture. Convinced that all the essential qualities of a submarine to operate in the Atlantic could be condensed into a vessel of about 800 metric tons provided a single screw was accepted, Walter's firm proposed a design for the Type XVIIA in October 1943.[28] All the desired features were incorporated into the design except that only ten torpedoes were carried, all in side-mounted tubes. A vessel of such size, with a hydrogen peroxide turbine, could be expected to achieve 26 knots submerged and be more manoeuvrable than its larger predecessor, the Type XXI. The proposal was accepted, but the usual modifications during development of the design increased the displacement considerably. The final figure of about 926 metric tons submerged caused the predicted submerged speed to drop to slightly under 25 knots. Procurement and production difficulties then postponed the construction of the Type XVIIA, and at the war's end only the sections for one vessel and some of the machinery were finished.

The design office at BdU submitted a counterproposal to Walter that was based on the smaller Type XXIII. This design was named the Type XXVIA and included a displacement less than 1,000 tons. Its full complement of torpedoes were preloaded, saving space.[29] Further modification led to the XXVIB with a predicted submerged speed of 21.5 knots. A series of final design decisions, the last made by Dönitz during the war, were concluded

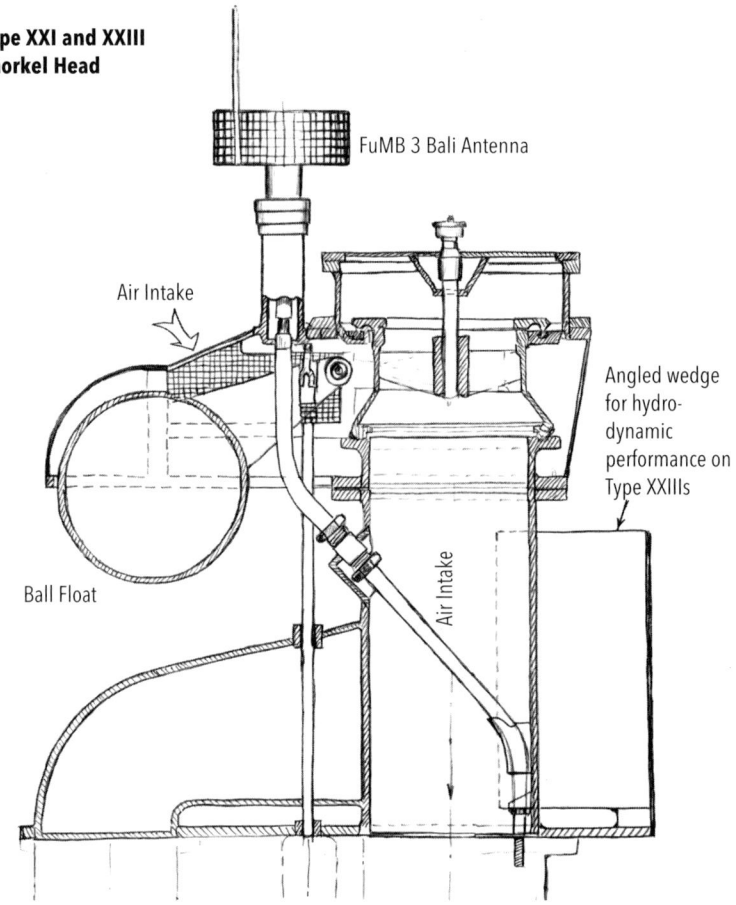

Type XXI and XXIII Snorkel Head

FuMB 3 Bali Antenna

Air Intake

Angled wedge for hydro- dynamic performance on Type XXIIIs

Ball Float

Air Intake

The standard ball float snorkel head on Type XXI and XXII U-boats. Note that on some Type XXIIs a steel wedge was welded to the front of the mast to improve hydrodynamics. *(Author's collection)*

in early 1944. In these meetings Dönitz was presented with the new Walter Type XXVI in two different versions: XXVI with anti-aircraft armament and XXVIW without. These designs were shown on 22 February 1944 along with a successor to the XXI, designated XXVIE, that was equipped with pre-loaded, side-mounted torpedo tubes and an increased battery capacity to power the Type XXI's larger electric motor incorporated into the design. The XXVIE was assessed to be inferior to the XXVIB and dropped.

Dönitz chose between the two remaining designs. The decision was made on 28 March 1944 after it was determined that the efforts to introduce increased anti-aircraft armament on the diesel U-boats in the autumn and winter of 1943–44 had failed to decrease sinking by Allied aircraft. The decision was made to invest in the Type XXVIW with its Walter turbine, closed conning tower and completely streamlined hull devoid of anti-

U-2540 (XXI) 'Wilhelm Bauer' in Bremerhaven, Germany, after being stricken from commission. The Type XXI ball float snorkel mast has two pipes, with the exhaust exiting underwater through vent holes. The snorkel mast on the Type XXIs and XXIIs was retrofitted after these U-boats' final designs were approved and the prefabrication process started. The snorkel design proved problematic on the high-speed Type XXIs and caused their operational delay and ultimate production cancellation by the Kriegsmarine in favour of the H_2O_2-powered Type XXVIW before the end of the war. *(Author's collection)*

aircraft guns.[30] It was the closest to a true submarine design produced anywhere in the world at that time. Orders were placed for the series *U-4501–U-4600*.

This new U-boat was given an advanced integrated pneumatic snorkel ring float design. The port-side pipe and induction system line was eliminated. The Type XXVIW was intended to operate with a two-cycle engine, though the final motor selected for the design was the MWM used in the very successful Type XXIII. Once the snorkel became a standard fitting on all U-boats it was generally considered that the air requirements of a two-

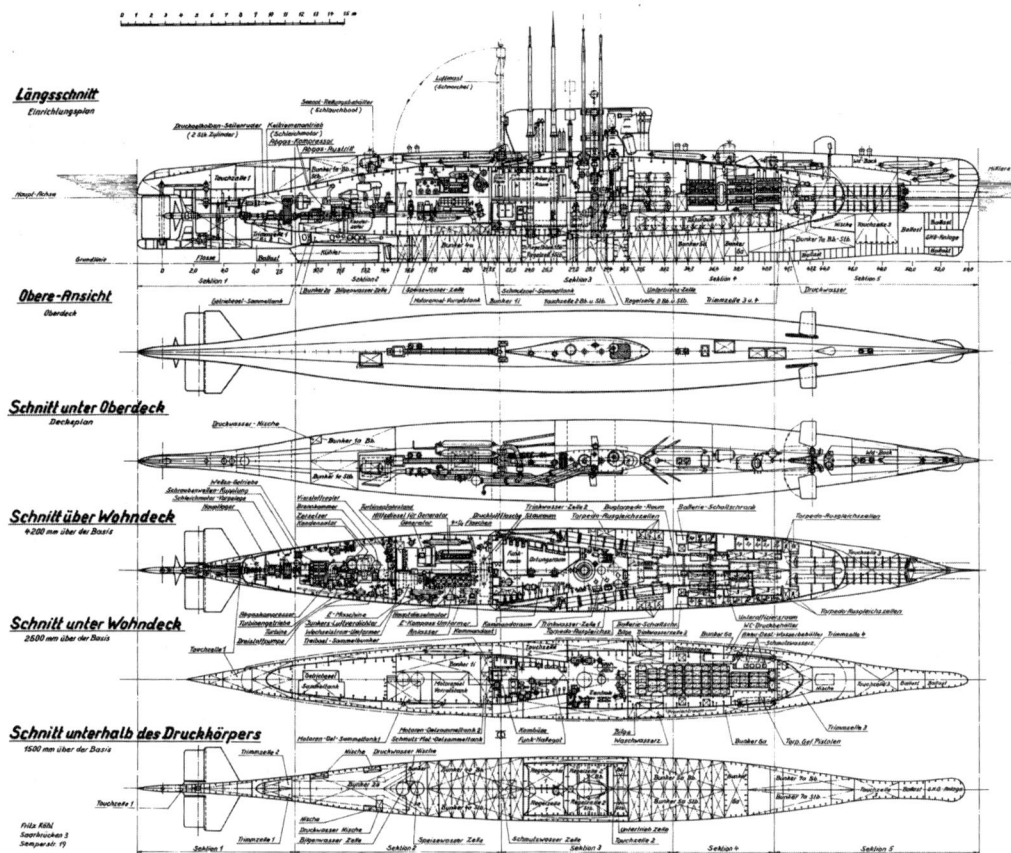

cycle engine were just too high to allow the operation of a snorkel. However, tests made in 1944 with the Type XXVIW engine proved that this combination was practical.[31] Thus, the Type XXVI was designed with a folding snorkel mounted in the aft deck after it was concluded that the extensible mast design on the Type XXI was unsound.

Admiral Eberhard Godt served as Dönitz' Operations Chief during the war and succeeded him as Chief of the BdU. Godt was directly involved with high-speed U-boat designs and their future employment. In his postwar interrogations by Allied Naval Intelligence he revealed that it was on the future design of the Walter turbine-powered Type XXVI that the future of the U-boat arm had rested, not the Electro-boat Type XXI:

Type XXVI was to be the perfect U-boat, incorporating all the advantages of earlier experience and the extremely high speeds available with Walter propulsion units. The high speed was of limited duration and was only to be

Type XXVIW U-Boat Plan

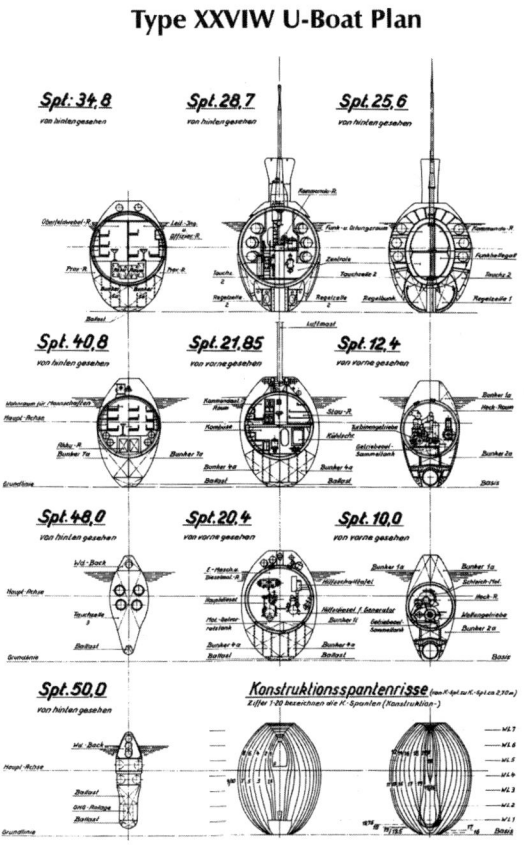

The H_2O_2-powered Type XXVIW with a pneumatic snorkel head mounted to the rear was the ultimate underwater convoy attack design that replaced the Type XXI. With a projected underwater speed of 25 knots and ten torpedo tubes, this nearly-true submarine design was designed to allow the U-boat to enter into the centre of a convoy at high speed submerged, launch its full complement of torpedoes and withdraw just as fast submerged, avoiding all surface escort vessels. Both the Royal Navy and Soviet Navy built copies of this design after the war. *(Author's collection)*

used in attacks. A diesel for cruising at snorkel depth and a small battery and electric motor for quiet evasive running were to be used for all other purposes, conserving the Walter unit fuel for attacks. This was to be a high-speed run into the centre of the convoy, release of all 10 torpedoes and high speed retirement. There was no expectation of ever operating the boats on the surface.[32]

The final sentence of Godt's quote underscores the significant role of the snorkel in the employment of high-submerged speed U-boats. This was a conclusion that was reached by the US Navy, who assessed that the Type XXVI was closest to the 'ideal submarine' designed during the war.[33] Both the Royal and Soviet Navies built copies of the XXVI design and used it as the basis for further submarine development.

Part II:

EVOLUTION OF OPERATIONS AND TACTICS

Chapter 6

Operations, Experience Reports and Evolving Tactical Procedures, June 1944–April 1945

In the wake of 'Black May' BdU pursued a series of technological developments with the goal of increased survivability. By May of 1944 the snorkel emerged as the single most important achievement to this end as U-boat commanders and their crew became more adept in its function during combat patrols. The loss of the Bay of Biscay ports quickly eliminated the mid-Atlantic as an operational area given that Type VIICs did not have the endurance or range to conduct operations there from Norwegian bases. However, the snorkel gave them the ability to patrol with near impunity along the shallow coasts of the United Kingdom. In the period June–August 1944 BdU's focus was the English Channel in order to counter the invasion of Normandy. Starting in September, U-boats opened an inshore campaign that shifted alternatively from the east coast of England, to the North Channel and Scottish Coast, to the Irish Sea and the west coast of Ireland, and finally back to the English Channel. The U-boats' focal points were the inlets, estuaries and convoy embarkation/debarkation points. Drawing on the experience in shallow water gained by the Type VIIs, the larger snorkel-equipped Type IXs began to deploy in greater numbers back to the North American coast, where they re-entered the St Lawrence River and patrolled off the ports of Halifax, Boston, New York City and Cape Hatteras for the first time in nearly two years. During these ongoing operations new technical improvements to the snorkel were introduced, anti-radar coatings were applied to the snorkel floats and upper mast, and a few Type VIIs received the anti-sonar coating known as Alberich designed to enhance acoustic camouflage. Looming in the background of these coastal operations, and being closely monitored by Allied intelligence, was the expected deployment of the new high-submerged speed Type XXIs that BdU hoped would enable the eventual return to the convoy battles of the mid-Atlantic.

There was never an updated release of the U-Boat Commanders Handbook first printed in 1942 and reprinted in 1943 that codified the new snorkel-enabled tactical procedures. U-boat commanders had to learn by doing in the last year of the war. Due to the pace of operations and lack of communications, a cycle of experience reports were issued that was employed to educate the U-boat force. U-boat commanders would maintain communication silence and only broadcast their patrol report summary one or two days out from their return to port, or in written form only once they arrived. BdU quickly assessed them to see if there was a new tactic or procedure learned during the patrol. If one was identified, it was broadcast out to all operating U-boats and often included in the training curriculum of the training flotillas. These U-boat experience reports and evolving tactical procedures issued by BdU are presented below, often along with the Allied intelligence summaries produced when they were intercepted through Ultra. What they clearly demonstrate is how the snorkel evolved U-boat operations and tactics during the last twelve months of the war and that a U-boat's actions during this period must be understood within this context.

In January 1945 Dönitz declared the age of 'Total Undersea War' in a communique to his U-boat force. While this was a term already in use among the various U-boat flotillas and BdU, the snorkel had more than proved its worth over the last six months. The snorkel saved the U-boat from destruction. It allowed it to remain submerged for the entire wartime patrol, limiting proven Allied detection techniques. While it might have been stating the obvious in his message, Dönitz knew the morale and propaganda value that it carried.

This chapter will focus on the transformation of tactical procedures that were driven by operations in European waters. The final U-boat patrols off the North American coast that culminated with *Gruppe Seewolf* will be detailed in Chapter 9.

June 1944

Upon learning of the Normandy invasion at 3.05am on 6 June, BdU directed snorkel-equipped U-boats currently on standby towards the Allied invasion zone along the Normandy coast. Despite the concern for the formidable Allied anti-submarine defence expected at the entrances to the English Channel, Dönitz reasoned that he had no choice but to send his eight

Gruppe Landwirt and four *Gruppe Mitte* snorkel boats there in an attempt to forestall the invasion. As an afterthought, he decided to countermand his previous order and send in non-snorkel-equipped U-boats from Brest as well.[1] The stakes were just too high not to deploy all available combat-ready U-boats to the invasion zone despite the risk. If Germany lost the fight for the beaches of Normandy, then they would probably lose the war. Every sacrifice had to be made at this moment, Dönitz reasoned.

This decision fundamentally altered U-boat operations for the rest of the war. Operations in coastal waters by U-boats had all but ceased in the prior years. The last U-boat that entered the English Channel was in 1940. It was nearly a year since a U-boat had prowled near the US East Coast. It was unknown by BdU whether the Allies possessed new technology to hunt and destroy U-boats in the shallows. As Hessler wrote 'thus U-boats fitted with a Snorkel installation with which they were still unfamiliar, were being sent to face an unknown threat in an area considered, even in 1940, as too dangerous for such operations'.[2]

Twelve months after the 'Black May' of 1943, Dönitz had tried every conceivable option to regain the initiative in the Atlantic. None worked as the Allies proved too adept at outmanoeuvring his U-boats with their convoys, while locating surfaced U-boats and sinking them with their aircraft. While his U-boats were now equipped with a new Tunis aerial that gave them an advantage in identifying approaching Allied aircraft, and additional anti-aircraft guns to fight them off if they were caught on the surface, none of these innovations were decisive enough to allow his U-boats to regain the initiative in the mid-Atlantic. His new Electro-boats, with their promise of high-submerged speed on which so much hope was placed, were still six months or more away from being ready for operational employment. For now, Dönitz only had one still relatively unproven technology to employ – the snorkel.

Intelligence officers in OP-20-G knew that BdU placed considerable faith in the new snorkel as they received transmissions that reinforced new operating procedures just days before the Allied invasion of Normandy. BdU reminded U-boats that their greatest threat was Allied aircraft equipped with radar:

General Orders for June: After comprehensive expansion of his anti-submarine defence, the enemy is now in a position to patrol the whole Atlantic and its approaches with anti-submarine forces. The most dangerous weapon in this defence is the anti-submarine aircraft equipped with locating gear, which tries day and night to take the U-boat by surprise, and which homes anti-submarine vessels onto it.

Due to this threat, BdU reinforced that 'surface cruising beyond charging times is thoughtless and is forbidden'. The critical factor to countering radar-equipped Allied aircraft was the snorkel. The sum of all recent experiences became Current Order No. 20, broadcast on 31 May at 10pm and 10.59pm to all U-boats. This order formed the basis of future snorkel-based operations and was modified accordingly throughout the rest of the war. In brief, it stated:

Current Order Number 20 prescribes conduct when using snorkel as follows:

Several U-boats have used snorkel with success for submerged cruises lasting several days. Use of snorkel for battery charging lasted 4–5 hours daily. 500 tonners [VIIC] without altered blower coupling tend to smoke. In this case, operating snorkel at night, manning periscope at the same time, in order to discover any [aircraft] which are searching with searchlights or flares. Snorkel can be located by radar, though only at distances considerably shorter than those at which radar can locate a surfaced U-boat. To avoid surprise by surface vessels, interrupt snorkel operation every 20 minutes for hydrophone sweep. If you have a non-smoking snorkel, use it in daytime too, manning periscope simultaneously. IXC boats (750 tonners) man both periscopes. Pay strict observance to snorkel instructions. In order to collect more data, carry out snorkel operation in fairly rough sea too. (2200/31)[3]

A total of twelve snorkel U-boats that included *U-275* (VIIC), *U-269* (VIIC), *U-984* (VIIC), *U-621* (VIIC), *U-441* (VIIC), *U-764* (VIIC), *U-953* (VIIC), *U-212* (VIIC) from *Landwirt* and *U-767* (VIIC), *U-1191* (VIIC), *U-988* (VIIC), and *U-671* (VIIC) from *Mitte* made their way into the English Channel. These last four were ordered to proceed to the latitude south of Ireland, then into the Channel. These were followed by another nine non-snorkel boats that sailed from Brest to the area between Lizard Head and Hartland Point. Strong Allied air attacks occurred, with more than fifty that first night. On the first night of the invasion, one snorkel and five non-snorkel U-boats were damaged and radioed their intent to return to base. During daylight on 7 June, all U-boats proceeded submerged into the target area, two more non-snorkel boats were lost and two others damaged the following night. By 10 June, two of the nine non-snorkel U-boats that left Brest for the Plymouth area were sunk, while five were forced to return damaged. It became apparent to BdU that a non-snorkel U-boat could not proceed further towards the invasion zone. *U-740* (VIIC) and *U-821* (VIIC), both non-snorkel equipped, were ordered to return, but they did not as *U-740* fell victim to air attack on 9 June and *U-821* was lost on the 10th respectively.[4]

BdU subsequently ordered the non-snorkel U-boats in Lorient, St Nazaire and La Pallice to establish a double reconnaissance line between Brest and Bordeaux. Their objective was to await a second potential invasion along the Biscay Coast. They were ordered to lie on the bottom in less than 10m of water, a procedure formerly forbidden due to the fear of mines laid in the shallows by Allied aircraft. This danger was disregarded under the circumstances as this procedure allowed the U-boats to remain on station and reduce their battery recharge time. These U-boats, however, were identified and attacked nightly by Allied aircraft. Once the threat of an Allied landing on the Biscay coast passed, Dönitz debated where to employ these U-boats. His obvious choices were to the English Channel or the North Atlantic. He decided against either given the recent losses of non-snorkel U-boats. Their chances of survival were low without a snorkel. These U-boats were ordered back to port, where they were to be retrofitted with a snorkel as a priority.[5]

U-boats that entered the English Channel could not send regular reports. Surfacing risked immediate identification either through visual observation or radar. Instead, U-boat captains began to radio short reports of their experiences to BdU just before arrival at their bases.[6] A review by BdU of the losses in the first week was telling. Not a single snorkel-equipped U-boat was lost.[7]

With losses mounting in the English Channel, Dönitz weighed his options for the continued employment of his U-boats. He longed for the days of the mid-Atlantic convoy battles of 1941–43 where his U-boats made a measurable impact against the Allied war effort. After deliberation on whether to continue the U-boat war or withdraw his fleet from operational areas, he decided upon the former. But now the focus was containment not a tonnage war. He had to buy time for the new Electro-boats to be deployed. Dönitz recorded this decision in the BdU KTB on 14 June: 'The present successes and those attainable in the future with the old submarine types do not alone justify the high expenditure in labour, armament and material on submarine warfare at home, and especially the high toll of life in the battle of the Atlantic.' Yet, he countered that:

The submarine war cannot be allowed to cease, since once it has finally succumbed it would not be possible to take it up again. To parry with the enemy is, although a proverb, a tactical, technical, and above all a psychological necessity. The submarine arm has shown itself capable of withstanding the most difficult times. Once again she must carry her self-assertion into the battle with new weapons, even in the face of heavy loss, and without having abandoned the cause even temporarily.[8]

The U-boat war continued as its focus shifted to coastal operations. Dönitz's logic, based on what he knew at the time, was not faulty. However, post-war analysis revealed that the assets he tied down, while significant, were far less than he believed. While the Type XXIII did deploy operationally before war's end, the Type XXI did not due to significant design challenges.

The experience reports Dönitz required came in slowly. His U-boats no longer sent frequent wireless transmissions during operations given that they increasingly remained submerged for longer periods of time. Most U-boats did not send a report until they arrived safely back in their pens on the Biscay coast. This limited the ability of BdU to directly influence operations due to a loss of near real-time tactical reporting. BdU recorded this impact to operations as follows:

> In considering the operational possibilities the periodic change from a favourable to a doubtful summing-up is striking. Reason for this can be attributed to the insufficient information at the disposal of operational staff. As the boats were continuously submerged and therefore could not transmit any immediate messages by radio, their reports were only received after arrival back in port, i.e. 8–14 days later. It was therefore always possible that the impression gained from these messages had changed and new boats arriving there met with quite a different situation, that is, more difficult conditions. A current, rough summing-up of the situation was only possible by studying intercept reports of enemy's sightings and attacks on submarines.[9]

Three U-boats that entered the English Channel were equipped with experimental rod aerials on their snorkels. These were *U-764*, *U-441*, and *U-621*. All three boats were given orders to transmit reports from the operational area. BdU even gave them specific instruction to depart the operational area to broadcast.[10] However, no reports were sent as some U-boats decided to remain submerged, and those that tried to transmit found that the rod aerials on a snorkel mast proved problematic. Out of the three U-boats, *U-441*, was subsequently sunk.

The first and only U-boat of the original five sent into the English Channel that returned was *U-984*. Upon its arrival on 5 July, Oberleutnant Heinz Sieder reported 'that operational conditions in the Seine Bay area were every bit as favourable as indicated hitherto'. He struck HMS *Goodson* on 25 June, 40 miles north of Jersey, damaging the frigate, which was subsequently towed to port and scuttled. On 29 June he encountered the small convoy ECM-17 30 miles north of Cape Barfleur, damaging one American steamer and sinking three others. His war patrol into the English Channel reaped 30,090 tons. Sieder was awarded the Knight's Cross on 8 July for this action. No doubt this gave a brief boost to morale across the U-boat arm, even though Sieder lost his life when his U-boat was sunk in the Channel on 2 August.

On 5 July *U-671*, under the command of Oberleutnant Wolfgang Hegewald, arrived at Boulogne after departing Norway. Hegewald cruised around the west coast of Ireland and transited through the English Channel. He sunk no Allied vessels, but his cruise was viewed as a success.[11] *U-671* had done the unthinkable. It crossed the Channel at a time of incredible Allied anti-submarine defence and survived.

Out of twelve snorkel U-boats that departed Brest for the Channel, three were sunk and two failed to reach the operational area. These losses were viewed as tolerable by BdU. However, in looking at the U-boats that arrived from Germany via Norway and around Ireland, only two U-boats out of eight survived the journey, *U-671* and *U-480*. According to Hessler, 'such heavy losses proved that we had given too difficult a task to these inexperienced crews and quickly scratched any idea of routing boats from Germany via the North Sea and Dover Straits, a step which was being seriously contemplated'.

Based on the reports from *U-984* and *U-671* alone, BdU decided to continue operations in the English Channel, but only with boats based in western France. The view expressed by BdU at the time was that 'in terms of supplies lost to the enemy, these sinkings, alone, would have warranted an even greater sacrifice on behalf of the German army in its grim, bloody defensive battle. Furthermore, as, from now on, only experienced crews would be sent into the Channel, it was reasonable to expect that losses might remain within tolerable limits'.[12]

OP-20-G analysed the events of June with some alarm, noting the operational use of the snorkel:

Not until late in June were there any definite indicators that U-boats had succeeded in penetrating the cross-channel invasion area east of Cherbourg, indicating the effectiveness of allied a/s measures as well as the inherent difficulty of submarine operations in restricted waters. Currently about 10 U-boats are estimated in the channel area, most of which appear to be equipped with snorkel. *Restrict information herein to those who need to know.*[13] [Author's emphasis]

The ability of Allied aircraft to detect the snorkel mast with radar during a U-boat's approach to the Channel, while transiting past the Faroe Islands, was a serious concern for BdU. Regarding those snorkel-equipped U-boats directed to the Channel, they were given a wide latitude in their freedom of manoeuvre, contrary to years of prior operational guidance developed during the height of the convoy battles in the mid-Atlantic.[14]

During June the passage of U-boats south of Iceland became difficult. *U-998* (VIIC/41) was damaged by air attack and returned to Norway, where it was decommissioned. *U-804* fought off a British Mosquito in the same area while going to the rescue of *U-998*, noting that the aircraft used a German recognition signal to confuse the U-boat's crew. *U-804* (IXC/40) returned to Bergen on account of three seriously and five slightly wounded members of the crew. *U-715* (VIIC) was recorded as lost. It was the second snorkel-equipped U-boat that attempted to make the passage. *U-802* (IXC/40) reported its snorkel out of order when it sent its required passage report. *U-423* (VIIC), the third snorkel-equipped U-boat to make the passage, was soon considered lost as well. BdU then ordered that 'outward-bound boats to put about if snorkel is unserviceable, and passage only to be continued if boat is already west of longitude AE 91, condition of snorkel then to be reported with "passing report"; steer for west coast of France. Boats were again ordered to proceed submerged in this area using snorkel since defence inadequate against strengthened forces of Mosquito aircraft.'[15]

By the end of June, the snorkel became the dominant driver of U-boat operations. A U-boat cruise was often terminated if the snorkel was faulty. Tactics continued to evolve after each successful cruise, as recorded by Ultra. On 19 June U-boats operating in the English Channel received the following message from BdU:

In spite of all difficulties an unconditional effort must be made by every Commanding Officer to reach the assigned op-area north of the Bay of the Seine. There the prospects of success are the greatest and most effective for easing the land battles. Enemy defence will be limited by their own heavy traffic. Use every means to attain this goal … Marbach (U-953) was not located in any instance while using snorkel.[16]

Several days later, on 29 June, the following Ultra intercept was recorded:

Some chasing is greatly hampered as a result of hydrophone and radar conditions. It is possible to lie on bottom undisturbed. Cannot surface. Take every opportunity to use snorkel, so that you will have freedom of action upon signing the enemy. Using snorkel is favourable when there are distant hydrophone bearings all around the U-boat, because then hydrophone listening is made difficult for the enemy. U-764 (Bremen) crew submerged for 18 days without surfacing. (1703/26). All Channel-bound U-boats whose snorkels become defective are now to discontinue and put into Brest. Those coming from Norway in the Baltic shall return if they have not crossed (63° North) 09 – 30° West.[17]

In the month of June three developments brought on by the initial success of the snorkel set the stage for the next ten months of U-boat operations. First, the snorkel asserted itself as the dominant technical development within the U-boat arm introduced since the events of 'Black May'. Construction priorities were now driven by snorkel retrofits in the Biscay bases and German shipyards. Second, operations shifted from the mid-Atlantic to the English coast. Third, new tactical procedures began to develop. Among the most important was that U-boat commanders were allowed freedom of manoeuvre given the emerging issues with two-way wireless communications. As U-boats spent more time submerged they had to become creative with their refuse by flushing it out through the toilet or storing it in containers. To conserve oxygen, new onboard routines were established on U-boats centred on snorkelling times when oxygen flow was at its greatest. Sitting on the bottom, otherwise known as 'bottoming', became common as crews could do this to conserve battery power and oxygen. As crews rested quietly in their bunks, overall movement was kept to a minimum. 'Bottoming' soon became a preferred offensive and defensive tactic. U-boats could enter a high-traffic area and 'bottom' while waiting for the sounds of an approaching Allied vessel or convoy. Then it would rise gently off the bottom and launch its acoustic homing torpedoes without ever breaking the surface, even with a periscope. After a torpedo attack or during an Allied pursuit, a U-boat could quietly shift positions and 'bottom' again to hide. U-boats could no longer use the safety of deep water to evade their pursuers, but hiding on an uneven bottom, or near an existing shipwreck, obscured a U-boat's sonar signature from a searching anti-submarine vessel. The benefits of 'bottoming' were placed into Experience Message 113 titled 'Silent Trim' broadcast on 1 July. This was based on the report made by Oberleutnant Fritz Kallipke of the non-snorkel-equipped *U-397* (VIIC), who operated as part of the reserve *Gruppe Mitte*. He sailed from Stavanger, Norway, on 8 June to form a patrol line, then returned to the port on 24 June. The message read: 'U-397 (Kallipke) lay 25m level in patrol line for fourteen days. Engines. He used electric engines only for drill, routine times, to look around. This achieved: (one) reduction of diesel charging time (two) increased hydrophone ranges (as a result of reduction of owner noises) (three) fuel savings.' (1920/30).[18] U-boats also learned to use the current in the shallows to drift in or out of an operational area with engines off in order to make a noiseless approach or getaway. The U-boat arm was evolving. Even morale was back up for the first time in a year.

July 1944

Snorkel retrofits in Biscay ports were BdU's top priority in early July. Once the retrofit was complete, U-boats were deployed into the English Channel. U-boat crews often received a few hours of snorkel training before being sent against the Allies. Four U-boats made their way into the Channel in July. These were *U-763* (VIIC), *U-672* (VIIC), which was sunk, *U-741* (VIIC), and *U-953* (VIIC). Snorkel procedures continued to be refined based on reports from returning U-boats. These were immediately broadcast out to the U-boat fleet as new experience messages.

A refinement to the original snorkel instructions contained in Current Order No. 20 was broadcast in early July. In order to obtain the shortest charging times in a Type VIIC it was recommended that 'Starboard Diesel passage at 280 revolutions with subsidiary charging, port Diesel charging only. Valid only for boats without adapted spring coupling for blower. Other boats to proceed according to own experience.'[19]

Two new orders were soon issued. First was Serial Order 21, which was designed to prevent torpedo failures that occurred due to pressure variations while snorkelling.[20] These issues were apparently encountered by U-boats making the long passage from Norway into the operational area. Their longer cruises meant more frequent periods of snorkelling, which in turn increased the fluctuations of atmospheric pressure within the U-boat. Dramatic drops in low pressure often occurred when an operating snorkel float was inadvertently submerged below the surface while operating the diesels. Unanticipated effects often resulted.

This was followed by Special Order No. 14 directed at U-boats departing German and Norwegian ports for the operational area west of England. It stated that all U-boats were to proceed submerged only using their snorkel, from the time they parted from their escort until they reached large square AL. All snorkelling was to be done in darkness, during fog, bad visibility, or in heavy sea. Snorkelling was to occur for short periods of thirty to forty-five minutes, especially if it had to be done in good visibility or calm seas.[21]

BdU transmitted an experience report out to the U-boat fleet on 6 July based on Sieder's successful cruise the month before in *U-984*:

Charging during cruise to operational area is very difficult due to many hydrophone bearings. Therefore take advantage of every opportunity to use snorkel. Omit attacks on sweep groups during cruise to operational area and in operational area, as these usually travel at low speed and with serpentine course. Shoot only in case of emergency or when conditions for firing are good. Save torpedoes for operational area. Best chances of success on lines of traffic there. Wait for large ships.[22]

U-763, under the command of Kapitänleutnant Ernst Cordes, left La Pallice on 10 June and returned to Brest thirty-six days later on 15 July after a successful patrol in the English Channel. He reported that 'remaining on bottom in case of pursuit by search group proved its worth'. He was operating at a depth of 60m when he was attacked. Cordes evaded his pursuers by rising from the bottom 'noiselessly and drifting with the current, without starting the engine'. He used this manoeuvre consistently during a thirty-hour hunt and avoided all Allied attempts at an accurate depth charge attack. He also stated 'during snorkel cruise on a dark night when snorkel was extended 3–4m, accurately placed depth charges [by aircraft], but with snorkel extended to normal distance, numerous runs-in by aircraft with inaccurately placed bombs, no searchlights. With normally infrequent showing of snorkel, numerous anti-submarine run-ins with inaccurate depth charges. All run-ins without Searchlight'.[23] What Cordes' report revealed was that if proper snorkelling depth was maintained, Allied airborne radar was less likely to identify the snorkel head as a target. At the end of his cruise Cordes noted in his KTB that 'the phrase "Total Undersea War" gave a psychological boost to the crew'.[24] This phrase soon began to circulate among the U-flotillas. More than a catchphrase, it began to resonate as crews that returned from patrol shared stories of how they never, or rarely, broke the surface in feats of increasing record-setting underwater endurance.

Cordes noted in his report that a bottomed U-boat, properly resting on the sand, received weaker concussions from depth charges. BdU added to the broadcast of his experience report to the U-boat force that this was already 'an old observation' and that U-boat commanders were reminded of it again. Lying on the bottom, however, could also be dangerous, as in the case of *U-672*. On 18 July, when lying bottomed, this U-boat received damage from a destroyer that had picked up a motionless and 'doubtful' sound contact. Due to severe damage, *U-672* was scuttled by the crew the following day.[25]

Oberleutnant Karl-Heinz Marbach, the commander of *U-953*, provided an interesting experience report regarding his month-long cruise into the English Channel:

Encountered no defence worth mentioning either on cruise or on return. During two different attacks on convoys, both successful, U-boat met with no defence, and was not attacked afterwards. Poor sound conditions confirmed; therefore went to bottom in case of hydrophone bearings while en route. Day and night aircraft observed. U-boat not ventilated during the day. Barrage balloons observed only with slow convoys. No traffic east of supply lane. Lay on bottom en route when headed against the current; daily run about 40 miles.

BdU annotated his rebroadcast experience report to the U-boat forces with: 'Pay attention to faint noises for auxiliary motors of sub chasers. Anti-submarine groups frequently remain stopped. Only by observation of the auxiliary motors did Marbach learn of the presence of the search group, which then suddenly started up on the screws.'[26] He received the Knight's Cross on 22 July for his successful patrol, even though he sunk no confirmed Allied ships. He returned to Germany to commission *U-3014*, a new Type XXI, after the Allies surrounded the U-boat base at Brest. *U-953* was assigned a new commander, Herbert Werner.[27] Once the Biscay bases became surrounded, U-boats that had received a fixed snorkel, or that would not receive an operational snorkel, were simply decommissioned in their pens. The crews of *U-256* (VIIC), *U-267* (VIIC), *U-270* (VIIC), and *U-382* (VIIC) were sent to Germany to commission new Type XXI U-boats.

The same day that Marbach was awarded the Knight's Cross for bravery, BdU broadcast further refined guidance on ventilating a U-boat while snorkelling. It was noted that: 'The experience of one Channel boat indicates that it is better to ventilate the boat with one diesel engine running for 3–5 minutes rather than by equalising pressure through snorkel, having first produced pressure below atmosphere by means of the electric compressor. Boats are to note their experiences on this subject in their KTBs.'[28]

BdU recorded in their own KTB how difficult underwater navigation was when conducting a cruise almost entirely underwater. This was a new challenge for U-boats, who earlier enjoyed the ability to routinely take navigation fixes from the surface. This proved particularly difficult when operating in coastal shallows. The below reference by BdU refers to a situation with *U-763*, though it was not mentioned by name. *U-763* found itself outside Portsmouth harbour through an error in underwater navigation.

Fortunately it was not noticed or fired upon among the peaceful traffic with riding lights set which lay at anchor there. In spite of most exciting circumstances, as for instance while diving in front of an approaching ship when the boat touched bottom at 9m leaving the conning tower sticking high out of the water, boat still managed to reach the open Channel by snorkel sailing. In so doing boat had to pass by a number of ships at the closest range.[29]

Several other interesting developments related to the adaption of the snorkel occurred in mid-July. BdU began to realise that sinking claims had to be verified through Allied reporting if possible, as they noted how their own commander's claims were not correct. This was not necessarily caused by a wilful attempt on the part of U-boat commanders to inflate their success in the hope of achieving a Knight's Cross like Sieder. Rather it reflected the new trend towards continually submerged operations where torpedoes were fired at sound contacts and sinking verification was done through hydrophones.[30]

OP-20-G began to slowly build a picture of the changing U-boat war. It many respects it was learning at the pace of BdU given the fact that changing tactics and procedures were based on experience reports from returning U-boats rebroadcast to the fleet. Allied intelligence was simply following the developments as they happened, as in the case of ventilation and communication: 'On 26 June they were likewise informed that "in cruising underwater air can be changed by using electric compressor with pressure up to 200 mbar below normal. Then equalise pressure with snorkel in 1.5 minutes." Snort dipoles can be used when: transmitting and receiving on H/F, possibly receive on VL/F, and with radar detection gear.'[31] Later experience showed that successful wireless transmission from a dipole was far too problematic, if not impossible. OP-20-G noted with dissatisfaction that this was a direct cause of in the drop in signals intelligence.

In their overall assessment of the month, OP-20-G highlighted that the Battle of the Atlantic was 'quiet'. This was in part due to a general reduction of wireless traffic that was a by-product of nearly exclusive submerged operation brought on by the snorkel. OP-20-G began to see the snorkel as a success and that U-boats so equipped might start operating in other coastal areas.[32]

One of the main reasons for the drop in Atlantic operations was caused by the BdU directive to have all available U-boats retrofitted with a snorkel. Retrofits took time, up to a month, if done properly. BdU now recognised that the snorkel was not just a defensive technology, but one that could allow their U-boats to return to the offensive and operate in areas that were long regarded as too dangerous. From French bases to German shipyards, snorkel retrofits were the priority. As one Ultra intercept revealed: 'In the Biscay ports, as a matter of policy any U-boats which can be equipped with a snorkel in the shortest time to begin priority.'[33] Back in Germany the installation of snorkels was not easy or efficient. This had almost nothing to do with the technical issues, but the organisation and bureaucracy in place at the shipyards and U-boat pens. A summary of several Ultra intercepts on the issue provide the context:

Every command was involved and countless messages went back and forth probing, querying, demanding, protesting, and reporting every aspect of snorkel and its installation from parts lost en route to last-minute adjustments and breakdowns onboard. Everything possible was subordinated to the task of installation. The date of snorkel completion for an individual boat was practically its war readiness date. Disagreements between dockyard officials and operational commands were aired vigorously. On 11 July COMSUBs West informed Commanding Admiral U-boats (Admiral von Friedeburg at Kiel, in charge of U-boat administration) that 'Stubborn attitude of construction committee with respect to Front demands is intolerable in the present situation.'[34]

Even the inbound Japanese submarine *I-52* (MO MI) that was scheduled to arrive in Lorient was to receive a snorkel installation. However, it was sunk by Allied aircraft on 24 June south-west of Cape Fear before it arrived.[35] This was the first indication that the snorkel design was being passed to the Japanese through a technology transfer.[36] Four snorkel-equipped U-boats had made their way to the Far East before the war's end. These U-boats provided the Japanese with the practical installation knowledge to adopt their own snorkel design. When Germany surrendered in May 1945 the following U-boats were taken over by the Imperial Japanese Navy: in Singapore *U-181* (IXD2) was renamed *I-501* and *U-862* (IXD2) *I-502*; in Surabaya *U-195* (IXD1) became *I-506*; and in Batavia *U-219* (XB) became *I-505*. The snorkel and a version of Alberich were both incorporated most notably into the design of the I-400 class of Japanese submarine aircraft carriers.

August 1944

U-boat operations in August were characterised by transition. As the Allied breakout from the Normandy beachhead began, the U-boat bases along the Biscay coast became encircled. Remaining snorkel-equipped U-boats were ordered into the English Channel and told to conserve enough fuel to return to Norway.

The priority in the Biscay U-bunkers was now the completion of snorkel retrofits on remaining U-boats. U-boats were ordered to shift ports along the Biscay coast to gain access to the parts required to complete these retrofits. Once completed, these boats were ordered to evacuate to Norway. U-boats that could not complete a retrofit were decommissioned. This ended the phase of the Battle of the Atlantic romanticised in countless German memoirs and blockbuster movies. The Biscay bases had provided the ability to send numerous Type VII U-boats out into the mid-Atlantic, where they formed Wolfpacks that threatened the very survival of the

United Kingdom in 1940–43. With the Biscay bases evacuated, those same Type VIICs could no longer conduct extended operations in the Atlantic from Norway due to their limited range. But, snorkel equipped, those same Type VIICs could effectively operate along the shallow coast of the U.K.

On 7 August BdU issued their order of priority for Biscay U-boats with 'the aim of all measures is to prepare all boats for action as "Snorkel" boats'. If they could not be retrofitted, they were to be decommissioned and the crews re-apportioned.[37] Delivery of snorkels to Biscay ports from Germany were ordered to be accelerated with the intent of retrofitting another ten U-boats by the middle of August.[38]

The often quick snorkel retrofits, both in Biscay ports and particularly Norwegian bases, resulted in catastrophic mechanical failures. A lack of crew training and experience also contributed to faulty operation of the new device. Time and again U-boats returned after starting their patrol due to snorkel breakdowns. Out of eight snorkel boats that departed Norway in June for the Channel, four arrived while *U-423* (VIIC), *U-478* (VIIC), *U-715* (VIIC) and *U-1225* (IXC/40) were all lost en route to the Atlantic. Hessler recalled the discussion in BdU at the time, noting how they were 'forced to assume that, with crews only imperfectly trained, the boats in question had occasionally found it necessary to surface; an assumption supported by comparison of their plotted positions with those contained in intercepted British radio messages'.[39] If a U-boat surfaced, it was likely to be located and attacked by Allied aircraft.

There is no known record of an Allied air attack on or near the relative position of *U-865* (IXC/40), despite Hessler's assertion. The cause of its loss remains unknown. However, a snorkel defect was the likely reason, as annotated in the BdU KTB after *U-865* failed on six occasions to respond to calls to report its position.[40] Other U-boats encountered similar problems. *U-1229* returned to Trondheim with at out of order snorkel in mid-July due to problems with both its ventilation intake and exhaust trunking.[41] In mid-August, *U-543*'s (IXC/40) last message was sent on its return passage in which it noted it had experienced a snorkel breakdown. *U-396* (VIIC) also began a return passage after starting its cruise due to a snorkel breakdown. Several snorkel-equipped Type IXCs disappeared without a trace after departing Norway. No corresponding Allied reports exist to suggest they were attacked and sunk. In these cases it should be assumed that a snorkel defect or improper venting of the batteries after a snorkel run resulted in the possibility that the U-boat flooded uncontrollably, carbon monoxide poisoned the crew, or a battery explosion occurred.

In Norway, Horten became the main base for snorkel retrofits, fixes and training before U-boats departed on their operational patrol. In August,

U-248 (VIIC) and *U-772* (VIIC) went through several days of snorkel training at Horten before departing for the English coast. New training routines were established in these early days at Horten that continued throughout the war as Norway transitioned into the main base of operations for the inshore campaign.[42]

U-boats that returned to Norway reported that they operated their snorkel continuously after completing a battery charge. These used their snorkel to proceed on full diesels while remaining submerged. *U-309* (VIIC) snorkelled for about three and a half hours per day, while *U-621* (VIIC) snorkelled for two hours per day.

BdU watched the summer battles in France unfold with concern. On 4 August the Allies broke out of Normandy at Avranches. As noted in the BdU KTB:

> The situation developed with such rapidity that the few troops still in Brittany were forced to make a hurried retreat to the fortresses by enemy reconnaissance spearheads and terrorists. This has caused great disorder in the fortresses, which means considerable interference to dockyard working and calls into question the completion of boats and installation of snorkel.[43]

BdU requested the direct intervention of OKW to rectify the priorities at the various Biscay ports that required to be defended. Order was re-established at the northern ports and retrofits continued. The Allied threat to the northern bases was greater than to those in the south. All remaining U-boats in port had to be retrofitted with the snorkel immediately. As per BdU, U-Boats 'which cannot be fitted with snorkel even in La Pallice or Bordeaux to be decommissioned and crew to return home for transfer to new boats'.[44]

OP-20-G followed the progress of rapid snorkel retrofits and evacuation to Norway as they intercepted several of the above mentioned BdU communiqués. At the start of the month, twelve of the twenty-nine U-boats still in the northern ports were equipped with a snorkel, while eleven were in process of being retrofitted. Six U-boats lacked retrofit kits. Among the latter were four decommissioned boats that were being provided with substitute commanders and temporary crews for transfer purposes.[45]

As snorkel retrofits continued, Dönitz issued a personal communiqué on 21 August that exhorted all U-boats operating in the Channel to make a final effort, as the Western Allies began their eastward breakout in France:

> In the stern battle against the enemy storming us from the West you are in the foremost line now as before … I know what hardiness, toughness and

endurance you must bring to bear in order to endure the hardships and unceasing attacks. But I also know that you, my U-boat warriors, carried on by the old spirit of attack, think only of destroying the enemy. Be assured that I follow your battle continually and that you are always in my thoughts.[46]

Three days later, on 24 August, U-boats operating in the Channel were ordered to 'begin return for operational area on your own initiative if increased defence seems to be too hard on the crew and to endanger the U-boats too much, and the prospects of success are too small'.[47]

At the end of August BdU took stock of three months of English Channel operations. On 28 August their KTB noted:

> The effect of the snorkel was certainly decisive, and operation in the Channel without it would have been quite out of the question. Only a few months ago it would have seemed impossible that a boat could operate for 42 days without breaking surface once. Only by means of the snorkel was it possible to operate close to the English coast again and to bridge the intervening gap between the operation of the new and old types of boats.[48]

During the last three months, thirty snorkel-equipped U-boats had conducted forty-five sorties against the English Channel and Cornish coast. The tally as identified by BdU was: five escort vessels, four landing craft (8,404 tons), and twelve other ships sunk totalling 65,249 tons; and another one escort vessel, one landing craft, and five ships damaged for 36,000 tons. In addition there were three minelaying missions that, according to British records, resulted in the sinking of one and damage to two ships. In total, twenty U-boats were destroyed. BdU calculated the loss rate against sorties as being 45 per cent, and 66 per cent when compared with the number of boats employed. While this might appear to be a high rate of loss for limited gain, BdU justified the sacrifice by stating that the '20 boats concerned were, after all, obsolete by this time. The loss of 1,000 men, of whom 238 – or about 25 per cent – were picked up by the enemy, was also not too high a price to pay for the results actually achieved.'[49]

Due to a lack of reporting by U-boats operating in the English Channel there were almost no experience messages transmitted to the fleet by BdU. One that was sent mid-month was Order No. 23. This addressed the issue of density layers in U-boat operations. This was an aspect that had been under consideration for some months by BdU. Enough experience reports were received for the following guidance to be issued:

Current Order No. 23 – August 1944

Density layers of water and listening conditions. Investigations concerning the salt content and temperatures of density layers in the areas of open sea have proved that layers of water of different temperature and different salt content circulate and displace each other. Since the acoustic range is strongly influenced by raising and falling temperatures, it is continually changing.

As Result of Investigations.

1. Measure density of water, with boat in action.

2. If listening reception seems poor, vary diving depth higher or lower, to obtain better signal strength. Also alteration of diving depth downward can improve listening conditions.

3. Since known underwater hydrophones work through measurement of sound, in case of pursuit, work with density measurement and supervision of the signal strength of the acoustic interception. Go into water layers unfavourable for sound transmission.[50]

The first four U-boats to open the inshore campaign against Great Britain departed Norwegian bases at the end of August. *U-296* (VIIC) was ordered to North Minch, *U-482* (VIIC) to North Channel, and *U-680* (VIIC) to Moray Firth. One Norway-based U-boat, *U-244* (VIIC), was ordered to Reykjavik, Iceland. These four U-boats were issued the following 'essential points' by BdU that guided the opening phase of the inshore campaign:

1. Approach unobserved, make your appearance by surprise. The first attack should lead to success, since some of the areas have not been occupied for a very long time. In general, at present neither alert nor very strong defence is to be expected. After being observed, act according to the situation: haul in along the coast, remain on bottom, or if necessary move off temporarily.

2. Choose times for using snorkel skillfully, always charge quickly and keep batteries well charged. Channel U-boats have determined that convoy vessels with noise-producing buoys cannot hear well by hydrophone; U-boats using snorkel have at times passed close by unobserved. Snorkel can be located inexactly at night by aircraft, but this radar does not permit the carrying out of an aimed attack without searchlights or flares. Attack will therefore be recognised in adequate time. During attacks without searchlights the bombs fell so inexactly that no damage of any kind resulted.[51]

Based on the operational experience in the English Channel, BdU decided to give U-boat commanders tactical authority for the conduct of their patrols. Hessler described this change as follows: '... realising that continuous snorkelling in the face of heavy enemy opposition imposed great strain on the crews – particularly the newcomers – we permitted those Commanding Officers working in inshore waters to decide for themselves whether to withdraw to the westward, or, in case of excessive strain, return to base before expending all their torpedoes'.[52]

As the inshore campaign began, the first Mediterranean snorkel-equipped U-boat was completing its retrofit. *U-407* (VIIC) received its snorkel in Salamis, Greece. The retrofit was begun in July by Deutsche Werke. Snorkel testing started in the Eleusis Bay on 3 August and the installation was completed by the 18th of that month.

In Germany the new Electro-boats were being commissioned. On 25 August the 31st U-boat Flotilla (Training) in Hamburg commissioned *U-2328* (XXIII). Two days later *U-2326* (XXIII) was ordered by BdU to continue passage to Swinemünde. These two Electro-boats were among six that had been identified in Baltic radio traffic by Allied intelligence since the middle of July 1944. On 28 August *U-2507* (XXI) completed its acceptance testing on the Elbe River and proceeded to Hamburg.[53]

September 1944

The snorkel proved that the diesel U-boat fleet could still operate successfully against Allied anti-submarine defences, especially in shallow coastal waters. The question for BdU was how best to employ them. The answer was driven by the loss of the Biscay bases that significantly limited the U-boats' operational range. The BdU KTB captured the operational shift as follows:

> The west is no longer available as a base for operations. Its place has been taken by Norway and one or two ports in home waters, since those in the former were not sufficient. The operational possibilities are therefore limited. The IXC boats can no longer operate in the Caribbean and along the Gold Coast without refuelling. For these the Newfoundland area and American coast are of increased importance. The St Lawrence River can be added to these, as it can be sailed again with snorkel boats. Operation of Type VIIC in the Channel will as a rule no longer be possible, as the outward and return passages alone last 7–9 weeks, and by that time as far as one can see the boats would no longer be in a condition to operate in such a difficult area. For these therefore, there only remains the coastal waters around England, such as the Moray Firth, Minch, and North Channel, as well as waters off Reykjavik.[54]

The snorkel-equipped fleet of U-boats threatened to escalate the Battle of the Atlantic all over again by shifting its main emphasis from the mid-Atlantic to a close-in blockade of the British Isles.

The coastal waters of the United Kingdom were abandoned as an operational area by BdU in 1940, but now Type VIICs equipped with a snorkel proved capable of conducting effective operations in these shallow coastal waters. Areas of concentration included the Minch, North Channel, Bristol Channel and Irish Sea. The English Channel became an important operational area again in December, after the start of Operation *Wacht Am Rhein* (Watch on the Rhine) in the west.

A new set of orders was issued by BdU that authorised U-boat commanders to exercise significant independence in the conduct of operations. Long-submerged U-boat patrols devoid of wireless communication meant that centralised control by BdU was no longer feasible. U-boats were ordered to report their situation immediately upon their return to port. These reports were then utilised by BdU in evaluating Allied shipping lanes and operational areas for further U-boat activity. BdU then promptly sent out wireless messages to outbound U-boats with this detailed information. German naval intelligence and B-Dienst reports were included in these assessments. Outbound U-boats often received their initial patrol areas by sealed written orders brought onto the U-boat and opened several days out of Norway. It was left up to the U-boat commanders how best to proceed based on the wireless intelligence assessments broadcast by BdU. Some returning U-boats only submitted written reports upon arrival, deciding not to send any wireless reports before entering the safety of a Norwegian fjord. In response, the 11th U-Flotilla took on a greater role in shaping operations as command elements in Horten, Bergen and Trondheim now had better intelligence of viable patrol areas around Great Britain. They utilised this information to direct outbound U-boats to the best possible areas of success before BdU ever got involved. At this stage of the war, time was a critical factor. BdU slowly acquiesced some operational authority as the situation dictated, though never completely.

This operational shift was noted by OP-20-G. They accurately reported expected U-boat operations along various coastlines for the coming month in a bi-weekly intelligence assessment to the US Fleet on 1 September.[55]

The commanders of the U-boats that returned back to Norway in mid to late August provided much-needed experience to BdU. Their reports revealed that Allied aircraft could detect a snorkel if it was riding high out of the water. BdU quickly issued out new guidance on 10 September, amending the original Order No. 20 as follows:

Addition to Current Orders No. 20:
Location:
Current Order 20 has been amended as follows 'The Snorkel can be

discovered and measured by enemy radar instruments. When extended the normal distance of approximately 0.5m above the surface of the water the Snorkel produces an impression on a radar set only 30% that of a surfaced U-boat; on the other hand, then extended 2 to 3 metres high the impression produced is 60 to 70% (surfacing would then be better). Therefore a considerably extended Snorkel can be measured exactly and attacked with bombs in the same manner as a surfaced U-boat, while a Snorkel at normal height can, to be sure, be discovered, but cannot be measured exactly enough for dropping bombs. Seaway and swell further reduce possibilities for radar.' (Under Current Orders No. 20, sentence 4 strike out from 'Snorkel' to 'to be located').[56]

A new Experience Report went out on the 14th:

Experience Report to U-boats 152: 'behaviour after firing torpedoes, especially in the vicinity of the coast: move away from the place of firing and then, but not until then, lie on the bottom in order to escape direction-finding and hydrophone pursuit. According to experiences in the channel destroyers always drop depth charges in the place of firing. The place of firing is the most reliable clue for the pursuer since poor hydrophone conditions make latter contact with the U-boat difficult.'[57]

A combination of the July experience report on German Search Receivers (GSR) usage, and the recent reminder of how easily a snorkel mast could be identified if improper depth was kept resulted in a more experienced employment of GSR and trim by U-boats. This began to frustrate Allied detection efforts, as noted by OP-20-G on 15 September: 'The difficulty recently experienced by anti-submarine groups in locating U-boats evidently is the result of GSR equipped snorkel.'[58]

Two-week cruises were soon exceeded. The snorkel and Alberich-equipped *U-480* concluded a sixty-three-day cruise, of which forty days were spent completely submerged. The cruise of *U-482* under the command of Kapitänleutnant Hartmut Graf von Matuschka Freiherr von Toppolczan und Spaetgen to the North Minch was one of the first of the inshore campaign. *U-482* departed Bergen, Norway, on 16 August after completing mandatory snorkel training. It headed first to a patrol area south of Iceland, through the Faroes and the Shetland Islands, then moved south towards the north coast of Ireland before returning back to Bergen on 26 September after a forty-two-day patrol. Freiherr von Toppolczan und Spaetgen spent fourteen days in the operation area of the North Channel, from 27 August to 9 September. He fired on a destroyer on 27 August but missed, without notice. His U-boat was detected on the 30th, but never located by Allied destroyers and search aircraft. *U-482* remained at the mouth of the North Channel for eight straight days, without detection even after a 'strong defence was set up'. Of particular note was the benefit of 'the shallow depth of the water' that 'let us sit on the bottom (60m near Inishtrahull)'.

Twice destroyers passed directly overhead the bottomed U-boat without any detection or concern by the crew. Freiherr von Toppolczan und Spaetgen even offered that multiple U-boats could be deployed in the same area and provided recommendations to prevent fratricide while on patrol: 'If multiple boats are used, the escorting boat must attempt to send a beta or an alpha signal after attacking so as to sound the alarm to boats with up or down snorkels so that they are not hit below the surface, given the small nearby escort.'

He found that underwater 'navigation is not a problem because there are beacons on the English and Irish coasts running according to the nautical radio service and there are lighthouses on the Irish coast used as in peace-time. (The lighthouse at Tory Island is used as a landmark when snorkelling at night.)' He concluded that:

> Snorkelling has proven itself and is highly regarded by the crew. No prob-lems. Battery charging on one side diesel travel with attached charging, one side strictly charging. If more snorkelling is done after charging is complet-ed, then use diesel electric – 5.5 nautical miles …
>
> Snorkelling is still possible at Sea 5 …
>
> The behaviour of the crew during the first enemy trip was good. Work at all posts was good, any problems in the equipment were quickly remedied and that made success possible …
>
> The rearrangement of duty operations by moving the mealtimes into snorkelling time and doing the night rest during the day went rapidly and was worth it. The state of health was good. The underwater trip to and from the operations area, 10 and 17 days, did not constitute any special demand on the crew and was very unhurried.
>
> Staying in the heavily watched operations area near the coast with almost continuous hydrophone readings from noise buoys, destroyers and particu-larly depth charges and ASDIC – for which mostly no one knew whether, how or by whom they would be picked up, constituted considerable mental stress. Experience, familiarity and not least, increased courage through suc-cess finally allowed acceptance of this stress with stoicism.

A common side effect on near continuous underwater travel was that:

The air defence weapons were deployed for the first time on the next to the last day of the undertaking. They all failed. For the 2cm weapons, the problem was rusted ammunition from the upper deck container. For the 3.7[cm], it was the difficulty of moving the rounds within the cover and the problem with the loader as well as the securing and firing latch. Because the boat was only equipped with tracer ammunition and it only surfaced for short periods at night, no function test was done; instead only a 2cm automatic weapon was changed and the weapons were kept ready. The reasons for the problems could not be determined until a function test was done after we had come in for rest.

The distance *U-482* travelled after leaving Bergen on 16 August 1944 was 2,729 nautical miles, of which 256 were surfaced and 2,473 submerged. This was an impressive cruise that resulted in one destroyer, two tankers and one freighter claimed sunk for a total of 18,000 GRT.[59] In reality, *U-482* sunk two tankers, one transport, one corvette and a rescue ship for a total of 32,621 GRT. This included the sinking of the *Empire Heritage*, one of the largest tankers afloat at the time (15,702 GRT).

U-482 spent about thirty-eight out of its forty-two patrol days submerged. This was now the average. Matuschka received the German Cross in Gold for his successful submerged patrol upon arrival back in Bergen on 26 September.

Word spread through the U-boat force that with the snorkel a U-boat could easily stay submerged for a month. In terms of human endurance, no other human-crewed submarine of any navy at any point in history had remained submerged for this long. Interest grew about the physiological impact such a lengthy submerged cruise had on the crew's well-being. The Kriegsmarine commissioned medical studies accordingly (see Chapter 7).

The U-boat exodus out of the Bay of Biscay ports continued. Bordeaux evacuated first, followed by Brest. *U-256* departed on 3 September for Norway with a new crew as Korvettenkapitän Lehmann-Willenbrok was ordered to remain behind and blow the U-boat pens with torpedo warheads. *U-155* sailed on 9 September from Lorient after a delay of several days. *U-673* (VIIC) sailed from St Nazaire on 13 September and evacuated the senior officer and staff of the 3rd Coastal Defence Division. *U-267* was recommissioned with a fixed snorkel and sailed out on 23 September with several officers attached to the base, precious metals from the dockyard, and a new Allied aircraft radar set from a shot down aircraft. Also in St Nazaire was the previously decommissioned *U-255* (VIIC), which workers attempted to recommission with a fixed snorkel. It lacked cam shafts and other essential parts, with the cam shafts scheduled to be delivered by sea plane on 9 October. However, installation of a fixed snorkel and the training of a new crew would take six weeks. *U-255*, however, never left the Bay of Biscay again until the end of the war, as it was utilised to shuttle supplies between the fortress garrisons of St Nazaire and La Pallice. The last U-boat to leave La Pallice was *U-382*, which sailed for Norway on the evening of 10 September.[60]

Along the coast of England, *U-248* joined *U-296* in the North Minch area. Both were recently outbound from Norway. *U-398* (VIIC) and *U-484* (VIIC) stalked the North Channel. As the recent experience report from *U-482* suggested the possibility of success in the area, additional boats were dispatched with *U-963* (VIIC), *U-985* (VIIC), *U-309* (VIIC) and *U-953* (VIIC) coming from French ports and *U-1004* (VIIC/41) and *U-743* (VIIC) from Norwegian ones. *U-743* was never heard from again. A snorkel defect cannot be ruled out for its demise.[61]

The snorkel became a key feature of each U-boat's patrol. When it failed to work properly it could have a major impact on the success of the mission. *U-680* was the first U-boat to reach the east coast of Great Britain. *U-680* was patrolling the Firth of Moray when it reported being depth charged so severely in that area that its snorkel, periscope, hydrophones, ballast tanks and valves were all damaged. BdU signalled to the boat's commander, Oberleutnant Max Ulber, that he could use discretion to move off the coast or return back to Norway with torpedoes and fuel acknowledging 'that constant operations underwater with snorkel against strong enemy defence places very great demands on inexperienced crews'.[62]

U-985 experienced a serious mechanical problem on 2 September, just days after starting its patrol. The upper deck door was left open and it laid across the snorkel well. The snorkel mast became bent when it was lowered back down, and the cable that ran to the dipole on the snorkel head snapped.[63]

A total of twenty U-boats were now Norway bound. Most sent a required weather report 300 miles west of Ireland. OP-20-G looked at their rate of movement and concluded correctly 'their average speeds of 60–75 miles per day indicate that they are travelling almost entirely underwater. They were given optional routes and heading points but informed to use their own judgement. Particularly they were advised [by BdU] "to get into the less strongly patrolled middle Bay of Biscay unobserved. Let a U-boat [lie] on bottom time-to-time and make extensive avoiding movements in order to deceive anti-submarine groups."'[64]

Experiences gained by U-boats operating inshore around England increased BdU's confidence in coastal operations. BdU recorded the factors that contributed to their U-boat's success as follows:

Reasons:

a) Density layering caused by coastal tides adds to the difficulty of picking up boats by hydrophone and ASDIC, and makes snorkel sailing possible under hydrophone direction-finding to signal strength of 2, but special care must be taken to make all-round search about every 15 minutes.

b) Ground echoes and density layering make location of boats lying on the bottom considerably more difficult.

c) Lying on the bottom prolongs duration of submergence.

d) Exploitation of currents makes quick, noiseless alteration of position possible.[65]

On 18 September the 11th U-Flotilla in Bergen and its U-boats fell under the jurisdiction of Commander-U-boats West Kapitän Zur See Roesing. He was previously in charge of training; however, his command began to play a greater role in directing U-boat operations for the reasons previously discussed.

Brest was going to capitulate imminently. Korvettenkapitän Winter radioed BdU: 'U-base and 9th Flotilla has been forced to capitulate after several days of brave fighting. Battles before the naval school. U-base going off radio. Hail our Führer.'[66]

In the Mediterranean, *U-596* (VIIC) sailed on its first patrol with a retrofitted snorkel.

OP-20-G's assessment for September was more sombre than in recent months:

> Losses and U-boat kills were moderate during September, reflecting both lack of enemy offensive operations as well as difficulty of locating and attacking snorkel-equipped U-boats ... For first time in two years U-boats again appear to be operating in the Gulf of St Lawrence. The only U-boat in US coastal area now appears to be homebound after torpedoing one ship South of Hatteras and unsuccessfully attacking another two NW of Bermuda.[67]

The U-boat in question off Hatteras was *U-512* (VIIC) and represented the first patrol off the US coast in two years (see Chapter 9), although this U-boat stayed well out to sea in deep water between the 200m line and Bermuda. It never saw the coastline. Not until 1945 did U-boats again sail within eyeshot of the US coast.

With concern over the new Electro-boats growing within Allied commands, the Western Allies conducted air raids on the dockyards of Kiel and Stettin.

October 1944

U-boat patrols against England's coast slowed in October. BdU analysed the results of their shift in focus from the English Channel to the English coast. October proved to be a transition month. Returning U-boats from Biscay ports that had received makeshift or incomplete snorkel installations now had them overhauled to full working versions with dipoles mounted on their masts. New snorkel retrofits were completed, thereby increasing the overall number of snorkel-enabled U-boats available to BdU. Most important was Dönitz's direction that his U-boats conduct shallow water operations against the coast of England based on his acceptance that the snorkel's success represented a paradigm shift in the Battle of the Atlantic.

As U-boats returned to Norway or Germany, they revealed disappointing results in their reports. *U-714* (VIIC), which was the last U-boat to patrol the south-west approaches to the Irish Sea, headed back to Norway on 24 September, arriving at Farsund on 20 October. *U-262* (VIIC), patrolled the same area several days earlier before returning to Flensburg on 5 November. Both U-boat commanders reported no targets other than heavy surface defence and sound buoys. Three U-boats remained on station in the North Channel. Several others departed back to Norway after unproductive patrols. *U-248* reported being forced off the coast by patrols during a night-time snorkel run. Oberleutnant Emde reported that he missed a T5 shot against a destroyer. *U-398* reported 'no traffic. Operation along coast difficult, strong air and anti-submarine activity.' *U-398*'s Captain, Korvettenkapitän Johann Reckhoff, suspected traffic was being routed through St Georges Channel and the Minch. He suggested that U-boats leave the area for ten days so that defences weaken in response before returning to the area.

BdU was frustrated by a lack of sinkings. Experience Message No. 165 was broadcast on 5 October and again on the 7th. Both messages were intercepted by Ultra:

Experience Radio Transmission No. 165
In recent days, a total of four boats operating in the North/Bristol Channel have not reported any traffic. However, a rather large number of escort convoys have certainly passed through this area. The failure to find the traffic can only be explained by the boats not being on the escort paths reported by radio above or deep in the traffic funnel, but rather further out to sea.
The following can be said in this regard:
1) It must be each commander's absolute ambition to get to the attack. This includes courageous approaches and dogged but considered perseverance in promising areas, even under heavy defence.

2) Boats operating outside the lochs on the English coast should get as close as possible to the narrowest points that traffic has to go through. According to reports from boats, the enemy area defended from the air and the sea for catching boats extends to about 150 nautical miles from the coast. Defence outside and inside is of the same strength; inside maybe it's even less attentive. Inside, one can certainly find traffic; outside in the broader area, the chances are much worse with the same defence.

3) Shallow water less than 200m deep is in most cases particularly favourable for operations (see Experience Radio Transmission no. 160).[68]

This apparent admonishment was not warranted. What BdU did not know was that inbound convoys were being routed through the southern approaches at this time, leaving U-boats few targets of opportunity along the northern approaches.[69]

U-boat operations were transforming. Admiral Dönitz weighed in personally in Experience Message No. 171, which was also intercepted by Ultra:

Why the U-boat War? The most decisive front in this war has once again become the front against the western powers. The heart and head of this front on the enemy side is England. England is an island … Yes, the final decision itself may depend upon the revived U-boat war.

This statement was followed by a warning not to be timid in the approach to the shallow waters of the enemy coast:

The experiences of many Commanding Officers have shown that the snorkel permits cruising without great detours. The snorkel allows the U-boat to remain in sea areas close to the coast in spite of very strong patrols and to achieve successes there. Directives concerning conduct in these areas and against enemy defence will be sent currently. I require the Commanding Officers to make the most energetic use possible of the singular capacity offered by snorkel and to become master of the enemy defence. Go right up to the sources of enemy traffic and attack there. It goes without saying that there will be sea and air defence. Avoiding it or facing it is the measure for the aggressive spirit and ability of the Commanding Officer. I shall call to account without mercy all Commanding officers who fail to make the most of all means at their disposal for fulfilling the assigned tasks in the consciousness of responsibility and the aggressive spirit of our arm of the service.[70]

The focus on the shallows continued with Experience Radio Transmission No. 172 on 18 October, which was not intercepted by Ultra:

[U]Boats operating off the English coast must approach close to the narrowest parts of channels and lochs … Outside, the [U]boat is nothing more than a 'stationary mine'. Our experience is that the interior defence is less attentive and the low water depth is not a disadvantage. Stay on the bottom and do sound and ASDIC location. Favourable water layering makes finding boats through sound and ASDIC more difficult.[71]

It is very interesting that BdU described the use of a U-boat in deep – or what in Naval parlance might be termed as 'Blue Water' operations – as being little more than a 'stationary mine'. U-boats were to manoeuvre into the shallows to find Allied merchant vessels.

Dönitz weighed in once again following up Experience Message No. 171 and 172 with his own demand that coastal operations were now the main focus. Each U-boat commander had to be reminded of this before each patrol and Dönitz applied the threat of a court martial to ensure they all understood his point clearly.

Addendum from the Commanding Admiral
Experience Radio Transmission no. 171 must be made the subject of the most serious training for all training officers at all training sites.

The behaviour of the boat being censured is unworthy of the spirit of attack that has distinguished the submarine branch since Prien going to Scapa, since Kretschmer, Wellner, v.d. Ropp, Jenisch, Dresky and all the countless other commanders of patrols that have always gone directly into enemy harbour entrances/deep into enemy fjords and river mouths. The behaviour of the boat being censured is unworthy of the men and women of our Volk who have given their all in recognition of the last decisions.

Express reference is made to the many addresses by the Commanding Admiral. As I write, court martial proceedings against a commander for cowardice before the enemy are in progress hardened by the ruthless desire of the leadership to expunge weaklings. Reminder [sic] Radio Transmission No. 171 and the addendum must be read aloud in commanders' briefings prior to going out on a trip against the enemy.[72]

If there was any doubt by U-boat crews regarding the shift to shallow water coastal operations, this above transmission left none.

In accordance with Dönitz's direction, Experience Message No. 173 was issued that informed crews not to be defensive when they heard:

'Hydrophone bearings (of screw noise, buzz saws,* noise-making buoys and the like) which appear near the enemy coast, especially in the vicinity of the shipping lanes, which are naturally strong.' They were told to focus on important sounds of 'high signal strength'.[73]

U-boats that patrolled off the English Coast in September began to return back to Norwegian bases during the second half of the month. As the reports from *U-1004* (VIIC/41), *U-281* (VIIC), *U-309* (VIIC), *U-953* (VIIC) and *U-1199* (VIIC) were received by BdU, they revealed 'good prospects' despite 'strong defences', yet no successes.[74]*U-979* (VIIC) returned on 10 October after a successful patrol off Reykjavik, where it claimed two ships sunk. However, only the US-flagged cargo ship USS *Yukon* (5,969 GRT) was damaged by a torpedo on 22 September. *U-979* was subsequently attacked by HMS *St Kenan* and sustained a bent attack periscope but, following the new shallow water tactics, Kapitänleutnant Johannes Meermeier bottomed at a depth of 20m and evaded his pursuer's ASDIC, probably under a thermocline layer. An experience report was later issued by BdU about this event.

Even though *U-281*'s cruise was not successful in terms of tonnage sunk, it nevertheless helped develop and refine snorkelling procedures. Kapitänleutnant Heinz von Davidson filed the following report:

Travel with snorkel:
In spite of the lack of any practical snorkelling experience when they moved out, the crew quickly entered into the snorkelling routine and attained the necessary trust in the equipment. The safe work of the technical personnel is particularly worth noting. Snorkelling was done up to Sea State 6 with lots of fog. Up to this sea state, we were only moderately successful at moving at snorkel depth with rough seas and fog outside. The pitch controller was reset every hour, so the commander and the watch officers were at the periscope. The periscope remained relatively clear until recent days with the periscope being continually heated. When we stopped to listen after about 20 minutes of snorkelling (for about 3–5 minutes), we always stopped snorkelling and put the snorkel down for longer pauses (10 minutes) every now and then so

---

* The U-boat crews used the term *Kreissäge* (circular saw, often just 'saw') or *Rattelboje* (rattle buoy) to record when they heard the British-built acoustic decoy code-named 'Foxer' deployed by Allied vessels. Foxer was used to confuse German acoustic homing torpedoes. It consisted of two pipe noise makers, that each consisted of two pipes connected together at their ends but allowed to vibrate against each other as they were towed through the water. They were towed about 20m (220 yards) behind the ship. The cavitation noise generated by the pipes vibrating together was much greater (10 to 100 times) than that coming from the ship's propeller. German acoustic homing torpedoes were thus likely to detonate safely against the Foxer given that they were tuned to home in on the sound frequencies generated by the loudest cavitation sound.

as to make it difficult for aircraft to find us. No air-dropped bombs and no spotlight flights during the entire trip with the snorkel. Daily before dawn, the boat was ventilated through the snorkel mast again with the diesel engine off. By rescheduling all of the needed work (reloading torpedoes, repairing the diesel engine, etc.) in the snorkelling time/time between snorkelling and ventilation, by saving one meal per day and the greatest rest in the remaining period, air consumption was reduced to the point that we got by with 9 potash containers per day, with CO_2 content tolerable at 2.5–3 per cent. The garbage was removed through the toilet and flooding equipment without difficulty with only used potash containers and large solid waste remaining in the boat.

Because the GHG (the rectifier in the NAG) is partially out, the information about traffic and [anti-submarine vessels] is incomplete from October 5 on.

In attempts to repair the GHG, there was no success in spite of the greatest exertions of all the radio personnel and the co-operation of all the electronic technicians. There is absolutely a need for at least one of the radio personnel, such as the flotilla senior radio master, to have a truly thorough training in GHG. Company-sponsored training would have the most success.

Navigation:
The most important tool was the plumb line, which worked without any problems to the end. The plumb line converter remained turned on all the time in areas with plumbable depths (up to 500m). It was determined that the available current charts did not offer information that was in any way sufficient. It is recommended that U-boat experience about current, displacement, etc. in the individual operating areas be collected and evaluated. The boats will then have them as an overview. When navigating along the Norwegian coast, travel on the 200m line was maintained in the North Sea. Here there were only very minor displacements compared to the experiences in the deep channels along the Norwegian coast. The approach point was found very accurately without any optical equipment.[75]

One area of continued frustration was the lack of responses from U-boats to demands by BdU for wireless reports. This situation continued to affect BdU as it impacted how it could direct U-boats to favourable operational areas based on fresh intelligence. For example, on 19 October BdU ordered *U-246* (VIIC), *U-978* (VIIC) and *U-1006* (VIIC/41) to 'send report in accordance with Channel Operational Order No. 2, Serial No. 36 IV as soon as you reach the Latitude of Square GO 13'.[76] No responses were received despite the fact that these U-boats were crossing the Faroe Islands, where BdU believed that there was opportunity for U-boats to surface and transmit a message. BdU sent out another reminder three days later to send in wireless reports.[77] It should be noted that in the case of *U-1006*, it had been sunk by an Allied surface vessel on 16 October.

Without a signal recognition from their patrolling U-boats, BdU simply had no knowledge of the tactical situation until a U-boat returned to port. Hessler detailed how the snorkel and coastal operations fundamentally altered U-boat communications during the last year of the war. He stated how commanders '… preferred to remain submerged, and to surface only to rectify some serious outboard defect – such as a sticky snorkel valve – or to transmit the required wireless reports on entering the Atlantic and leaving patrol. At this stage of the war the transmission of a radio message was an event in itself.' BdU noted that nearly 80 per cent of snorkel-equipped U-boats maintained radio silence during the whole of their patrol, except to report their arrival at the escort rendezvous position the day before entering a Norwegian base. Indeed, many commanders failed even to do this and merely waited off the coast until they could join up with the escort detailed for another boat.[78] While a lack of wireless transmission frustrated BdU operations, a lack of wireless transmissions also meant a lack of actionable intelligence for OP-20-G. U-boats were no longer being located through Ultra at the same rate they were just six months earlier.

Despite these issues, October proved to be an important month for BdU as U-boat losses began to drop. This proved a validation to BdU that the snorkel, and subsequent shift to coastal operations, was working. 'Neither in 1939 and 1940 nor during the US coastal battle of 1942 was the excellent protection of the coast, combined with the effects of tidal streams, so manifest as it was now,' Hessler noted.[79]

Technical problems with the snorkel continued, but were reported with less frequency as improvements were introduced. *U-1226* (IXC/40) reported that its snorkel piston was not working properly and had to raise the mast by tackle. As a result BdU decided to redirect it to act as a weather boat.[80] It went missing around 23 October. *U-1200* (VIIC) returned to Bergen due to a defective snorkel on 17 October after only ten days at sea.[81] The snorkel was fixed and the U-boat left for patrol a second time on 19 October. It subsequently went missing and was positively identified in 1999 in the English Channel. The cause of sinking remains unknown. A snorkel defect cannot be ruled out.

Allied intelligence tracked Norway's now central role in late war U-boat operations. OP-20-G recorded that both 'Trondheim and Bergen have become major bases for Atlantic operations, while Kristiansand is only the initial calling point for Type IXs en route to Baltic for repair bases.' US Navy intelligence analysts believed: 'Trondheim has nine U-boat pens with a total capacity for 13-15 U-boats.' It was estimated on 15 October that the last four pen roofs would be completed during November. 'Bergen has six U-boat pens with a total capacity for nine U-boats. Roofs to complete by November 1st.'[82] The assessment was close to reality. Trondheim was home to the 13th U-Flotilla. Three U-boat bunkers were planned, Dora I–III. Work on Dora I began in early 1941 and was completed in November 1943. It consisted of five U-boat pens. Dora II began shortly after construction of Dora I, and was to have four additional pens, two wet and two dry. A lack of skilled labour prevented this bunker from being more than 60 per cent completed by war's end. An Allied raid against Dora I was launched on 22 November consisting of 170 RAF bombers, but was called off mid-flight due to poor visibility. Dora III was planned, but cancelled due to a lack of resources. Dora I's five covered U-boat pens could support seven U-boats, while Dora II's four pens supported six. In Bergen, the home to the 11th U-Flotilla, construction of the Bruno bunker began shortly after the successful invasion of Norway in 1940. It was originally planned to have ten covered U-boat pens, but only seven were completed by the autumn of 1944, with one dedicated for fuel storage. The six covered pens could support nine U-boats. Horten boasted no U-boat pens, and was not home to any U-flotilla, but its role in Norway was significant. Allied intelligence did not place any significant importance on this Norwegian port, possibly due to a lack of U-boat pens. However, it became the main snorkel training and repair facility for all Atlantic-bound U-boats, as discussed in Chapter 2.

November 1944

OP-20-G's 'Secret' level assessment to US Navy Fleet Commands distributed on 1 November contained three main themes. First, it made the point that U-boat activity in the Battle of the Atlantic had ebbed to its lowest point since the US entered the war, though it noted that U-boats continued to patrol along various coastal regions. This observation was made in the context of the convoy battles of previous years and was not an absolute reflection of ongoing U-boat operations. Second, it ominously raised concern that the U-boat force was still potent and that a renewed offensive into the North Atlantic was anticipated. Third, it continued to track the production of the Type XXI Electro-boat, while wondering when they might be deployed operationally. The word choice that was applied to the Type XXI's readiness was 'efficacy', a clear indication that Ultra intercepts contained growing concerns from within the Kriegsmarine about potential technical issues, as previously noted in Chapter 2.[83]

Allied intelligence was right to be concerned about a renewed offensive spearheaded by the Type XXI when they intercepted a message sent from Berlin to Tokyo on 10 November that stated:

> The U-boat war is the first and principal offensive task for the German Navy. All measures are being adequately prepared for the construction of new U-boats. With these U-boats the superiority gain for a time by the enemy through technical advances will be overtaken. The renewal of the tonnage war is at the same time the most effective contribution of the Navy to the total conduct of the war by Germany, and this contribution may have the most profound military and political effects. Let the Anglo-Saxons calmly believe that the U-boat war is over; we will teach them better.[84]

While BdU longed for a renewed tonnage war in the mid-Atlantic led by Type XXI Electro-boat Wolfpacks, the reality was very different.

Significant improvements to the snorkel were introduced into the diesel fleet. The Type II non-flange snorkel for VIICs was now being retrofitted in increasing numbers, and snorkel heads and masts were receiving the anti-radar Wesch mats for the ball and ring floats. These steps improved snorkel use, cutting down on technical failures, as well as increasing protection while snorkelling by reducing its radar signature. Morale increased throughout the U-boat fleet as confidence in the snorkel grew and U-boat losses dropped dramatically.

An example of the growing confidence and proficiency in the snorkel's use was the new record set for submerged endurance. *U-1199* (VIIC), commanded by Kapitänleutnant Rolf Nollmann, caught the attention of BdU and Dönitz after its first operational war patrol with a snorkel. Nollmann departed Bergen on 14 September and returned on 5 November after conducting a shallow water patrol off the coast of Peterhead and Aberdeen for thirty-one days. The amazing aspect of the patrol is that *U-1199* spent a total of fifty out of fifty-three days completely submerged, completing the longest submerged snorkel patrol to date. The previous record was set by *U-480* in the previous month. BdU recorded: 'Boat ran submerged the whole time, crew most enthusiastic about snorkel.'[85] Nollmann concluded his report with: 'Surface groups were only slightly experienced and never contacted the U-boat. *Shallow water is the best protection*.' [Author's emphasis][86] Experience Message No. 193 was issued shortly after Nollmann's patrol that was a verbatim copy of the last paragraph of *U-1199*'s KTB:

> Shallow water is best protection against search gear. Boat was not intercepted and we felt absolutely safe on the bottom. Snorkel completely tested,

50 days submerged without surfacing. I have a feeling of complete superiority with the Snorkel. Unfortunately the possibilities for hydrophone listening along the coast are poor, which results in unfavourable tactical positions to the enemy if picked up by hydrophones.

Morale of the crew good and conviction that the U-boat arm again has superiority over the enemy.[87]

Nollmann provided some interesting insight into Allied countermeasures:

Countermeasures: long-term air during the day, not dangerous, dropping of depth charges for effect. Hunting groups of corvettes or fishing trawlers with ASDIC escorting at all times. Little experience, nothing found. Shallow water is the best protection. At irregular times, the air and sea along the entire path separate with depth charges. Listening is very bad. Vessels are not found on the group listening apparatus until they are very close. Trawlers in line abreast on the escort path are dangerous, chasing U-boats with a net or wires. Recognition signal: clattering like chains. The group listening apparatus shows corvettes or destroyers with ASDIC in the background. Camouflaged as harmless fishing vessels.[88]

BdU noted with satisfaction that 'the losses in October have decreased again satisfactorily. In all, 6 boats were lost through enemy action. This reduction in loss is entirely due to the introduction of the Snorkel.'[89] Snorkel-equipped diesel U-boats were patrolling as lone wolves, but in increasing numbers, from the English Coast to the St Lawrence River. A renewed emphasis on operations against the North American coast by Type IX U-boats was imminent. Snorkel-equipped U-boats patrolled off Gibraltar and proved frustrating for Allied hunter-killer groups.

The previous five months of U-boat snorkel experience culminated in the newest directives and experience messages being issued by BdU in November than in any month prior or after. Snorkel tactical procedures were now codified. Below is all of the snorkel-related tactical guidance issued by BdU in November that was identified through captured U-boat records and Ultra intercepts.

On 13 November Dönitz issued new guidance to the entire U-boat fleet:

From Atlantic U-boat Services
Message No. 186. Repeat on Northern Waters Service
A) Now that the snorkel's teething troubles have been overcome, the following picture emerges clearly for the past five months experiences reported by the boats equipped with it:

1) The snorkel has to a large extent put the boat beyond the reach of its most powerful enemy, the locating aircraft, and has thus enabled it to operate in areas protected by strong air patrols.

2) It mostly eliminated the effectiveness of submarine-hunting aircraft because the most important preliminary condition for hunting submarines, which is the locating aircraft getting to the location where a submarine is submerged, is not met. Because it is no longer possible to use onboard radar devices to find a snorkelling U-boat at a great distance, submarine-hunting vessels are forced to rely on the much shorter ranges of their hydrophones and underwater-locating devices.

3) The losses have thus been significantly reduced.

4) The high number of total snorkel operations, with underwater patrols of up to 70 days, shows that the strain on health is perfectly bearable, and that the mental strain has become less, because the nervous tension of waiting for surface location before surprise aircraft attack when on surface passage, particularly in the approach areas, has been done away with. Compare Biscay passage in February 1944 with the approach between the Shetlands and sorrows in October 1944. The instructions which were wired to a number of boats two or three months ago concerning caution and consideration for the exceptional strain on the ship's company during snorkel passage were issued at a time when very little experience was available about the practical effects of the snorkel. Subsequent experience and practice has made these instructions obsolete and they no longer apply.

B) The capability of operating in areas with heavy aerial surveillance led to the use of boats in the Channel, the North Channel–Minch and the east coast of England, meaning areas that had to be abandoned by boats back in 1939–40. Experience on operating in areas of shallow water shows:

1) Operating in water depths under 100 metres is quite possible.
The strong layering of water due to bodies of water flowing in and putting the boat on the bottom makes it much more difficult for the enemy to find the boat using hydrophones and other locating devices.
That means increased chances for unnoticed close approaches and attacks and easier evasion of enemy defences.

2) Success was only achieved by boats operating in points of enemy traffic congestion, meaning penetrating deep into enemy lochs and coastal escort routes where enemy traffic has to go for navigational reasons.
Operations 'further outside' have proved futile, the chances of being approached by an enemy (other than the defence) in the open sea are negligible.

3) Because of the enemy's efforts to keep boats away from its traffic routes,

it generally has stronger defences 'outside' than inside. For the reasons indicated in 1) and 2), avoiding defences is easier 'inside' than outside.

4) The number of underwater sounds in coastal waters is naturally much larger than in the open ocean. In addition to hydrophone readings from propeller noises of all types, there are lots of 'war-related' noises to be registered, such as detonation of air-dropped bombs and depth charges, sounds from minesweepers' detonation devices, and all sorts of ticking, hitting or spinning noises that can be heard well outside the registration range to 'bluff' U-boats.

5) As long as it was not yet possible to form a general impression of the situation, it was natural that this multiplicity of noises, by contrast with the open Atlantic, should exercise a certain influence on the commanders. The following is now the correct attitude to adopt towards these noises:

a) It is obvious that there are lots of different types of hydrophone readings near the coast. Letting oneself be affected or daunted by them means a negative effect on the task of going against the enemy and destroying it; it is therefore wrong and must be rejected.

b) It is obvious that hydrophones should be used along with other devices to warn against danger. However it is wrong to be a slave to them.

The hydrophone is first of all for finding the enemy.

c) It has now been determined:

The snorkel has given the boat the capability of operating in shallow water. It is therefore the commander's duty to use this capability to evade enemy defences or push through them and destroy enemy traffic at its exit point.[90]

An expanded version of the above message was issued out to U-boat commanders via the training flotillas as Current Order No. 1, issued November 1944.[91] This was followed by Current Order No. 2 that provided complete technical guideline for uniform snorkel operation across the fleet. Clear warnings were issued – learned from practical experiences – that highlights how improper venting or overpressure of the batteries could jeopardise the U-boat.[92]

U-boat commanders were issued guidance on firing torpedoes from a submerged position simply based on hydrophone contacts. A preferred U-boat tactic was to bottom their U-boat outside a major port or shipping channel and await a sound contact, then blow tanks and slowly rise off the bottom to an appropriate firing depth and launch an acoustic torpedo. Patrolling near the surface where a periscope was utilised for visual target acquisition became the tactical exception and not the rule. Using the new

T5 acoustic homing torpedoes allowed commanders to strike sound targets from depths of 30m. This was a dramatic change from the pre-snorkel days when line-of-sight target data was required and plugged into the torpedoes' firing mechanism.

Current Order No. 67 – Issued November 1944
Firing torpedoes on the basis of firing data obtained by sound detector.
I. The captain can gain the best idea of the tactical situation by visual means. The periscope is therefore the most reliable instrument for observation. The captain should try to obtain his firing data by means of the periscope.
II. Under present wartime conditions however, U-boats may find themselves in a situation where use of a periscope is impossible. It is then a question of making the best use of the situation, if possible for firing purposes. This is all the easier if the U-boat is equipped with sound-detector apparatus and search gear. Captains who are solely dependent, however, on the sound detector must be clear on the following possibilities of attack.

A) U-boats can be in such a position that individual ships or convoys are passing overhead before they have had the opportunity of using their periscopes. In this case it is considered possible to make a rough estimate of the general course, speed and range, using sound-detector and stop watch only. The use of a 'Zaunkönig' torpedo or a Lut-fan for attacking from astern, will, in such cases, have certain prospects of success.

Special attention must be paid to the following:
1) The firing of torpedoes is up till now only possible from a submerged depth of 22 metres. Therefore endeavours should be made to fire from a depth of 20 metres.
2) As soon as it is suspected that a ship will pass overhead, an attempt should be made as soon as possible to estimate speed and general course in order that only slight alterations will be necessary when the ship is actually overhead.
3) Stop engines when the ship is directly overhead and continue checking the range referring to the estimated speeds until the moment of firing.
4) Prompt decision must be made by the Captain, which type of torpedo is to be employed (Lut or Zaunkönig).
5) Directly after firing, the U-boat must dive to a greater depth (at least 50 metres), in order to avoid the possibility if torpedoes passing overhead, when travelling to a higher level. (When firing Zaunkönig torpedoes, speed should not exceed 3 knots
6) Rapid grasp of the situation and speedy manipulation of the firing control apparatus and torpedo tube is absolutely necessary.

B) If a ship does not pass directly above a U-boat, the firing data obtained by sound detector alone, are generally not sufficient to ensure the success-ful use of torpedoes.

The captain is not in a position to judge by sound detector alone his posi-tion and range in relation to an individual ship or convoy. It is not suffi-cient to know the enemy's speed only when firing a torpedo. In spite of these inadequate particulars if the captain has the impression that the sit-uation is favourable, he should fire, if he foresees no further opportunities of attack during the operation, or for example when leaving the area of operation or when returning to base.[93]

Wireless communications continued to be a problem and new guidance was issued out in the form of Current Order No. 80 to address the issue. BdU admitted that: 'Long Snorkel cruises make heavy demands on the aeri-als.' Noted defects included ground shorts caused by: split insulators (for-mation of hair-breadth cracks which are often hard to detect); rust on insu-lators, cable ends and bulwark leads; and broken rod insulators and rusted supports.[94] OP-20-G tracked the difficulty of wireless communication between BdU and operational U-boats with interest.[95]

Allied intelligence reported on the snorkel's ability to increase the effec-tiveness of the once thought defeated diesel U-boat. The Allies were per-haps as surprised as BdU was at the snorkel's tactical and operational impact. OP-20-G issued their 'Secret' mid-month assessment on 15 November that stated:

Enemy U-boat activity continues moderate although with somewhat increased effectiveness … With the aid of [the] snorkel U-boats have been operating much closer inshore in areas which previously they had found untenable because of air coverage. The recent enemy tactics appear to make use of the difficult sound conditions by lying on the bottom when being hunted using snorkel when charging thus obviating the necessity for surfac-ing while in operating areas …[96]

Commensurate with OP-20-G's statement on the snorkel's effectiveness, there were several U-boat patrols of note in November.

U-483 (VIIC) under the command of Kapitänleutnant Hans-Joachim von Morstein completed a patrol off the North Channel – the first using Elektra-Sonne for underwater navigation. *U-483* left Stavanger, Norway, on 3 October and returned to Bergen, Norway, on 21 November. It patrolled for fifty days in the area between Islay and Lough Swilly, alternating from Scotland and Northern Ireland, at the entrance to the Irish Sea. *U-483*'s KTB revealed how little time it spent on the surface compared with its time submerged. Its performance during this patrol became the standard for all future patrols around England. The total number of days this patrol lasted from the time it submerged after departing Stavanger to the time it surfaced at 3pm outside of Bergen on its return was a little more than forty-seven days. This represented 1,143 operational hours. Of that time, *U-483* spent a total of 1,139½ hours submerged and only 3½ hours surfaced. The time surfaced consisted of the following instances:

9 October – approx. sixty minutes to repair diving plane.

12 October – thirty minutes for a burial at sea of Funkmatt Hoffmann, Gustav, UO 3667/41 who died of pneumonia as a result of tonsil abscess after six days of illness.

14, 18, 19, and 20 November – thirty minutes each to send a radio messages upon nearing the Norwegian Coast on return passage.[97]

In looking at the causes of surfacing, only on 9 and 12 October would the hatches have been open with fresh air flowing through the U-boat without the snorkel being operated. If we subtract the two hours of radio transmission that did not require the hatches to be open, then the crew itself spent 1,141½ hours submerged. Statistically, this represented 99.8 per cent of the cruise submerged underwater, receiving fresh air only by the snorkel. It was an amazing feat of endurance at the time, and one that became commonplace among U-boats. Von Morstein annotated the KTB for this patrol as follows:

Snorkelling proved its worth. It was always possible to keep the battery well charged, and staying unnoticed was also done to the maximum.

Operating problems and breakdowns resulting from inadequacy of the equipment for snorkelling were a problem. For example, the forward diving plane broke down because it was overtaxed; the fan coupling in the diesel engine gave out, as did the echo sounder. Because of a breakdown in the forward diving plane, the return trip had to be made prematurely.[98]

Von Morstein sent a short report by wireless to BdU upon arrival back in Norway:

Favourable conditions for running on Snorkel inshore, little interference, even possible during the day. Shallow water, rocky bottom and layering give good protection against being picked up by hydrophone and radar. Slight diving depths (20–25 metres) are especially favourable in cases of overfall. Anti-submarine measures taken after attacks at first light, about twelve hours later strong defensive reaction in the vicinity of the scene of action. In one case 349 depth charges were dropped in 18 minutes.

To sum up, it can be said that it is perfectly feasible to operate inshore by using Snorkel and the operations carried out by other boats in the Channel, etc., show that this is not an isolated case.[99]

OP-20-G intercepted this short report and recorded it with interest.[100] They confirmed von Morstein's sinking of HMS *Whitaker* on 1 November.[101]

U-991 (VIIC) and *U-1202* (VIIC) occupied the Bristol Channel. *U-978* and *U-1200* operated between Havre and Plymouth. *U-246* (VIIC), under the command of Kapitänleutnant Ernst Raabe, was ordered to the English Channel, the first U-boat to return there in the last two months.

U-246 was about 120 miles south-west of Fastnet when it was damaged by depth charges from an unknown Allied surface vessel on 26 October. Raabe sent a short report to BdU by wireless stating only: 'Severe DCs – have begun return.' He previously reported the U-boat fit for operations in the English Channel as per BdU guidance. BdU used this incident to point out to all U-boats that 'all recent experiences show the U-boat is easier to [be located] in the open sea in great depths than right under the coast in shallow water. Radar and hydrophone conditions close to the coast are very poor and patrol is less strong and less alert.'[102]

U-255 (VIIC) was recommissioned in its St Nazaire bunker with a snorkel. It required piston cams to be sent by Heinkel He 115 seaplane, but that probably did not happen. Its snorkel installation was a 'starrer' or rigid one, where the mast was in a fixed upright position. The intent was to make the boat survivable for its journey from France back to Norway. Special technical snorkel instructions were issued to *U-255* from BdU via the U-boat base at St Nazaire to ensure safe operation.[103]

Only two U-boats, *U-802* (IXC/40) and *U-1009* (VIIC/41), reportedly returned to Norway after departing on their patrol due to faulty snorkel float values that month.

December 1944

Dönitz was satisfied that his U-boat crews had mastered the snorkel and proved its capabilities in the preceding months. During December weather reporting became critical in the final weeks and days before the launch of operation *Wacht am Rhein*. Simultaneously, U-boat patrols around the English coast increased in preparation for the land offensive. Dönitz was eager to test the limits of his snorkel-equipped U-boats even further and ordered a secret operation against Allied aircraft carriers at Scapa Flow. While his U-boats were not successful in locating any major Allied capital ships, they proved capable of remaining undetected outside one of the most heavily defended harbours in the world. *U-120* (VIIC) and *U-297* (VIIC) spent twenty days in the operational area without being discovered. Wireless communication and command and control continued to be refined with the snorkel's introduction.

OP-20-G noted in their December assessment with some alarm that *U-716* (VIIC), *U-869* (IXC/40), and *U-1233* (IXC/40) conducted successful experiments with the new Kurier flash transmission wireless sets in the Skagerrak. They noted 'in August during previous experiments with ten U-boats, BdU encountered great difficulty in receiving the U-boat short signals. However, on November 28th Kurier U-boats were told "Reception of signal is now good. A perfectly recorded signal at 1120A on frequency C confirms its utility." ...' Kurier could not be read through Ultra, and it was known by OP-20-G that this communication system was to be incorporated in the new Type XXIs. They also recorded that 'normal wireless transmissions continued to be a problem. Further analysis determined that faulty dipole antennas were to blame. U-boat commanders were warned on 18 December that "poor transmitting conditions can be traced to antennas which have become defective after long snorkel cruises. The latter put a great strain on the antennas."'[104]

Commanders continued to be impressed with the snorkel and its ability to allow U-boats to operate in the shallows. *U-300* (VIIC/41), under the command of Oberleutnant Fritz Hein, returned to Stavanger on 2 December after a sixty-day patrol off of Reykjavik harbour, where he sunk two vessels for a total of 7,559 GRT. Hein noted in his report:

> ... Guards are not very effective, they work based on listening, ASDIC only once for a short time. Depth charges for effect and suspected otherwise. Saws only for PC boats. Rattling head as reported for 'Nollmann' from dragging nets along the bottom.
> 3) Listening conditions changing depending on the seas, often very good for over 8 nautical miles.
> 4) Snorkelling done during the day and at night between small vessels.[105]

U-1003 (VIIC/41) reported upon its return from a month of operating in the North Channel that the crew became used to 'the constant underwater journey. Today I am delighted with the snorkelling and my crew as well. We feel very secure while snorkelling ...'[106] *U-1003* never fired a torpedo as it failed to locate any Allied ships. This was typical of many U-boats sent to a fixed operational area. This was one of the reasons BdU issued Current Order No. 4 (see below) in order to allow U-boats freedom of manoeuvre.

On 15 December the Bi-Weekly Intelligence issued by OP-20-G assessed U-boat operations as directed against coastal and inland waterways. It was noted that only four Allied vessels were hit by torpedoes in December so far, to include two merchant ships and one escort ship sunk, and another damaged. This was both shocking and revealing to Allied intelligence, who surmised that U-boats were simply not being offensive minded:

> These moderate losses are quite remarkable in view of the heavy shipping in the North Atlantic particularly at trade focal points where the majority of U-boats are concentrated. While the present doctrine of continuous submerged operations with snorkel has provided U-boats with a considerable degree of immunity from attack thus enabling them to move into probable hunting grounds it is evident that such tactics are not conducive to aggressive action.[107]

BdU grew concerned about their commanders' apparent lack of aggressiveness, believing that perhaps they were relying too much on sound while staying submerged and missing opportunities to attack. Experience Message No. 198 was sent to all U-boats on 18 December to address this concern:

> The fact that as a rule U-boats are forced to operate submerged in most op areas requires them at all times to make the most of opportunities to attack which present themselves during the day. Therefore, depending on the weather, be at periscope depth a great part of the time with only slight interruptions while in op area. Go deeper only if you know your U-boat is in a stratum in which the hydrophone definitely brings better results than the periscope. There is no such thing as an excuse that poor hydrophone conditions or a poor hydrophone set caused a chance for attack to be missed during daytime.[108]

More Allied vessels probably should have been sunk or damaged by U-boats at this time. While a lack of aggressiveness was certainly a factor, commanders and their crews, however, were also getting used to a world devoid of sight where operations were conducted by sound alone. The long submerged patrols were pioneering for their time. Both BdU and U-boat crews had to adopt accordingly under the pressures of combat without the benefit of normal experimentation and trials. For example, as submerged U-boat patrols exceeded fifty days, BdU issued Current Order No. 3 titled 'Switching to night routine to save current, air and potash cartridges' based on little scientific study except the reports of returning commanders.

Shifting crews to eat meals at night minimised air consumption as the U-boat was presumably refreshing air via the snorkel. It was also recommended that 'after the meal, a quick surfacing for ventilation can be made'.

BdU finally had to relinquish operational control over U-boats due primarily to the lack of wireless communication that reduced its ability to obtain and retransmit active intelligence on Allied ship locations. Commanders were formally authorised freedom to manoeuvre based on the tactical situation in Current Order No 4. BdU probably reasoned that this initiative might compensate for the perceived lack of aggressiveness. Specifically, if no targets were located in the original patrol area, a captain was allowed to follow:

> … his flair and hunter's instinct … If no prospects of success exist in the original area of operation, he may seek out another area. For example, to run closer to the coast, to penetrate deeper into the bays, and thus occupy the apparently more difficult areas. A report to High Command from the operational area, about a decision, is not required.[109]

The biggest news for U-boat crews was the land offensive that opened in the west starting on 16 December. Their role in setting the date for the launch of Operation *Wacht am Rhein* was not insignificant. *U-870* (IXC/40), *U-1232* (IXC/40) and *U-1053* (VIIC) were redirected from combat patrols to weather reporting. *U-1232* was headed for Canadian waters, while *U-870* headed for Gibraltar. Both were told on 3 December that: 'In order to judge the operational purposes of the enemy in the western area, it is absolutely necessary to have a clear picture of the weather situation over a large area. Therefore weather reports are of the greatest importance.'[110] The weather reporting in late November and early December by *U-1053*, *U-870*, *U-1228* and *U-1232* was rewarded with a message from BdU on 19 December: 'Your recent weather reports contributed decisively to determining the beginning of our great offensive in the west on 16 December.'[111]

On 16 December *U-978* (VIIC), under the command of Oberleutnant Günther Pulst, arrived in Bergen. He received a hero's welcome for his patrol. *U-978* was one of the first U-boats ordered to return to the English Channel in November to sink Allied vessels ahead of the land offensive in the Ardennes. Pulst operated there from 4 to 25 November and claimed the sinking of three steamers, declaring the Channel a 'very rewarding op area with good prospects for success'. He was promptly awarded the Knight's Cross 'for his distinguished execution of a Channel war cruise …'[112] Admiral von Friedeburg presented Pulst with his award on 21 December. He actually sank only a single US-flagged steamer for 7,176 GRT but could claim the new record for the longest snorkel patrol up to that time. *U-978* departed Bergen on 9 October and returned on 16 December for a sixty-nine-day patrol that took it around Ireland and into the western English Channel off Cherbourg. Pulst noted that the 'snorkel proved itself very well throughout the patrol'.[113]

Ten days later, *U-991* (VIIC), under the command of Oberleutnant Diethelm Balke, returned from his patrol into the Channel. His patrol lasted from 15 October until 26 December and surpassed Pulst as the longest snorkel patrol to date, setting the new record at seventy-three days. As OP-20-G noted from an Ultra intercept, Balke reported: 'Snorkelling undisturbed even when moon was out. No attack or run-in during the entire cruise in spite of the fact that snorkel around dipole was out of order from the time of departed from port on. Snorkel was camouflaged with a mat. Operated at water depths as low as 30m and as far as 0.8 miles from shore; enemy has not adjusted himself to the fact that U-boats operate with advantage in shallow water, therefore one is usually safest close to the coast.' His report of sinking a liberty ship off Fastnet and scoring two hits on a 14,000-ton troop transport in the Channel were unsubstantiated.

Immediately after the German offensive began in the west on 16 December, U-boats operating in the English Channel were told by BdU two days later that 'sinkings are of the greatest military importance right now'. Between 18 and 29 December an increasing number of U-boat attacks were reported by Allied vessels for a total of seven merchant ships and two escorts torpedoed. One of those Allied ships sunk was the troop transport SS *Leopoldville* (11,509 GRT) by the Alberich-coated *U-486* (VIIC). *U-486*, commanded by Oberleutnant Gerhard Meyer, had conducted one of the most successful late war patrols in the Channel. Departing Egersund on 26 November and returning to Bergen on 15 January, Meyer sunk 19,821 GRT, earning himself the German Cross in Gold.[114] His U-boat remained bottomed outside of Cherbourg when it launched an acoustic homing torpedo and sunk the Allied troop transport.

Although the cross-Channel supply lines of the Allies were never seriously threatened, OP-20-G noted that 'the U-boat was more than a mere nuisance. During the six weeks prior to the end of the war, approximately 18 ships were sunk or torpedoed there.'[115]

Snorkel defects continued, specifically with the Type IX retrofits. *U-1233* (IXC/40) returned to Bergen from its patrol a second time because of snorkel trouble.[116] *U-1233* was one of the very few Type IXs to receive a Type II snorkel mast. Its intake trunking was run forward of the boot heel, making it prone to being damaged when the snorkel mast was recessed back into the deck well. This was the likely cause of the trouble. *U-864*

(IXD2) navigated into Farsund due to snorkel failure and ran aground.[117] BdU conducted an assessment of the U-boat losses that had occurred in the past few months while on passage south of Iceland through the Faroe Islands passage and identified that more Type IXs were lost than VIICs. They recorded that 'the cause is not known, but it may be that the boats were lost through a break-down in the snorkel installation or were forced to surface because of snorkel trouble and were then destroyed'. An underwater minefield was placed in the area by the Royal Navy and known in U-boat crew slang as the 'Rosengarten' (Rose Garden). At times mines were observed free of the bottom and drifting on the surface, though there are no known reports of a snorkel U-boat striking one. BdU issued Experience Message No. 205 on 30 December stating in part 'commanders of IXC boats must therefore pay very particular attention to careful training of the crew in the use of the snorkel, and to most careful operation and servicing'.[118]

BdU summarised the developments of the past several months in their own KTB. They viewed Allied naval forces in coastal waters not occupied by U-boats 'since 1939' as 'inexperienced and unobservant' based on the reports provided by returning U-boat commanders. It was surmised that 'it is impossible to occupy only areas which offer the greatest opportunities for attack, e.g. the Channel, possibly also the North Channel and the Gulf of St Lawrence, as the enemy would discover this very quickly and would concentrate his defences on them'. This meant that by expanding the deployment of snorkel U-boats around the British Isles the enemy 'is now forced to defend himself from attacks on all sides, to divide up his forces to cover different areas and thus weaken them'. BdU also believed that occupying a wide operational area, to include North America, would provide intelligence 'of new measures and methods of enemy defence, and a better idea of the development of enemy dispositions'. BdU admitted in their assessment that they had 'expected to lose greater numbers of U-boats as more snorkel boats were sent to the more difficult operational areas' but that 'this did not occur' and 'on the contrary, there was a decrease compared to the losses incurred in 1941 and 1942', which 'illustrates the immense value of the snorkel'.

When the losses of U-boat per operational ones at sea just before the introduction of the snorkel were compared against those at the height of snorkel operations, a dramatic drop was evident. April/May of 1944 revealed a loss of twenty-three U-boats for forty-two at sea compared to seven lost for forty-nine at sea in the months of November/December. This resulted in a drop in loss rate of 55 per cent to 14 per cent. The conclusion reached by BdU was that the snorkel was the critical factor and that 'this sudden change at the end of 1944 not only gave the captains and crews in action at the time new faith in this weapon, it also showed that the basic idea of this new type of boat, namely the "undersea boat" with its higher submerged speed and greater staying power, was justified, and opened up great possibilities for success. This change also made it clear to the enemy that the danger from submarines was by no means over.'[119]

The snorkel underwent two improvements during the autumn. First, Type VIICs were being equipped with a Type II snorkel mast that eliminated the flange joint. Not all received this as even in the last months of the war Type I snorkels were being installed on VIICs. Only nine Type IXs are believed to have received a Type II snorkel mast. Most of the Type IXs received the Type I, which might have contributed to their increased losses due to snorkel problems. The other improvement was the application of the anti-radar mats on snorkel heads that significantly reduced the return signal generated by Allied radar sets.

When BdU surveyed the operations of the last few months they recognised that the sinking of enemy vessels was low, but this was a function of mathematics from their perspective. The average number of days in the operational area was significantly reduced compared with 1942 as a result of the much longer passage at a slow snorkelling speed, but also owing to a disproportionate time spent in port. In August 1942, out of 100 days the average U-boat spent forty in harbour and sixty at sea, of which forty were spent in the operational area. In December 1944 U-boats spent sixty-three days in harbour and thirty-seven at sea, only nine of which were in the operational area. The most surprising revelation of the survey was the fact that U-boat losses amounted to eighteen in four months – just over 10 per cent of those at sea. This was no higher than the losses recorded in the latter half of 1942. From BdU's perspective, they could rightly believe they were now back on the offensive.

This shift in thinking by BdU might appear academic, but for the U-boat force it was a strong morale boost to know that their survivability had dramatically increased from the days of 1943. This also gave BdU the impetus to expand operations from the coasts of England and Newfoundland to the American East Coast. Hessler noted regarding morale that 'this changed situation in the latter part of 1944 has not only given the crews of old-type boats new faith in their weapons, but has also shown the new-type boats, with their high submerged speed and endurance, to have been rightly conceived and promising of great achievements …'[120]

Knowing that snorkel-equipped Type XXIs and Type XXIIIs were on the way provided an illusion of a future resumption of the convoy battles of the

1941–42 period, though it ignored the realities of the ground war inexorably drawing closer to German ports and industrial centres.

The OP-20-G bi-weekly secret assessment of 1 January echoed many of the above themes:

> Coincident with the German land offensive, enemy U-boat activity has increased in Central English Channel where up to five U-boats have been operating with some success … Inshore snorkel operations finally began to pay dividends during December with six merchant ships and one escort sunk in three ships torpedoed in the south-west approaches and English Channel area and one escort sunk and one merchant ship torpedoed off Halifax. Difficulty continues to be experienced in locating and effectively attacking snorkel, as a result of which few U-boats were sunk during the month.[121]

Allied intelligence acknowledged the difficulty in finding and destroying snorkel-equipped U-boats now that German tactics had evolved and experience using the new device had become codified across the U-boat fleet.

As the Battle of the Atlantic entered 1945, Dönitz could be pleased under the circumstances. The snorkel had seemingly countered the Allied radar-equipped aircraft that drove his U-boats from the mid-Atlantic eighteen months ago, and the new Electro-boats were expected to complete their work-ups in the Baltic shortly.

January–May 1945

The inshore campaign continued unabated off the coast of England for the next five months with U-boats sinking Allied vessels until the very end of the war. *U-1023* (VIIC/41) was under the command of Kapitänleutnant Heinrich-Andreas Schroeteler (Knight's Cross recipient on 2 May 1945), who sunk the Norwegian minesweeper HNoMS *NYMS-382* (twenty-one dead and ten survivors) in the English Channel on 7 May after firing a T5 acoustic torpedo before surrendering on 10 May at Weymouth, U.K. *U-2336* (XXIII), under the command of Kapitänleutnant Emil Klusmeier, departed Larvik on 1 May, the eve of the end of the war, to sink the Canadian-flagged *Avondale Park* (two dead and thirty-six survivors) and the Norwegian-flagged *Sneland* I (seven dead and twenty-two survivors) from convoy EN-591 outside the entry of Edinburgh shortly after 11pm on 7 May. *U-2336* returned to Kiel on 14 May, nearly a week after hostilities were over. The sinking of the *Sneland I* was the last Allied vessel sunk by a U-boat during the war in any theatre. These sinkings, like those occurring off the US East Coast at the same time by patrolling Type IXs, did little to alter the course of the war. The question often asked is 'Why did the U-boat

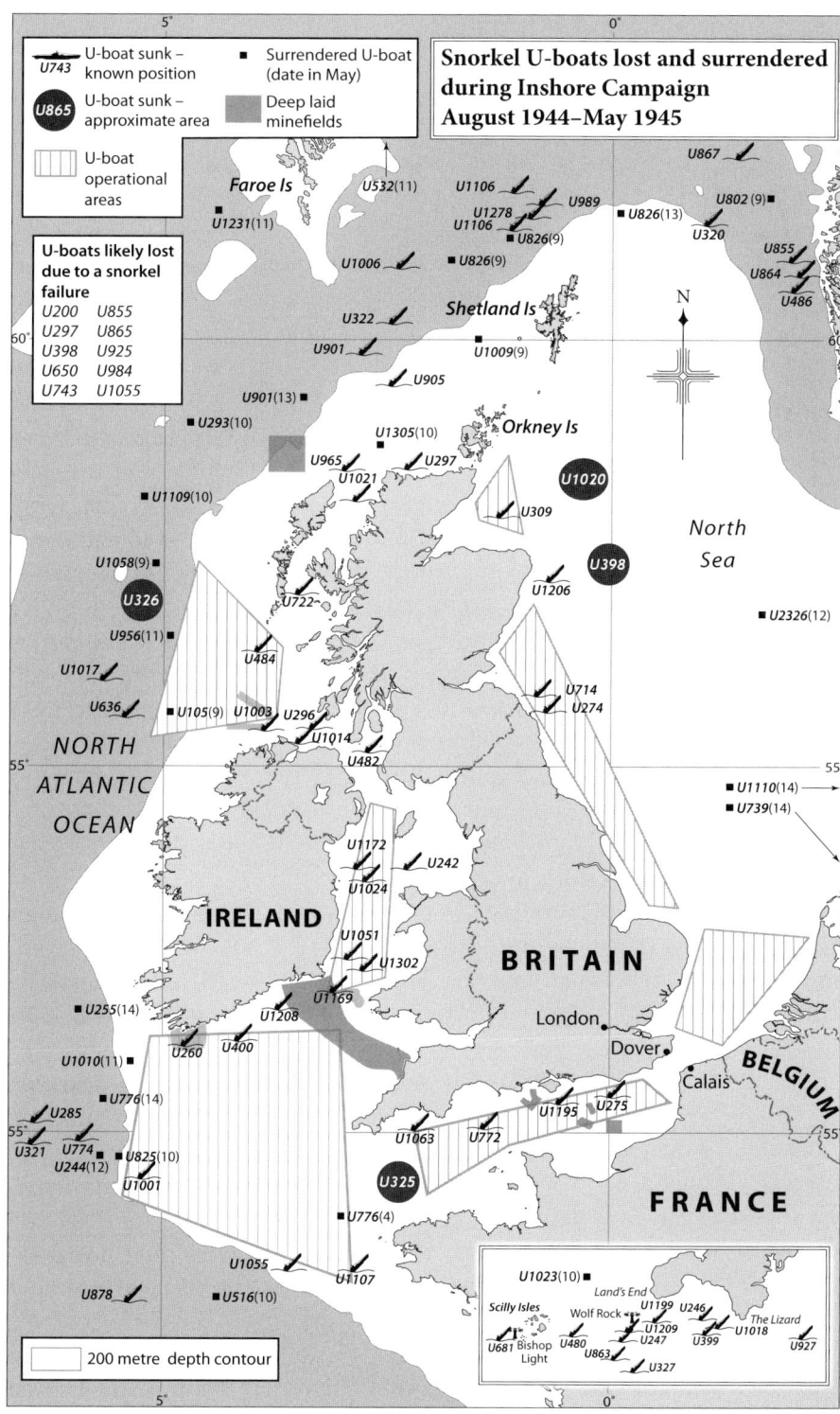

Snorkel U-boats lost and surrendered during Inshore Campaign August 1944–May 1945

Key:
- U-boat sunk – known position (U743)
- U-boat sunk – approximate area (U865)
- U-boat operational areas
- Surrendered U-boat (date in May)
- Deep laid minefields

U-boats likely lost due to a snorkel failure
U200   U855
U297   U865
U398   U925
U650   U984
U743   U1055

200 metre depth contour

war continue to the end of hostilities?' To answer that question, one needs to understand the role that the U-boat played as the Third Reich's only available strategic weapon in the last year of the war.

In a two-day conference at the Berghof, Hitler's Alpine retreat, which began on 12 April 1944, Admiral Dönitz explained to Hitler that based on captured British documents provided by the Japanese Attaché in Berlin, U-boats were tying down a disproportionate number of Allied naval vessels. Reichsmarschall Hermann Göring, who was also in attendance, added that there was a disproportionate number of Allied aircraft also tied down in anti-U-boat operations. This idea that a U-boat simply on patrol could impact the Allies in this strategic way, even when not actively sinking ships in a tonnage war, became Dönitz's new reality. Post-war assessments of actual Allied strategic assets tied down in hunting U-boats was far lower than Dönitz or Göring believed, but at the time they had little evidence to contradict their assessment. The conclusion Dönitz reached at the end of the meeting was 'that U-boat warfare must continue in spite of losses'. He came to this conclusion even before the snorkel was operationally proven.

In a subsequent meeting with Hitler on 3 December, Dönitz highlighted how his decision to continue the U-boat war was now confirmed through the successful application of the snorkel. He cited the recent patrol by Nollmann, which spent fifty continuous days underwater utilising the snorkel-equipped diesel U-boat *U-1199*. With the defensive withdrawal of the Luftwaffe back to the German border, the U-boat, arguably along with the V2 rocket, remained the only strategic assets of the Third Reich capable of reaching Allied shores. Unlike the V2, which was considered a *Verwaltungs* (Vengeance) weapon and meant to sow only terror among a civilian population, the U-boat had the potential to impact military operations. They could drop agents off at enemy shores, as they did multiple times in Canada and the US in 1944 and 1945. U-boats could patrol and sink Allied ships right up to the very entrance of Allied harbours, impacting men and supplies along the Western Front. U-boats could obtain important intelligence on Allied shipping, even if they sank no vessels. This latter point foreshadowed the future of submarine operations during the Cold War. Ultimately, a snorkel-equipped U-boat proved capable of operating in areas that previously it could not. For example, great enthusiasm was generated by successful operations off Gibraltar in December 1944 and January 1945, where previous U-boat losses reached over 80 per cent of those on patrol. Now U-boats remained on station for as long as ten days, scoring hits on Allied vessels while avoiding hunter-killer groups.

Dönitz believed that if the older boats could perform this successfully with a snorkel, the new snorkel-equipped Electro-boats could only increase the U-boat arm's operational prospects in the Atlantic. Dönitz's enthusiasm for his snorkel-equipped U-boats was so great, he pointed out to Hitler that future success in the Battle of Atlantic was not a question of 'if' his new boats could meet the challenge but of 'when' they would be made ready. Future success was now a dockyard and construction problem, meaning that it was entirely up to how fast the new U-boats could be produced. Such enthusiasm, based on actual achievements on combat patrols, at a time of the Third Reich's strategic withdrawal to the borders of Germany, was not lost on Hitler.

In a conference on 17 February, Dönitz informed Hitler that seven U-boats had just returned from around the British Isles and that 'these ships had to operate in narrow sea lanes and in shallow waters near the coast. They all report that enemy defences are not very effective. This proves therefore that the superiority of enemy submarine defences has been overcome by the introduction of the snorkel.'[122] Hitler informed Dönitz how he was satisfied with the outcome of coastal operations by snorkel-equipped U-boats. This was indeed rare praise at a time when the final German offensive in the west had failed, the Soviets were only 70km from Berlin, and Allied aircraft roamed the German skies with near impunity, laying waste to cities. Dönitz, perhaps with a hint of eagerness, replied that while the new Type XXIIIs would operate off the English coast, the new Type XXIs would soon deploy off the US East Coast. He again repeated this goal to Hitler in one of his last meetings with him on 1 March, despite knowing that technical difficulties existed on the Type XXI.

There should be no question that in the final months of the war the U-boat proved Germany's only remaining strategic asset that could strike out at the Allies in their home waters. While the U-boat's coastal operations both in the United Kingdom and off the North American coast did not alter the course of the war, they continued to the very end. If Dönitz was willing to continue to deploy U-boats in the face of overwhelming odds in April 1944 when they had little prospect of surviving a patrol due to radar-equipped Allied aircraft, he had no reason not to continue deploying them now that the snorkel all but eliminated that threat. There was no motivation for Dönitz to halt the Battle of the Atlantic with the Allied policy of unconditional surrender in place. The military leaders of the Third Reich understood all too well that this war would continue until the bitter end. There would be no 'Stab in the Back' as there was during the First World War when revolution broke out in the Kriegsmarine and war ended with German armies still on foreign soil. Dönitz remained convinced until the very end that his U-boats were making a difference to Germany's deteriorating strategic position and that each Allied ship sunk saved the lives of a German soldier on the battlefield. It should be no wonder that upon Hitler's death Dönitz was named his successor. The role the snorkel played in that decision was not insignificant.[123]

January was a high point for BdU in the inshore campaign and it proved a growing concern for Allied intelligence. Operation *Wacht am Rhein* was still under way in the west. It was a significant Allied intelligence failure that raised concerns. If the Wehrmacht's build-up and operational intent for this offensive had been overlooked, what other military surprises were being prepared, Allied intelligence analysts pondered. In the Atlantic there were considerable U-boat successes off Gibraltar, which pointed to an expansion of U-boat deployments to areas beyond England. The first indication of U-boats deploying against the US East Coast for the first time in years was now intercepted in traffic with the movement of *U-869* (IXC/40). Simultaneously, BdU introduced the Kurier system and special ciphers that were unreadable by OP-20-G. The new Type XXIII Electro-boats made their combat debut off England, while U-boats deployed successfully into the shallows of the Thames Estuary and circumnavigated Ireland for the first time in the war. Entire Allied anti-submarine task forces were ordered against single U-boats in hunts that lasted weeks and often ended unsuccessfully for the Allies. The confirmation of a U-boat's sinking often eluded the hunter-killer task force as their target never surfaced. The Battle of the Atlantic transformed into a war of sounds and electronic blips played out on sonar and radar receivers. Ultra's impact diminished.

At the end of January, the Western press began to publish reports about the 'New U-boat war'. This prompted the Japanese Naval Attaché to inquire with BdU if this was in fact the case. The answer he received was sent back to Tokyo on 8 January from Berlin: 'The sudden onset of a new U-boat war, as announced by the enemy, is not to be expected, for we have already been in the new U-boat war since the equipping of snorkel.'[124]

This was a factual and interesting self-assessment by BdU. The introduction of the snorkel opened their new offensive and the appearance of operational Electro-boats was viewed as a continuation of that offensive, not something new. BdU appeared to accept inshore operations as normal by January 1945 and not something interim as they had thought six months earlier.

Dönitz announced in his weekly broadcast to the U-boat force on 27 January that:

The war at sea has entered a completely new stage through use of the snorkel, which makes it possible for U-boats to remain underwater for weeks at a time. The more adroit the U-boats can become in use of the snorkel against the enemy, the greater their success will be … The Führer has ordered that the U-boat war is to be intensified by all possible means.[125]

The emphasis on Hitler's comments was clearly a nod to the support Dönitz had gained through his efforts.

Allied Intelligence Assessment
At the start of 1945 the US Navy produced an assessment of current U-boat operations that highlighted what they knew at the time. The following report by U.S Naval Reserve Lieutenant W V Quine issued on 16 January provided an overview of the evolution of U-boat warfare into 'Total Undersea Warfare' and the challenges it presented to the Allies. He also revealed how influential Dönitz's views on military matters became to the Führer in the final months of the war. The relationship between Dönitz's ascendency within Hitler's inner circle and the success of snorkel operations should not be underestimated. Excerpts from the long report follow:

16 January 1945
Memorandum for Captain Wenger
Subject: Review of current situation U-boats, January, 1945.
1. 'Total Undersea Warfare'.
With the successful conclusion in November of the snorkel's experimental period, U-boat Command introduced the phrase 'Total Undersea Warfare' into current orders. The phrase undoubtedly anticipated the arrival of Type XXI and XXIII, but also applied to currently available operational U-boats. Another new type large U-boat, the Type XXVI, was mentioned recently by the Japanese Naval Attaché.

There is no reason at present to believe that Admiral Dönitz will not live up to his threat. The U-boat branch has made a remarkable recovery since the fall of France. Despite severe losses in counter invasion activities, the organisation maintained its discipline and withdrew to Norway in good order. Failure in the channel during the invasion summer was probably expected. But morale was kept up. With admirable tenacity the U-boat authorities have adjusted themselves to changes at home and have persisted in subordinating everything to one end: the reopening of the Atlantic Battle.

4. Appreciation of various aspects of 'Total Undersea Warfare'.
a) Snorkel is admittedly a success, enabling U-boats to cruise, charge batteries, and ventilate without surfacing. It has enabled U-boats to return to areas

heavily patrolled by aircraft. A submerged cruise of 70 days is possible and crews can stand it. It has even increased the scope of U-boat operations, for shallow coastal waters are now favourable areas. The U-boat is, of course, still bound to the surface for the maintenance of its life, but the area exposed has been reduced to a minimum, and even this can be camouflaged. The exhaust should be from 1 to 1.5 metres below the water once snorkelling has started. Smoke trails, however, remain a problem.[126]

This excellent wartime document provides immense insight into what was known by Allied intelligence in January 1945 abut the evolution of German U-boats in the age of 'Total Undersea War.' It specifically revealed what was working and the overall Allied capability at that time to counter new U-boat tactics and technical innovations. Perhaps the most important part of the document is the recognition that the snorkel fundamentally altered the Battle of the Atlantic. It clearly shifted the paradigm from primarily surfaced to submerged operations, forcing significant changes almost overnight in how U-boats navigated, communicated, attacked their targets and hid from their Allied pursuers. Ultra's impact was diminished as little could be done to interdict a U-boat that no longer surfaced or communicated as frequently as it did through early 1944. As the end of the war in Europe loomed, and with the German Army and Luftwaffe clearly on the defensive, we see the U-boat overcome the 'Black May' of 1943 to emerge as an offensive threat to the Allies.

Irish Sea
U-Boats operated off the North Channel and southern coast of Ireland throughout the war, but none had ever dared enter the Irish Sea or circum-navigate Ireland itself. The first sortie into the Irish Sea was attempted in November 1944 with the results not being known until January. The first U-boat to enter the Irish Sea was *U-1202* (VIIC), commanded by Kapitänleutnant Rolf Thomsen. He departed Kristiansand on 30 October and returned to Bergen on 1 January after a sixty-four-day patrol. He sank one ship, the American Liberty Ship *Dan Beard* (7,176 GRT), on 10 December in the St Georges Channel. He claimed another four steamers sunk, but these were never confirmed by any Allied reporting. Thomsen relied on hearing 'violent explosions' to confirm the sinkings.[127] He report-ed on 3 January to BdU that 'Irish Sea, St George's Channel very favourable operations area, heavy convoy traffic, continual arrivals. Medium sea defence, continual air day and night. Despite this, the boat snorkelled undisturbed close under land.'[128]

Navigation was benefitted by the fact that: 'England and Ireland are using lighting as in peacetime.'[129] He received the Knight's Cross on 4 January for his efforts, as noted in the OP-20-G interception of a BdU communique: 'His initiative was promptly recognised by the award of the Knight's Cross "for his outstandingly performed war cruise …"' Thomsen's success prompted BdU to send other U-boats to the Irish Sea with an average of three to four U-boats a month. Provided with the latest detailed information on shipping lanes, traffic and defence, these U-boats claimed other successes. During January alone, six Allied ships were torpedoed, and four others attacked in the Irish Sea. This area remained a profitable operational area until the end of the war, with another five Allied vessels sunk or torpedoed here in April.[130] By war's end a total of nineteen U-boats were ordered into the Irish Sea, with varying success.

Introduction of the Type XXIII
Due to their limited range, the Type XIIIs launched from Norway and patrolled the eastern approaches to Scotland and England, returning to base after their two torpedoes were expended. All Type XXIIIs utilised their snorkels and remained completely submerged for the duration of their patrols, which averaged approximately thirty days. *U-2324*, under the command of Oberleutnant Hans-Heinrich Haß, conducted the first Electro-boat sortie of the war. A total of six Type XXIIIs conducted nine combat patrols, sinking a total of 14,601 Allied GRT. Not a single Type XXIII was ever located or attacked during a patrol.

Arctic U-boats
The U-boats assigned to the Arctic were among the last to be retrofitted with a snorkel. These snorkel boats were employed against the Murmansk convoy route in the Barents Sea. Keeping with the shift in operational employment to convoy embarkation/debarkation routes close to the ports, these U-boats shifted focus to the Kola Peninsula and in the entrance to the Kola Estuary that led to the port of Murmansk. On 6 March Dönitz sent a wireless message where he stressed the relationship between the Arctic convoys and the land operations on the Eastern Front, adding that:

> Snort makes it possible to attack convoys effectively in a position close to the coast, even at seasons when daylight is of long duration. Our own hard-hitting torpedo Luftwaffe will be put into operation when weather conditions are suitable. Intention: (a) to intercept convoy according to air reports. Attack in full force, surfaced when it is dark. However, do not pursue in daylight, but a quick retreat, in order to get to the Murmansk coast in any case in good time in the second disposition. (b) Form a wedge of U-boats at once

in unobserved disposition off the convoy's homing port (Murmansk). Use your radar; don't overestimate carrier night air.[131]

One incident worth noting occurred with *U-668* (VIIC). This boat received its snorkel retrofit in Narvik during November 1944 after completing its fourth combat patrol. During its sixth patrol, while under the command of Kapitänleutnant Wolfgang von Eickstedt, *U-668* ran into a snorkel defect while operating in Kola Bay on 11 March. The intake pipe burst, allowing water into the port-side diesel engine. The damage was considerable. 'A flask had broken with the piston sleeve and the valve push rod was severely bent.' Because the snorkel had allowed the U-boat to operate so close to the coast without detection, von Eickstedt felt secure enough to move closer to the coast near Murmansk and put the boat on the bottom, where it came to rest at a depth of 250m under the Arctic water. The damage was repaired within fifty-six hours utilising shifts of three men. *U-668* was again fully operational and back on patrol on 14 March.[132] It returned to Narvik on 17 April, completing a forty-eight-day patrol.

U-992 (VIIC) sent out a short report at the request of BdU that was intercepted by OP-20-G. Under the command of Oberleutnant Hans Falke, *U-992* departed Bogenbucht, Norway, on 16 January 1945 and headed to the entrance of the Kola Estuary. Falke reported:

> Boat reports 8 February in AC 8826 [T5] on search group, detonation after 5 minutes 53 seconds, 5 February in 8855 Russian escort destroyer sunk, on 13 February from convoy a vessel (probably a freighter) sunk with [T5]. Boat had shot at the passing convoy by night by sound, certain sinking of a piston driven vessel after 2 minutes determined. On 14 February sank a tanker from convoy 7000 GRT. Boat reports further best shooting opportunity directly off the entrance to the Kola Estuary, boat had snorkelled unmolested in AC 8859 close under the coast, snorkel icing insignificant, began return transit.[133]

Like many snorkel U-boats that conducted attacks by sound without any visual verification, Falke's sinking claims were not accurate. The only confirmed sinking was against the British corvette HMS *Denbigh Castle* (1,060 GRT), which was sunk on 13 February within the entrance of the Kola Estuary. Also interesting is the fact that icing was not a real concern on the function of the snorkel float.

Snorkel Problems
Throughout the end of the war the snorkel dominated operational readiness. No U-boat sailed into the North Atlantic without a retrofit snorkel,

and none could operate effectively if it was damaged during operations. Below lists the known U-boats that suffered a snorkel defect, as recorded in BdU's KTB, from January to April 1945. It many cases either improper use of a snorkel or a snorkel defect could result in the U-boat's loss.

U-1004 (VIIC/41) departed for a patrol from Bergen on 1 January and returned on the 11th just before entering the Shetland Straits due to a snorkel breakdown.[134] It did not depart again until 27 January for its second and last patrol after its snorkel was repaired. *U-1014* (VIIC/41) departed Bergen on 8 January on its first patrol and returned five days later on the 13th, also due to a snorkel breakdown. After repairs it departed on 18 January for Malin Head, only to be sunk in the North Channel on 4 February by depth charges from the British frigates' HMS *Loch Scavaig*, HMS *Nyasaland*, HMS *Papua* and HMS *Loch Shin*. A snorkel failure might have been the cause. *U-1276* (VIIC/41) left Bergen on 19 January and damaged its snorkel, forcing it to return on 22 January for repairs. It then departed on 28 January, sinking the British corvette HMS *Vervain* (925 GRT) off the southern coast of Ireland in the Celtic Sea on 20 February, then being sunk herself that same day by depth charges from the British Sloop HMS *Amethyst*.

On 2 February, *U-1022* (VIIC/41) and *U-864* (IXD2) returned to Bergen due to their snorkel and hydraulic oil systems being out of service. On 12 February, *U-275* (VIIC) broke off patrol in the English Channel and arrived at St Nazaire due to a snorkel defect that caused heavy water intake. *U-1021* (VIIC/41) began return transit to Bergen due to snorkel failure on 17 February. *U-1235* (IXC/40) returned to Bergen due to snorkel failure the following day. *U-963* (VIIC) began its return transit from the Irish Sea prematurely because its snorkel mast could not be lowered.

U-805 (IXC/40) broke off its patrol due to snorkel failure on 9 March. *U-483* (VIIC) began its return transit from the northern part of the Irish Sea when it was rammed while snorkelling on 12 March. Its snorkel was lost and its periscope bent, causing leaks into the boat and limiting its ability to dive. *U-1002* (VIIC/41) reported on the 15th that its patrol was interrupted due to the failure of the port supercharger clutch and a damaged starboard supercharger clutch. This resulted in limited snorkel operation and its attack periscope being out of service. However, *U-1002* moved off to the south-west for repairs. *U-294* (VIIC/41) was on a transfer cruise from Bergen to Narvik, but put into Trondheim due to snorkel breakdown on the 17th. *U-997* (VIIC/41) reported on the 22nd that it was on return transit after suffering damage to its snorkel after a depth charge attack. The U-boat began to take on water through the diesel air intake head valve and snorkel drain. *U-979* (VIIC) arrived Bergen again due to snorkel breakdown on the 29th. *U-881* (IXC/40) broke off its patrol due to snorkel breakdown on the 30th.

How many U-boats were lost solely to a snorkel failure is not known.

Final Experience Messages and Tactical Changes

The number of Experience Messages and Tactical Modifications issued from January until April were far fewer than the preceding six months, as operations with the snorkel were largely worked out by December 1944. As U-boats spent long periods underwater and snorkelled for hours near the surface, especially in rough seas, the 2cm deck guns often became damaged or even torn off. On 20 January Experience Message No. 214 was broadcast, stating: 'U-boats report isolated severe damage and sometimes loss of 2cm weapons due to snorkel travel in heavy seas.' The only recommendation was: 'If the situation permits, an attempt must be made to adjust the course and the travel at sea such that damage is avoided.[135]

This next Experience Message underscores the change in tactics when being pursued by Allied anti-submarine destroyers or other surface vessels. The recommendation was that when a U-boat was being hunted, it should not seek deep water, but do the opposite and head towards the shallows, as Allied commanders would not expect such a manoeuvre. The focus of the below experience report was *U-483*, which arrived at Stavanger on 23 November. *U-483* departed Norway on 3 October for a patrol off the North Channel. *U-483* hit the British frigate HMS *Whitaker* on 1 November in convoy SC-159, which set off a pursuit by Allied vessels. At the time, the U-boat's commander, von Morstein, reported more vessels sunk than had occurred because he was basing his sinkings only on sound reports and not visual inspection. He escaped detection because he manoeuvred his U-boat into shallow water, not deep water. BdU sent out a message on 16 January based on von Morstein's experience: 'Moral: when pursued, think what defensive measures the enemy is expecting. Do the opposite. The most unusual measures often lead to the best successes.'[136] Von Morstein received the German Cross in Gold in December for his efforts on this patrol.

Another Experience Report was sent out by BdU on 19 January that offered yet a different solution to a pursuit by Allied anti-submarine vessels. *U-486* (VIIC) departed Egersund on 26 November, returning to Bergen on 15 January after a fifty-one-day patrol. Commanded by Oberleutnant Gerhard Meyer, *U-486* sailed along the western coast of Ireland and into the English Channel off Cherbourg, where it sank a total of four Allied vessels totalling 19,281 GRT, including the troopship *Leopoldville*. His success prompted a report by BdU that was intercepted by

OP-20-G.[137] It should be noted that *U-486* was coated with Alberich. While *U-486*'s Alberich certainly offered the U-boat some protection, Meyer left the area at high speed by using his snorkel while running his diesels on full, the exact opposite of what *U-483* did. This again highlights how a snorkel could be used tactically.

Many of the U-boat commanders in the last year of war were in their early 20s and lacked experience. Most had never participated in a patrol in the early days of convoy warfare. Their first patrol was with a snorkel-equipped U-boat. The added complexity of handling a snorkel boat combined with sailing inexperience resulted in serious collisions around ports. So extensive was this problem that BdU sent out a warning on 24 January: 'Almost every CO of today is very young. The limited experience involved in this connection must be balanced by cautious navigation. Every collision incurred by careless methods of handling will be ruthlessly punished.'[138] BdU became aware through Allied reporting and intelligence gathered by B-Dienst that their U-boat commanders' claims of sinkings were inflated. This was because torpedoes were fired from submerged U-boats at sound contacts without any visual verification of the target. All U-boats were informed on 14 January to make visual inspection by periscope of any Allied vessel hit with a torpedo, if tactically possible.[139]

A major change in snorkel guidance was issued on 30 January by BdU. Up to this point snorkelling to charge a battery was conducted at night. That guidance now changed. 'A clear night with full moon and glass-like sea is most unfavourable for snorkel cruising. Two U-boats report well-placed aircraft bombs, dropped by sight under these conditions. Under these circumstances snorkelling seems better by day, as aircraft can then be sighted with periscope.'[141]

In February, BdU announced, 'Once an air contact is made by FuMB, submerge unless snorkelling or in emergency.'[141] This was reiterated on 10 February in Experience Radio Transmission No. 218.[142] Now that U-boats were frequently bottoming, BdU offered guidance on how to avoid being stuck and to prevent damage.[143]

Lack of aggressiveness by U-boat commanders was a continued issue identified by BdU. Some new commanders were perhaps reluctant to take their U-boats into shallow water or snorkel amidst Allied anti-submarine vessels, preferring to stay in deeper water. This was the exact case with Oberleutnant Bernhard Schwarting, who commanded *U-905* (VIIC), and Oberleutnant Erwin Dohrn of *U-325* (VIIC/41). Schwarting was 32, having just celebrated his birthday in January, and Dohrn was only 24, with a birthday coming up in March. Both men were on their first combat patrols. Their hesitation to enter the shallows resulted in BdU sending out the following admonishment on 19 February as a reminder to all other U-boat captains: 'In the all-out push to destroy the enemy (the Commanders should have) gone into an area where the enemy is to be encountered with certainty (therefore into the Channel or the Irish Sea).'[144]

A message sent in early February highlights the already discussed issues with wireless communication and the freedom of action granted U-boat commanders in situations where they were operating without effective communications back to BdU. Citing the three separate examples, the below guidance was sent out by BdU on 19 February in Experience Message No. 222A: 'It is the commanding officer's duty to bring the weapon entrusted to him into action without fail and only to reflect how and where this is possible. Even if no reproach can be made to the commanding officers according to the book, they must, however, be reproached for lack of initiative.'[145]

In March BdU guidance reminded U-boat commanders of tactical procedures. On 2 March, BdU advised that: 'It is evident that enemy aircraft are carrying out intensified search for snorkelling U-boats, possibly even without radar. The basic principle is still to cruise as carefully as possible. Therefore: Do not surface east of 15W unless surfacing is necessary to send a radio message, in special cases for night attacks, or for repairs.'[146] This was followed by an Experience Message from an unidentified returning U-boat the same day. 'COs confirm the old experience, that the greatest danger occurs in the vicinity of the firing position after one has made an attack. Therefore get away from firing position after attack; do not go to the bottom immediately. Basic principle: Do the opposite from what the enemy expects of you, for instance, move off into shallow water. They have added no new tricks to their defence.'[147]

Oberleutnant Werner Riecken returned to Trondheim after a sixty-five-day war patrol to the English Channel on 2 March 1945 while commanding *U-1017* (VIIC/41). His patrol to the western Channel resulted in two Allied vessels sunk for a total of 10,604 GRT. His short report upon arrival resulted in a Top Secret Experience Message No. 229C broadcast out to the U-boat fleet shortly after his arrival. Two points he made were that U-boats were hard 'to find in shallow parts of the ocean' and that 'if recognised, move in the direction the enemy considers improbable, e.g., towards land'. There is no evidence that this message was intercepted by Allied intelligence.[148] What this message reinforced was the idea to use the shallows for hiding from pursuit, and when pursued, to head inshore and not into deeper water. This report also recommended that a U-boat move head-on towards or away from an Allied hunter to reduce its underwater profile.

These final experience messages sent by BdU demonstrate how even in the final months of war Dönitz's U-boat fleet remained a highly organised and efficient military organisation.

Chapter 7

Crew Health

The men serving on snorkel-equipped U-boats conducted their wartime patrols under conditions that had few comparisons among the world's navies. Commanders and crew alike conducted complex tactical tasks while under extraordinary psychological and physiological stress brought about by operating up to seventy days in a world of sound, devoid of natural light, where constant barometric pressure differentials threatened to shatter eardrums and reduce oxygen levels, where the spectre of carbon monoxide poisoning lurked at every snorkel use. They conducted their snorkel patrols without the benefit of full scientific or medical testing, all the while under wartime threat of destruction by Allied hunter-killer groups and often in the harshest of all maritime environments – the North Atlantic. No submariners of any other navy came close to this underwater feat of endurance during the war. Even Allied intelligence acknowledged this achievement in classified reporting.

Initial scientific and medical testing occurred onboard *U-235*, *U-236* and *U-237* during a two-month period of snorkel trials that lasted from October to December 1943. The snorkel was deemed safe to operate for the crew if it was properly used.[1] However, this conclusion was based upon the belief that U-boat crews would only remain submerged for several days at a time. Wartime reality proved very different.

Two post-war reports prepared by members of the Kriegsmarine medical staff provide unique detail on the impact of the snorkel on crews. Dr Hellmut Uffenorde was a lecturer at the University of Kiel and a former consulting otologist at the Sinnesmedizinischen Forschungsabteilung (SIMPA) des Marine Sanitätsamtes MOK Ostsee (Research Division for the Physiology of the Sensory Organs attached to the Medical Department of the Naval Station of the Baltic Sea). He authored the 'Otological Experience with Snorkel-Equipped U-boats'. Dr Guenther Malorny served as the primary carbon monoxide tester of the snorkel-equipped U-boats from the autumn of 1943 until May 1944. He authored 'Carbon Monoxide on U-boats'.

Dr Malorny concluded that before the introduction of the snorkel there was no concern about carbon monoxide (CO) poisoning onboard U-boats. No one suspected what the impact was until the first testing began in the autumn of 1943. He explained that 'the significance of the carbon monoxide for the crews on U-boats was not sufficiently estimated by the [snorkel] engineers. When I succeeded in demonstrating that a series of inexplicable accidents were caused by the effect of CO, expensive modification of construction had to be made later.'[2]

It remains unclear what he meant as no documentation has been located that details the 'expensive modification'. In terms of the weaker GW engine, though, the S-curve pipe configuration in the exhaust trunking may have been engineered on purpose to help reduce the backflow of water into the exhaust piping. Thus the strain on the GW engines was reduced when trying to clear the line, aiding in the prevention of toxic smoke in the diesel motor room.[3] Other modifications came in the form of new snorkel cams that replaced the return cams and made the diesel engines less sensitive to increased back pressure during snorkel operations. It was also recommended that each snorkel-equipped U-boat receive a Draeger CO indicator.[4] However, both of the latter technical fixes were not present on all vessels.

Initial testing was done only on VIICs and the high rate of CO gas exposure alarmed Malorny. Normal CO exposure to crews on non-snorkel-equipped VIIC, IXC, and IXD2 U-boats was measured at 0.013–0.038 per cent of oxygen. On a VIIC snorkel-equipped U-boat with GW engines this increased during normal snorkel operations to 0.08–0.12 per cent of oxygen. But when the snorkel head dipped below the sea surface due to inclement weather or a tactical manoeuvre while the diesel engines continued to run, this could increase to 0.4–0.7 per cent or higher, which could be fatal.[5] It was determined that a high concentration of CO would induce acute poisoning within fifteen minutes and a loss of consciousness or death in forty-five minutes.[6]

The toxic effect of carbon monoxide is based on its rapid bonding to the body's haemoglobin, which is approximately 300 times greater than that of oxygen. The first serious symptoms of CO poisoning appear as soon as 30 to 40 per cent of the haemoglobin has combined with the carbon monoxide. At 0.05 per cent CO exposure 30 per cent of the haemoglobin in the body will combine with carbon monoxide. According to Dr Uffenorde: 'If air containing 0.2 per cent volume of the CO is breathed for one hour, about one half of the haemoglobin is combined with CO. But, even the concentration of 0.07 per cent volume CO is sufficient to saturate 50 per cent of the haemoglobin if the period of its influence is prolonged accordingly.'[7]

This latter point is extremely important and highly relevant to the last year of the U-boat war. When the snorkel was invented and tested, all those involved believed that a U-boat would only remain submerged for only several days while operating the snorkel. No one believed a U-boat crew would remain submerged for a week, let alone two or more months, until they actually did that. There was no prior medical experience to draw upon that would offer any guidance on crew health. German U-boat crews on their own were in fact pioneering submarine science under the least favourable conditions of a wartime environment.

The increase in CO gas was compounded by the continual drops in pressure caused by the submergence of the snorkel float valve below water. Dr Uffenorde conducted several late-war tests and determined that when the snorkel float valve was inadvertently shut while the diesel engines continued to run the pressure in the U-boat could drop 200–300mbr in a few seconds, thus reducing the oxygen content in the air from what is normal at sea level and dropping it to what it is at 4,000m (13,200ft). In these circumstances medical staff had to rely upon aviation medical science to deduce the effects as human beings began to experience the ill effects of high altitude at that pressure and elevation. Not only was this detrimental to human physiology, but the drop in pressure could also prevent the internal communication tubes from carrying any voice commands from the control room to any other part of the U-boat. This meant that someone would have to physically run from one part of the U-boat to another to issue an order, if one was required, during these situations.[8]

Dr Uffenorde concluded that:

There was no opportunity to investigate in detail the otological problems connected with the carbon monoxide poisoning during the snorkel warfare towards the end of the war, though many experiences indicated the seriousness of the danger. Especially on the boats of the type VIIC which were put into action in the beginning of the war, it happened repeatedly that men of the cruise definitely became unfit after several months of snorkel cruising.[9]

His comments are revealing. The Type VIIC experienced a unique problem in terms of their GW engines not being efficient enough to exhaust all the built up CO, especially when the snorkel head submerged during operation, thus causing a longer exposure to accumulating toxic bonding in the haemoglobin. Type VIIC snorkel U-boats were exclusively employed in

European coastal waters and their cruises typically ran for about four to eight weeks. While the Type IXC and IXD2 MAN engines could handle the back pressure more efficiently and vent the CO better, their cruises lasted longer; sometimes even double the length of a snorkel-equipped Type VIIC. This meant that in both cases the crews were likely to be equally unfit to immediately return to duty upon completion of their cruise. One can also imagine how difficult it might have been to conduct any tactical manoeuvres onboard such a U-boat after remaining submerged for two months or more under the increasing effects of carbon monoxide.

After almost a year of snorkel operations it became clear that the additional stress brought upon U-boat crews was taking a toll. A communique issued by BdU on 10 April 1945 to *U-965* (VIIC), *U-978* (VIIC), *U-714* (VIIC), and *U-309* (VIIC) stated 'a very long stay in the operational area can lead to serious appearances of exhaustion among the crew. The [commander] must himself decide in such cases [when] a return passage should be begun prior to exhausting the special fighting power of the boat.'[10] So concerned was BdU of crew exhaustion brought on by extensive underwater patrols that even in the death throes of the Third Reich permission was given to U-boat commanders to terminate their war patrol if they felt that the crew was operating beyond their psychological and physiological limitations. This sort of care and concern by BdU obviates the sort of post-war rhetoric that casts Dönitz and his U-boat men as fanatics. If that were the case, he would have ordered them to attack at any cost without any regard for their health or well-being.

Psychological Challenges

Coastal operations around the United Kingdom, and especially the English Channel, thrust U-boat crews into a world of continuous sounds that initially lasted weeks, then months. Earlier in the war a U-boat could not spend more than twenty-four hours submerged before it had to completely surface to refresh its oxygen and charge its batteries. During this process the crew was placed in shifts to conduct watches that allowed them to feel fresh air and see the world around them. If the surface weather was good, hatches were often opened to allow those below to experience the fresh breeze. When not actively engaged in a convoy battle, most of the crewmen were rotated up on deck to conduct routine drills and maintenance, further exposing them to direct sunlight and fresh air. In the deep blue of the mid-Atlantic, U-boat crews could dive deep below storms and often enjoy a serene submerged experience where the only sound they might hear was the call of distant whales or porpoises. During the inshore campaign initiated through the snorkel's introduction, all of this routine changed.

Deprived of their sense of sight, crews operated by sound alone. There was the constant pinging of ASDIC, assorted Allied noise-makers designed to thwart detection devices or acoustic homing torpedoes, the constant churn of the sea in the shallows, the drone of turning screws from vessels only metres overhead, and reverberating shockwaves of depth charges that bounced off the bottom.

During the first operational employment of snorkel-equipped U-boats, BdU requested short reports on crew health to be sent by wireless when possible, with longer reports to be filed in writing upon return to port. While operating in the Western Approaches of the English Channel at the end of June and early July 1944, Oberleutnant Heinz Sieder, the commander of U-984 (VIIC), sent a short wireless report of his experiences. Sieder noted his successful operation in shallow water thanks to the snorkel, but concluded somewhat ominously that 'perfect health essential, otherwise there are casualties on the way'.[11]

Among the first discomforts that the crew had to deal with was the stench. During periods of three-to-four week cruises in the northern latitude where daylight lasted for twenty hours, U-boats often dared not raise the snorkel for ventilation. Consequently, the atmosphere, which was always pretty foul, 'was further polluted by the stench of decaying waste food and other refuse'. Crews attempted to get creative by expelling waste through new air-pressure toilets (these were a new feature created for snorkel-U-boats), others tried to pack refuse into tins and dispose them at night through the 'Bold' discharge tube. Finally, in July one commander hit upon the idea of stowing all refuse, including packing cases, into a dedicated, empty torpedo tube and firing it every three or four days. Thus, the tube could no longer be used for its intended purpose, but the result was a success and this procedure, 'known as a Mullschoss (rubbish shot)', was adopted by most snorkel-equipped U-boats. 'Thereafter, when a boat returned to base, the first dockyard workmen to arrive onboard no longer recoiled from the open hatch.'[12]

Foul air was a nuisance, but oxygen was critical. Crews adopted new procedures to conserve oxygen on a snorkel boat. Ship cleaning, torpedo maintenance and meals were put off until the night when the snorkel was run. Crew members generally lay on their bunks most of the time, unless on watch. 'A few commanders even extinguished the lighting to discourage conversation and other oxygen-consuming activities.'[13]

Bottoming a U-boat became a favoured tactic when operating in the shallows. In fact, if a U-boat was low on its batteries or simply trying to conserve diesel, it was not unusual for U-boats to lay quietly on the bottom during the day only to rise to the surface at night for recharging and shifting operational areas. However necessary it was, there was a psychological impact on the crew. This was especially true in the areas of high Allied anti-submarine activity outside ports where the crew could hear constant ASDIC pings and surface vessels crossing back and forth above them, never knowing when a depth charge might be dropped on to their U-boat. It was common for U-boat crews to endure such conditions, without ventilation by snorkel, for as much as thirty hours, as in the case of *U-763* (VIIC) as recorded in its KTB on 6 July 1944 while south of the Isle of Wight.[14] As Hessler wrote after the war, 'Even the bravest – and one must grant that these pale-faced U-boat men were brave – could not fail, eventually, to become adversely affected by such conditions.[15] The psychological impact of extended underwater combat operations was compounded by physiological pressures.

Physiological Challenges

Crew health became such a critical factor in the successful operation of a snorkel-equipped U-boat that it was required to be reported by every vessel entering the English Channel once it reached a position west of Ireland. Once BdU received the acknowledgement that the crew's health was satisfactory, the U-boat was permitted to move south-east into the English Channel to conduct independent operations. This requirement was specifically driven by the impact of the underwater transit by snorkel from Norway, through the Faroe Islands passage.[16]

The concern over exhaustion continued through the rest of the war. For example, in September 1944 *U-1228* (IXC/40) broke off its search for the stricken *U-867* (IXC/40) and made for Froisfjord (Frafjord) along the Norwegian coast 'on account of exhausted state of crew'. BdU noted in their KTB that: 'Exhaustion was probably due to break down of snorkel.'[17]

The maintenance of crew health meant a management of oxygen under the constant threat of carbon dioxide, and even more problematic, carbon monoxide poisoning. Carbon monoxide remained a persistent threat, especially when a snorkel was damaged. Sixteen snorkel-equipped U-boats have been identified as sinking by unknown/unconfirmed causes. These are *U-180* (IXD1), *U-297* (VIIC/41), *U-396* (VIIC), *U-398* (VIIC), *U-650* (VIIC), *U-683* (VIIC), *U-743* (VIIC), *U-855* (IXC/40), *U-865* (IXC/40), *U-857* (IXC/40), *U-869* (IXC/40), *U-925* (VIIC), *U-984* (VIIC), *U-1055* (VIIC), *U-1200* (VIIC), and *U-1226* (IXC/40).[18] Many of the aforementioned U-boats reported snorkel problems and returned to base for repairs immediately after starting their patrol, including *U-396*, *U-865*, *U-857* and *U-1226*. It remains a distinct possibility that any of these U-boats might have met its demise by this silent killer. Hessler details how this might have occurred through the experience of *U-218* (VIID), which dealt with carbon monoxide poisoning during operations off Land's End on 20 June 1944:

> ... 0400. Bomb or depth charge concussion has apparently fractured a tappet lever on the port diesel. Starboard diesel started; but owing to insufficient exhaust pressure the safety valve lifts and the exhaust gases escape into the boat, filling all compartments and necessitating the wearing of escape apparatus.
>
> 0500. Surfaced to ventilate the boat.
>
> 0503. Naxos gives three separate warnings, amplitude 4 to 5. Dived to 80 metres.
>
> 1200. Several men suddenly taken ill during the forenoon. By noon two-thirds of the crew are suffering from severe headache and stomach ache, nausea and retching and are no longer fit for duty. The remainder, also complaining of bad headache, keeps things going. There are several cases of fainting through over-exertion and carbon monoxide poisoning.
>
> 1230. Rise to periscope depth in an attempt to ventilate with the port diesel.
>
> 1240. Port diesel starts, but exhaust pressure is too low to empty the snorkel mast. The safety valve lifts again, filling the boat with exhaust fumes, which cause further cases of poisoning.
>
> 1250. Electric compressor started in an attempt to draw out the fumes and replace them through the snorkel valve. The state of the crew continues to deteriorate.
>
> 1400. Surfaced to change the air in the boat. I cannot wait until dusk.
>
> 1406. Dived. The boat is thoroughly ventilated. By evening there is only a slight improvement in the state of the crew. Milk is issued to counteract the effects of the poisoning. Six men, in a state of collapse, given injections of lobelyn sympatol to stimulate heart action ... [19]

Carbon monoxide poisoning was indeed a silent killer. Many crews began to suffer from it long before the U-boat commander or anyone else realised what was happening. If quick action was not taken, a crew member might forget to turn a trim wheel or open a valve, causing their U-boat to slip into the depths and never rise again. In Mid-October BdU sent out Experience Message No. 177:

> 1) On multiple occasions, lack of crew experience while snorkelling has led to a build-up of smoke in the boat and a subsequent disablement of the crew members by CO gas. Some commanders report that cases of poisoning have not shown up until several hours after ventilation. The general weakness is then so pronounced that surfacing and opening the hatch are only possible

with great effort. The bridge crew was hardly in a position to continue on their feet. In one boat, these phenomena occurred again after a half-hour ventilation after build-up of smoke on the water.

2) Lessons: CO gas is odorless and tasteless. It does not lie in a layer on the bottom, like CO_2 gas. Ventilate over water one hour or more if possible. Later do some more ventilation for short periods, if possible over water always using diesel or electric compressors through the snorkel. Connect the ventilation over water:

a) If travelling with diesel, one diesel ventilation through the air intake plus air exhaust through the exhaust circuit.

b) If travelling with an electric engine, suck air out from the end rooms or push it in with the air intake. Running the exhaust and the air intake at the same time doesn't do anything.[20]

On 30 October, BdU again reiterated the warning of the dangers of carbon monoxide poisoning.[21]

When the snorkel head closed inadvertently while the diesel were running, pressure could drop by 400–500mb inside the U-boat within seconds – especially if the diesel blowers were turned on. The crew would experience immediate pain that could result in popped ear drums and bloody noses as best. Some of the immediate and lasting effects felt would be severe fatigue, rapid breathing or shortness of breath, nausea or vomiting, fast heart rate, headache, insufficient urine production, or respiratory distress syndrome.

The constant up and down pressure, as well as lack of sunlight and reduced oxygen, affected the crew in varying ways. BdU wanted to understand this impact and how best to mitigate any lasting effects so that a crew returning after a sixty- to seventy-day underwater patrol could be recuperated quickly and returned to duty.

A series of naval conferences were hosted by the German Institute of Submarine Hygiene on order of the Kriegsmarine to better understand the health impacts of long underwater cruises. A report by the Japanese Attaché in Berlin was intercepted by Ultra via Bletchley Park when it was wired to Tokyo. The report was based upon the interpreted review by Japanese Surgeon Lieutenant Commander Xubayashi. The Ultra intercept was further annotated by a British medical staff officer.

The report noted that long underwater cruises brought on a variety of symptoms and ailments. Constipation increased due to the mandatory reduction of sound that caused restriction on the use of toilet pumps. That meant crew could no longer count on regular bowel movements and had to wait for times that were appropriate due to tactical conditions. While this could be considered a minor impact, long underwater patrols also caused a reduction of red blood platelets that resulted in a lack of blood clotting. The report noted that:

> A temporary decline in the blood building process is marked among engine room personnel. Recovery follows return to port. Although the principle cause is high temperature and humidity, a subsidiary cause is the lack of vitamin C. Ultraviolet ray treatment is effective, and apart from carrying this out at base, it is to be installed in the submarines as well. As far as the submarine rations alone are concerned, tests for [vitamin C] in the blood have shown a deficiency.

Vibrations from the diesel engines caused a concern as it related to the partial paralysis of the knee joints in crewmembers who were stationed in the engine room. It was thought that the addition of rubber floor mats might reduce the stress, although it was noted that recovery soon followed a return to port. There was also the thought that the increase of carbonic acid gas acting concurrently with vibration might cause a change in the toxicity in the sympathetic nerves. The medical staff went so far as to place a subject in an experimental air chamber with 2.5 per cent to 3 per cent carbonic acid gas for five days. The results showed an absence of deep sleep in cerebral electrical tests, though a short period of deep sleep occurred just before dawn. Work performed in the chamber during the experiment resulted in many mistakes.

Concern was raised about the concentration of carbon monoxide gas in the U-boat and that further research was required. In order to counter the threat of this silent killer, BdU put a silicone gel used to purify and deodorise the air inside the U-boat known as 'Kieselgelaktivkohle'. This carbon-activated gel was combined 'with the ventilating system. Ozone is ineffective. To deodorise the sewage tank, 30 to 40 granules of "Auroramin" for every 100 litres are thrown in daily.'

Fatigue and strain were a long-standing concern, and made worse by extended underwater duty. Studies were made of how quickly a body could recover from the strains of patrol before a crewmen might be 100 per cent ready to return to sea, both physically and physiologically. It was noted that:

> Soporifics are unsuitable for the treatment of fatigue while at sea as they interfere with the carrying out of duties: a vegetable sedative Haldrian (valerian) is preferable. Caffeine and Pervitin are only used in exceptional cases. The internal use of 'Sepileln' consisting of sodium salts of various organic and inorganic acids produces 'Alkalosis' and seems to be effective in curing and preventing fatigue.

As noted by the British doctor reviewing the translation, 'Hypophyses V L Hormone ("Anteron" is best for exhaustion)'. It was recommended that after a return to port regular exercise, or sports, be pursued. An Alpine climate combined with ultraviolet ray treatment was thought to be an 'excellent' means of recovery. It was also recommended that while resting, smoking and other activities that might greatly stimulate the sympathetic nervous system should be avoided. 'The ideal is strict relaxation in a sanatorium for instance.'[22] U-boat crews, however, did not have the luxury of relaxing in an Alpine environment for a month in between each war patrol.

Chapter 8

Allied Countermeasures

The snorkel was treated as a 'secret' development by the Kriegsmarine when it was introduced. Allied intelligence certainly intercepted wireless traffic about its existence through Ultra intercepts. However, it appears that the best information came from captured German crewmen picked up after their U-boat was sunk or scuttled.

The British Admiralty's Naval Intelligence Division's C.B. 04051 (103) Interrogation of U-Boat Survivors, Cumulative Edition, June 1944 was the first known assessment of the German snorkel. The document revealed that the equipment as well as its basic technical schematics were known to the British at the very start of the Normandy invasion. While this document was descriptive, it did not contain any analysis of the snorkel's operational or tactical potential as U-boat tactics had not yet evolved. Consequently, the report did not assess any impacts to ongoing Royal Navy Escort or Support Group tactical responses during a U-boat hunt.[1]

This information acquired by British intelligence was accurate. It is clear that by June they had gained knowledge of the Type II non-flange mast as well as the replacement of the pulley system with a hydraulic piston lift. Both design improvements were starting to be fielded broadly across the U-boat fleet, as in the case of *U-480*, which received a second snorkel installation that summer, upgrading from the Type I to the Type II. The Admiralty report understood that the snorkel was intended for charging, but clearly did not opine the consequences of a non-existent U-boat profile on their detection gear, or the possibility that U-boats could remain submerged for almost their entire patrol. In November British forces that occupied the former German U-boat base at Salamis, Greece, found technical renderings of the Type II snorkel mast installation for Type VIICs, the first such technical documents of their kind obtained by Allied intelligence.[2]

Four months later, US Naval Intelligence observed the stark drop off of actionable intelligence, defined by immediate, readable Ultra intercepts or HF/DF map plots that allowed them to 'fix' a U-boat's location. The report noted the decrease in wireless transmissions and change in Enigma keys, as well as the atmospheric conditions that impacted reception in the North Atlantic. These observations prompted OP-20-G to publish a memorandum notifying US Naval leadership about the impact of these developments to anti-U-boat operations. What the report did not mention was the fact that a number of the intelligence impacts were caused by the introduction of the snorkel, suggesting that OP-20-G did not fully comprehend the correlation. A contributing factor to the lack of understanding was that most snorkel-fitted U-boats were being employed almost exclusively around the coastal regions of the British Isles and not in the convoy lanes of the North Atlantic.

A few statements of note in the 24 November 1944 report are of interest. 'The problem of fixing U-boats in the Atlantic has become more difficult and will probably continue so …' for the following reasons: 'Approximately 90% of the D/F cases have involved U-boat transmissions of the ration of 30 seconds or less. Such short transmissions make it difficult to obtain any large number of high quality bearings.'; 'the use of Norddeich Off Frequencies has become more general for all types of transmissions. It has been our experience that fewer bearings are obtained on all frequency transmissions of short or medium duration, thereby resulting in less accurate fixes'; 'U-boats have been maintaining a rigid condition of radio silence. We have noted U-boats on patrol in various areas in the North Atlantic for periods as long as 30 or 40 days without making a single radio transmission'; and 'ionospheric disturbances, in the North Atlantic in the winter have a detrimental effect upon D/F fixing'.

This resulted in the conclusion by OP-20-G that 'the accurate locating of U-boats by means of Ultra information has progressively become more and more difficult'.[3]

The OP-20-G memorandum balanced the fact that the dramatic reduction in reliable U-boat position signals was assessed as not impacting operations too significantly given the fact that few U-boats were operating in the mid-Atlantic. The report assumed that if traditional Wolfpack tactics were reinstituted in the spring of 1945 then a natural increase of signals would result in a resumption of accurate U-boat position information. Like the Admiralty report of June, this US Navy intelligence assessment failed to appreciate the paradigm shift introduced by the snorkel.

Overnight the snorkel rendered Allied radar detection almost ineffective and significantly reduced the value of Ultra in fixing U-boats for hunter-killer groups. Yet, a review of US and British intelligence reports revealed that it took both countries about six months to appreciate the snorkel's impact on their anti-U-boat operations and implement effective counter-measures.

This was revealed by Ladislas Farago, who served as the Chief of Research and Planning in the US Navy's Special Warfare Branch (OP-16-Z) during the Second World War. Writing after the war, he offered how unprepared the Western Allies were in the face of snorkel-equipped U-boats. The US Tenth Fleet was organised in May 1943 at the very height of the North Atlantic convoy battles as the first anti-submarine command. Its mission was to find, fix, and destroy German U-boats. To this end, its supporting missions included the protection of coastal merchant shipping, the central-isation of control and routing of convoys, and the co-ordination and super-vision of all US Navy anti-submarine warfare training, anti-submarine intelligence, and co-ordination with the Allied nations. The Tenth Fleet had no organic naval vessels. Its commander, Admiral Ernest King, used Commander-in-Chief Atlantic's (CINCLANT) vessels operationally, and CINCLANT issued operational orders to escort groups originating in the United States. The Tenth Fleet was also responsible for the organisation and operational control of hunter-killer groups in the Atlantic.

The Tenth Fleet was 'misled in its appreciation of the snorkel by reports that tended to emphasise the deficiencies of the device', according to Farago.[4] Interrogations of German U-boat prisoners early in 1944 who had participated in the first snorkel trials and training in the Baltic spoke despairingly of the device. At this time no U-boat had conducted an oper-ational cruise and not even the German U-boat command understood the device's full potential. OP-16-Z produced a number of intelligence broad-casts that disparaged the device through the Tenth Fleet. By the summer of 1944 the Tenth Fleet dismissed the snorkel as a viable technological solu-tion for the U-boat. This assessment changed by the late summer and early autumn of 1944 with the approach of *U-518* (IXC) off North Carolina in August, followed by others off Canada (see Chapter 9). *U-518* sank the SS *George Ade*, 100 miles from the US East Coast – the first American-flagged ship sunk by a snorkel-equipped U-boat. All Tenth Fleet efforts to hunt down this U-boat failed, leaving it concerned.[5]

The Allies had no tactics or technology to counter the new threat, which was the responsibility of the US Navy's Tenth Fleet. Farago noted in the early 1960s:

In a very real sense, then, the snorkel thus succeeded in doing exactly what Doenitz hoped it would accomplish: it provided effective protection from the U-boats' most dangerous foe, the planes of the escort carrier groups. The protection was so effective, indeed, that from September, 1944, through March, 1945, the escort carrier groups managed to sink but a single U-boat, and a non-snorkeller at that, although they accounted for forty-six U-boats during the prior sixteen months.[6]

The Allies devised a simple division of labour in terms of counter-U-boat operations from 1942 onward. The US Navy's hunter-killer groups were given the responsibility for the central Atlantic and US East Coast, while the British and Canadian air and surface forces were responsible for their respective coastal regions as well as the North Atlantic. This generally placed the burden of counter-U-boat operations on the US Navy from 1942 until early 1944, when U-boats were non-snorkel equipped and operated in Wolfpacks. Once the snorkel was introduced the burden of anti-U-boat operations shifted to the British and Canadian forces through to the end of the war. This included the development of new tactics. It is made clear in reviewing available primary documents that by the end of the war the British and Canadian Royal Navies appreciated the fact that they were fighting a very different U-boat foe, and adapted accordingly. The US Navy and US Coast Guard, however, did not have that same appreciation due to a lack of operational experience against snorkel-equipped U-boats.

Allied Air Operations
In order to destroy a U-boat, it had to be located. By the spring of 1944 location and destruction was predominately carried out by radar-equipped Allied aircraft. The British Air Ministry published ORS/CC Report Nr. 325 on 5 January 1945 titled *Operational Experience Against U-Boats Fitted with Snorkel*, which summarised the negative impact the snorkel had on Allied air operations against U-boats during the previous six months.[7] The report began: 'Throughout the past few months the German U-boat fleet have been fitted with a "Snorkel" pipe, about 16' in diameter and showing some 2–3 feet above the water, through which the air for the Diesels can be sucked in and the exhaust expelled. The consistent use of this device has very considerably reduced the efficiency of [aircraft] detection of U-boats – probably by a factor of about 10, and produced a return to close-in submarine warfare.'

Based on past operational results the following 'recommendations and statements of fact are considered to follow fairly definitely from the scanty data on operations:'

1. Snorkels are usually seen by their wake and 'smoke', this 'smoke' is however only produced on some occasions, much more frequent in winter.

Theoretical investigation in progress may enable this effect to be predicted. The average citing ranges are average 'smoke' 7 miles, (two cases of
20 miles!), wake 4½ miles, snorkel itself about 1 mile.

2. An improvement in efficiency of two- or three-fold could be obtained by
use of binoculars throughout.

3. Very little use has in fact been made of binoculars, even for recognition.

4. The operational range of detection on a ASV Mark V (4 miles) is about
one third of the operational range on surfaced boats (13 miles), but

5. Radar efficiency is very low and sees more than Force 3 – because of the
sea returns.

6. The proportion of snorkel U-boats seen snorkelling and subsequently
attacked while visible, or less than 15 seconds dived, amounts to 70% of
attacks.

7. Hence the depth charge setting for snorkels should be that proper to
'snorkel depth' itself.

8. The sighting range in Leigh-Lights* at night is so low (about 400 yards
media) that visual bombing holds out little hope. Radar bombing and or
homing weapons will be essential.

It was noted in the study that U-boats could clearly be identified through
the wakes left by the periscope or snorkel. In the last several months
snorkels could be identified seven times greater through the 'smoke' trail.
This 'smoke' was probably vapour caused by a snorkel riding too high out
of the water, exposing its exhaust vent. However, the British assessment
identified that the smoke, which was usually described as grey in colour,
was 'presumably largely water mist that became clearly visible and much
more frequent in cold weather'. The results up to November, according to
the assessment, 'show so low a proportion of 'smoking snorkels' (9 out of 22
= 40 per cent) that this phenomenon must be due to some special weather
conditions, more frequent in winter than summer'. It was made apparent by
the study that the British pilots were not utilising binoculars during their air
patrols and that a periscope or snorkel that was not smoking could be identified by binoculars at about 4.5-mile range, while the naked eye could only
identify it at a range of 1.9 miles. Despite this fact, the study stated that very
few periscopes or snorkels were in fact either first sighted or even recognised using binoculars. Even when air patrols used binoculars, they

---

* Leigh-Light refers to the 22-million candlepower, 24in searchlight mounted under RAF aircraft
designed by Squadron Leader H de V Leigh. This device, when used in conjunction with active
radar, allowed Coastal Command aircraft to identify surfaced U-boats at night and surprise them,
without alerting them in advance by dropping flares. This tactic worked well until the introduction of the snorkel.

assessed that periscopes were identified only 16 per cent of the time, while snorkels only 33 per cent. By binocular 'recognition' it was meant 'to identify the vague phenomenon: wakes, smoke, odd looking waves, etc. which are usually first seen'. The study also looked at the rate at which binoculars could identify a periscope or snorkel when radar contact had provided a rough bearing an exact range. It was determined that a binocular was used to confirm a radar bearing 19 per cent of the time. All this led to the conclusion that 'there is room for considerable improvement in the use of binoculars, both regular scanning by lookouts detailed for the purpose whenever the neck disability is more than 5 miles and for recognition of radar blips. The second point could be met by the second pilots always keeping a pair of binoculars ready focused.' What this assessment did not consider was the fact that U-boats predominately snorkelled at night as directed by BdU, limiting the effectiveness of visual identification even further.

A separate detailed analysis was conducted on daylight attacks against U-boats by aircraft during the period June to December 1944. This study focused on U-boats that submerged once they were attacked on the surface. The report was divided into attacks that occurred when a U-boat had been submerged for less than fifteen seconds, submerged between fifteen and sixty seconds, submerged more than sixty seconds, and were lost while the aircraft was manoeuvring to attack. The study found that whether the U-boat was identified operating with just a periscope or snorkel separately, or the U-boat was identified operating both simultaneously, it was impossible to obtain a kill once the vessel began to submerge. The kill rate per attack when the snorkel and/or periscope were still visible was only at 17 per cent. This was 50 per cent less than the 43 per cent kill rate for a completely surfaced U-boat. The study went on to state 'the number of snorkel sightings leading to targets visible, partly visible or dived less than 15 seconds (41% of sightings, 74% of attacks) is so high that the DC's against snorkels should have the depth setting proper to the boat actually snorkelling'. This data does support that the U-boat dipole mounted on the snorkel mast was effective in identifying attacking aircraft, giving U-boats the advantage of diving before an air attack commenced. A fifteen-second advantage was enough to gain survivability against an air attack regardless of how far out the aircraft identified the snorkelling U-boat. The realisation that snorkel 'smoke' was a marked advantage caused British Coastal Command to issue a memo that declared this study was only permitted to be circulated among those engaged in 'Air Anti-U-boat Warfare'. Not even the Royal Navy was notified of this observation in order to maintain strict secrecy over this operational advantage. Given that this memo was issued on 22 March 1945, at the end of winter, it probably contributed little to the anti-U-boat effort. However, it does show how seriously the snorkel altered the balance sheet against Allied aircraft.

One effective Allied aircraft tactic against snorkel-equipped U-boats introduced was the use of sonobuoys. U-boat commanders noted in their short reports to BdU that Allied aircraft dropped sonobuoys in areas where their snorkels were presumably seen to alert other aircraft or anti-submarine groups to the U-boat's diving points. All U-boats were warned of this tactic on 15 February by BdU, suggesting it was a recently employed tactic. There were two types of sonobuoys, one for listening and one for HF/DF.[8] The HF/DF buoy was less effective as snorkel-equipped U-boats rarely transmitted wireless signals. It was the direction-finding buoy that was used with effect during the last six months of the war against the snorkel-equipped U-boat.

Sonobuoys were originally intended to be dropped manually from blimps. Parachutes were added when the decision to deploy them from manoeuvring aircraft was made. They were equipped with a stored, self-erecting antenna. The first operational passive broadband sonobuoy was known as AN/CRT-1. The operational frequency of the AN/CRT-1 was 300Hz to 8kHz, which was within the audible range of the human ear. The operator had to make real-time decisions based on his ability to distinguish various underwater sounds. The problem was that in shallow water the operator had to contend with a host of other noises caused by waves, currents and density layers, making identification of a U-boat operating on electric motors or even drifting with engines off problematic. An improved version, the AN/CRT-1A, also known as the Expendable Radio Sonobuoy (ERSB), had an increased frequency band of 100Hz to 10 kHz and lighter weight (12.7lb).

The improved sonobuoy contained enough battery power for four hours of continuous operation. It was not until June 1944 that these new sonobuoys were being employed by US aircraft squadrons operating in the central Atlantic. It was not until the autumn of 1944 that a single British aircraft squadron received the device for employment.[9]

As an approximation, an aircraft equipped with eight sonobuoys could hold contact with a U-boat for sixty to ninety minutes, and if equipped with twelve, for as long as three hours.[10] This was ample time to vector in a surface hunter-killer group or squadron. The drawback was that calm water was required to achieve these contact times.

The British also took a careful look at operational and practice data recording radar returns against the snorkel.[11] The data the British collected was identified by their own intelligence analysts as 'scanty'. The S-Band equipment, while operational, could not be compared effectively with the X-Band, which was not yet operational. However, in looking at the MK.V Liberator it was noted that the operational range to identify a periscope or snorkel was 4.7 miles compared with the average of 12.9 miles by day or 14.3 miles by night for this specific equipment on surfaced U-boats. It was thought that the ratio of a third would appear promising until it was realised that this fact implied the majority of these contacts would appear inside the 'sea returns' and thus be almost impossible to recognise by sight. The study predicted that in a calm sea the MK.V Liberator had a ratio of 10:1 to identify the snorkel or periscope, while the MK.III Wellington's ratio was 6:1. In moderate seas the ratios were respectively 50:1 and 30:1. In rough seas it was considered next to impossible to make a radar contact. The conclusion was that the S-Band's operational range against snorkels 'appears to be about one-third of that on surfaced U-boats'. In addition 'detection of snorkel radar in seas of Force 3 or higher is much more difficult than in calmer seas'.

While the above data was based on daylight attacks, a sobering assessment of night-time attacks was also made. The study concluded: 'The sighting range of the snorkel at night is so low that the technique of attack hitherto used, i.e. radar contact – visual sighting – release of bombs by visual judgment – holds out little hope of success. It is suggested that either radar bomb sites or homing weapons or both are essential.' This observation is interesting when compared with the procedures outlined to German U-boats by BdU that snorkelling should be carried out at night. This meant that if proper guidance was followed then a snorkel-equipped U-boat's survivability against aerial identification and attack was very high. No calculations were made by the British in their report between snorkels camouflaged with anti-radar matting and those without. The process of covering snorkel masts with the Wesch anti-radar matting became commonplace in the autumn of 1944 and served to reduce the ability of Allied radar detection even further than already indicated in the above assessment.

The British knew the U-boats were there but were now unable to easily locate them or even effectively employ their aircraft and radar technology against them. The study noted that 'of the conclusions drawn some are practically certain; others are open to some doubt as based on small numbers. It is however, considered that, in view of the urgency of the snorkel problem, these probable conclusions should also be drawn.' Indeed, there was a snorkel problem. Six months into this problem the Western Allies were still struggling to identify probable countermeasures against an enemy that they thought was defeated in May 1943, but that had now returned with a vengeance.

Given the negative impact that the snorkel had on British air-based anti-submarine efforts, a series of meetings were convened starting on 22 November 1944 that were intended to address the issue. Meetings followed on 15 December, 19 January 1945, 29 January and 13 March to identify solutions to the troubling snorkel trend. These meetings were held in Room 71/II at Whitehall in the Air Ministry and were chaired by Sir Robert Renwick Bt, who looked for updates from Air Commodore H Leedham, CB, OBE, as the DCD (Director of Communications Development), and Dr A C B Lovell, as the TRE, on 'actions taken by the DCD and TRE (Telecommunications Research Establishment) to provide anti-Schnorkel measures …' In the first meeting in November it was stated that 'methods that could be introduced into existing equipment which it was anticipated would give some 20%–25% increase in the ratio of the snorkel responses as against those of sea returns'. In addition, Commodore Leedham believed that either X-Band or K-Band could be used but at least another month of experiments was required. It was confirmed in December that ongoing trials suggested that modifications to both the Wellington and Warwick systems would allow them to better pick up smaller targets. X-Band trials were still ongoing. It was also recommended that American detection systems be included in the testing programme.

In the 19 January meeting it was expressed that significant delays caused by wrongly specified equipment had prevented Coastal Command from equipping their aircraft with the new detection system modifications. K-Band was given the highest priority and X-Band results were promising. By 29 January, Coastal Command aircraft were finally receiving modifications to their radar sets that would allow for better detection of smaller targets. Interestingly, it was noted that the tests being performed off Llandudno, North Wales, in the Irish Sea against British submarine test targets had to stop due to the presence of actual U-boats in the testing area. The first X-Band-equipped Warwick Mk V aircraft were expected to be delivered in late March or early April.

The Air Ministry wanted to increase their chances of a successful attack against a snorkel-equipped U-boat by 20 per cent. Most of their recommendations, however, were not implemented until the spring of 1945. The US was not involved in these meetings, primarily as they were not directly engaged in the snorkel war to any great extent. British findings were to be made available to the US primarily because it was thought they would 'interest them'.[12]

BdU issued new guidance on 3 March 1945 to their U-boats based on changes introduced by British Coastal Command air patrols. Specifically, Message No. 226C reminded U-boats to maintain depth discipline when snorkelling and avoid being observed.[13] Seven days later, on 10 March 1945, a follow-on message was sent, followed by further guidance to maintain a low snorkel profile in calm surface conditions embodied in Message No. 228B.[14]

What BdU did not calculate was that with the coming of spring, North Atlantic storms gave way to calmer water, as noted by the reference in Message No. 228B of a sea state 1. This increased the potential of a U-boat's identification through a raised snorkel or periscope by Allied radar or visual recognition.

Allied Surface Operations

From the start of the war until mid-1944 BdU did not believe that U-boats could patrol effectively along an enemy's coast. This self-imposed operational limitation was due to the belief that Allied aircraft combined with the critical limiting factor of a U-boat's requirement that it had to surface in order to recharge its batteries simply prevented extended coastal operations.[15] Just prior to the Allied invasion of Normandy the Admiralty conducted an assessment of the potential for U-boats to operate in the shallows, titled 'Inshore Operations by U-boats', where they concluded that once a U-boat conducted an attack in the shallows it would immediately proceed to deeper water in order to withdraw. The idea that a U-boat would 'bottom' at the scene of the attack, or move closer inshore, was 'considered unlikely' by the Admiralty.[16] This view changed before the end of the war.

The Royal Navy's 'support group' was the corollary to the US Navy's 'hunter-killer group'. The number of support groups in the North Atlantic grew to seventeen Royal Navy and seven Royal Canadian Navy by November 1944, the predominant number being assigned to the critical area of the United Kingdom's coast.[17] Despite the advantage held by the Allies in the number of anti-submarine surface vessels operating in familiar home waters equipped with state-of-the-art search gear, they found that hunting a snorkel-equipped U-boat in the shallows was difficult.

The first Allied experience against a snorkel-equipped U-boat in coastal waters occurred in the English Channel in the days immediately following the Normandy invasion. One particularly graphic account is provided by Lieutenant Commander Allan Easton (Distinguished Service Cross recipient), who commanded the destroyer HMCS *Saskatchewan* at the time. Operation *Neptune* was the code name for the Allied protection of the invasion area from U-boats operating in the English Channel. HMCS *Saskatchewan* was operating as part of 12th Escort Group in that operation. On 7 June, one day after the Normandy invasion, Easton's ship was on escort duty accompanying four other vessels when a 'low rumble was heard, the unmistakable sound of an underwater explosion' at around 8pm. No one knew exactly what it was. The flag went up from the other escort communicating that it was searching for a contact it made via ASDIC. 'Action stations' was now called onboard HMCS *Saskatchewan*. A search began and a salvo of hedgehogs was fired that exploded without hitting any target. Three destroyers were now searching for the original contact with active ASDIC. The ASDIC officer onboard Easton's destroyer, Sub-Lieutenant Coyne, noted ominously that: 'I think the Channel is not going to be an easy place to locate submarines.' He elaborated on his statement to Easton: 'In the few days we've been in these waters, the H.S.D. [Higher Submarine Detector] and I have been watching the sound effects and so on of the ASDIC and they're very confusing. Fish appear to be very plentiful. The tides may have something to do with it. To my mind the outlook isn't particularly bright.' He concluded his observation, while observing four destroyers now searching for a U-boat, that: 'It's not like the clear water of the mid-Atlantic, sir. There's the place for good ASDIC condition!' At that very moment an explosion was heard, immediately followed by a column of water that shot up into the air a mere 100 yards abaft Eaton's destroyer.[18]

As Easton observed the area of the explosion there were no track marks left by a typical torpedo's stream of bubbles in the water. He correctly concluded that a defective electric-drive acoustic torpedo had self-detonated just four seconds before hitting their stern. As was the custom in a U-boat hunt, the destroyer's loudspeaker was switched on as it was connected to an ultra-short range telephone on the bridge. It was assumed that the acoustic torpedoes had a short range so everyone was alert searching the immediate area. Eight minutes after the first explosion a report came over the loudspeaker from one of the other destroyers: 'Torpedo just passed down starboard side running very shallow leaving slight swirl behind it. Heard on hydrophones. No explosion.' The ASDIC operator on a nearby destroyer picked up multiple contacts, then almost immediately dismissed them as fish. The same false signals were heard by Easton's ASDIC operator. Then a third destroyer picked up something slightly different and turned slowly to starboard to investigate when the slender pipe of a periscope broke the surface, just abaft to starboard.

The periscope was indeed from a U-boat operating within 20m of the surface among four searching destroyers. Seeing the destroyers, the U-boat retracted its periscope and began evasive manoeuvres that quickly broke contact. Twenty minutes later a hydrophone operator noted that he distinctly heard blowing tanks. HMCS *Saskatchewan* quickly turned and gave chase, letting loose a salvo of depth charges, but they did not hit the mark. After the first detected torpedo the crew had dropped a trailing noise maker into the water that was designed to detonate acoustic torpedoes. It was a good thing, because no sooner had the depth charge explosions stopped echoing over the hydrophones than another explosion abaft of Easton's destroyer was heard, accompanied by a column of water 100ft high. Another acoustic torpedo had been detonated by the noise maker.[19]

The U-boat Eaton encountered was *U-984* (VIIC), which reported firing two T5 torpedoes and a LUT acoustic homing torpedo at a group of three destroyers on that day. Oberleutnant Heinz Sieder claimed 'one missed, one detonated too soon, one probable hit after 7 minutes'.[20] On both attacks against HMCS *Saskatchewan* Sieder set the running depth of the T5s at 4m. Both were launched at periscope depth. After the third torpedo, Sieder ordered the U-boat to bottom in order to reload the tubes. He believed that an hour later he was accurately located on the bottom by two destroyers that bracketed him with depth charges. While the destroyers had detected an ASDIC return they did not know it was *U-984*. The lights flickered onboard the U-boat and sea water began to leak into the bow compartment, but the boat withstood the concussions.

U-984 remained bottomed until the afternoon of the 8th as the destroyers criss-crossed the area. Sieder knew the destroyers were utilising a well-drilled tactic to starve the U-boat of oxygen and battery power in order to force it to the surface, where it was vulnerable. However, *U-984* was a snorkel-equipped U-boat. At noon, Sieder decided to lift off from the bottom and move closer to shore, to the area of Ushant, France, where he planned to snorkel to recharge batteries and refresh oxygen. He noted in his KTB that 'the air condition was exceptionally bad in the last 12 hours. The men literally gasped for air. A certain amount of relief was provided by breathing with potash cartridges. (Mouthpiece of the escape lung connected).'[21] By 9pm *U-984* was snorkelling close to the coast. Sieder then decided to return to Brest, where he could recharge the batteries in a long snorkelling run, instead of the two it would require in the operational area.

U-984 returned to Brest on the 10th and after some minor repairs went back out to the operational area two days later. Sieder's second foray into the English Channel was an extraordinary example of the snorkel's new ability. He penetrated the Allied defensive screen and reached the invasion area off the Cotentin Peninsula. In the five days from 25 to 29 June he sank a British frigate, HMS *Goodson*, and subsequently sank three vessels and damaged one off the invasion beaches of Omaha and Utah. The Allied vessels were from Convoy ECM-17 and carried military equipment and troops for the invasion. His total tonnage for this patrol was 30,090 GRT. BdU noted in Sieder's KTB after it was turned in: 'Exemplarily executed enterprise carried out with high attack spirit. The Commander carried himself on 7.6 and 25.6

with iron calmness and toughness towards the destroyer and took advantage of every opportunity for attack. The attack on the convoy on 29.6 was a tactical masterpiece with magnificent success. The experiences of the boat are valuable.'[22] Sieder was awarded the Knight's Cross on 8 July 1944 for his patrol.

Back on the surface, the rest of the night and following day were quiet. Then at around 7.30pm on the 8th a deep underwater explosion was heard and the previous night's attack and counter-attack with a U-boat was repeated. Torpedoes were fired, missed their target or prematurely exploded, followed by ASDIC contacts, depth charges, and in Easton's words, 'dead or unconscious cod rising to the surface.'[23] This U-boat, if it was an actual U-boat, was not *U-984* as Sieder had already departed the area. If the encounter had occurred in the mid-Atlantic in 1943 the U-boat would have probably been destroyed in short order as clear ASDIC returns would have been acquired. Here in the shallows, four destroyers could not zero in on a U-boat due to the benefits gained from the rocky bottom, thermoclines and current.

The next afternoon Easton's squadron fell in with six British destroyers that formed a line of ten abreast that began to search for U-boats. This was a formidable defensive line at the western end of the English Channel. The weather was overcast, with a rain squall, though visibility was still good at 3 miles. At some time after 5pm a puff of smoke was seen in the distance. Two destroyers began to turn towards the smoke, with one opening fire from its deck gun. Easton recalled:

> On that instant I knew exactly what she was firing at. I altered course towards the smoke and rang for twenty-five knots as I saw our neighbour turning, too. A minute later the smoke had disappeared and nothing whatever was to be seen. What we had observed was a new German invention in operation, an invention with which we were acquainted but not familiar. It was the snorkel …'[24]

Easton and his fellow commanders were briefed on the German secret invention before the invasion. He recalled that in his briefing it was noted that the snorkel was to allow U-boats to operate in British coastal waters by allowing it to recharge batteries without surfacing. The report went so far as to note that it was equipped with a radar antenna on the snorkel head that would allow it to identify aircraft and surface ships. However, Easton noted: 'It did not occur to us that a [snorkel] would smoke.'[25] This fact was kept as an Allied secret, as previously noted. Not surprisingly, the U-boat evaded all ten destroyers.

Improved detection of a snorkel-equipped U-boat was the Allies' first priority. The snorkel evolved U-boat tactics to a degree that traditional detection techniques were rendered nearly irrelevant overnight. Usual detection sources such as the HF/DF of wireless signals, surface radar returns, or visual sightings of a surfaced U-boat could not be relied upon. ASDIC was only effective at short range and when used in shallow coastal water could not effectively discern rock from wreck from U-boat. During the convoy battles of previous years ASDIC had proved effective in maintaining contact with a U-boat after an initial detection, often from a visual source such as a surface vessel or aircraft that subsequently vectored in an escort vessel. From mid-1941 until mid-1943 most U-boats were initially detected through radar or visual identification on the surface, not by a chance ASDIC contact.[26]

As BdU shifted focus from open-ocean convoys to specific coastal embarkation/debarkation routes, so did the support groups. Support groups were assigned coastal patrol areas with the intent that they learned all the sub-surface ASDIC signature returns given off by the shallow sea floor and various wrecks. This was believed to be a critical factor in the future success of hunting U-boats as the knowledge gained of the bottom conditions made the difference in distinguishing a U-boat sonar signature from a known sub-surface anomaly.

In August the Admiralty conducted a preliminary analysis of the problem that continued to hold true for the remainder of the war. Through the use of Ultra intercepts, analysis showed that search groups had probably passed over U-boats ten times, but made only one contact. The U-boat on the other hand, had detected 65 per cent of the escorts that passed within 3 miles of them by using their own hydrophones. At this range a U-boat had an excellent chance of slipping through the search screen or manoeuvring around their flank.[27] Captain R Winn came to the judgement at the end of August that a U-boat was able to remain 'submerged for up to ten days without presenting any target detectable by radar or visually except at short range'.[28]

U-boats operated with two main weaknesses prior to the introduction of the snorkel. First, a U-boat could not remain submerged for more than twenty-four hours without surfacing completely to recharge its batteries. Second, when operating in the deep open ocean of the North and Central Atlantic, a U-boat's sonar signal was often clear and distinct. Allied escort vessel tactics prior to the introduction of the snorkel were to leverage these two weaknesses in a 'hunt to exhaustion' whereby the U-boat, once identified through ASDIC, would be pursued until it was compelled to the surface after a loss of electric power caused by drained batteries. Once on the surface, the U-boat could be destroyed by surface gun fire or ramming. This tactic worked only when a U-boat was identified by ASDIC and contact maintained. In the shallows, density layers, thermoclines, currents, rocky bottoms, other wrecks as well as the tactic of bottoming for long periods, significantly diminished the effectiveness of ASDIC. Additionally, a U-boat only had to raise its snorkel mast just a few metres above the surface to recharge its batteries or suck in fresh air required for it to run full diesels and escape at high speed, thereby presenting the Allies with a very difficult target. Allied tactics had to change.

In September 1944, after four months of hunting U-boats in the English Channel, the Admiralty changed their conclusion on U-boat tactics. They now put out guidance that when a ship was torpedoed in waters where a U-boat could bottom effectively, that it would do so if immediate anti-submarine attacks occurred.[29] They began to realise that a U-boat no longer attempted to run for deep water; its best defence was to hide in the shallows. By October 1944 the Admiralty issued new guidance:

> U-boats can now operate inshore and are likely to adopt static tactics in place of the mobile tactics which we have been used to dealing with. Static tactics involve the use of curly and gnat torpedoes fired from U-boats which endeavour to lie in wait on the course of convoys. When no targets are available U-boats are likely to move with great caution and charge by snort [i.e. snorkel] mainly by night. On approach of a hunting force [the U-boat] will probably bottom or may drift with tide near bottom.[30]

In addition to ASDIC, another source of submerged U-boat identification was through the sound emitted from inside the vessel. The Admiralty was interested in learning if there were ways to improve U-boat identification through hydrophones. The Admiralty Research Laboratory in Teddington, Middlesex, published a classified study on 22 February 1945 titled *Supplement to the Detection of Schnorkel by Hydrophone*. This was part of a series of reports designed to show the 'probability of recognition of Schnorkel over a yearly cycle on various hydrophone systems'. As a baseline the probability model was based on a snorkel-equipped U-boat charging its batteries at a regular snorkel depth cruising at 2–3 knots. A subsequent report considered propeller noise in the calculus among other operational conditions, as well as practical results from test trials being carried out. What is interesting is how limited the report was given that it was nearly one year since the first snorkel-equipped U-boat became operational. The analysis factored in the rule that pressure is inversely proportional to distance, as well as the impact of temperature gradients based on the report

'Sound Beam Patterns in Sea Water' issued by the Woods Hole Oceanographic Institute, Massachusetts, on 10 October 1944. This latter point is interesting as it shows how little the Admiralty understood the impact of temperature gradients, especially now that the U-boats had moved back to operating inshore.

The study looked at all hydrophone and sonar systems across the spectrum of distances. It was based on depths of 150ft and 900ft, with the former having a bottom reflection coefficient of .3 and the latter being evaluated with a bottom reflection coefficient of both .3 and .7. All probabilities were modelled across sea states 1–4. Looking at a sea state 2, in 150ft of water with a bottom reflection coefficient of .7, we see that in order to have a 60 per cent chance of picking up a snorkelling U-boat that is charging its batteries, a 50ft vertical rod hydrophone has the best chance at 14,000 yards, followed by 15ft ASDIC at 10kc/s being 6,000 yards, 15ft ASDIC at 20kc/s being approx. 4,200 yards, a non-directional hydrophone suspended from a sonobuoy being 3,900 yards, and finally a non-directional hydrophone suspended from a ship being less than 2,000 yards. A calm sea would give greater distances, while a sea state 4 would reduce them significantly. These averages were compounded in shallow water by the extensive noises heard from a wide range of other vessels and differing gradients. The study was based on British submarine diesel noise trials. The results were not promising and confirmed the difficulty of submerged U-boat detection in coastal waters, already well known by support group commanders.

In addition to the use of technology, new search patterns were adopted by the search groups designed specifically to find a bottomed U-boat. These patterns were 'Scabbard' and 'Artichoke'. Both made the assumption that a U-boat would in fact bottom near the torpedoed vessel, bow pointed in the direction of tide. The search patterns were designed to improve the chances of ASDIC detection by hopefully encountering the bottomed U-boat abeam.[31] However, it is not clear if these patterns were routinely employed in practice as the tactical conditions of a U-boat encounter were often highly varied.

While the British wrestled with U-boat detection in coastal waters they also introduced a series of defensive measures designed to blind and confuse U-boats, which now operated almost exclusively in an underwater world of sound. Code-named 'Foxer', this noise maker was towed behind an Allied ship and was originally intended to confuse the German G7 acoustic homing torpedoes introduced in 1943–44. These were turned into buoys in the autumn of 1944 and employed in a static fashion around harbours and close-in waterways where Allied vessels manoeuvred to blind U-boats operating in these areas. BdU issued guidance regarding this Allied tactic to all U-boats on 3 January 1945:

> It has been determined that the enemy has noise-producing buoys which reproduce the noise of a buzz saw. Apparent purpose: (1) Attempt to deflect Zaunkönig (2) Blocking our hydrophones. Details on the buoy not yet known. The following observations are important and are to be reported: (1) Appearance of buoy, if it can be determined by chance observation through periscope. (2) Length of the towing connection. (3) Does the buzz saw noise also occur in noise-producing buoys? (4) Is the noise produced by the movement of the current or by a special mechanism?[32]

It was clear that BdU did not completely understand the buoy's tactical use. This tactic was employed some six months after the introduction of the snorkel and the inshore campaign, highlighting how long it was taking the Allies to adapt to the new U-boat tactics.

A post-war analysis of the inshore campaign revealed the Allied struggle with locating and destroying U-boats. In the period from July to mid-September 1944 twenty-six ships were torpedoed. During that time only three U-boats were found and located immediately by Allied support groups after a torpedoing. From the period mid-September to December 1944, where U-boats were completing their evacuation to Norwegian bases and snorkel retrofittings were being completed on the existing operational boats, the number of U-boat patrols against the British Isles decreased. However, three Allied ships were sunk with no U-boats located after the attacks. From mid-December 1944 until February 1945, twenty-three Allied ships were torpedoed with only three U-boats sunk immediately after the reported attack. This period of the inshore campaign proved the most effective for snorkel-equipped U-boats and the most concerning for the Allies. The final period was from mid-February until May, 1945. This period saw a marked increase in operational U-boats sent against the British Isles, which resulted in thirty-five Allied ships torpedoed and eight U-boats identified and sunk shortly after the attack. This suggested that Allied tactical improvements were proving effective, though the number of operational U-boats deployed also increased at the same time. During these four periods the number of U-boats sunk by aircraft proved dismal, with only one each for the first three periods and six in the fourth.

There were other U-boats sunk around the British Isles during these four periods of analysis, however, they were identified by chance. In the first period there were eight sunk, followed by two, one and twelve. These numbers reflected a combination of contributing factors that ranged from some

DEC. 23, 1944   THE ILLUSTRATED LONDON NEWS   719

THE NEW "LUNGS" OF THE U-BOAT: THE SCHNORKEL BREATHING SYSTEM.

DRAWN BY OUR SPECIAL ARTIST, G. H. DAVIS.

THE EXHAUST AND FRESH-AIR "PERISCOPE" WHICH ENABLES U-BOATS TO REMAIN UNDER WATER FOR LONG PERIODS.

In a joint statement on U-boat warfare, issued by President Roosevelt and Mr. Churchill on December 9, reference was made for the first time to a new device which enabled enemy submarines to remain submerged for long periods and to penetrate into areas denied them for three years; and on December 14, Mr. A. V. Alexander, First Lord of the Admiralty, added a warning that U-boats might still make heavy attacks. The new device, necessitated by our ceaseless anti-U-boat campaign, which has made it almost suicidal for a German submarine to surface either by day or night, is known in Germany as the Schnorkel Spirall, and in the Royal Navy by the terse sobriquet of the "Snort." Its purpose is the essential taking-in of fresh air, (1) to replace that which becomes foul in a submarine after a period of immersion; (2) to replenish the compressed air used for blowing the ballast tanks; and (3) to recharge the batteries which drive the electric motors used for under-water cruising. The "Snort," which might be described as a Diesel "periscope," consists of a streamlined tube which, when raised from its deck stowage recess, is nearly as high as the periscope proper, and which contains pipes for drawing in fresh air and carrying away the exhaust of the Diesel surface motors working with the U-boat submerged. On the appearance of an enemy, the "Snort" can be lowered, the Diesels stopped, and the electric motors used to put the U-boat into a dive. The Germans claim that the new device enables a submarine to stay under water for 20-30 days.

The Illustrated London News, 23 December 1944. Prime Minister Winston Churchill and President Franklin D Roosevelt jointly announced to the public on 9 December that German U-boats were now equipped with a device that allowed them to remain submerged. Five days later First Lord of the Admiralty A V Alexander followed up with a public warning that with the appearance of this new device heavy losses should be expected by the public. The day after this illustration was published the snorkel and Alberich-equipped *U-486* (VIIC) sunk the SS *Leopoldville* outside Cherbourg Harbour despite it having a Royal Navy escort, causing a significant loss of life among the US 66th Infantry Division being sent as reinforcements to the Western Front. *(Author's collection)*

Wartime image of a ball float snorkel head and attack scope of a U-boat above the waves. Very little of the snorkel mast was exposed above water if a crew maintained good underwater trim. This made the U-boat an exceptionally difficult target for Allied anti-submarine efforts. *(Author's collection)*

A U-boat snorkelling as seen from 200ft by a Royal Airforce Coastal Command aircraft on 29 April 1945 in the Irish Sea, between Dublin and Holyhead. This U-boat was *U-825* (VIIC) under the command of Oblt.s.Z Gerhard Stoelker on its second patrol into the Irish Sea. He was attacked no fewer than three times by an aircraft while snorkelling. The chance that a snorkel-equipped U-boat could be destroyed by an aircraft was less than 10 per cent. *(ADM 334, Public Records Office)*

U-boats transiting British waters without a snorkel in July–September on their return to Norway to a large increase of U-boats sent on patrol at the end of the war.

The Admiralty understood that the chance encounter provided the best opportunity to locate and sink a U-boat. This is revealed by the fact that out of thirty-seven U-boats sunk during the inshore campaign by surface vessels, only eleven were destroyed by surface ships escorting or supporting a convoy, while the other twenty-six were targeted by patrolling support groups.[33] Most U-boats sunk in the inshore campaign were encountered en

This unique camera footage shows an aerial attack on *U-825* on 29 April by depth charge at 8.14pm and twice on 30 April, the first being at 11.35am and the second at 7.50pm. *U-825* suffered no damage from the attacks and surrendered at Portland on 10 May as per Dönitz's orders. *(ADM 334, Public Records Office)*

route to their patrol areas.[34] Put another way, by April 1945 U-boats that reached the British coast found themselves in a very effective position. The Admiralty assessed that their escorts only had an 8 per cent chance of detecting a U-boat as it approached a convoy in coastal waters.[35] The key was interdicting the U-boat before it reached the coast.

Acoustic Camouflage

The Admiralty did take note of the use of rubber coating of U-boats during the war. Survivors of *U-485* were interrogated about this technology. The Royal Navy interrogator noted that the: 'Rubber covering was against our

ASDIC. His was one of the first boats to be so fitted, and he personally had had insufficient experience to be able to assess its value.'[36]

In the autumn of 1944 the Admiralty took serious note of the development. In a report dated 21 November 1944, it reviewed the possibilities of what the rubber was used for and concluded: 'In general, it is considered that there is a possibility of reducing echo strength from a submarine by protective coatings, and that any development along these lines must be carefully watched.'[37]

The November assessment was indeed correct that developments had to be 'watched' as Alberich reduced the ASDIC effectiveness and gave U-boats a marked advantage when operating in coastal waters.

Strategic Countermeasures

Air raids were employed as a strategic countermeasure to U-boats. Starting in the spring of 1943 and lasting through to the end of the war, Allied air raids hit German shipyards and production centres. The result was that most shipyards experienced work stoppages of three to four weeks that delayed the VIIC construction and operational readiness of existing boats. In the last twelve months of the war air attacks reportedly contributed to preventing some 150 Type XXIs from being built. Diesel production was hit hard when a raid on the factory in Augsburg delayed work for nearly four weeks in June 1944. Battery production at Hagen and Hanover was paralysed by air attacks, causing a scarcity in them after February 1945. It was determined that due to this shortage, only half of the ordinary number of batteries required for the Type XXIs would be installed after December.[38] Despite the strategic bombing campaign, more U-boats were at sea or operationally ready in May 1945 than at any point during the war.

Chapter 9

The American Coast,
May 1944–May 1945

The fact that German U-boats patrolled off the North American coast, and specifically the US East Coast, is not well known unless you are a generational resident of one of the coastal communities that dot the mid-Atlantic region or a sports diver who frequents the North East or North Carolina's Outer Banks. The North American coast became a prime hunting ground when the German U-boat operation known as *Paukenschlag* (Drumbeat) was initiated after Hitler's declaration of war against the United States. During the six-month period January–July 1942 U-boats cruised along the coast with near impunity, sinking Allied vessels. The U-boats' prime target was oil tankers making their way northward from the Gulf of Mexico. Due to the news blackout enforced by President Roosevelt's administration, the devastation wrought during the 'Tanker War' has never become part of the broader cultural memory of the United States. Arguably, the Outer Banks of North Carolina might be the exception as most of the torpedoed vessels were attacked there.

Most Canadians and Americans today, when informed that German U-boats cruised within eyesight of the North American coast or into the St Lawrence River, often respond with a 'I never knew they came that close' statement. True as that may be, there are several popular histories that cover that period. The three main works are Michael L Hadley's 1985 *U-Boats against Canada*, Homer H Hickam Jr's 1980 *Torpedo Junction* and Michael Gannon's *Operation Drumbeat*. However, only Hadley's work discusses U-boat operations off Canada until the end of the war, touching upon the final offensive during the period of 'Total Undersea War'. A more recent addition to this canon, Roger Sarty's *The History of Canada: War in the*

St Lawrence, provides an updated account of the U-boat war in the confines of Canada's main shipping channel.

While the operational goals and impacts of the 1942 U-boat offensive off the North American coast have been well documented, aspects of the latter war years have not. Less well-known is the fact that U-boats all but withdrew from North American waters over the course of the next two years due to the maturity of Allied anti-submarine defences, only to return equipped with snorkels to the St Lawrence River for the first time in more than two years in 1944 and cruise within eyesight of the US East Coast in 1945 in greater numbers than any time since 1942.

The appearance of snorkel-equipped U-boats off the North American coast has gone without any comprehensive historical treatment to date. During the last months of the war, U-boats patrolled and attacked Allied vessels within eyesight of the coast as the Western Allies reached the Elbe River in central Germany and the Soviets were fighting in the streets of Berlin. This chapter, like Chapter 6, will place the final U-boat operations against the North American coast in context through a review of the available BdU orders, Allied Intelligence summaries derived by Ultra intercepts, interrogation reports and individual U-boat KTBs. Every snorkel-equipped U-boat that deployed against North America from May 1944 until May 1945 is discussed below.

Operation *Paukenschlag* ended on the order of the BdU in July 1942 after an intense six-month period of U-boat operations. More than sixty individual U-boats participated in the operation and many conducted multiple patrols, which resulted in 251 Allied vessels sunk and thirty-four damaged off the North American coast.[1] There were as many as ten U-boats operating along the coast in any given month during this period. Most of these patrols were conducted by smaller Type VIICs operating from the Bay of Biscay ports in France. When BdU concluded the operation it established a policy of sending U-boats in singles or pairs to operate along the North American coast each month to tie down Allied anti-submarine assets and attack straggler merchant vessels. The focus of the U-boat war was now the convoy routes in the north and mid-Atlantic.

A survey of non-snorkel U-boat operations off the North American coast between August 1942 and May 1944 shows the low operational tempo maintained by BdU. During the twenty-one-month period between August 1942 and May 1944 a total of thirty-one non-snorkel-equipped U-boats were sent to patrol off the North American coast. From a statistical perspective that was an average of 1½ per month, noting that there were eight months without a single U-boat patrol along the North American coast. With some exceptions for mine-laying operations, these patrols rarely moved within eyesight of the coast. In fact, U-boats approaching the North American coast after 1942 did not enter the Gulf of St Lawrence (after September 1942) or come close to the US East Coast, staying primarily beyond the 200m line that marked the continental shelf.

Non-Snorkel U-boat Patrols sent to the North American Coast post-Operation *Paukenschlag*

Month Year	U-boats off Canada/US	Month Year	U-boats off Canada/US	Month Year	U-boats off Canada/US
AUG 42	3/2	MAR 43	0/2	OCT 43	0/2
SEP 42	4/0	APR 43	1/1	NOV 43	0/0
OCT 42	0/1	MAY 43	0/2	DEC 43	0/0
NOV 42	0/0	JUN 43	0/0	JAN 44	3/0
DEC 42	0/0	JUL 43	0/2	FEB 44	1/3
JAN 43	0/0	AUG 43	1/0	MAR 44	0/0
FEB 43	0/0	SEP 43	1/0	APR 44	1/0
				MAY 44	1/0
				Total	16/15 (31)

All non-snorkel-equipped U-boats that operated off the North American coast during this period were Type IXs except for five Type VIICs and one Type XB. Two of these Type VIICs were minelayers that quickly returned to port (*U-566* and *U-230*, deployed July 1943). The one Type XB minelayer (*U-233*, deployed May 1944,) was sunk south-east of Halifax on 5 July 1944. Of the remaining twenty-eight U-boats, fifteen patrolled Canadian waters, while thirteen patrolled a variety of locations along the US East Coast. The last non-snorkel U-boats to enter the St Lawrence River were dispatched in August and September of 1942 and included *U-165*, *U-513*, *U-69*, *U-106* and *U-43*. From the second half of 1942 until the beginning of 1943 there was little activity off the North American coast. Out of the thirty-one U-boats that deployed there, eight were destroyed during their patrol. Three were sunk by air and five were sunk by surface attack. Two of the three sunk by air attack were in the Bay of Biscay returning from a successful patrol off the North American coast. The loss ratio for patrols off the coast during this period was 19 per cent (six of thirty-one). No more than one patrol was made by any U-boat off the North American coast during this period. The patrols were well spaced and at no point were there more than two U-boats in any given operational area. This level of inactivity was a significant drop from the first half of 1942. Allied vessels and anti-submarine assets transiting and operating along the US East Coast could be forgiven for falling into a sense of complacency during this period.

During the last eleven months of the war, from May 1944 until April 1945, a total of thirty-seven snorkel-equipped U-boats deployed off the North American coast. This more than doubled the monthly post-*Paukenschlag* non-snorkel-equipped U-boat average to 3.3 per month with thirteen deployed to Canadian waters and twenty-four to the US East Coast (to include *Gruppe Seewolf*).

Snorkel U-boat Patrols sent against North America

Month Year	U-boats off Canada/US	Month Year	U-boats off Canada/US
MAY 44	1/0	DEC 44	0/2
JUN 44	0/1	JAN 45	0/0
JUL 44	2/1	FEB 45	2/3
AUG 44	3/0	MAR 45	0/9
SEP 44	1/1	APR 45	0/6
OCT 44	3/1	Total	13/24 (37)
NOV 44	1/0		

All snorkel-equipped U-boats that deployed during this period were Type IXs except one XB that was redirected in the last weeks of the war. Unlike the non-snorkel-equipped U-boat patrols of prior years, these were conducted with extended underwater periods. The patrol length against North America was often more than double those against the United Kingdom in terms of days at sea. While U-boat patrols against the United Kingdom's eastern coast might last twenty to thirty days, and the western coast (to include the Channel and Irish Sea) fifty to sixty days, the patrols against North America could last ninety to 120 days.

U-boats took a well-travelled route from Norway to North American waters that proceeded south of Iceland through the Faroe Islands, passing over the underwater British minefield known as the 'Rosengarten'.[2] Their patrol started out submerged as British Coastal Command aircraft were active in the area. Once a U-boat passed Iceland they often cruised surfaced towards the Flemish Cap in order to make up time. Once they neared the Flemish Cap or a longitude equivalent, they submerged, often for fifty or more straight days. They used the 200m line as an underwater navigation aid, following it south-west until they reached a latitude that matched their specific deployment area. Then the U-boat typically headed due west towards the coast. Like their VIIC counterparts patrolling against Great Britain's coast at this time, the long submerged cruises quickly corroded flak guns and damaged dipoles, hydrophones and other sensitive gear. U-boats operated with damaged snorkels and little or no wireless communication.

Crews had to fix their problems on the spot or function with severe handi-caps. There was no help available as the supply U-boats known as 'Milch Cows' that often assisted U-boats in the mid-Atlantic had all been sunk by this time. The crews had to be self-reliant. They had to avoid Allied aircraft at all costs. Being caught on the surface for any reason meant almost certain destruction as inoperable flak guns left the U-boat defenceless. Most U-boats operated with radio silence. Neither BdU nor Allied intelligence ever knew exactly where they were. The U-boat crews lived in a world of sound, devoid of natural sunlight, where the air they breathed was not just foul, but low on oxygen and high on carbon dioxide content. Losses among Type I snorkel-equipped Type IXCs were already high, as previously noted, and their problematic snorkel installations were compounded by even longer trips that tested men and equipment to the extreme.[3]

Despite these handicaps, these U-boats sailed into the Gulf of St Lawrence and St Lawrence River, up to the water's edge along the coast of Maine, within eyeshot of Halifax Harbour, Boston Harbour, into Long Island Sound, and well within the 100m line from New Jersey to Cape Hatteras. While they never represented a threat as they once did during the 'Second Happy Time' of Operation *Paukenschlag*, many U-boats proved capable of sinking Allied vessels while avoiding detection and escaping entire US hunter-killer task groups. These U-boats survived. Of the thirteen snorkel Type IXs that sailed against Canadian waters, all returned or sur-rendered with the exception of three. One was sunk by surface attack, one by air attack (a very rare occurrence for snorkel-equipped U-boats) and one went missing for unknown reasons, probably a snorkel defect. Of the eight-een snorkel U-boats that patrolled against the eastern United States (not including *Gruppe Seewolf*), eight were lost. Five were confirmed sunk by surface attack, one was possibly sunk by surface attack (either *U-879* or *U-857*) while two went missing for unknown causes (*U-1226* and either *U-879* or *U-857*), also probably due to defective snorkels. Of the six U-boats that constituted *Gruppe Seewolf*, only two survived. If we do not include the U-boats of *Gruppe Seewolf* (for reasons discussed later in this chapter), those missing from unknown causes, or the four that simply never left European waters due to the cessation of hostilities (*U-541*, *U-1228*, *U-1231* or *U-802*) the survivability rate of snorkel-equipped U-boats during the last eleven months against Allied sea and air patrols was 67 per cent. Analysing this percentage further, we find one U-boat was sunk outbound off Portugal (*U-154*), so it never reached its patrol area. Two more were caught on the surface south-east of Newfoundland (*U-1229* and *U-881*) outbound to their patrol area. That raises the survivability of those snorkel-equipped U-boats that reached their patrol area to 80 per cent. *U-869* was probably a victim of a catastrophic snorkel failure and not an active U-boat hunt, so it should be classified as an 'unknown' loss (see Chapter 10 case study). The loss of only one U-boat to Allied aircraft underscores the effectiveness of the snorkel's ability to negate radar-equipped aircraft. These statistics and qualifications might seem irrelevant given that a U-boat sunk was a U-boat lost, but what they reveal is a fact that a U-boat's greatest vulnerability was entering/leaving port or while en route to its patrol area. Once a U-boat reached the coast around Great Britain or North America, it became significantly harder to identify and destroy, as previously discussed in Chapter 6.

The final eleven months of U-boat patrols off North America should be understood in context. These U-boats returned into the narrows of the St Lawrence River, and prowled for weeks within eyesight of the lights of major embarkation/debarkation points such as Halifax, Boston and New York. They returned to the shallows from New England to the Outer Banks, where they operated only miles from land for the first time in more than two years. Most survived their patrol. This was by no means a small accomplishment given the physiological and psychological strains of the long submerged cruise, the deterioration of equipment brought on by sea water corrosion and constant dampness, and the preponderance of Allied anti-submarine task forces hunting these U-boats during transit.

The above two tables reveal that there was a marked increase in ordered U-boat patrols against the North American coast in the last eleven months of the war after the snorkel was introduced. Some 92 per cent of all snorkel-equipped U-boat patrols against Canadian waters occurred in a seven-month period during the second half of 1944, while 78 per cent of ordered patrols against the US East Coast occurred in the last five months of the war. This dramatic increase of U-boat activity against North America represented a density of U-boats that was only surpassed by Operation *Paukenschlag* nearly thirty months earlier. This did not go unnoticed by Allied intelligence.

BdU's initial patrols against Canada were an attempt to surprise the Allies in an area previously believed to be inaccessible to U-boats due to increased Allied defences. The shift south to the US East Coast was both an expansion of that tactical concept, but also in conjunction with the December offensive in the west, Operation *Wacht Am Rhein*. Lastly, *Gruppe Seewolf* was an attempt to surprise an Allied convoy in transit across the North Atlantic, a repeat of the idea that the Allies would not be prepared for such an operation. After the convoy was initially attacked, these U-boats would then proceed to points along the US East Coast to operate individually.

BdU wanted to gain updated intelligence regarding the North American coast and operational experience with a snorkel-equipped U-boat in this area and it started to achieve this in the spring of 1944. *U-107* (IXB), commanded by Kapitänleutnant Volker Simmermacher, departed Lorient on 10 May 1944 on his third patrol. This was his second off the North American coast and the first snorkel-equipped U-boat patrol sent to operate in this area. He was originally directed towards Cape Hatteras, but then redirected north to Nova Scotia.[4] Simmermacher reported his experience to BdU as follows upon return to port:

> The snorkelling device proved itself well on the trip. The snorkel was used in the varying visibility and sea conditions (up to sea condition 6) in the travel through Biscay, in the Atlantic and along the North American coast, both day and night … Even though no absolute generalisation can be made from this experience in a single undertaking, the snorkel has proven itself to be a very useful tool that has provided substantial support for the U-boat in its operations and made many operations possible for the first time.[5]

BdU received confirmation that a snorkel-equipped U-boat could reach the North American coast and conduct a successful operation close to shore and survive. What is remarkable is that this patrol occurred a month before the BdU unleashed its snorkel-equipped U-boats into the Channel and four months before it shifted exclusively to coastal operations in the Atlantic.

As *U-107* was returning, *U-802* (IXC/40), under the command of Kapitänleutnant Helmut Schmoeckel, departed Lorient on 16 July bound for the Gulf of St Lawrence and his second patrol in Canadian waters. OP-20-G tracked his progress closely, noting that his U-boat was snorkel equipped. The intelligence came from a BdU wireless transmission that drew on recent snorkel experiences by *U-107* and other U-boats now operating in the English Channel:

> Schmoeckel, snort equipped, who operates off Halifax in U-802 late March and early April, is now heading for the Gulf of St Lawrence. He has been told that since the area has not been occupied since 1942 'Great surprise successes are possible, as traffic is heavy. Area can be well navigated with snort. Cruise unobserved, contact traffic in narrow channels, especially the mouth of the St Lawrence River. Part convoys to England and return and to and from the St Lawrence River to Belle Isle Straits, (July to November)' were described in the area as of 1944. A lengthy review of the 1942 situation was also given. Finally he was urged to 'get right on in there' since 'surprise appearance after such a long time promises the greatest prospects of success'.[6]

BdU was so convinced that the snorkel offered a significant advantage in the confines of shallow water that *U-802* was soon followed that summer into the Gulf of St Lawrence and the St Lawrence River by *U-541* (IXC/40), *U-1221* (IXC/40), *U-1223* (IXC/40) and *U-865* (IXC/40).

With the effort against the Gulf of St Lawrence in full swing, intelligence was still needed about the current defences along the old hunting grounds off Cape Hatteras. *U-154* (IXC), under the command of Oberleutnant zur See Gerth Gemeiner, was directed specifically towards North Carolina. *U-154* departed Lorient on 20 June, its departure identified by OP-20-G, which vectored in a task force to intercept the U-boat before it ever left European waters. *U-154* was sunk outbound on 3 July by depth charges from the US destroyer escorts USS *Inch* and USS *Frost* off the coast of Portugal. *U-154* was identified as a submerged contact by the USS *Inch* at 9.11am and attacked by 'Mk 10 projectors'. At the time of the contact *U-154* was cruising shallow. In response to the abrupt depth charge attack Gemeiner launched two torpedoes five minutes later, 'one missing astern and the other missing ahead' of the *Inch*.[7] *Frost* was called in to assist in the attack. Gemeiner took his U-boat deep and began evasive manoeuvres, as noted by the sonar operator onboard the *Inch*. *Frost* commenced a depth charge run at 10.38am that resulted in an 'exceedingly heavy underwater explosion felt by all personnel on *Frost* and *Inch* eleven minutes after *Frost* dropped depth charges.'[8] Confirmation of the sinking came in the form of German military raincoats, miscellaneous items and human remains that surfaced amidst a growing oil slick. OP-20-G recorded a communiqué sent to Gemeiner by BdU on 19 July. Clearly BdU did not know that *U-154* was already lost.[9]

This information, compiled from prior U-boat patrols and the code reading carried out by B-Dienst of Allied convoy traffic, underscores what a target-rich area North America still presented to BdU this late in the war. With snorkel-equipped U-boats, BdU believed they could catch outbound convoys at their embarkation and assembly points. The communiqué from BdU raised the concern that a U-boat that remained submerged for extended periods in the warmer waters of the South Atlantic might become too uncomfortable for the crew given that it was not expected to surface. To alleviate that discomfort, the U-boat would alter its patrol by heading north.[10]

The next opportunity BdU had to gain operational intelligence off the US East Coast was by *U-518* (IXC) commanded by Oberleutnant Hans-Werner Offermann, who was awarded the German Cross in Gold on 6 November 1943. *U-518* was originally ordered to patrol off Panama but Offermann elected to go to Cape Hatteras as he 'did not consider the Panama operational area very promising'. As noted by OP-20-G: 'since being D/F'd

12 August, *U-518* has been hunted by both the Guadalcanal and Core Groups, which attacked a series of sound contacts about 500 miles East–North East of Bermuda 15 to 17 August. *U-518* was informed on 7 August that it could alter its original operational area if it saw fit.'[11] This was Offermann's second patrol, his first being with the non-snorkel-equipped *U-518* in the Caribbean in February 1944. Despite being hunted by several task forces, the snorkel-equipped *U-518* evaded its pursuers.

U-518 never saw Cape Hatteras, preferring to maintain its position at the 200m line that ran along the continental shelf or in deeper water to the east. However, *U-518* was in fact the first snorkel-equipped U-boat to patrol near Cape Hatteras and only the sixth U-boat to do so in two years. As this was his first snorkel patrol, Offermann took the liberty of adapting snorkel procedures. During his patrol *U-518*'s routine was to submerge by day and almost always fully surface as soon as it got dark. Offermann only submerged again if there was a specific threat, and only utilised his snorkel to charge the batteries and to ventilate the U-boat just before dawn so that the air would be refreshed before the long day submerged. This was bold behaviour compared to the almost continually submerged operations of *U-107* and *U-802* in the Gulf of St Lawrence. Offermann's tactical decisions suggests he was not convinced of the snorkel's capabilities.

Both *U-802* and *U-518* were not only operating in proximity to the coast, but both were collecting valuable operational intelligence for BdU. OP-20-G knew this and tracked both U-boats accordingly, based on what they anticipated were their locations. As neither U-boat was sending wireless transmissions during their patrols, Ultra or direction-finding stations could not be used to pinpoint their positions despite being actively hunted by Allied task forces. Both U-boats returned safely to port to provide BdU with needed intelligence reports.

OP-20-G had some foreknowledge of this increase in U-boat patrols when in mid-August 1944 they intercepted the following wireless message from BdU sent in the clear: 'All U-boats in American waters to report situation as soon as possible. Reports are urgently needed for sending out new U-boats.' At that time there were three snorkel-equipped U-boats in the operational area, with *U-107* (IXB) returning from Canadian waters, *U-802* (IXC/40) still in Canadian waters and *U-518* (IXC) operating off Cape Hatteras at the 200m line.[12] The reason why information was needed was in preparation for increased operations against the North American coast to begin that month. *U-802* acknowledged the BdU message on 20 October while 500 miles south-east of the tip of Greenland, stating that the last seven reports it sent were never acknowledged.[13] This was the first time *U-802* had been heard by BdU in two months, underscoring the pattern of radio silence and atmospheric issues with North Atlantic wireless communications.

In keeping with BdU policy to keep one or two Type IX U-boats off the North American coast, particularly in the Nova Scotia–Newfoundland area after the end of Operation *Paukenschlag*, assessments of Allied naval defences were continually kept updated. In March 1943, almost one year after the end of Operation *Paukenschlag*, returning U-boats off the North American coast reported seeing 'the usual American patrol, unwatchful and relatively unpractised, consisting of destroyers, corvettes and PC-boats. Temporarily strengthened when (U-boats are) noticed. Aircraft irregular.'[14] This was based upon the fact that outside of specific hunter-killer task forces, general coastal patrols were not kept informed of specific U-boats operating off the coast. OP-20-G kept that intelligence closely guarded as 'Top Secret'. They released 'Secret' assessments to the Fleet Commands that were purposely very general in order not to compromise the fact that the German Naval Enigma codes had been broken. In many cases, there just was not enough intelligence to provide specifics. For example, on 15 February 1945 OP-20-G released: 'General situation appears substantially unchanged since last bi-weekly. However anticipate a gradual increase in U-boats at sea during next fortnight … Two U-boats not well fixed in Western Atlantic may be patrolling off New York and Halifax from recent contacts in these areas. Alternatively the latter may be in the Gulf of Maine.'[15] What OP-20-G was actually tracking was the most significant deployment of U-boats off North America in more than two years.

Without active two-way wireless communications between U-boats and BdU the best OP-20-G could hope for with Ultra at this point in the war was an assessment of future operations based on what transpired during the last two to three months. They noted on 30 September in their more broadly distributed 'Secret' bi-weekly dispatches out to Fleet Commands that they should 'anticipate continued enemy activity in the Canadian area wherefore U-boats currently are estimated of which one probably homebound. For first time in two years U-boats again appear to be operating in the Gulf of St Lawrence. The only U-boat in US coastal area now appears to be homebound after torpedoing one ship South of Hatteras and unsuccessfully attacking another two NW of Bermuda.'[16] OP-20-G did not have a sense of the increased U-boat activity yet to come.

U-boats continued to patrol and attack shipping along the North American coast, and specifically the US East coast through the last days of the war. The U-boat remained the only strategic weapon system that Germany possessed and could employ globally. Dönitz's long-standing view that every Allied ship sunk made it easier for a German soldier on the front line remained a key principle, even after he turned over the reins of BdU command to Admiral Godt. With the onset of Operation *Wacht am Rhein* in December 1944, U-boat activity dropped off along the North American coast as assets were focused in the Channel and around the United Kingdom. As the winter turned to spring and the Western Allies began their drive across Germany, a surge in U-boats against the US East Coast occurred. While their efforts resulted in little tonnage sunk, the idea remained that the U-boat could still take the war to the enemy's shores relatively safely with the snorkel.

The severe losses of U-boats in 1943 were reversed with the introduction of the snorkel. U-boat commanders and crews knew that. They knew their chances at surviving a patrol were better with a snorkel in early 1945 than at any point in the previous twelve months. The snorkel offered a psychological and morale boost to the crews, as well as for the German population. This was clearly capitalised upon by the Ministry of Propaganda in early 1945 through several news reels that introduced the snorkel (see Conclusion).

Alternatively, commanders who were not aggressive enough were admonished in radio traffic and threatened with court martial. There was also the potential of being reassigned to ground combat formations. On 31 January 1945, at the height of the Soviet winter offensive against Germany's Eastern Front, Dönitz sent out a message to the entire Kriegsmarine meant to reinforce morale. He noted that 'the Führer has once more explicitly ordered the Navy to see to a speedy intensification of the U-boat war'. Dönitz went on to describe his priorities as protecting necessary sea routes, guarding U-boat exercise and training areas along the German coast, and that non-essential personnel were to form a new 'Marine' combat division that would be deployed on the Eastern Front. He concluded by stating that each member of the Kriegsmarine must 'mentally adopt himself to the hour. We must become harder. Moaning and groaning is unmanly and shortsighted. Nothing is achieved by empty, defeatist chatter.' Dönitz ended with a final warning:

> For those officers who not fulfil these requirements, proved themselves of negative value through chattering, through inordinate [behaviour] or through miserable cowardice, and so not only failed to carry out their task as leaders but actually damage our power to resist I have no use as officers. I shall release them and place them at the disposal of the Army regardless of rank or position.[17]

This was not an idle threat. At that moment the Kriegsmarine formed two

Marine Infantry Divisions along the Eastern Front under the training cadre of SS officers. These two divisions were employed under Reichsführer-SS Heinrich Himmler's new military command *Heeresgruppe Weichsel.*

Generally speaking, the odds of surviving a three-month war patrol in a snorkel-equipped U-boat was better than a three-month combat tour in an infantry division on the Eastern Front. Under these circumstances there should be no surprise that U-boats continued to operate with vigour along the North American coast through the final days of the war.

Canadian Waters

As *U-107* returned from the first snorkel patrol in Canadian waters off Nova Scotia and Halifax, *U-802*, under the command of Kapitänleutnant Helmut Schmoeckel, was en route to the St Lawrence River. On 20 July BdU radioed guidance out to *U-802*. While some of the information was based on *U-107*'s recent experience, the latter part of the transmission was based on the cruises of *U-106* (IXB) and *U-43* (IX). Both were non-snorkel U-boats that operated in the St Lawrence River in September and October 1942. *U-802* was now the first U-boat to return to the river in almost two years. The intelligence *U-802* might bring back was critical in shaping additional snorkel U-boat operations in the area. BdU gave Schmoeckel his orders: 'Surprise appearance after so long a time promises greatest chances of success with low defences. Strike therewith!'[18]

One of the key issues that *U-802* and patrols of other Type IX U-boats off the North American coast experienced during the period of 'Total Undersea War' was problematic wireless communication due to constant submergence. This is a point that requires continued underscoring as it answers many questions about U-boat behaviour in North American waters during the final months of the war. Schmoeckel noted in his KTB on 15 August:

> For 24 hours I have received no further Radio Messages because the very low frequency transmitter no longer comes in, and shortwave roll-call no longer takes place (according to Radio Message). Therefore I must expose the snorkel for a longer time to pick up the missing radio messages over the tactical frequency.

Schmoeckel was using the dipole attached to the snorkel mast to receive VLF signals. Again on 17 August he noted:

> Sometimes only extended the snorkel head without running the diesels because snorkelling is only for receiving Radio Messages. Because I cannot

hear very low frequency, shortwave roll-call is not there, I must listen for a longer time on tactical frequency to pick up all Radio Messages. In the operational area I will probably no longer be able to achieve this.[19]

U-802 was tracked outbound by OP-20-G through the wireless messages sent by BdU. A hunter-killer task force was vectored into the expected path of Schmoeckel. On 19 August, *U-802* was ambushed by the USS *Bogue* hunter-killer group while proceeding in the middle of the mid-Atlantic. While running on the surface at approximately 4.10am, a US aircraft approached from astern and switched on its searchlight. The crew attempted to use the 2cm deck gun but it failed, probably due to sea water corrosion during the extended underwater cruise around the northern British isles. It dropped a light buoy and two depth charges. Schmoeckel ordered a crash dive and escaped without any reported damage. An Allied surface ship approached the area of the buoy but made no attack run. OP-20-G noted it was 'possibly sunk'.[20]

It was increasingly difficult for Allied intelligence to confirm U-boat sinkings among snorkel-equipped U-boats that remained submerged, especially as they maintained radio silence. A month later OP-20-G conceded on 12 September that *U-802* had survived the attack and moved towards the Gulf of St Lawrence as far as Cabot Strait. It based this assessment on the assumption that *U-802* had 'likely torpedoed the SS Livingston, then moved offshore and was again being hunted by Bogue'. However, OP-20-G's assessment was wrong. It was *U-541* that had sunk the *Livingston* after it arrived in the operational area several weeks after *U-802*. Tracking multiple U-boats that were running silent often led to incorrect assessments by OP-20-G.

On 9 September, *U-802* was in the centre of the St Lawrence River. At 2pm Schmoeckel noted in his KTB:

Stopped. Boat lies on a density layer at periscope depth and remains lying like a plank. Every 20 minutes all around sweep through the periscope. Because the water is murky sighting by aircraft is hardly possible. I lay here in a tactically favourable position, 7nm from land and can overlook the entire mouth of the river. If there is any traffic at all in the Gulf then it must pass by here. Since my entrance into the operations area on 31 August I have, except for depth charge scare on 4 September and the two small boats although we were almost continually on the convoy route, observed no traffic.

He also noted that: 'At night to snorkel I set off a bit to the north because the sound gear cannot be relied on.' On the 11th he wrote: 'due to strong marine phosphorescence I believe that snorkelling by night is not advisable. Therefore I remain lying stopped during the night, to charge in the twilight and by day. The capacity of the battery has dropped to 2/3.'[21] During coastal operations U-boat commanders often bottomed their U-boats for a variety of reasons. Some did this during the day to conserve air and batteries as they waited for the sounds of Allied surface vessels. Others, like *U-802*, did so due to the possible danger presented by marine phosphorescence.

While surfaced *U-802* made a 'Borkum' detection and subsequently dived at 1.45am. Schmoeckel noted how an Allied aircraft kept patrolling along the north–south line that *U-802* had patrolled over the last seven days.[22] What Schmoeckel did not know, and OP-20-G was slow to recognise, was that *U-541* was now operating in the area and had sunk the British-flagged *Livingston* at the mouth of the Gulf of St Lawrence on 3 September. This was a potentially dangerous situation for both U-boats, who were now using sound to locate the enemy and operating in confined narrows. If one or the other made an incorrect determination on a sound contact they could fire an acoustic homing torpedo and inadvertently sink the other.

While at periscope depth in the St Lawrence River off of Sainte-Anne-des-Monts on the 13th, *U-802* thought it was getting ready to encounter a convoy. The following combat action illustrates the new shallow water tactics that became the standard method of attack and evasion in the last ten months of the war. These tactics were not anticipated by the Royal Canadian Navy, who continued to evaluate their adversary's action within a pre-snorkel framework. At approximately 3.30pm with calm winds, mirror flat sea and no swells, a mast head was seen bearing 123 degrees. Schmoeckel called 'Action stations' for the first time during their cruise. He noted:

Three destroyers in line abreast formation at a distance of 2–3nm from one another. General course of the enemy 270°. I attempt to pass through between the northern and centre destroyer, because I suspect a convoy behind. Course 180°.

A few minutes later:

Centre destroyer, already on NW zigzag for a long time, bears 90°T. Turns to the SW zigzag. Enemy bow left target angle 30°, range = 4,000 metres. Hard to port, new course 60°. Northerly destroyer is about 3 nm away. Continuous sound gear impulses are heard.

At 3.59pm:

Centre destroyer bears 170°, target angle right 60°. Destroyer suddenly turns towards at target angle 0° and goes to high speed (smokestack smokes). Apparently he has detected me with his sound gear. Hard to port. Enemy zig-zags back and forth. It seems he doesn't have me.

At 4.02pm:

T5 shot from tube V on destroyer, bow right target angle 50°, enemy speed 20 knots. Steering WS, range = 500 metres, depth 4 metres. Torpedo detonation after 20 seconds. Three minutes later: Am overrun at depth 25 metres by loud destroyer propeller sounds. Apparently the northern destroyer.

At 4.10pm:

Went to depth 2A +10 [170m]. Sinking sounds heard. Course 150°. It was probably a destroyer group proceeding independently, because behind the destroyers no mastheads were seen. A remote escort for a convoy by destroyers appears unlikely to me in this sea area.

Schmoeckel then set a course change to 180° and moved towards the coast. 'The depth charge series that followed were heard increasingly farther off,' he recorded, as the Allied destroyers did not expect their quarry to head towards shallow water. By 6pm Schmoeckel altered course to 90°, then back again to 180°. *U-802* counted five depth charge series as it crept away towards the coast and shallow water. Shortly after midnight *U-802* came to rest on the bottom about 3,000m from the coast. 'The capacity of the battery has decreased considerably since the last measurement. We now have only half that of a new battery. At the moment the battery is practically empty. With the last current I had I just reached the coast. Intention: remain lying 24 hours.'

The tactic to head into shore and bottom after an immediate attack worked. *U-802* escaped Allied retribution. Schmoeckel slowly made his way back out of the St Lawrence River the following day. Another tactic he used on his way out was to drift with the current and hide in the water density layer. As noted on 17 September:

The surveillance of the corner between the south bank of the St Lawrence River and Anticosti Island seems to be especially strong. Therefore I intend to remain lying stopped for 24 hours. According to calculation of the current during this period I should drift most of the way through … I lie at the lower edge of the water layer.

These were difficult circumstances for *U-802* as it crept slowly out of the river with the defences now alerted to the presence of a U-boat. As noted in the KTB on the 19th: 'The few possibilities to snorkel here exist in the twilight. By day there is continuous air [cover] here, nights very strong marine phosphorescence. By attempting to a great extent to lay stopped I attempt to slowly increase the level of my battery.'

On 21 September an incoming wireless message was received from BdU: 'Boats in American waters: 1.) As soon as possible, report situation even by Short Signal. Reports are important for the operation of new boats. 2.) This applies especially to "Schmoeckel", "Gemeiner" and "Petersen".' Current intelligence and situation awareness was required from the radio silent *U-802*, *U-154* [which had been sunk] and *U-541* as there was now three more outbound U-boats and another two only days away from departure to North America as BdU increased the operational tempo.

However, *U-802* could not send a message due to active Allied surface patrols and the fact that the leads to the deflector antennas were not working. *U-802* continued to cruise underwater without surfacing to transmit. On the 28th, BdU repeated its request to Schmoeckel for a report. In his KTB, Schmoeckel recorded that he could not afford to surface:

> Because my FuMO is out of service, I believe that here in this area where no U-boat can pass without aircraft attack, it is not prudent to proceed on the surface to repair my antennas – leads of the net deflector antennas. Also I must accept that my anti-aircraft weapons, after 6 weeks submerged cruise, are no longer ready to fire. I can only begin all this work after moving off to a remote sea area.

Inoperable deck guns became a major problem for snorkel-equipped U-boats that remained submerged for far longer than their non-snorkel-equipped predecessors. Extensive maintenance of the deck guns was required during patrols, but this was next to impossible to conduct so close to the enemy's coastline. Again on 29 August and 3 October, BdU radioed their impatience: "'Offermann", "Schmoeckel", "Heuter" suppose, that on return transit, situation report will be remembered.'

On 4 October, Schmoeckel recorded in his KTB that he was overrun by a vessel while at periscope depth. He did not detect the vessel as *U-802*'s listening gear was damaged, probably during the depth charge attack of 19 August. The faint propeller sounds picked up shortly before the U-boat was overrun were thought to be *U-802*'s own propeller.

U-802's cruise into the St Lawrence might not have sunk the tonnage that BdU hoped, but it did demonstrate that the snorkel and new shallow water tactics were highly successful in avoiding Allied detection. Even more interesting was the fact that the crew's endurance proved capable of handling such a long underwater journey. For nearly eight weeks, between 14 August and 11 October, *U-802* operated almost exclusively submerged. During seventy-two days in the operational area *U-802* logged 2,497 nautical miles submerged and only 6 nautical miles surfaced. *U-802* surfaced briefly three times during this patrol; twice to empty bailers and once to mount the 2cm deck gun. This was an incredible feat of crew endurance in a snorkel-equipped U-boat, and the first in a distant, confined operational area. *U-802* returned to Bergen on 11 November. Schmoeckel's experiences were shared throughout the Type IXs now heading west. Among the concerns noted in his report filed upon return on 23 November was wireless communication:

> Because of heavy interference in the radio direction finder and later breakdown of the snorkel round dipole, conditions for receiving were very difficult because the tactical situation forced underwater movement almost all the time. The lack of shortwave appeals frequently forced us to snorkel simply for radio transmission purposes …
>
> It has become necessary again to acquire an underwater transmitting and receiving antenna.[23]

The third snorkel U-boat to deploy to North American waters was *U-1229*, under the command of Korvettenkapitän Arnim Zinke. *U-1229* departed Trondheim on 26 July en route to Canada. A previous departure on the 18th resulted in *U-1229* returning to port due to snorkel problems, as previously noted. Zinke's movements were tracked by OP-20-G. Allied intelligence noted that *U-1229* departed the Baltic on 13 July and transited south of Iceland on 8 August to reach a point in the Flemish Cap by the 19th.[24] *U-1229* was sunk on 20 August 1944 in the North Atlantic south-east of Newfoundland by depth charges and rockets from three Avengers and two Wildcat aircraft (VC-42) of the escort carrier USS *Bogue*. However, *U-1229* was a victim of circumstance. Zinke decided on his own authority to travel surfaced during the middle of the day instead of using his snorkel, according to the statements made by the surviving crew after capture. Simultaneously, a US Naval task force was hunting for *U-219* (XB), which was expected to transit to Penang with cargo for Japan. The Admiralty confirmed for OP-20-G that the U-boat they sank was in fact *U-1229*.[25] This was the only snorkel-equipped U-boat sunk in American waters by Allied aircraft. There were forty survivors, including the chief engineer, who were picked up by ships of the task force and brought into the Bristol Airfield at

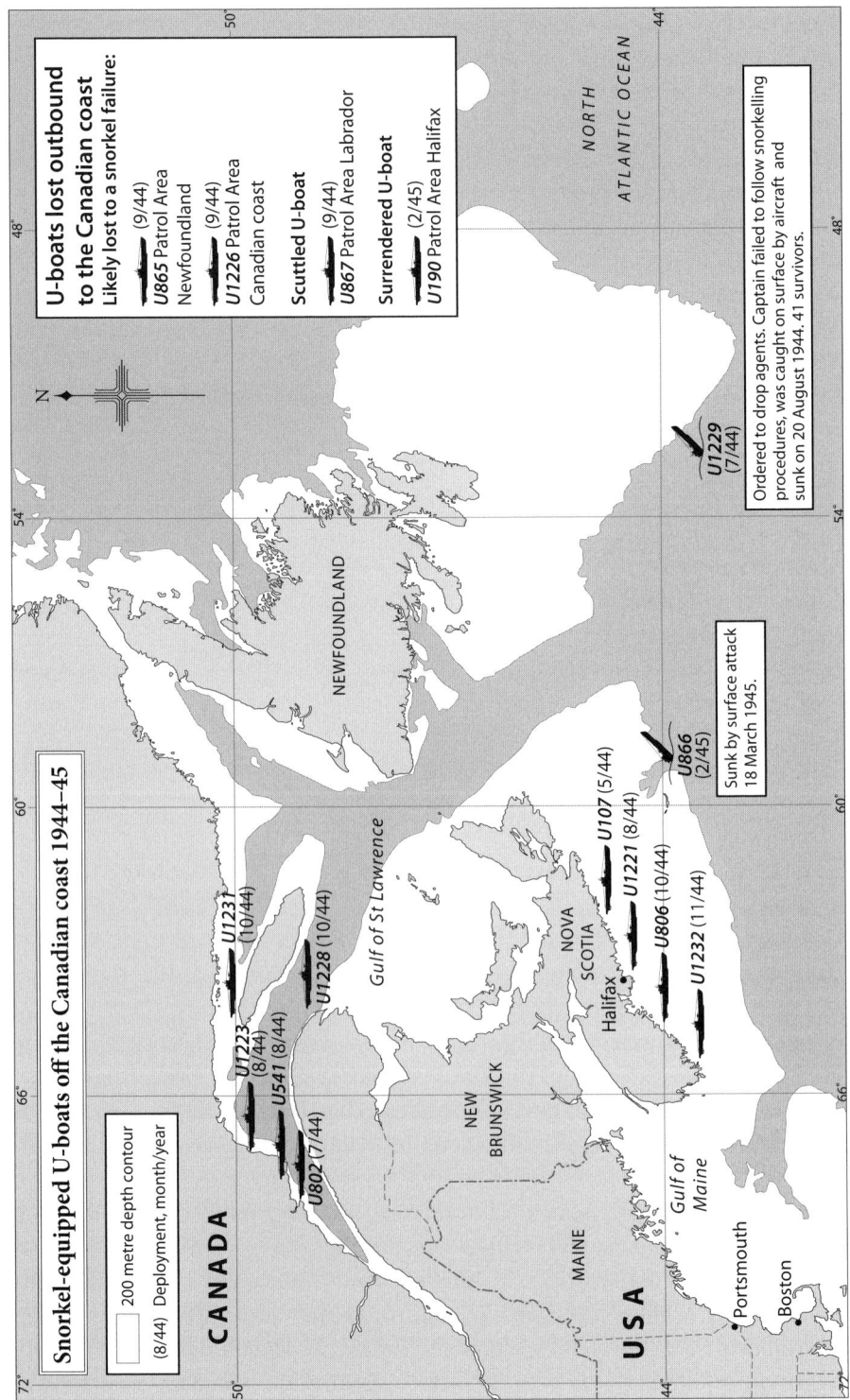

Snorkel-equipped U-boats off the Canadian coast 1944–45

200 metre depth contour

(8/44) Deployment, month/year

U-boats lost outbound to the Canadian coast

Likely lost to a snorkel failure:

U865 (9/44) Patrol Area Newfoundland

U1226 (9/44) Patrol Area Canadian coast

Scuttled U-boat

U867 (9/44) Patrol Area Labrador

Surrendered U-boat

U190 (2/45) Patrol Area Halifax

Ordered to drop agents. Captain failed to follow snorkelling procedures, was caught on surface by aircraft and sunk on 20 August 1944. 41 survivors.

U1229 (7/44)

Sunk by surface attack 18 March 1945.

U866 (2/45)

U107 (5/44)

U1221 (8/44)

U806 (10/44)

U1232 (11/44)

U1231 (10/44)

U1228 (10/44)

U1223 (8/44)

U541 (8/44)

U802 (7/44)

CANADA

NEWFOUNDLAND

Gulf of St Lawrence

NOVA SCOTIA

Halifax

NEW BRUNSWICK

MAINE

Gulf of Maine

Portsmouth

Boston

U S A

NORTH ATLANTIC OCEAN

Argentia, Newfoundland. A preliminary interrogation was made of the U-boat crew at that location. A selected group was later sent to the United States for a more comprehensive interrogation, which would include questioning a spy.

U-1229 was not just on a normal patrol. Zinke had a special mission not disclosed to the crew. He was to land a spy, Leutnant Oscar Mantel, in Canada. Mantel was known to the crew as being onboard to serve as a '*Propagandamann*', but that was the cover employed by the 40-year-old, who spoke 'very good English'. Mantel was a resident of New York City from 1929 until his return to Germany in 1941 before the US entry into the war. His interrogation inadvertently initiated the near panic by the US Tenth Fleet of the possibility that U-boats were preparing to attack US cities such as Boston, New York and Washington DC with ballistic rockets (see below section on *Gruppe Seewolf*).

Ten days after *U-1229* departed for its ill-fated secret mission, *U-541*, under Kapitänleutnant Kurt Petersen, recipient of the German Cross in Gold, departed Lorient. His orders were to proceed towards the Canadian coast. Petersen and *U-541* were no strangers to North American waters. He first departed Kiel on his first war patrol on 4 November 1943, sortieing out into the North Atlantic, where *U-541* participated in a number of unsuccessful Wolfpacks. He returned to Lorient on 9 January 1944. His second patrol began on 29 February with an intended operational area of the Caribbean. However, *U-541* was redirected towards the US East Coast while en route. This was in fact one of the few U-boat sorties off the US East Coast since the end of Operation *Paukenschlag* in 1942.

U-541 maintained a patrol between Bermuda and the area south of Cape Hatteras. It never cruised within sight of the coast. Petersen noted in his KTB that he observed surface traffic near the coast, probably along the 200m line. *U-541* was not snorkel equipped during this patrol. This was the main reason it stayed so far out to sea. It was unsuccessful in its attack on an unescorted tanker but it did stop two Swiss-chartered vessels carrying refugees and took two US citizens as prisoners back to France. While the patrol was unsuccessful in sinking Allied vessels, it did bring back useful intelligence about the current state of Allied anti-submarine efforts along an operational area that few U-boats had visited in two years.

Upon arrival in Lorient on 22 June 1944, *U-541* began a snorkel retrofit that was completed in July. *U-541* was the third or fourth Type IX to be retrofitted with a snorkel. It went into dry dock on 28 June and was refloated on 25 July. Independent snorkel training prior to its departure was not identified in the KTB, but was probably coupled with sea trials in the Bay of Biscay on 3 August. Now snorkel equipped, *U-541* departed on its third patrol. Petersen departed Lorient on 6 August. Within twenty-four hours *U-541* found itself snorkelling across the Bay of Biscay on full diesels as it was attacked by aircraft and hunted by what Petersen thought was an Allied destroyer. *U-541* escaped thanks to the snorkel and reached the Atlantic. On 24 August received a wireless transmission from BdU identical to the one received by *U-802*. The wireless message directed *U-541*'s destination as the mouth of the St Lawrence River and provided two-year-old intelligence about the area. The message did not mention the previous clandestine U-boat patrols sent there. It is not clear if Petersen knew he was operating in the same area and at the same time as *U-802* when he received the message.

On 5 September, *U-541* recorded seeing both the Cape Ray and Cape Anguille lighthouses 'burn as in peacetime' as it passed thru the Cabot Strait into the Gulf of St Lawrence. On 3 September, *U-541* sank the British merchant steamer *Livingston* (2,140 GRT), then submerged as it entered the Gulf. *U-541* continued submerged until the 8th, when it surfaced at 2.32am during a dark, overcast night in medium to bad visibility after detecting a sound contact. Petersen believed this target was an auxiliary carrier given its long flat deck. Prior to this, the practice had been to snorkel for two to three hours between 1am and 4am. It can only be surmised that Petersen surfaced due to the poor visibility with the expectation that his U-boat would not be spotted. However, surfacing prompted an engagement with several destroyers at close range. Star shells lit up the surface 'as in daylight' and a destroyer came within 300m while firing its 2cm gun, causing damage to the conning tower. No crewmen were injured and Petersen ordered the U-boat to dive. *U-541* fired a 'reverse shot' at the destroyer, claiming an explosion and sinkings sounds were heard, though the Allies recorded no ship hit that night.

With several destroyers now searching for the U-boat, Petersen followed the new snorkel guidance by running shallow and bottoming in 113m of water. *U-541* stayed there for nearly six hours before surfacing again on 9 September. Perhaps learning a lesson, *U-541* remained submerged during the rest of its patrol in the Gulf and into the St Lawrence River. It snorkelled routinely each day after midnight as prescribed by regulations and operated successfully among destroyers that routinely depth charged the area. It was noted in the log that *U-541*'s exact course was not known because the gyro and magnetic compass were out of service, yet the U-boat continued to manoeuvre in the shallows without significant trouble using dead reckoning. An interesting facet of operating in shallow water was noted on the 18th when *U-541* went to periscope depth for a shot on a target that was heard, but it was identified as being too far away. As noted in the KTB, 'due to water layers, visibility range is greater than listening range'. Another feature of snorkel operations along the North American coast was the lack of radio communications. In this case *U-541* received nothing from BdU from 3 to 25 September. As noted in the KTB: 'Because in the Gulf no very low frequency reception is possible, today is the first Radio Message received since 3 September.'

Once Petersen departed the Gulf of St Lawrence he began to surface in an attempt to send a radio message back to BdU. The first time *U-541* surfaced after leaving the Gulf of St Lawrence was on 30 September, having remained submerged for twenty-one straight days. He transmitted on 3, 5 and 7 October but received no confirmation response from BdU. On 9 October, Petersen noted in his KTB that 'because up to now the boat has not been heard, constructed an emergency antenna to transmit. A 14m-long copper wire is attached to the starboard after net deflector and raised with 4 Aphrodite balloons. Reception was 2 volume levels better. Boat was heard well by Control for the first time, see the Communications Report.' The use of Aphrodite balloons for communication became standard practice by U-boats whose transmissions were not being received.

U-541 arrived in Flensburg on 11 November. It could not return to France as the bases had been evacuated in September due to the Allied advance out of the Normandy bridgehead. While transiting south between Denmark and Norway on 6 November, Petersen transmitted his assessment to BdU, which was picked up by Ultra. He was convinced the area around 46N 57-15W (100 miles east of St Louisburg) was 'very promising territory'. He described the defence as 'weak air and sea in and before the gulf. After successes there was slight day air patrol; one harmless search group of destroyers or minelaying boats was heard on hydrophone each day. After being observed, because of sinking mentioned above (*Livingston*), U-boat advanced as far as St Lawrence River without difficulties.' OP-20-G believed that 'on this basis three Type IXC were dispatched from the Baltic to the exact spot. *U-1228* was also directed to this area.' However, there appears to be no direct connection, as all the U-boats with the exception of one, which soon entered Canadian waters, had departed before Petersen's message. OP-20-G did note the weak defence possessed by the Canadians in a handwritten annotation in the margin of the weekly report: 'Canadians have no "Support Groups", they have seven western local groups with four to five ships per group. They have 7 air squadrons, 28 VLR [Very Long Range]; 65 LR [Very Long Range]-78L [not known].'[26] Petersen's cruise, along with that of *U-802* to the St Lawrence, demonstrated the viability of complete underwater operations in a contained environment. Petersen's experience was recorded by BdU in Top Secret Situation Report No. 2 sent out to other Type IXs.[27] BdU concluded Petersen's third cruise, and his first with a snorkel, as 'in all a good, joyful combat patrol of the experienced commander'.

As *U-802* and *U-541* were still operating in their respective areas, BdU sent another four U-boats towards Halifax and the St Lawrence following similar tracks as their predecessors. *U-1221* (IXC/40), under command of Oberleutnant Paul Ackermann, departed Bergen for Nova Scotia on 20 August. There, Ackermann conducted a twenty-eight-day patrol entirely submerged. Out of 1,135 nautical miles patrolled, almost half – 527 – were conducted while operating the snorkel. He spent weeks patrolling within 10km of the shoreline outside Halifax. There was one exception. On 16 October Ackermann surfaced for about one-and-a-half hours and cruised 6.3nm as the sea was too rough to snorkel in shallow water. While he did not get specific in the KTB, he was probably afraid of being bounced off the bottom in a sea state of 4–5 while snorkelling. As with other U-boats in North American waters, none of Ackermann's transmissions to BdU were received.

As the war drew to a close, many of the crew went to sea with the knowledge that their homes were either being overrun by the Western Allies or the Red Army. Despite the weight of this, they continued to perform as required.

U-1223 (IXC/40), under the command of Oberleutnant Albert Kneip, departed Bergen on 28 August for the St Lawrence River just eight days after *U-1221*. Wireless communications remained a constant problem. It took five separate requests for a passage report from BdU before Kneip received one his radioman could read.[28] *U-1223* was one of ten U-boats at that time, that included *U-245* (VIIC), *U-285* (VIIC), *U-398* (VIIC), *U-482* (VIIC), *U-484* (VIIC), *U-680* (VIIC), *U-925* (VIIC), *U-979* (VIIC) and *U-1221* (IXC/40), which were all equipped with the new Kurier transmission system. All of these aforementioned U-boats were informed by wireless on 15 August that: 'Kurier receiving station will Guard all 4 frequencies continuously for reception, as per Guarding Plan. Check transmitters operate at times given. Send signals only when 'check transmitter' is heard.'[29] On 1 September Kneip was directed by BdU not to remain on station as a weather boat, which was typical of westbound U-boats, but to proceed directly to the St Lawrence River.[30] Only one message from Kneip was intercepted on his outbound journey on 22 September. His transmission to BdU noting his position east of the Grand Banks was reciprocated with the following message the next day:

OP area has not been occupied since 1942. Great surprises are possible, as traffic is heavy in area. Area was abandoned ((by German U-boats)) in 1942 as a result of the appearance of aircraft with radar, which made charging more difficult. Area can be well navigated with snorkel (see also Channel Experiences). Cruise to area unobserved; interception of traffic in narrow channels especially in BA30 ((mouth of St Lawrence)) ((should be)) effective.[31]

U-1223 spent a month underwater before heading home. There was no further intercepts from 23 September until 6 November. Due to a lack of any KTB for this boat it is not clear if Kneip ever sent a transmission by Kurier during this time or if he remained submerged for the duration. On 7 November BdU sent a message to Kneip that read: 'According to a press report 47 men were lost from a steamer sunk by a U-boat in your area. Assumption: One of your successes.'[32] On 21 November BdU requested Kneip to send a situation report 'without fail as soon as you are in the open sea on return cruise' suggesting that there was growing anxiety with the lack of transmission.[33] *U-1223* sank the Canadian frigate HMCS *Magog* (1,370 GRT) and damaged the British-flagged *Fort Thompson* (7,134 GRT). These attacks occurred within the light of the Matane lighthouse, where one can look across the river and see the other side. Kneip sent a positive wireless report on 26 November that confirmed BdU's belief that the North American coast was '... promising, as shipping is regular and there is little anti-submarine activity'.[34]

Despite the promising report in December, the effort shifted to the US East Coast. By the time the report was received only one final U-boat had been dispatched in February to Canadian waters. That U-boat was *U-190*, discussed below.

U-865 (IXC/40), under the command of Oberleutnant zur See Dietrich Stellmacher, departed Trondheim on 8 September 1944 for a coastal patrol just off Newfoundland. This U-boat departed just nine days after *U-1223* but never arrived at its destination. No Allied attack report has been identified to date that corresponds with the U-boat's likely westward course. Was *U-865* a victim of a sea mine dropped by British aircraft off the Norwegian coast or did it suffer a mechanical defect with its snorkel? A careful review of the BdU KTB reveals the possible cause.

U-865 received its snorkel retrofit in May 1944. It left Trondheim on 27 July, 1 and 10 August, returning to port after two, three and four days at sea respectively due to continued snorkel failures. After each return, the engineers in Trondheim worked to correct the unknown deficiency. *U-865* was recorded lost by BdU on 7 October due to a suspected snorkel failure, probably during its passage south of Iceland, but the actual location remains unknown.[35] What might have happened is conjecture since we do not know the exact cause of the original malfunction. A defect in the intake might have caused excessive flooding of the boat, forcing it to dive uncontrollably into the depths and resulting in a crushed hull. Alternatively, a defect in the exhaust piping might have resulted in a build-up of carbon monoxide. One by one the crew might have passed out and the U-boat, as in the prior case, slipped into the depths. There was also the possibility of a battery explosion caused by improper venting after snorkelling. The exact cause may never be known, however, we know that a snorkel failure is a primary culprit.

U-1226 (IXC/40), under the command of Oberleutnant August-Wilhelm Clausen, departed Horten on 30 September with the initial intention to report on North Atlantic weather in advance of Operation *Wacht Am Rhein*.[36] On 2 December, BdU declared *U-1226* lost at sea. Its loss was emblematic of current U-boat operations. Oberleutnant Clausen's last wireless transmission was received by BdU on 23 October after clearing the Faroes Island passage. He reported that his snorkel lifting lever was out of order and that the port-side double 2cm gun was not working.[37] He received an order from BdU to remain in the southern half of AK (a German naval grid square south-east of Greenland) and act as a weather boat. BdU assured Clausen that in the area 'snorkelling was not necessary' and that when he returned to base, he should do so with the snorkel 'in a fixed position', meaning upright. In the meantime, he was given freedom of manoeuvre if the 'enemy' was sighted.[38] BdU concluded: 'This order was not received. She is believed to have been sunk by aircraft in AL 10/20 while repairing her snorkel.'[39] However, there is no known Allied attack report for this location and date. It is highly likely that the U-boat's snorkel failed and caused *U-1226* to sink between Iceland and the Canadian coast.

The loss of two U-boats to possible snorkel failure caused BdU to send a warning out to all U-boats on 30 October:

> Improper servicing while snorkelling have on several occasions led to smoking up of the U-boat and resulting injury to members of the crew from carbon monoxide gas. Several COs report that evidence of poisoning does not appear until several hours after ventilation has taken place. General weakened condition of the crew is then so pronounced that surfacing and opening of the tower hatch is possible only by exerting the greatest energy. The bridge crew was hardly in a condition to stand on its feet. In the case of one U-boat, these conditions did not appear until the U-boat had been ventilated for a half-an hour on the surface after smoking up.[40]

The patrols against Canada continued. *U-1228* (IXC/40) was commissioned on 22 December 1943 at Deutscher Werft, Hamburg-Finkenwerder. Its commander was Oberleutnant zur see Marienfelde. *U-1228* began its testing and training cycle at the end of December 1943, which was followed by extensive trials in the Baltic. In July 1944 it arrived at Howaldtswerft in Hamburg for its final overhaul, where its snorkel retrofit occurred. After initial snorkel testing was complete, anti-aircraft gun testing and crew combat training followed. *U-1228* returned to Stettin for a bridge enlargement in August, then back to Kiel in preparation for its first combat patrol.

U-1228 departed for Horten on 5 September, arriving two days later. From 7 to 10 September it conducted final snorkel training with the Argu-Front. It then departed Horten for Kristiansand, and then departed the latter port to begin its patrol on 13 September along with *U-867* (IXC/40). On 14 April Marienfelde recorded in his KTB that 'since departing while proceeding submerged the port shaft or the port diving plane beats at low speed settings so loud that submerged attack seems questionable. I decide to run into Bergen.' Marienfelde experienced for the first time the difficulty in communicating with the dipole mounted on the top of the snorkel mast. He annotated in his KTB as he manoeuvred towards Bergen that 'sent Radio Message concerning snorkel via round dipole antenna, was not confirmed. Ended Snorkelling. Surfaced to send radio message.' *U-1228* entered Bergen on 15 September. After about twenty-four to twenty-six hours of repair work, Marienfelde departed for his patrol at 7pm on the 17th.[41]

As *U-1228* proceeded on its patrol, another snorkel boat headed towards North American waters. *U-867*, under the command of Kapitän Arved von Mühlendahl, radioed that both his diesel engines had been lost due to heavy weather. He was dead in the water and required a tow. *U-867* was still close to the Norwegian coast, just west of Stadlandet, Norway, so Marienfelde changed course at 6am on 18 September to rendezvous with the stricken U-boat. Mühlendahl departed Kiel on 9 September with a mission to establish an automatic weather station on Labrador before crossing paths with *U-1228* at Kristiansand. Upon receipt of the wireless message, BdU instructed Mühlendahl to head towards the coast staying submerged until his batteries ran out. Meanwhile, both *U-215* and *U-858*, in addition to *U-1228*, were ordered to rescue the stricken *U-867*. Mühlendahl's message was intercepted by the Allies and British Coastal Command aircraft were directed to the area to attack *U-867*. British Mosquitoes located *U-275* off Utvaer, Norway, by happenstance en route, and attacked that boat believing it was their intended target, *U-867*. *U-275* suffered significant damage, but later limped back to port.

At 5.37pm on 19 September, *U-867* was found and attacked by another RAF Liberator (224 Sqn, coded Q, pilot Flt Lt H J Rayner), but the six dropped depth charges overshot. The pilot reported that the U-boat was already losing oil before the attack and that dinghies were visible alongside. Apparently, this attack, coupled by the lack of rescue, caused the crew of *U-867* to scuttle the boat while the British circled overhead. Some twenty-one rubber dinghies holding fifty crewmen bobbed in the rough seas. *U-215* and *U-858* both heard the detonations from close by and headed towards the area, but the latter U-boat was attacked by another Liberator at 8.10pm. Despite their proximity, *U-215* and *U-858* were unable to reach the survivors. The search was abandoned on 22 September and *U-867*'s crew was lost at sea.[42]

Marienfelde had attempted to reach the stranded *U-867* by snorkelling during the day in order to reach him by nightfall. The heavy seas caused the U-boat to breach the surface several times due to long swells at around 4.15pm on the 18th. A Hog Fish active sonar device was detected and Marienfelde decided to surface and remain there in an attempt to reach *U-867* as quickly as possible, noting in the KTB: 'I decide to remain on the surface, because assistance in the first night is best.' He surfaced at 8.57pm. At 10.55pm a searchlight turned on at 90° 30–50m to the right of the bow just as the FuMB picked up a loud tone. A Sunderland flew over at an altitude of 15m and dropped four 'bombs' abeam to port. Simultaneously, cannon fire from the aircraft ripped across the water, while flares were dropped. Marienfelde sent a wireless message off to BdU stating he had been attacked. He then ordered his U-boat to dive at 11pm. No second attack occurred. At 2.25am on the 19th Marienfelde submerged and proceeded to snorkel the rest of the way to the stricken *U-867*.

U-1228 dived and continued its approach submerged while running the diesels on snorkel. Unknown damage had been done to the snorkel system, as recorded in the KTB:

02.25 At the beginning of snorkelling heavy smoking of the boat. Exhaust gas piping probably damaged by aircraft bombs. A diesel operator was felled from breathing fumes.

03.20 Surfaced due to failure of the snorkel. When starting the diesel to blow and proceed heavy exhaust gas entry through leaking loosened sealing. The entire crew located below deck was affected because donning of the rescue breathing devices was not fast enough.

19.09 Norwegian Sea. All men out of the boat. Crew on the over deck. Both engines stopped. FuMO 'Gema' manned by the watch officer with a rescue breathing device. Boat ventilated. Unconscious: chief engineer, doctor, both engine operators, crew that remained below deck.

04.20 After the chief engineer, doctor came to, the boat was somewhat ventilated, and crew has been allowed to come up. The boat is prepared for diving.

04.40   With FuMO. 2 aircraft detected bearing 270°T, range = 4,500 and 8,500 metres.

1st approach from 270°T, from range = 3,000 metres, repelled with 3.7cm.

2nd approach from 180°T, range = 1,000 metres, repelled with 2cm.

3rd approach from 70°T, range = 2,500 metres repelled with 2cm. Aircraft was not seen, only fired at by radar, and immediately turned away.

After the 3rd approach when flying off in 60°T at range = 9,000 metres dived. A new approach recognised in the FuMO during the dive manoeuvre, no bomb attack.

05.00   After ship blocked off due to exhaust gas. One diesel operator still unconscious. Most of the crew is still not fit for duty.

I decide against a new attempt to surface and attempt to get the diesels operable for surface operation and to return with the available battery.

Boat would have to proceed on the surface for hours for ventilation, especially the after ship, plus at daybreak run with E-motors with limited ability to crash dive and anti-aircraft defences manned.

Headed for the coast with 1 motor KF.

05.10   Masch.Ob.Gefr. Mittler, dead.

Marienfelde recorded that 'during the submerged transit with the strong carbon monoxide presence and air stinking of exhaust gas, except for a few, the entire crew fainted or is incapacitated'. *U-1228* continued submerged despite the risks as one by one the crew began to pass out near death. At 4am Marienfelde noted after being submerged for twenty-three hours and 'despite their own frequent faintness, Ass.Artz Dr Duge and San.Ob.Mt Kuchenbecker were most excellent in the care and revival of the especially strongly poisoned and exhausted, likewise Ob.Masch. Lehmann in depth control and on surfacing.' He finally ordered the U-boat surfaced at 6.15am after twenty-five hours submerged as each hour that passed his crew grew weaker. A total of ten crewmen were completely incapacitated, with most of the rest of the crew only capable of limited action. By the end of the day on the 20th, *U-1228* had reached Bergen for repairs, its second attempt at its first combat cruise thwarted. This incident highlights the extreme challenges faced by snorkel-equipped U-boats as nearly four-fifths of the crew were incapacitated and the rear compartments were shut down as the craft attempted to work its way back to base, all the while being hunted by Allied aircraft. This episode also serves as a blueprint for how other potential cases of carbon monoxide poisoning could incapacitate a crew and sink a U-boat.

The crew of *U-1228* was extremely lucky. The initial smoking gave a visual sign that the snorkel was damaged and the quick surfacing by Marienfelde probably saved his U-boat. Without the smoke, he and the crew may not have recognised the carbon monoxide creeping through the U-boat until it was too late for anyone to act. If anyone in the control room had taken the wrong action, the U-boat could easily have been sent to the surface, where waiting Allied aircraft might have dealt it a deadly blow, or it might have been descended uncontrollably into the depths, where an equally devastating fate awaited. The incident was recorded by OP-20-G, probably due to *U-1228*'s harrowing escape and resilience:

> U-1228 was attacked homebound on 18 September 5 times and suffered severe damage. The CO kept the U-boat submerged even though the snorkel became defective, until the battery ran out … the crew was stricken but survived.[43]

Between 21 September and 11 October, *U-1228* went through a complete overhaul. The following actions were taken while in port: new packing of the exhaust installation, repair of the snorkel exhaust valve, replacement of the gyrocompass sphere, overhaul of the float valve, overhaul of the attack periscope, and offloading of torpedoes (two damaged by bombing on the broken off first patrol). Masch.Ob.Gfr. Mittler was buried at the Bergen Honour Cemetery. *U-1228* transited to Hatvik-Bergen, where fresh provisions were loaded and the snorkel repaired. The intake piping was warped at the conning tower and had to be replaced. The German Cross in Gold was awarded to Ob.Masch. Lehmann by the Flotilla Commander for his performance onboard the stricken U-boat.[44]

At 10pm on 12 October, *U-1228* departed once again for its patrol off the North American coast. Nine days later, on the evening of the 21st, *U-1228*'s snorkel failed while running both diesels. Suddenly the air stopped flowing in through the snorkel head. The snorkel's float valve was not visible in the dark. The decision was made to wait until twilight the following morning to surface and determine the cause. The U-boat came to periscope depth at 8am on the 22nd and the ball float was seen hanging askew. Due to the sea state being 4–5, it was determined that outbound transit had to continue and that the snorkel head would be fixed at the next available opportunity. While the investigation was ongoing, sound bearings were heard on multiple occasions, forcing Marienfelde to remain submerged as he continued outbound between Iceland and the Faroe Islands. With overcast conditions, *U-1228* surfaced at 8pm in a sea state 3. Crew members scrambled onto the deck, reached the port-side well that held the snorkel mast and determined that the pivot pin of the snorkel ball float had fallen out 'because the weld-ing did not hold'. The intention was to 'remove the snorkel head, further dismantle on the bridge (taking it below into the boat is not possible due to the size) and repair the float valve in the boat. Removing the snorkel head is very difficult in the often overcoming seas on the foreship.' After more than two hours of maintenance the decision was made to 'manhandle' the snorkel head onto the bridge, where it was lashed down with steel wires. *U-1228* then proceeded to dive. This was very risky. If the snorkel head was lost then they had little choice but to turn around or risk heading to their operational area with an increased chance of being located and sunk.

In the early morning hours of the 23rd, *U-1228* surfaced in the morning twilight. Work recommenced on the snorkel float. With less than an hour of work complete, *U-1228* dived, only to resurface at 10pm to commence work again. This process continued until the 27th, when it was determined that the snorkel head had been fixed. On the 30th the repaired snorkel head was reinstalled back onto the mast and *U-1228* dived to test the sea repairs. At 4am on the 30th, eight days after the initial problem, Marienfelde recorded that the 'valve does not open'. Later that night, *U-1228* surfaced and again the snorkel head was disassembled on deck and additional adjustments were made after three hours. *U-1228* dived, raised the snorkel mast, turned on the snorkel and it proved mobile again. Marienfelde noted in the KTB with exuberance: 'So it moves after all! After eight days of work it's finally done at the cost of the failure of the snorkel round dipole antenna, which is only operable for shortwave reception.'

While *U-1228*'s snorkel struggles might have been extreme, this episode reinforces how important the device was to successful operations at the end of the war and the lengths to which a commander would go to ensure its technical effectiveness. Also obvious is how deadly shoddy dockyard work could be during the retrofit process. Admittedly, snorkel maintenance in port was often completed quickly to get the U-boat operational. Unfortunately for Marienfelde, his snorkel troubles were not over.

On the 13th he began his underwater approach to the Canadian coast, using the snorkel to charge diesels and vent the U-boat. On 22 November the ventilation valve started to get stuck at periscope depth. Marienfelde planned to move towards the coast, then surface to conduct yet another emergency repair of the snorkel head. He tried one last time to snorkel and found that the float valve would stay open as long as the U-boat did not cruise below 12m – half the normal snorkelling depth and very dangerous. Under these circumstances Marienfelde decided to manoeuvre towards '"Connoire Bay"', because from the Nautical Handbook it seemed uninhabited and going under the coast without the sounder seems most favourable there. A lengthy repair seems likely because a broken float guide pin or bent float guide bolt is anticipated.' At 5am on the 24th, *U-1228* surfaced less than 10km south of the bay. Further progress towards shore was stopped 'due to failure of the Echolot and unpredictability of the gyrocompass sphere deviation'. Such equipment malfunctions presented an incredible navigational challenge inshore. Examination of the float valve commenced and Marienfelde recorded that: 'At the float, nothing is seen. Dispensed with removal of the float valve because after lubrication and working it is free again. So control room lubrication of the snorkel appears absolutely necessary. However, there was still the suspicion that the root cause is damage to the float guide bolt, which in these conditions can only be maintained consistently by repeated lubrication.' *U-1228* dived, started the snorkel and found it working again.

On 25 November, Marienfelde determined that he would not sail directly into the Gulf of St Lawrence as directed by BdU. All of Marienfelde's efforts resulted in a single sinking at the mouth of the gulf. At 2.30am on the 25th a single Gnat torpedo was fired at a destroyer zig-zagging in the centre of the Cabot Strait. The torpedo hit its mark, sinking the Canadian corvette HMCS *Shawinigan* (900 GRT). All hands were lost. Marienfelde's only close call came on 4 December while snorkelling after midnight. Marienfelde believed his U-boat was heard, but not detected by ASDIC. The following day the float valve jammed again. Finally, the decision was made to turn back towards Norway and complete the patrol.

Marienfelde decided to change up the snorkelling procedure and snorkel at moonrise so that with better visibility there would be no reason for all-round listening with the hydrophones that required a halt to the snorkel's operation. This avoided the related flooding of the intake tube and a complicated draining procedure. Starting on 13 November and ending on 4 December, *U-1228* spent twenty-two days submerged in the channel between Cape Britton Island and Newfoundland. Despite the snorkel trouble, Marienfelde's patrol consisted of 1,324 submerged nautical miles, with only six surfaced during this period. It was an amazing feat of endurance, ingenuity and patience.

Upon his return Marienfelde made his report and proposed a number of changes to the existing snorkelling procedures to increase the efficiency of operation and conserve air. Of interest was that *U-1228* was fitted with an experimental diesel exhaust; it may have been the only U-boat to receive this modification. The normal diesel exhaust on a U-boat was designed to expel gases just above the waterline. *U-1228* had a modified exhaust with an exhaust port below the waterline, possibly about 1m below the surface. This was approximately the same level below the surface at which gases would be expelled by the snorkel exhaust outlet if the snorkel mast was raised. While no technical document has been located to explain the reason for the modification, this was almost certainly done as a result of the successful introduction of the underwater exhaust in the snorkel. The idea was that when a U-boat was surfaced the gases expelled underwater limited any smoking that might be used to identify the U-boat and also reduce its infrared signature. This is hinted at in the KTB.

However, just like the snorkel exhaust, if the sea state became too high, instead of being a metre or so below the water surface, the exhaust exit could fluctuate from several metres above the water surface one minute to 5 or more metres below the surface the next. This proved to be too much back pressure for the diesels. They overheated and could only be run at low RPM or not at all. The diesels proved so sensitive to back pressure that, as the crew of *U-1228* discovered, it made a difference which side (lee or windward) was higher. In order to get around this problem Marienfelde used the lowered snorkel mast in the deck well to exhaust the diesel gases as it sat several metres above the waterline and was not impeded by a higher sea state. He noted this in his KTB: 'Utilised the snorkel in a fixed, resting position to exhaust the boat when running on diesels due to high sea state.'[45] A novel use of the snorkel indeed!

During this first operational cruise *U-1228* travelled 3,534 nautical miles underwater and 3,331 surfaced. Despite its many technical issues, *U-1228* spent a total of thirty-three out of seventy-three days entirely submerged. With all the trouble experienced on his war patrol, BdU admonished Marienfelde in the clear across the wireless for not continuing close into shore where the Allied traffic was expected, despite the snorkel and gyro compass problems. He was made an example of to other U-boat captains that they had to maintain their aggressiveness despite challenging technical and tactical circumstances.[46]

U-1231 (IXC/40), under the command of Kapitänleutnant zur See Hermann Lessing, departed Bergen on 18 October, just five days after *U-1228*. His destination was also the St Lawrence River. *U-1231* received a snorkel in Wesermünde during its final overhaul. It was also at this time that the upper snorkel mast received an anti-radar rubber coating. This was one of the first installations of the coating and it received strong praise from Lessing after the patrol. Many U-boats that conducted patrols from the autumn of 1944 through the end of the war received the coating along their snorkel mast and around the snorkel head. At the end of August, *U-1231* completed initial snorkel training at Kiel before departing for the Baltic, where anti-aircraft practice was completed and the UAK issued their final approval. *U-1231* made its way to Norway for the usual three days of snorkel training, deep diving and final combat service drills. During snorkel testing it was noted that metal shavings had fallen into the periscope well during assembly at Kiel that caused 'binding and clicking'. Servicing in Bergen was required to fix the issue. After clearing the periscope housing, *U-1231* departed submerged to the Canadian coast. After it crossed the Atlantic without incident, *U-1231* began its underwater patrol of the Gulf of St Lawrence, St Lawrence River and Nova Scotia.

Lessing's use of the snorkel was not without incident. As during Marienfelde's patrol, the snorkel became the final determinant of operations. On 20 October Lessing noted 'snorkelling had not gained much, because the diesel was flooded twice due to operating error (starting when undercutting)'. Five days later, on 25 October, he wrote:

> Began snorkelling. While initiating the snorkel mast a bang was heard, that was first thought to be an aircraft bomb far off. The snorkelling and starting attempt failed, because the diesel could not work against the outboard pressure. The bang must have been the bursting of the exhaust gas piping outside the pressure hull. Two Diesel-Machinists and an E-motor Machinist fell out briefly from mild carbon monoxide gas poisoning.

He continued: 'Still no final conclusion. Must surface to determine. I decide to move off on a NE-course, to surface in a less busy area east of Iceland at light and examine the exhaust gas piping.'

On 26 October, *U-1231* surfaced to examine the issue. 'Surfaced to examine the blowing [with exhaust gas] piping, in the process blew with diesel. Works after all. Discovered a crack of about 20–30 cm aft of the heat equalisation sleeve on the starboard blowing [with exhaust gas] piping.' The crack was only partially welded due to increased waves and poor weather. Lessing then ordered *U-1231* to conduct:

> … submerged transit to fill the battery as well as grind in the intake and exhaust valves of the starboard diesel. The diesels suffered a bit while snorkelling as a result of the heat exchanger being torn in the exhaust gas piping and therefore they had to continually work against increased pressure. It is necessary to remove the exhaust valves of both diesels, grind them in as well as repack the exhaust gas piping. This done by shutting down one diesel during the night cruise.

During *U-1231*'s outbound cruise and time spent in its patrol area, only a single transmission from Lessing was intercepted on 10 November.[47] On 4 December, while in the middle of the St Lawrence River, south of Pointes-des-Monts, Lessing noted in the KTB that:

I decide to leave this area because icing of the snorkel valve caused by the cold appears concerning and I expect no more success here. Additionally, I still intend to catch the Halifax traffic off this harbour, to still achieve successes there. The time of year allows ice and therefore the shutting down of ship traffic is to be expected.

Here the icing of the snorkel valve drove Lessing's decision to shift his operational area. *U-1231* arrived at its operational area on 20 November and departed on 2 January. *U-1231* returned to Farsund, Norway, on 31 January 1945 without achieving a hit on any Allied vessels. *U-1231* spent forty-three days underwater, one of the longest such patrols for a Type IX off the North American coast. Overall, during its patrol *U-1231* cruised 8,695 nautical miles, of which 5,367 were underwater. Out of 106 days, eighty were spent utilising the snorkel.

Lessing noted the following in his KTB's conclusion for this patrol:

3) Initially the snorkelling caused some difficulties because snorkelling in high seas was different than in Horten in calm water. A particular difficulty occurred from tearing a thermal expansion joint in the exhaust piping because the diesel had worked against increased pressure during the first submerged transit period and by the packing often leaking etc. the diesel room was regularly heavily filled with smoke.

I had received a rubber protection [on the snorkel head] against [radar] detection before beginning the journey. Based on my observations, this worked well since, despite being located [by an enemy radar] once at Volume 5 [as heard by the radar detector operator in our boat], I was not detected.

4) The crew had great confidence in snorkelling and felt totally safe. The smoking that occurred was always accepted with equanimity. Mild CO poisoning occurred only in the diesel personnel when the E-machinist and 2 stokers temporarily fell …

6) A significant change was mandatory sleeping, which was carried out strictly to save current and air. A certain variety was offered through records and storytelling sessions. The elimination of resulting waste was made through a bow torpedo tube. This was continually flooded from outboard and drained into the bilge, where the water was filtered through a makeshift strainer to prevent excessive clogging of bilge strainer and the strainer in the main bilge pump. Before reloading the torpedo tube used for waste discharge first ran with the tube empty, and some of the existing remnants were eliminated. The refuse shot was made with the boat placed 3–5 degrees bow down, whereby it proved necessary to launch approximately 3–4 times, so that everything went out.

The state of health of the crew remained good. There were only several cases of conjunctivitis that, except for one case that turned out to be an ulcer, could be cured with the existing resources. The embarked San.Feldw. [corpsman] has proved himself well. I believe that the embarkation of a doctor is unnecessary because the necessary treatments can be performed by a San. rank.

While *U-1231* sank no Allied vessels on its patrol, it was never identified or attacked by Allied anti-submarine assets. OP-20-G noted in a 17 December Intelligence Summary that *U-1231* was unallocated for twenty-three days, which again confirms how the snorkel impacted the Allies' ability to find U-boats conducting submerged patrols in their operational area.[48]

Twelve days after *U-1231* departed, *U-806* (IXC/40) left Kristiansand for its operational area off the Canadian coast under the command of Kapitänleutnant Klaus Hornbostel. The snorkel for *U-806* was retrofitted in May 1944 at Kiel. Between 18 and 19 May 'experimental cladding' was installed on the snorkel while in dock at the Deutsch Werke. This cladding was probably an anti-radar rubber absorber applied around the snorkel head. *U-806* then conducted snorkel training at Horten from 22 to 24 October. On the 30th Hornbostel set course for his patrol area off Nova Scotia.

Snorkelling began the day of departure. On the next day an autumn storm brought sea state 6 conditions. Hornbostel noted in the KTB that 'in the prevailing sea conditions (about 6) the untrained personnel still have considerable difficulties with depth control'. This lack of control probably caused the snorkel head to dip under the sea, causing the float valve to close while the diesels sucked in fresh air through the intake piping. In such circumstances back pressure was generated that brought immediate discomfort to the crew until the snorkel head once more breached the surface. During his outbound trip Hornbostel began to conduct 'refuse shots' as early as 1 November. This was a new technique employed on long submerged patrols to prevent the need to surface the U-boat and throw rubbish overboard.

BdU initially requested that *U-806* occupy a weather station in Naval Square BD 4654 on 4 December, but *U-806* made exceptionally good progress and was already nearing the Nova Scotia coast. The weather reports were required to support the final timetable for Operation *Wacht Am Rhein* scheduled to begin at the end of month. Hornbostel made a quick weather report from the U-boat's current position so that BdU knew where he was. As *U-806* approached the 200m line on 12 December, Hornbostel noted that he would proceed surfaced that night for the last time before running entirely submerged and relying on his snorkel only to ventilate the U-boat. By 3am on the 15th *U-806* began to navigate by the glow of the lights from Halifax, and at 4.10am Egg Island lighthouse came into full view. As Hornbostel noted: 'from now on the navigation in the operations area was continually checked by lighthouses'. While navigation was seemingly not a problem thanks to a well-lit coast, communication was.

Hornbostel struggled with the same poor long-range, two-way wireless communication problem that plagued many, if not all, of the snorkel U-boat patrols operating off the North American coast in 1944–45. In this case, he wrote in the KTB: 'While resident in the operations area Radio Message receiving was only by the snorkel antenna because the Radio Direction Finder antenna was out of service. Reception during entire time was difficult but possible.' As discussed in Chapter 2, constant snorkel use caused the interior of the boat to become damp and electronics began to short and work improperly. While the cause of the RDF antenna's problem was not diagnosed or noted in the KTB, it is possible that the dampness was a potential cause of the problem.

U-806 patrolled at a rate of 50 nautical miles per day as it crept along on electric motors and snorkelled as required. Hornbostel conducted a slow, switchback pattern right outside of Halifax Harbour. It was noted that there was a persistent use of 'rattle buoys' outside the harbour entrance. These Allied devices were designed to drown out the sound of the screw noise that came from surface vessels to prevent U-boats getting an accurate sound bearing at close range. In addition, the buoys could throw off the T5 acoustic homing torpedo. While operating at a depth of 40m on 17 December, *U-806*'s crew heard propeller sounds that quickly grew louder, all around the boat. The forward net deflector of the U-boat became hooked on a net and was torn off the boat with a loud clang. Hornbostel noted that two patrol vessels stopped, probably to investigate. It is clear this Allied action was not seen through the periscope by Hornbostel, but instead discerned by sounds interpreted onboard the U-boat. Did the two patrol vessels note that their net had caught something and stopped to investigate? Did they realise that they had just had a close encounter with a German U-boat? Hornbostel dived to 70m and changed course to the south, creeping along in the shallow water as the sound of propeller screws and rattle buoys prevented accurate listening. The conclusion drawn by Hornbostel was that he was overrun by an outbound convoy.

U-806 snorkelled, recharged its batteries, and planned the next day's operations. Hornbostel made a very dangerous, but necessary decision – he surfaced the U-boat at 4.16am after coming up to periscope depth to conduct a full sweep of the area. After the incident with the convoy, a persistent rattling was heard from outside the U-boat and it had to be fixed. Noise could give away the U-boat's position. He confirmed that the net deflector was torn off, and that a hatch on the conning tower cladding associated with the radio direction finder had become loose and was fixed. Within ninety minutes of being surfaced *U-806* was again below the waves in a sea state 3 condition snorkelling to recharge its batteries. *U-806* encountered a steamer and patrol vessels on the 18th and was again overrun at a depth of 30m without any engagement. In the early hours of the 19th, *U-806* surfaced and Hornbostel ordered what was left of the net deflector removed due to continued rattling.

Hornbostel finally decided to attack on 21 December after nearly five days patrolling outside Halifax and numerous encounters with convoys and patrol vessels. At 7.47pm in a sea state 3–4, with overcast skies and good visibility, Hornbostel saw a small convoy of four Liberty Ships proceeding in a double row. He called 'Action stations' ten minutes later, followed by the order to fire a 'two-fan from Tubes I and III on the starboard forward steamer' at 7.55pm. Both missed as he had misjudged the heading of the steamers. He now ordered a shot from Tube V on the port steamer at 8.04pm. A hit was heard at two minutes and thirty-one seconds. He came up to periscope depth at 8.38pm and noted its stern deep in the water, with the other steamers and patrol vessels gone. He had struck the British steamer *Samtucky* (7,219 GRT). He then moved off the coast, expecting the Canadian defences to be alerted and begin searching for the U-boat.

Hornbostel's next attack came on 22 December, when he fired a three-fan from Tubes I, III and IV at a steamer being escorted by a flower corvette. Tube IV did not fire due to a mechanical malfunction. One of the other two torpedoes' direction mechanisms also appeared to malfunction as the torpedo was heard passing by the conning tower on the starboard side to aft – a potentially dangerous situation known as a circular shot.[49] The third torpedo detonated after nine minutes of running, missing its target. On 23 December at 1.11am a radio message was received from BdU. This was the first message received in several weeks. *U-1232* was to be expected in the operating area shortly after it departed, eleven days after *U-806*. A situation report soon followed. This message was picked up by OP-20-G but not recorded in its daily summary:

U-806 is estimated on patrol in the Halifax–Gulf of Maine area having been told on 21 December that U-1230 'is presumably in the same op area as you are', A fresh U-boat, U-1232, which was reporting weather, is now in the vicinity of Sable Island probably moving into Halifax area. They were told that based on experience from U-1221 'success may be expected only directly off Halifax; act accordingly'. The defence was described as 'little weary patrolling without ASDIC. Off Halifax none, elsewhere little day and night air'.[50]

On the 23rd, *U-806* was conducting a snorkel run to ventilate the boat south-east of Halifax when it noticed a Catalina overhead. The U-boat conducted a crash dive at 1.30pm. Hornbostel noted in the KTB that:

> During this crash dive the torpedo from Tube IV, which had been withdrawn about 3m, slipped out of the steel band, damaging the torpedo retaining bolt and hit with the pistol against the outer tube door. Pistol is unusable, battery chamber bulkhead torn, torpedo also unusable. Tube IV is in service again after replacing the retaining bolt.

A U-boat's torpedo tube was its only offensive and defensive weapon as the deck guns had long since been removed. Ensuring operability and being self-sufficient so close to an enemy coast was imperative. Within hours *U-806* was manoeuvring back towards Halifax Harbour again.

At approximately 2pm on the 24th Hornbostel observed another convoy of eight steamers leaving Halifax under the escort of a flower corvette. *U-806* was approximately 15 nautical miles from the harbour entrance. 'Action stations' was called. A shot was fired from Tube V at 2.37pm and HMS *Clayoqot* was hit and noted as sinking at 2.40pm. A second corvette quickly made its way to the defence of its stricken sister ship. *U-806* quickly fired a second shot at one of the steamers, but missed. Four depth charges were heard as well as machine gun fire. *U-806* had been at periscope depth, but now Hornbostel ordered evasive manoeuvres. In the past, U-boats would move off as quickly as possible to deeper water. Deep water offered manoeuvrability and put depth between the U-boat and exploding depth charges. This was also what Allied anti-submarine commanders were trained to expect from a U-boat commander. However, with the advent of the snorkel and inshore operations, the opposite tactic was taught to U-boat commanders and expected by BdU. The following procedure conducted by Hornbostel was emblematic of this new tactical concept.

At 2.47pm, just seven minutes after hitting the corvette, Hornbostel gave the order to dive to 60m. His U-boat was operating in water that was only 75m deep. His next order was to head towards land, passing directly under the convoy he had just attacked. He heard six depth charges, far off, as the convoy defenders were conducting defensive operations based on old U-boat tactics, expecting the U-boat to be heading out to sea. At 3.10pm, just thirty minutes after the attack, Hornbostel set the U-boat down in 68m of water. He recorded the manoeuvre in the KTB as 'decision: Lie on the bottom here'. While the crew sat motionless in their bunks or stood quiet at their stations, all around them the sound of the Allied search could be heard for the next ten hours.

> In this period about 100 depth charges, however not very close, no damage. About twelve patrol vessels (turbine and piston propulsion) ran out of Halifax. Because the boat was directly on the route from the shooting location to Halifax, the boat was frequently overrun. All destroyers and corvettes have ASDIC (partly buzzing, partly single impulse), only a few employ saws.

The U-boat was never located. In the early morning hours of 25 December Hornbostel ordered the U-boat raised and it set off to the south-south-east on electric motors – silent running. He stayed 10–20m off the bottom, while all around he heard the sounds of increased searching, even having a destroyer pass directly overhead with active ASDIC, but he was not identified.

Hornbostel wrote up his analysis of the Allied defensive action in his KTB and noted:

> In the period up to darkness the shooting location and the immediate vicinity was intensively searched with ASDIC, however there were a relatively small number of depth charges (about 100 units) more or less randomly thrown. Not finding the boat is primarily due to the fact that there was a very irregular, rocky bottom.

The key to *U-806*'s survival was that that the rocky bottom helped mask his acoustic signature from Allied ASDIC and the new U-boat tactic of bottoming, closer inshore near the attack location, was certainly not expected by Allied anti-submarine commanders. Even if a possible signal was heard by a searching corvette, it might be disregarded due to the working assumption that a U-boat had already departed the area.

U-806 moved off to the southern area of Nova Scotia, where it spent the next week in search of additional Allied vessels. At midnight the U-boat received a greetings from BdU that read: 'To all U-boats. Heartfelt wishes for the New Year to submarine crews at the enemy. I am with you in thought. The years change, our slogan remains the same: Attack, run, sink!' *Sieg Heil*! Komm.Adm.U-Boote' This was followed by:

> U-boat men!
> The past year has shown us that we can again fight with the improved boats.
> In the coming year the striking power of our weapon will be strengthened by

new boats. It is our responsibility to bring them to full effect. For the year, we promise we will continue to employ them unconditionally and ruthlessly in the fight for the freedom of our people.

– ObdM und BdU –

By 'improved boats' it was meant U-boats retrofitted with snorkels. The Type XXI Electro-boat was referenced by 'new boats'.

A heavy Allied defence was noted the following week due to the recent attack. As a result, *U-806* had no further successes. With supplies and diesel beginning to run low, another problem occurred. The snorkel, the improvement that made the 'new boats' so successful, as noted by BdU, stopped working. At 3.41am on 4 January, Hornbostel noted the following in his KTB:

> Snorkel mast cannot be lowered without surfacing. Surfacing is not possible in the current defence conditions. Intention: In about 8 days return transit must be started due to fuel and provisions inventory. Because moving off and repair of the snorkel cannot be accomplished in this period, decide on return transit. Even during the testing and training period of the boat in the homeland it was clearly determined by the UAK and the Agru-front that snorkel safety was totally inadequate in its present form (weak, long linkage, with pressure hull pass through and joints not greasable). Despite final adjustments and overhaul a half year later, no changes. However this is absolutely necessary because otherwise it cannot meet the demands of a 4-month patrol.

Hornbostel's commentary on the snorkel revealed a problematic retrofit and rushed testing. *U-806* headed back to port. Hornbostel came across an outbound convoy a few days later but he noted in the KTB that he could not send a warning signal to BdU because only a 'short signal' transmission over the snorkel antenna was possible and it was not expected to be received. In order to make a long-range wireless transmission U-boats still had to surface. Finally, on 8 January, *U-806* began to run on the surface for a short period of time, marking the official end of its snorkel patrol off Halifax. With only two brief exceptions, it had maintained a constant underwater patrol for twenty-eight days. This was by no means a record, but the fact that Hornbostel did so outside one of the busiest Allied harbours was impressive. On 27 February, *U-806* arrived safely at Flensburg, Germany, after a long return route south of Iceland.

U-1232 (IXC/40) was commissioned in March 1944. It was commanded by Kapitän zur See Kurt Dobratz, who at the age of 40, was one the oldest

U-boat commanders to conduct an operational patrol during the war. Dobratz began his military service as a commissioned Kriegsmarine officer in 1922 but transferred to the Luftwaffe in 1935. While in the Luftwaffe he not only served in various staff positions but also as a fighter pilot, conducting eleven sorties while part of I.KG 26 in 1941. He transferred back to the Kriegsmarine in 1943. *U-1232* was his first U-boat command. During the post-commissioning period, Dobratz was noted as having ordered a cutaway hull modification to *U-1232* (see Chapter 2). Being a former Luftwaffe pilot, Dobratz was probably very cognisant of the value of hydrodynamics.

U-1232 conducted the normal training and work-up routine in the Baltic during the spring and early summer of 1944 before arriving back in Hamburg, where it received its snorkel retrofit during the four-week period between August and September. *U-1232* departed Kiel for Horten on 28 October, arriving three days later on the 31st without incident. Snorkel training and final check-outs occurred in the first week in November. On 7 November, Dobratz departed Horten for Kristiansand, then left there on the 11th to begin his first combat patrol. This first part of this consisted of sending weather reports until mid-December, due to the final planning for the upcoming German offensive in the Ardennes, as previously noted. By the end of the month *U-1232* had arrived off the Newfoundland Banks, where Dobratz began an impressive snorkel patrol. BdU was clear in its direction to Dobratz when it transmitted on 18 December: 'Go close to points of heavy traffic concentration as given in transmitted situation reports,' and on the 22nd: 'Occupy sea area around main port [Halifax].'[51]

The KTB for *U-1232* has not been located and information about the patrol can only be gained by Ultra intercepts. After Dobratz sent his last weather report on 17 December, he was not heard from for more than a month. His wireless transmission, which was intercepted on 23 January, was indeed good news for BdU and their inshore efforts.

From: Dobratz
1) Started return January 14th.
2) Constant traffic of independents and convoys day and night from Sambro Lightship to BB 7564 ((44.15N-62.55W)) and 7535 ((44.33N-62.45W)). Shuttling defence vessels with Saws and deterrent depth charges on the 100 metre line. After attacks traffic decreased for as much as 7 days, strengthening defence with ASDIC. I was never discovered. Slight day and night air ((garbled)) convoys. Snorkelling and surface charging inside the 100 metre line was undisturbed. Lights ((were operating)) as ((light)) measure, R/Bs as in peace time. Hydrophone produced better range than visibility. At times snorkelling (pressure below normal) and periscope iced over.

3) December 31st in BB 7561 ((44.21N-62.55W)) miss of 2 on Liberty Ship. January 2nd in 7564 ((44.21N-62.55W)) sank destroyer of 'Somers' Class. January 3rd in 7538 ((44.27N-62.45W)) spread of 2 on 20,000 ton Passenger Ship, detection after 3 min 45 sec. January 4th in 7535 ((44.33N-62.45W)) sank 7,500 ton Tanker and 6,000 ton Passenger Freighter from Westbound Convoy, missed single shot on 5,000 tonner. January 14th in 7527 ((44.27N-63.25W)) sank 2 Tankers of 9,400 and 8,000 tons and 2 Freighters of 7,000 and 6,000 tons from westbound convoy.

4) All BB75 ((Halifax Area)).

5) Was rammed by Corvette after the last shot. Out of order: attack periscope and U-boat aiming sight. Out of order on the way out: twin mountings completely broken, D/F apparatus partially clear for use, is taking water badly. Snorkel round dipole soaked.

6) Missing Ser NAS: 20/11 164; 26/11 126, 127; 20/12 389; 6/1 329, 336, 337, 341, 342; 12/1 386 to 389; 13/1 302 to 309.

7) 2 T-3A, one of them only partially clear. 88 CBM.

8) CD 1426 ((41.51N-45.34W)). East 2, Sea 2, 1012 MB.[52]

This intercept reveals how difficult it was to receive wireless messages, with almost none received between 20 November and 13 January. This example highlights how Ultra might not produce a complete or accurate message because some of it might be garbled. For purposes of comparison, the BdU record of the message, marked as Top Secret, noted that in item (4) it was the echo-locaters, not the direction-finder, that was damaged.[53] In this case the US Navy analyst made a translation error.

The next day Dönitz initially sent a single-worded message at 10.17am: 'Bravo!'[54]

This was followed at 8.21pm that evening with the following:

Dear Dobratz,
I have today personally proposed to the Führer the Knight's Cross for you. The answer of the Führer was the single word: 'Immediately'. I congratulate you heartily on the award.[55]

On 25 January both Dönitz and Admiral Godt sent Dobratz another congratulatory message on his accomplishments. That same day OP-20-G assessed the actions of both *U-806* and *U-1232*, whose patrols overlapped, as follows:

Two U-boats returning from patrols off Halifax have made situation reports. U-806 (Hornbostel) stated 'Insignificant defence near and ahead of convoys and independents before and after the first time U-boat was observed. Appearance of DDs and corvettes after 2nd time U-boat was observed. This time all used ASDIC and deterrent D/Cs. U-boat was never spotted.' (0012/20).

(Note: This U-boat reported the torpedoing of the 7,219-ton British MV *Samtucky* 21 December. The latter was beached and considered a total loss. The latter also sunk the HMCS *Clayoquot*, an AM, 24 December. Both these attacks occurred off Halifax.)

U-806 has stopped en route home to report weather in the vicinity of 57N 30W and was told she could surface at night in that area since it was free from attack.[56]

Both sinking claims were accurate, with *Samtucky* being part of Convoy HX-327 and *Clayoquot* part of XB-139. This confirmed that these vessels were part of ship convoys and not stragglers encountered by *U-806*, adding further credence to the account recorded in *U-806*'s KTB. OP-20-G also noted *U-1232*'s successful snorkel patrol along the coast, noting that it was 'never discovered'.[57]

The Knight's Cross to the Iron Cross was bestowed on Dobratz on 23 January while he was still on patrol. Dönitz highlighted to Hitler the capability of a snorkel-equipped U-boat, utilising Dobratz's patrol as an example.[58] This was a very successful inshore patrol against two convoys, SH-194 and BX-141, given that Allied naval forces had already been on alert for snorkel-equipped U-boats since the autumn of 1944. Ultra intercepts had previously noted how U-boat commanders such as Kneip (*U-1223*), who operated off the mouth of the St Lawrence during October, had reported 'Op area promising' on 25 December, and Altmeier (in *U-1222*), who operated off Nova Scotia in November, said, 'Successes may be expected only directly off Halifax' on 22 December.[59] Dobratz's sinking claims, however, were not correct, demonstrating how difficult it was to verify the result of a torpedo hit while submerged. As noted in the OP-20-G Intelligence Summary: 'Actually this U-boat sank 26,804 tons *which, incidentally, is still a pretty good haul* [author's emphasis].'[60]

It is interesting to note that even Commander Knowles, who wrote the assessment, was struck by Dobratz's success. After his successful return to Norway on 14 February, Dobratz was reassigned to Chief of Staff at BdU. His years of staff experience and highly successful patrol was put to good use in the challenging operational environment. Dobratz became the last Kommandierenden Admiral der U-Boote (Admiral of U-boats) during the final days of the war. On 26 February BdU sent a wireless message to all U-boats noting Dobratz's success and his reward of '... big fat steamers by the good Lord, and with the Knight's Cross by the Führer'.[61] His success was turned into Experience Message No. 231 A, giving direction for operations along enemy coasts, which was broadcast out on 21 March to the rest of the U-boat force.[62]

U-1232 was the last U-boat to depart for Canadian waters in 1944. The shift in operational U-boat patrols further south to the US East Coast was now under way. In early February 1945 three U-boats, *U-857* (IXC/40), *U-866* (IXC/40) and *U-879* (IXD2), all departed to a point initially '150 miles south-east of Halifax' under orders to send weather reports once a day while en route.[63] The patrols of *U-857* and *U-879* will be discussed below in the section on the US East Coast operations, but *U-866*'s will be detailed here due to its fate off the Canadian coast.

U-866 was commissioned on 7 November 1943. It followed the standard training and retrofit schedule as most late-war Type IXs. It snorkel was received in Bremen in August 1944. *U-866*, commanded by Oberleutnant Peter Rogowsky, arrived in Horten from Kiel on 23 January, where it conducted final snorkel training and trials. It reached Bergen on 2 February and departed for its first patrol on the 6th. After several weeks of weather reporting, Rogowsky was given orders to proceed west on 4 March. On the 5th, *U-866* reported from a position located at 47.30N-41.30W that was approximately 880km due east of Cape Race lighthouse at the tip of Newfoundland.[64] Four days later, BdU recorded *U-866* as being off Halifax. Rogowsky was subsequently directed (along with *U-857*, which was directed to Cape Hatteras) that: 'If no traffic there, go along the coast.'[65] *U-866* was ordered to operate off Halifax, and this was confirmed again by BdU in a message transmitted on 31 March to Rogowsky stating that: 'Dobratz ((1232)) achieved great successes in your op area only because he went in close to the entrance ((to Halifax Harbour)).'[66] It is likely that Rogowsky never received that transmission. It is believed that *U-866* was encountered just east of Nova Scotia along the 200m line and subsequently sunk on 18 March at position 43.18N-61.08W by depth charges from the US destroyer escorts USS *Lowe*, USS *Menges*, USS *Pride* and USS *Mosley*. There is a possibility that this was *U-857*, however, when comparing the last reported positions of both U-boats and calculating the miles to the sinking point, it is likely that it was *U-866*.[67]

While some westbound U-boats might pass through Canadian coastal waters en route to the US East Coast, *U-190* (IXC/40), under the command of Oberleutnant Hans-Erwin Reith, was the last U-boat directed against Canada during the war.

U-190 was commissioned on 24 September 1942. It arrived in Lorient after completing its fourth patrol on 20 June 1944 as the fighting for

Normandy was under way. The U-boat's commander at that time, Kapitänleutnant Max Wintermeyer, was replaced by Oberleutnant Hans-Erwin Reith. *U-190* immediately underwent a retrofit for a Type I snorkel installation, which was completed at the end of July. On 17 August *U-190* departed at 9.45pm en route to Flensburg. On its first dive just two hours after leaving Lorient, *U-190* raised its snorkel mast, initiated intake procedures and immediately encountered problems. The engine room filled with heavy smoke caused by the 'new gaskets' installed as part of the snorkel exhaust configuration. An Allied aircraft turned on a searchlight and approached the location after apparently detecting the snorkel mast by radar. Reith ordered an immediate crash dive. A patrol of Allied destroyers was soon detected approaching the area. After a tense five hours of evasion, *U-190* came up to about 25m and began a second snorkel attempt. From 5.30am to 6am the snorkel system was run with full diesels in order to cross the dangerous Bay of Biscay as quickly as possible. The snorkel exhaust system was not working properly and by 11.30am it was realised that the crew was suffering the effects of carbon monoxide poisoning. It was estimated that a full three-quarters of the crew was affected and Reith ordered the U-boat to surface for complete ventilation.[68]

U-190 came up at 11.50am, then dived again at 12.15pm. The twenty-five minutes on the surface appeared enough time to allow the U-boat to dive again and remain submerged for nearly ten hours. While no commentary exists in the KTB on this point, the crew probably worked to repair the snorkel exhaust line as they successfully snorkelled the following day. However, a new problem developed that was possibly linked to the repairs they tried to make. The next day, the 19th, *U-190* snorkelled for the first time at 6.36am and ended the snorkel run at 7.17am, turning the boat around to head back to port due to a 'leak in the snorkel installation' that caused the boat to take 'on much water'. Due to the presence of Allied aircraft, *U-190* remained submerged. Reith attempted several more snorkel attempts the next day, then finally 'bottoming out' on the 20th. A link-up was made with a German escort and *U-190* made it back to Lorient at 8.30am on 21 August.

U-190 remained in Lorient for approximately thirty-six hours undergoing emergency repairs to the snorkel system. Reith departed at 8.45pm on 22 August. No other problems were recorded in the KTB related to the snorkel and it completed its fifth cruise, designated an evacuation and not a war patrol, at 4pm on 4 October when it arrived at Flensburg, Germany. *U-190* moved to Bremen for 'overhaul and streamlining' in mid-October, then arrived in Kiel on 26 January 1945. On 7 February *U-190* topped off with fuel, conducted a final trimming trial and departed for Horten on the

10th, arriving on the 14th. During its time in Kiel the snorkel installation was likely to have been overhauled, given the makeshift retrofit conducted in Lorient. During five days in Horten *U-190* conducted final snorkel testing and sea trials. Reith departed on the 19th for his first patrol, heading first to Kristiansand, then Stavanger, before finally heading westward towards its operational area off Halifax on the 23rd.[69]

U-190's sixth and final war patrol was reconstructed from the interrogation report of the boat's commander and crew, as well as surviving documents not destroyed before it surrendered to Canadian forces. Among the surviving documents is the distance log that accurately recorded the time the U-boat spent cruising surfaced or submerged, and while submerged, how often it ran the snorkel (while running the diesels) or the electric motors. This latter report is rare among surviving late war U-boat documents. It is extremely useful in evaluating the performance characteristics of a typical Type IX with a functioning snorkel operating off the North American coast.

During *U-190*'s final war patrol that began in Horten and ended off the Nova Scotia coast, it spent seventy-nine days at sea before it surrendered. Of those, seventy-seven days had detailed operational data recorded. That represents a total of 1,848 hours. In total, *U-190* only spent approximately 209.95 hours surfaced, the equivalent of 8.7 days, or put statistically, *U-190* spent 89 per cent of its patrol submerged. We can break this down even further by splitting the patrol into two phases, Phase I being the time it departed Norway, transited south of Iceland and reached the start of its operational patrol area. Phase II represents the time it spent off Nova Scotia in its operational patrol area. Phase I lasted thirty-nine days and Phase II thirty-eight days. During its transit to the operational area *U-190* had more opportunities to surface for prolonged periods of time. It also ran submerged on diesels, utilising the snorkel for longer periods as well. During Phase I *U-190* spent 206.95 hours surfaced in transit (or 8.62 total days). Statistically this represented approximately 78 per cent of the outbound cruise submerged. During this phase it operated the snorkel for 119 hours (or 4.96 days), representing a usage of approximately 13 per cent during the outbound cruise. If we look at Phase II, we see a startling change. While in the operational area, *U-190* spent three hours surfaced, probably to transmit a wireless message or take a navigation fix. Statistically, this means that *U-190* spent 100 per cent of thirty-eight consecutive days submerged. During this time it snorkelled (running diesels) for 200.75 hours (or 8.3 days), representing 22 per cent of its operational patrol, the rest of the time spent running on electric motors. Another interesting statistic is that outbound in Phase I, *U-190* averaged 4.5 hours a day snorkelling, with fif-

teen days seeing an average use of nine hours. We know that the end of hostilities concluded *U-190*'s patrol prematurely, but the statistics reveal clearly the operational potential of a functioning snorkel and trained crew.
Through the use of the snorkel *U-190* successfully avoided all anti-submarine assets during the entire cruise. If the interrogation of the radio operator was accurate then the single documented radio transmission to *U-190*
by BdU intercepted by OP-20-G was never received. This again underscores
the communication issues experienced by snorkel boats in North American
waters.[70]

The snorkel-equipped U-boat patrols off Canada proved beyond any
doubt that these craft could transit the North Atlantic and sink ships while
operating in the shallows outside busy harbours with near impunity. Their
experiences during the autumn of 1944, to include new tactics, were shared
with those U-boats dispatched to patrol further south along the US East
Coast in 1945.

US East Coast

The first Type IX snorkel-equipped U-boat assigned to US waters was
U-154 (IXC), under the command of Oberleutnant Gerth Gemeiner.
U-154's snorkel was retrofitted at Lorient in May and it departed there on
20 June 1944 for a point east of St Augustine, Florida, according to Ultra
intercepts.[71] However, *U-154* was sunk fourteen days later on 3 July, north-
west of Madeira, Portugal, by depth charges from the US destroyer escorts
USS *Inch* and USS *Frost*. We do not know if Gemeiner's snorkel malfunctioned at any point, forcing his U-boat to surface while he was hunted. This
remains a distinct possibility.

Gemeiner's U-boat was not the first directed to the US East Coast after
the end of Operation *Paukenschlag* in 1942. Yet the mass sinkings of Allied
ships off the US East Coast that year was replaced by two years of near
quiet. The appearance of U-boats was rare, and the sinking of an Allied ship
even rarer. Alerted in advance through Ultra, the US Navy's Tenth Fleet had
some forewarning of inbound U-boats that avoided the Atlantic-based
hunter-killer task groups.

When U-boats did manage to slip past their Atlantic pursuers and arrived
near the US East Coast prior to January 1945, they remained well beyond
the continental shelf in almost all cases. U-boats no longer cruised within
eyesight of the coast, preferring to remain in the deeper water between the
coast and Bermuda and the continental shelf marked by the 200m line.
Unlike the dark water of Canadian inlets and the St Lawrence River, where
heavy fog, strong currents, thermoclines and rocky bottoms could easily
offer a U-boat a place to hide, especially from ASDIC when bottomed, the

US East Coast south of Maine offered little natural protection. Much of the coast offered gently sloping sandy bottoms, and while the cold, dark waters of the Labrador Current north of Cape Hatteras offered some protection from aerial observation, the warm Gulf Stream-washed shore of the southern states could boast clear visibility to depths of 30m or more, offering little natural protection for a patrolling or 'bottomed' U-boat. From the Gulf Stream to the south of Cape Hatteras only clear, warm water prevails. Tactically, these conditions are not favourable for continuous submerged, inshore operations. There was also a concern by BdU that a U-boat could not stay submerged for long periods in tropical or sub-tropical waters as the inside of a U-boat might become too uncomfortable for the crew. While there was no operational difference between snorkel-equipped U-boats assigned to patrol off the Canadian coast and those assigned to the US East Coast, tactically their experiences were very different.

Oberleutnant Hans-Werner Offermann and his *U-518* (IXC) returned to Kristiansand from his patrol off Cape Hatteras on 24 October with a positive report for BdU. Offermann departed one month after *U-154*, following Gemeiner from Lorient on 15 July after receiving a snorkel retrofit the previous month. Offermann's original operational area was to be the Caribbean, where a recent patrol by the non-snorkel-equipped *U-539* (IXC/40) proved highly successful.[72] However, Offermann was granted freedom of manoeuvre by BdU on 7 August and he chose to head towards Cape Hatteras.[73] He was the first snorkel-equipped U-boat off the US East Coast and the first to return to the Outer Banks in almost a year since the non-snorkel-equipped *U-129* (IXC) patrolled there in December 1943. He had been preceded by the non-snorkel-equipped *U-541* just five months earlier, although Kapitänleutnant Kurt Petersen (IXC/40) kept to deeper water between Bermuda, Georgia and Florida, never manoeuvring near the 200m line and sinking no ships.

Offermann's *U-518* was hunted just like Gemeiner's *U-154*. Alerted through Ultra, US Navy's Task Force-62, followed by the Croatan Group, attempted to follow up on an initial sound contact to pursue and sink the U-boat in European waters rather than wait for it to arrive off the US East Coast.[74] Unlike Gemeiner, Offermann successfully avoided his pursuers through the use of his snorkel, even though he did not remain submerged as often as his counterparts. He clearly felt safe in his operational area. Offermann reported his observations to BdU. BdU subsequently turned them into the 'current intelligence' for all future U-boat patrols to the area.[75]

After the return of *U-518*, further deployments of U-boats to the US East Coast did not resume until the end of December 1944. An exception was *U-1230* (IXC/40), which deployed in the first week of October. Its purpose, however, was not to conduct a standard combat patrol but to drop off agents. This patrol will be detailed below in the section on *Gruppe Seewolf*.

The first snorkel-equipped U-boat with specific operational orders to patrol inshore along the US East Coast was *U-869* (IXC/40) under command of Kapitänleutnant Hellmut Neuerburg. *U-869* inaugurated the operational shift from Canadian to US waters in early December, when it was ordered to patrol the mouth of the Delaware River and focus on traffic from the port of Philadelphia. *U-869* did not return from its patrol and it will be discussed as a specific case study in Chapter 10.

U-1233 (IXC/40), under the command of Korvettenkapitän Hans-Joachim Kuhn, followed *U-869* to the US East Coast on 24 December. *U-1233* was retrofitted with a snorkel in Kiel in October and November before heading to Horten for its final snorkel trials and training. Kuhn was originally expected to follow Neuerburg a few days after his departure on the 8th, but he immediately experienced snorkel difficulties. *U-1233* attempted to depart on 18, 21 and 22 December and each time returned to Horten (initially), then to Bergen for repairs.[76]

When Kuhn finally departed he continued to run into the problems typical of Type IXs that winter in the North Atlantic, namely communications. When *U-1233* presumably reached a point west of Ireland, BdU sent Kuhn his deployment order recorded in the BdU KTB as 'proceed towards Cape Hatteras, on the surface as much as possible'.[77] BdU requested *U-1233* to report five times between 19 and 22 January without a response.[78] BdU grew concerned at Kuhn's lack of reports and sent him a message, which was intercepted by Ultra on 24 January, which read: 'If you so far have been transmitting without success, probably antenna cable is soaked or is short-circuited by [break in] insulation. Relief measure: Bring reserve transmitter into tower; draw antenna through storm hatch with Aphrodite Balloon.'[79] This is important to note, because Kuhn was directed to Cape Hatteras through a wireless order from BdU on 12 January.[80] It is not clear if Kuhn had orders to patrol at some other location along the US East Coast before receiving the wireless transmission to head towards Cape Hatteras, or if the 12 January order constituted his original patrol objective. BdU then sent a follow-on order around 26 January, stating '... occupy at your discretion either the area given in heading orders or that of *U-1232*, off Halifax'.[81]

No KTB for *U-1233* exists. We do not know what transmissions it received from BdU or what affected Kuhn's decisions. It appears from the following transmission from Kuhn that he received the message on 26 January and decided not to manoeuvre towards Cape Hatteras, but stay further north along the coast. On 4 March Kuhn sent what was probably his only report that was received by BdU since *U-1233* departed. Intercepted by

Ultra, it stated that Kuhn had been on his return cruise since 2 February. Based on his report, *U-1233* reached a point almost 100 miles due south of Montauk, Long Island, at the 200m line, and proceeded north-east along the continental shelf until it reached an area near Halifax, then turned east to head back to Norway without sinking any vessels. It is likely that Kuhn reached the 200m line at some point at the end of January, spending no more than seven to ten days submerged along the coast while cruising north-east in deep water. Kuhn reported picking up weak sound bearings of 'independents' along the Gulf of Maine. He had experienced poor visibility, encountered 'weak patrolling with buzz-saws', and identified no 'air nor land radar'. Whether he fired torpedoes at Allied vessels is not known. What followed next were the reasons he most likely decided to return to Norway. Kuhn reported: 'Damages on cruise: Twin mounts destroyed, 3.7cm unusable, round dipole (flexible cable), air target periscope [sky scope], in op area echo sounder.'[82]

Kuhn was faced with no way to fight off enemy aircraft while on the surface. An inoperable echo sounder meant he could not cruise close to shore and expect to manoeuvre effectively against targets. With the sky scope and dipole inoperable, he also had to snorkel blind. Yet, we know that these reasons did not constitute a life-threatening situation for the U-boat. It is also not clear how this damage occurred. BdU received the message and recorded in their KTB 'U-1233 (Kuhn) reported return transit from BD 1770. Only has sound bearing in CB 11. CA 35, BA 99. Sea damage on outbound transit: anti-aircraft weapons, air search periscope. In operations area [echo sounder].'[83]

According to Ultra, BdU responded to a report from Kuhn on 5 March that questioned what was contained in his previous transmission. By the response from BdU: 'On what do you base your reports of traffic near Halifax, Newfoundland Bank, and at 41 degrees? Report visual and hydrophone observations, especially of convoys. Attacks, number of torpedoes used. How closely did you approach the order traffic concentration points?'[84] Kuhn never responded. He was asked again by BdU to respond on the 7th, but again no response was received. Kuhn had probably surfaced briefly on the 4th to send his message, and then proceeded on snorkel south of Iceland and through the Shetland passage. *U-1233* returned on 28 March to Kristiansand, completing a ninety-five-day patrol.

Not a single U-boat departed for North American waters in January. Operations were focused around the British coast with the onset of Operation *Wacht Am Rhein* in the west. The next group of U-boats BdU ordered to the US East Coast were dispatched in February. This group consisted of *U-857* (IXC/40), *U-879* (IXD2) and *U-853* (IXC/40).

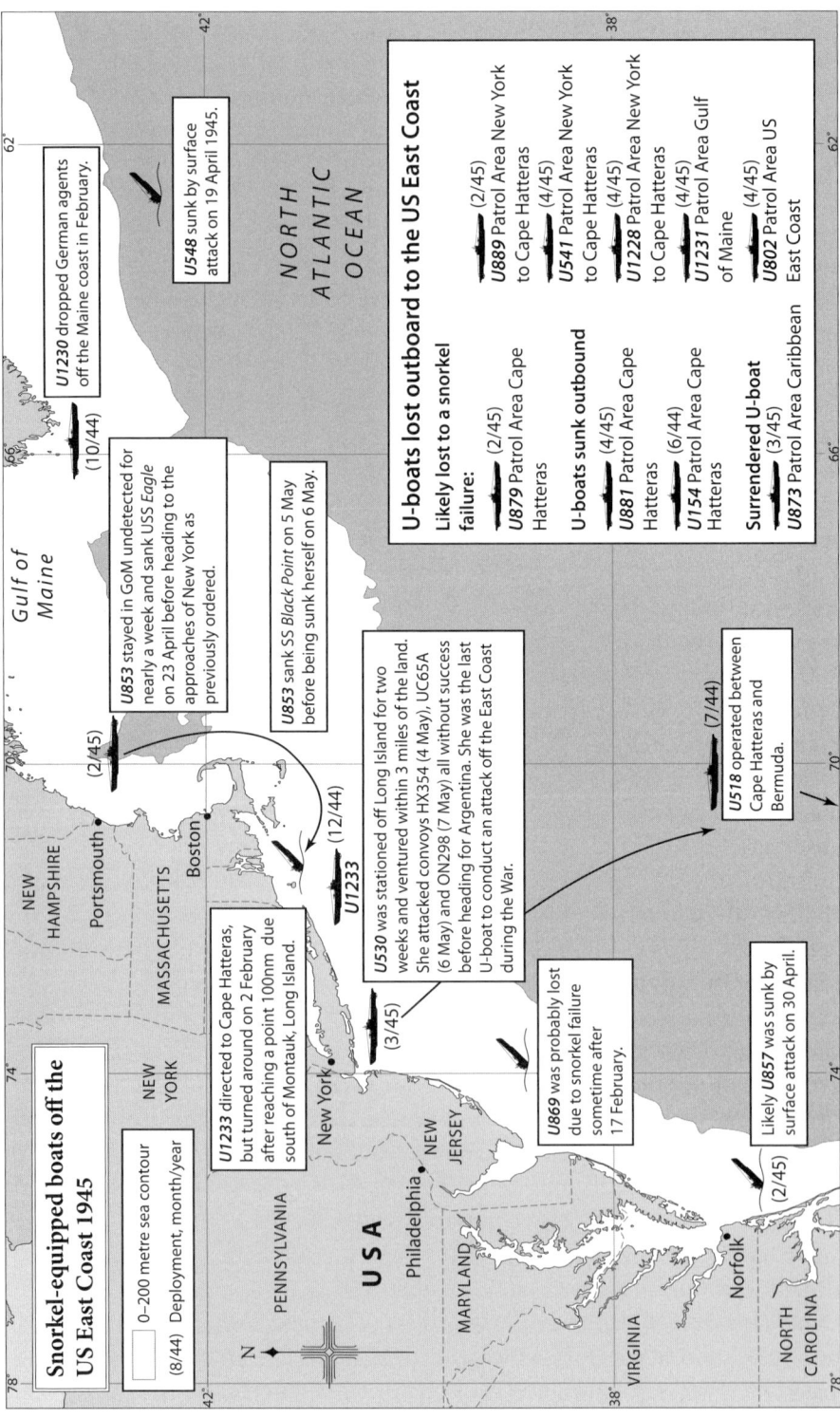

Snorkel-equipped boats off the US East Coast 1945

0–200 metre sea contour

(8/44) Deployment, month/year

U1230 dropped German agents off the Maine coast in February.

U548 sunk by surface attack on 19 April 1945.

NORTH ATLANTIC OCEAN

Gulf of Maine

U853 stayed in GoM undetected for nearly a week and sank USS *Eagle* on 23 April before heading to the approaches of New York as previously ordered.

U853 sank SS *Black Point* on 5 May before being sunk herself on 6 May.

NEW HAMPSHIRE

Portsmouth

(2/45)

(10/44)

MASSACHUSETTS

Boston

U1233 directed to Cape Hatteras, but turned around on 2 February after reaching a point 100nm due south of Montauk, Long Island.

(12/44)

U1233

NEW YORK

U530 was stationed off Long Island for two weeks and ventured within 3 miles of the land. She attacked convoys HX354 (4 May), UC65A (6 May) and ON298 (7 May) all without success before heading for Argentina. She was the last U-boat to conduct an attack off the East Coast during the War.

New York

(3/45)

NEW JERSEY

PENNSYLVANIA

Philadelphia

USA

U869 was probably lost due to snorkel failure sometime after 17 February.

U518 operated between Cape Hatteras and Bermuda.

(7/44)

MARYLAND

VIRGINIA

Norfolk

Likely *U857* was sunk by surface attack on 30 April.

(2/45)

NORTH CAROLINA

N

U-boats lost outboard to the US East Coast

Likely lost to a snorkel failure:

(2/45)
U889 Patrol Area New York to Cape Hatteras

(2/45)
U879 Patrol Area Cape Hatteras

(4/45)
U541 Patrol Area New York to Cape Hatteras

U-boats sunk outbound

(4/45)
U881 Patrol Area Cape Hatteras

(4/45)
U1228 Patrol Area New York to Cape Hatteras

(6/44)
U154 Patrol Area Cape Hatteras

(4/45)
U1231 Patrol Area Gulf of Maine

Surrendered U-boat

(3/45)
U873 Patrol Area Caribbean

(4/45)
U802 Patrol Area US East Coast

Under the command of Kapitänleutnant Rudolf Premauer, *U-857* departed Horten on 6 February 1945. It received a fixed snorkel while in its Bordeaux bunker in August 1944. This was to enable it to escape from the French port that was now under Allied siege by land and make its way back to Germany. At some point over the next few months an operable snorkel was installed.

On 6 February, *U-857* departed Horten for North America. Its last wireless transmission with a position was sent on 6 March and was picked up by Ultra. OP-20-G identified the position of *U-857* as 49.30N-33.30W but it was not entirely sure of the western fix.[85] Clearly the U-boat was on a southwest course based on its previous position of 51.30N-31.30W identified by Ultra. That put Premauer almost in the middle of the Atlantic between Newfoundland and Ireland. On 6 March it received its 'Guard America' message.[86] BdU sent a message on 8 March to *U-857* in special cipher that was not decrypted.[87] The content of this message is unknown and could contain any number of topics meant for the commander's eyes only. On 9 March OKM recorded in their KTB: 'U-857 (Premauer) area of Cape Hatteras. If no traffic there, go along the coast.'[88] It is possible that this was the message contained in the encrypted transmission. We also do not know if *U-857* sent a confirmation back that was not intercepted. BdU's confidence in *U-857*'s final operational destination may have been because Premauer received his deployment orders in writing before he departed.

On 15 March BdU transmitted a message of intelligence in the clear for the area of Cape Hatteras. This intelligence was based on the outdated observations by *U-518* and *U-541* during their patrols of the spring and summer of 1944. This was followed by intelligence for the area around Halifax on 16 March and Boston on 6 April.[89] None of these were directed specifically to *U-857* but to all U-boats operating off the North American coast. Before we can discuss what might have happened during the rest of Premauer's patrol, we need to look at *U-879* and *U-853* as their ultimate fates are intertwined.

U-879, under the command of Kapitänleutnant Erwin Manchen, departed Kiel for Horten on 27 January 1945 after completing its snorkel retrofit. *U-879* experienced a delay in transit since it could not pass the Skagerrak by dawn and probably did not want to risk being identified by Allied aircraft. Manchen briefly put into port at Frederikshaven instead.[90] After reaching Horten and going through the final snorkel training and testing, *U-879* departed on 6 February for North America. One day out of Horten, *U-879* reported via wireless that 'port diesel coupling adjusting collar is broken. Dockyard aid is necessary. Am returning to Horten.'[91] The issue was fixed and its patrol resumed on 9 February. BdU estimated that *U-879* was approaching Northern Ireland on 15 February and issued its 'Guard Ireland' circuit message.[92] On 25 February, BdU asked Manchen to send a position report, followed on 28 February by a request to send weather reports as soon as the passage report was transmitted. In addition, Manchen received an 'approximate cruising route' of 47.51N-31.45W that placed it south-east of Halifax out in deep water, but heading directly towards the 200m line east of Cape Cod.[93] This is important to note. Manchen did not transmit any reports as he probably never received the transmissions from BdU. On 3 March an impatient BdU sent another request to 'begin sending weather reports immediately', followed by yet another reminder the next day.[94] The lack of wireless reporting should not have been unexpected at BdU by this time. A request by BdU was sent on 5 March that finally received a response the next day with a simple position of 59.30N-23.30W.[95] This position report placed it south-west of Iceland. *U-879*'s progress to this point suggests he was cruising underwater mainly by snorkel. Manchen sent another position report on 7 and 12 March, now showing steady progress, suggesting he was cruising surfaced as normal procedure called for once the 'Rosengarten' was safely passed.

Manchen's transmissions contained little information except a position. His weather report for 12 March placed him at 53.30N-33.30W.[96] That day BdU also transmitted the 'Guard America' circuit to Manchen.[97] Later that day BdU sent a message to both *U-853* (IXC/40) and *U-879*.[98] *U-853* was requested to start sending one report a day, while *U-879* received a harsh admonition that read: 'It is incomprehensible why ordered reports are not coming in.' Manchen responded the next day with another position report of 50.30N-38.30W.[99] Another weather report came in placing *U-879* at 49.30N-40.30W, which was just north-east of the Flemish Cap.[100] Two more transmissions from *U-879* were acknowledged from BdU on 14 March.[101]

Manchen reported to BdU that 'situation continuously as reported by Cabolet (U-907). Guns in good order. 173 CBM'.[102] Later that day *U-879* was ordered not to send any further weather reports as it approached Newfoundland.[103] A final message from *U-879* was acknowledged to have been received on 15 March by BdU.[104] This was the last communication known to be received by BdU from Manchen. However, a final position report was noted in the Ultra intercepts on 16 March as 47.45N-42.35W.[105] This placed *U-879* at the Flemish Cap. *U-879*'s final operational destination was recorded by BdU on 18 March as being Cape Hatteras.[106] It is not known what *U-879*'s departing order was, as it may have been any point along the US East Coast south of Newfoundland. The transmission directing *U-879* to Cape Hatteras may have been a redirection order and not a confirmation of its original deployment location, unlike *U-857*, which appears to have received its order before departure given the lack of any intercepted wireless from BdU stating its operational area. This is important to note, because if this final transmission was not received by *U-879* – a very real possibility – then Manchen would have conducted his patrol based on his original orders. What we know for certain is that its approach grid along the North American coast transmitted on 28 February was to the east of Cape Cod, as previously noted.

U-853 (IXC/40), under the command of Oberleutnant Helmut Frömsdorf, departed from Stavanger on 23 February, two weeks behind *U-879*. All three U-boats – *U-857*, *U-879* and *U-853* – proceeded along similar patrol routes that brought them south of Iceland, east of Newfoundland, then south along the US East Coast. The lack of wireless transmissions that resulted in limited Ultra intercepts confused OP-20-G as to the actual locations of all three U-boats. On 20 April OP-20-G recorded the following in its Intelligence Summary:

Hatteras
U-853 (Frömsdorf) had evidently just arrived off Hatteras 14 April when she sank the 6959-ton MV Belgian Airman. Four days later U-853 torpedoed and sank Swift Scout, (8300-ton tanker), about 90 miles north-east of the first attack. This is the only U-boat presently estimated in this area although two more 740 tonners may arrive shortly. On 12 April Control [BdU] reported heavy traffic of independents at night SSE of Hatteras and told 'U-boats there they had "no limitations on attack areas"'.

All U-boats in the western Atlantic have been told that if 'after sufficient observation your assigned area appears unfavourable because of lack of traffic or poor weather, moving to other points of traffic concentration is permitted.' (2215/4).

Gulf of Maine
The 8537-ton US tanker *Atlantic States* was torpedoed off Cape Cod 5 April by one of two U-boats (U-857, U-879) now believed homebound south of Newfoundland. Probably one of these was attacked and sunk by TG 22.10 (4 Des) south-west of Sable Island on 19 April.

The traffic situation off Boston broadcast 6 April included the statement that Boston was an embarkation port for troop transports and the area between Cape Ann and Cape Cod was a warship practice area.[107]

U-853 was certainly not operating off Cape Hatteras. It is not clear where exactly *U-857* and *U-859* were at this time. The torpedoing of the

SS *Atlantic States* could be assigned to either *U-857* or *U-879*. However, it was probably *U-879* that sunk the vessel.

U-853's commander, Oberleutnant zur See Helmuth Frömsdorf, employed the new shallow water tactic of 'bottoming', which strained the skills of the US Navy and Coast Guard sonar operators alike. On 23 April the USS *Eagle PE-56* (430 tons) was torpedoed 3 miles south-south-east of Cape Elizabeth, Maine. The USS *Eagle* was towing targets for US Navy bomber exercises when it was struck amidships with a heavy explosion, broke in two and sank. The commander, four officers and forty-four ratings were lost, while one officer and twelve ratings were picked up about thirty minutes later by the USS *Selfridge* (DD 357). The *Selfridge* immediately began to drop depth charges on a nearby sonar contact. Several survivors of the USS *Eagle* reported briefly sighting a U-boat's conning tower with the same orange and red colours of the Golden Horseshoe that adorned the conning tower of *U-853*.[108] *U-853* was able to maintain itself in the Gulf of Maine undetected by any US Naval vessel or OP-20-G for nearly a week before heading south towards New York, where it sank the SS *Black Point* on 5 May.

U-853 was the last U-boat sunk off the North American coast and has the dubious honour of sinking the last Allied vessel there, the SS *Black Point*. However, *U-853* was not the last U-boat operating off the US east coast and certainly not the last one to launch torpedoes at Allied vessels. *U-853* was not unique in the sense that its captain was 'aggressive' or looking to be awarded the Knight's Cross, as many have opined since the war. Frömsdorf was doing his duty to the last, just like the dozen other U-boat captains off the North American coast were in those final months of the conflict.

After being detected by US Task Force 60.7, *U-853* subsequently tried to bottom, then creep towards deeper water, given that the surrounding flat and sandy sea floor provided little acoustic cover. It was sunk on 6 May, after a near twenty-four-hour pursuit and depth charge attack in water of less than 40m by destroyers under the command of Lieutenant Commander L B Tollaksen of the USS *Moberly*. His son, Ensign Tollaksen, correctly concluded of his father's actions some fifteen years after the event that *U-853* 'was the first "bottomed submarine" destroyed by the forces of CINCLANT.'[109] It is a distinction lost in the U-boat's often maligned and misunderstood history to this day.

The rationale for *U-879* being the U-boat that sunk the *Atlantic States* comes from November guidance by BdU that U-boats should use depth demarcations for accurate underwater navigation, as in the 2 November 1944 Experience Message 178: 'The most exact knowledge of own submerged speed stages at various screw revolutions, soundings, and lines of soundings, as well as the use of Elektrasonne offer opportunity for good fix. Make the most of every change to sound marked depths.'[110] The message was initially focused on inbound/outbound U-boats, but the practice was adopted in operational areas.

What this meant in practice was that U-boats traversing the US East Coast used the 200m line as their main navigational fix. Every U-boat detailed in this section demonstrated moving north–south along this line before turning west along a longitude equivalent to their patrol area. This is confirmed by looking at track charts of several surrendered U-boats such as *U-190*, *U-530* and *U-889*. All three U-boats travelled along the 200m line until they were on a latitude equal to their deployment area before heading close inshore. This would have ensured they conserved enough fuel for their operational area. There would be no reason for *U-857* to have veered west towards the coast given its initial operational area as Cape Hatteras. *U-853* was too far behind both U-boats to be able to have reached that area in time to sink the vessel, even though the Gulf of Maine was its patrol area. This leaves *U-879* as the main possible U-boat to have sunk the *Atlantic States* if it did not receive its final destination order of Cape Hatteras and proceeded instead to a previously ordered operational area. Given that BdU had sent intelligence reports regarding both Halifax and Boston, it stands to reason that Manchen did not receive the Cape Hatteras order but instead conducted his patrol between Halifax and Boston.

What we do know for certain is that on 14 April the unescorted Belgian-flagged merchant *Belgian Airman* (6,959 GRT) was torpedoed and sunk north-east of Cape Hatteras. It appears that the U-boat that sunk this vessel then proceeded north-east out of the area defensively, as if to avoid possible patrol vessels. At 3.25am on 18 April the unescorted US-flagged steam tanker *Swiftscout* (8,300 GRT) was hit on the port side by one torpedo about 145 miles north-east of Cape Henry, Virginia. The torpedo struck the No. 6 tank just abaft amidships and broke the back of the ship. The armed guards spotted the U-boat about 650 yards away and opened fire, but the attacker dived and fired another torpedo at 7.35am that hit abaft of the first hit and blew the hatch covers off. The bow and stern of the tanker were split and thrust above the water. The stern sank quickly but the bow was observed to sink and reappear several times before finally disappearing. The U-boat then proceeded back south-west towards the Outer Banks and on 23 April torpedoed and damaged the unescorted Norwegian-flagged tanker *Katy* (6,825 GRT) east of Kitty Hawk.

We know the fate of *U-853*; this U-boat did not make it further south than Long Island Sound. The fates of *U-857* and *U-879* are less clear. A previous assessment by OP-20-G that one of these U-boats was sunk on

19 April east of Boston at position 42.19N-61.45W by depth charges from the US destroyer escorts USS *Buckley* and *Reuben James* is not confirmed. According to Axel Niestlé, this attack probably resulted in the loss of a completely different U-boat, *U-548* (IXC/40). He is probably correct.

U-548, under the command of Oberleutnant Erich Krempl, departed Horten on 5 March, the second U-boat sent to the US coast that month. It received a 'Guard America' transmission from BdU on 28 March that was intercepted by Ultra.[111] The last weather report was sent by Krempl on 31 March north-west of the Azores. On 12 April it was ordered to the Gulf of Maine area. It was never heard from again and was probably sunk on 19 April 1945 in the North Atlantic south-east of Halifax, in position 42.19N-61.45W, by depth charges from the US destroyer escorts USS *Reuben James* and USS *Buckley*.

That leaves a confirmed sinking report on 30 April east of Cape Hatteras at position 36.34N-74.00W by depth charges from the US patrol frigate USS *Natchez* and the destroyer escorts USS *Coffmann*, USS *Bostwick* and USS *Thomas*. This sinking occurred just north of the torpedoed *Belgian Airman*. Whether this was *U-857* or *U-879* is unknown and a maritime survey of the wreck site might one day provide evidence of which boat was sunk. This means one of these U-boats met a fate probably similar to *U-869* (see *U-869* case study). Given the fact that *U-879* had technical issues early in its patrol and that it probably proceeded close to the coast, it stands to reason that it might have suffered a mechanical failure and now rests on the sea floor somewhere along the coast, perhaps along the 100m line, waiting to be discovered.

The month of March brought the largest deployment of U-boats to the US East Coast since 1942. The first was of *U-530* (IXC/40). OP-20-G did not identify this U-boat or *U-548* that preceded it earlier in the month.

U-530 departed Horten under the command of Oberleutnant Otto Wermuth on 3 March for the US East Coast. Wermuth received word of Germany's surrender while off New Jersey and made the decision to run for Argentina and surrender in a neutral port. As a result, the commander and crew were interrogated and what follows is the account of *U-530*'s last patrol from that interrogation.[112]

Wermuth was a native-born German who was 25 years old when he took command of *U-530*. He joined the Kriegsmarine in 1939 and volunteered for U-boat service in April 1941. He graduated in October that same year and was assigned to the training boat *U-37* as a watch officer. In July 1942, Wermuth transferred to the *U-103* as second watch officer and remained in that role until June 1943, when he assumed the duties of first watch officer until February 1944. Wermuth gained significant experience during the three patrols of *U-103*, seeing action in both the North Atlantic and off the African west coast. After completing U-boat commander training from March to July 1944, Wermuth took command of the *U-853* on 10 July for a short while, leaving command of that U-boat on 31 August. He had been selected by Admiral Hans von Friedeberg, Chief of the German Submarine Division, to command *U-853*, which was then in Lorient waiting for repairs. Due to delays to this work he was reassigned to Hamburg to take command of the *U-530*.

U-530 received its snorkel in Lorient during May 1944. It was among the first Type IXs to receive a retrofit and the crew had already mastered the technology during a 136-day cruise off Venezuela that summer, though the snorkel was not employed on the return trip to Germany due to 'faulty greasing'. In January 1945, *U-530* was in dry dock in Hamburg for an overhaul. It is likely that it received its anti-radar coating at this time on the upper portion of the snorkel mast, which was noted by the crew as having been present on its last cruise. After departing dry dock for an overhaul, *U-530* entered Kiel, which was the main supply base for U-boats departing on an operational patrol from mainland Germany.

At Kiel, *U-530* took on fuel and provisions. Wermuth stated that: 'U-530 had a fuel oil capacity of 245 tons, but at the request of the chief engineer he took aboard but 225 tons. This request was made for reasons of better stability. In addition to this, the craft had 5 tons of lubricating oil onboard. He stated that in Kiel he had taken onboard a one-week supply of fresh provisions including meat, vegetables, bread, etc., and a 17 week supply of special submarine foodstuffs.'

U-530 departed on 19 February and arrived at Horten on 23 February, where it conducted final diving and snorkel trials. On 3 March, *U-530* departed Horten for North American waters. According to the interrogation report, Wermuth:

… stated that he did not know the route chosen, but that it was to the north of England and that to reach it they travelled continuously submerged for approximately three weeks, charging their batteries at night by means of the Schnorkel device, with which the *U-530* is equipped. This undersea travel was for the purpose of avoiding air attacks, which he stated were terrible.

Regarding communication with BdU, he stated:

… that while in his combat area, as was the common procedure, he did not report attacks made or received. His only radio messages sent were daily weather reports. He said that the last contact he had with his commanding officer in Berlin was on 26 April, which was a message concerning defensive measures to be taken.

This was followed by:

> … a message over his regular wavelength to cease hostilities on 8 May. Subsequently he changed this date to 10 May. These messages instructed all submarines to cease attacks, to use navigation lights at night, to fly a blue flag, to travel only on the surface, and to proceed to the nearest United Nations port for surrender. Further, they ordered that detonators be removed from all torpedoes, that mines be deactivated and that all ammunition be dumped overboard.

Wermuth informed his interrogators that 'he did not believe these orders to be official but, rather, to be an enemy trick'. Yet, as noted by his interrogator:

> … whether he did or not, he attached sufficient weight to them to decide to quit his zone of action, according to his testimony, and to intern his submarine and crew in some neutral country. He said that Portugal and Spain were discarded as being too close to the battle zone. He said that at that time, though they knew that Argentina had broken diplomatic relations with Germany, they did not know that they had declared war and that he decided to come here for internment because it was far from the fighting zone and because he thought they would get better treatment here. He said that he did not learn that this country had declared war until he arrived in Mar del Plata.

Wermuth generally attempted to mislead his interrogators as he had been on patrol off Long Island and attacked Allied shipping there, though without success. While he was evasive in his answers, his crew was not. The fifth war patrol of U-530 is reconstructed as follows from the interrogation report:

> Followed 200-metre line northwards 30 miles from Norwegian Coast, turning north-west above Bergen. At 65°N. turned on south-western course, continuing use of snorkel for four hours each night, otherwise on motors at 60 metres …
>
> After passing 25°W U-530 surfaced four hours each night and a few days later, the whole night. After rounding the 100-fathom Newfoundland Bank she steered for 41°N-60°W, and from there by radio was ordered to operate off New York [harbour].

In mid-April Germany's strongest longwave station ('GOLIATH') went off the air; and when U-530 resumed the use of her Schnorchel about a week later, the reception from Nauen became progressively worse. Shortwave reception was still possible until the end of April.

On about 28 April, U-530 crossed the 200m line and remained for some two weeks south of Long Island, once coming within two or three miles of land. On about 4 May a spread of three Lut torpedoes was aimed at a convoy of 10 to 20 ships. Two torpedoes missed and the third got stuck in the tube and its battery exploded.

Two days later a very large convoy was sighted. Again a spread of two Lut torpedoes missed. A single Lut also missed a tanker. An hour later a single Lut also missed a tanker. An hour later a single T-5 missed a straggler from the convoy. One day later (7 May 1945) two single T-5 shots missed their target in another large convoy. During this period two blimps and one plane were seen in the periscope, and several aerial bombs fell fairly close to the U-boat. At this point it was decided to turn away from the operational area and try to re-establish radio contact.*

*(O.N.I. NOTE: Convoys HX 354, UC 65A and ON 298 were in this area during the period from 3 May to 7 May, and are probably the convoys referred to. HX 354 and ON 298 were badly scattered because of fog. No submarine contacts were reported by these convoys.)

This reveals how effective the snorkel was as this U-boat was never detected during attacks against convoys outside New York Harbour during the last days of the war.

The next six U-boats sent to the US East Coast were part of *Gruppe Seewolf* and are detailed below as Allied intelligence assessed them as a unique threat.

As the western Allies began their breakout from the Siegfried Line after a winter of stalemate along the German border, more U-boats were sent to North America. Some were redirected, including *U-873* (IXD2). This boat, under the command of Kapitänleutnant Friedrich Steinhoff, was originally ordered to the Far East with a load of mercury and optical glass. Then, its patrol area was changed to the Caribbean, making it the first U-boat to deploy there since July 1944. *U-873* reported its position in plain language about 700 miles west-south-west of the Azores on 11 May and it was escorted to Portsmouth, New Hampshire, to surrender.[113] This U-boat was equipped with both a Kurier transmission system and a cutaway hull before its deployment.[114]

U-889 (IXC/40), under the command of Kapitänleutnant Friedrich Brauecker, departed for the US East Coast from Horten on 5 April 1945. He never reached his operational patrol area and surrendered to the Allies on 13 May, entering Shelburne, Canada, for internment. As with other surrendered U-boats, a thorough interrogation report was produced and it is summarised below.

The commander, Kapitänleutnant Friedrich Brauecker, entered service in 1937. He saw action in the English Channel in command of a torpedo boat and was decorated with the Iron Cross, 1st Class in 1943. In August that year he transferred to the U-boat service, where he 'had been serving for 2 years on 740-tonners'. Brauecker took command of *U-889* on 4 August 1944 when it was commissioned.[115]

U-889 had fifty-five crew including an officer who was a 'commander's pupil' training as a future U-boat captain. This is very interesting as we see that even this late in the war, BdU was still functioning in a capacity to continue training officers for future operations. The U-boat training programme never slackened under the weight of Allied aerial bombing or the loss of its training ports in the Baltic to the Red Army. Despite the stress placed upon the U-boat service, it remained a highly effective organisation until the end.[116]

U-889's maximum load of fuel was 246.5 tons, but it left for patrol with only 230, probably due to the fuel shortages experienced within the Reich in 1945. 'Of this, 90 tons was spent in reaching the operational area and 90 was expected to be used in returning. This left 50 tons for use in the operational area, which C.O. figured would enable them to operate for their full period at one-half ton per day with a comfortable margin.'[117]

The interrogation report contained interesting commentary on the shift to shallow water operations. 'Instructions were that 100 metres was to be the depth limit, save in emergent necessity, notwithstanding that the depth gauge in the conning tower indicated to 200 metres.' The commander claimed that 'U-889's diving qualities were slightly better than usual in her class. Trim down, she could dive to 20 metres in 35 seconds. Venting of the individual battery cells enabled a steeper diving angle, as acid was prevented from spilling.' This comment was probably due to a hull modification that was made to the bow. Post-war pictures reveal that a slight bowing was added on the port and starboard sides of the boat's bow, going back a few metres. This was not the cutaway bow typical of some late-war Type IXCs, but different. It is the only known U-boat to have adopted this configuration. An Echo Sounder Type AN608 was installed for tracking depth, an important component for shallow-water operations.[118] Communications equipment onboard was standard.

The interrogation report noted that *U-889* was equipped with a 'new experimental device' designed to improve listening while snorkelling. This device was the new Zwiebel (onion) sonar system mounted at the front of the bow that greatly improved listening during snorkel use. It was an experimental set installed only on the *U-889*:

> It consists of 15 hydrophones installed inside dome on the bow, and is used to listen in a 60° arc on the bow while the U-boat is snorkelling. Insulation from the noise of the U-boat's diesels is achieved by rubber mounting behind the hydrophones and rubber baffles. It was stated that, although this experimental set enables listening in a forward direction while snorkelling, it was considered necessary to stop the diesels every 20 minutes for an all-round listening search on the main hydrophones.[119]

The snorkel installation was a Type I. The upper 5ft was covered with a 'rubberlike coding about 4 mm thick, having an embossed pattern; it is stated to contain iron fillings and to be effective against 10cm and 3cm radar [S- and X-Band radar], but is probably not the latest development. The captain believed that the combination of the anti-radar coding and the round dipoles gave him complete immunity against air attacks.' This statement by the boat's commander is telling. It demonstrates the level of confidence the snorkel provided to a U-boat crew, even late in the war.[120]

U-889 retained useful records when it surrendered, which included two logs. One was a rough day-book in pencil and there was a more finished summary in ink, which showed the boat's daily progress. A reconstructed plot chart suggests what other similar documents have shown, namely that US East Coast-bound, snorkel-equipped U-boats travelled along the 200m line before they turned into the coast to reach their patrol area.

Before departing Kiel on 26 March 1945, the commander of the 5th Flotilla, Korvettenkapitän Karl-Heinz Moehle, came aboard and gave a 'pep' talk to the crew. According to the interrogation report, this officer conveyed Dönitz's verbal order to all U-boat commanders that when Allied ships were sunk there were to be 'no survivors'. However, on this occasion 'he held no such converse'. What the crew was referring to was the fact that Moehle usually gave a verbal reminder to each U-boat under his command that the Laconia Order was in effect.[121] *U-889* arrived at Horton on 30 March and received another 'pep' talk from Kapitän zur See Hans Roesing, who was commander of FdU-West.[122]

After refuelling and taking on drinking water, *U-889* departed on its first patrol at 8.01pm on 5 April. *U-889* began its cruise towards the US East Coast through the Faroe Islands passage. *U-889* was given freedom of manoeuvre by BdU from New York to Cape Hatteras on 23 April.[123] The U-boat was at a position several hundred miles to the south-east of

Greenland heading south-west towards Newfoundland when it received the new guidance. At 11.12pm on 7 May *U-889* dived for half an hour because of an Allied aircraft overflight. It was on this day that news of the unconditional surrender of Germany was heard and Dönitz's Order recalling all U-boats to Norwegian bases was received.[124]

Reception of German wireless traffic from BdU was 'very poor aboard U-889' during May, with 'signal strengths varying from 0 to 1 (German scale). However, almost all control messages were eventually obtained from control repetitions.'[125] *U-889* finally surrendered on 13 May when it arrived at Shelburne, Nova Scotia, under Canadian escort.

The snorkel installation on the *U-889* provided 'very good service', according to the crew, and while crossing the North Atlantic the boat surfaced only occasionally to obtain navigational fixes. Interestingly, 'in order to obviate any necessity for surfacing an alteration of the attack periscope has been devised – incorporating a movable prism system – to enable the taking of star sights at periscope depth'. Snorkelling was carried out preferably from about 10pm to 7am and the crew reported 'no discomfort was felt in the boat'. Ultraviolet lamps were installed to compensate for the lack of sunlight due to continuous underwater travel. An unknown 'alteration was to have been made on the U-889, but was cancelled at the last moment, due to non-arrival of certain parts'.[126]

Among the records of *U-889* were experience messages of new U-boat tactics. The interrogation report noted 'from the captured standing war orders and from conversations with the [commander], interesting facts concerning U-boat tactics were learned'. These are summarised below:

Shallow water operations:
In North Atlantic U-boat operations that are in coastal waters, the present tactics are for the U-boat to proceed as quickly as possible to very shallow water after firing torpedoes. The CO stated that British destroyer tactics were of great assistance to the U-boat in shallow waters, as it seemed to be the firm conviction of the British that U-boats need plenty of water in which to operate and therefore they persisted in carrying out their searches towards deeper water. When the U-boat has proceeded to shallow water (even as shallow as 20 m), it is considered (A) to be reasonably safe if the hunt is being carried out on the side of the convoy away from the U-boat, and (B) to be quite safe if D/Cs are heard to explode in the deep water. The U-boat may bottom, if considered advisable, or may draw slowly away from the hunt, keeping as close as possible to the shoreline. The latter is the course chosen if the hunt is taking place in deep water, which they had been instructed in training schools will nearly always be the case. They have also been taught to fire

from shallow water where possible. Gnats [T5] and Luts [T3] enable them to do this without being suspected due to the random nature of the torpedo's course immediately previous to reaching its target. The [commander] stated that T3s and T5s carried by him had a firing range of 6000 m, which also facilitated firing from shallow water well beyond the escorts.[127]

'Creeping Attack':
Believed that directing and attacking ships always alternate. Avoiding action is to wait until attacking ship can be heard in U-boat (without hydrophones) then alter through 90° away from directing ship at full speed. When first DC explodes, depth may be altered if it can be estimated whether charges exploded above or below.

After 1 to 3 minutes, a further alteration of 90° is made in order to reach a reciprocal course, and U-boat rises to gain advantage of screening by attacking ship's wake.

The above avoiding action has been practised in the Baltic and the CO felt it had not been very realistic and would be very difficult when under actual DC attack. He felt that SBT released during second turn would increase chances of escape. He had not heard of multiple creeping attacks.[128]

Countermeasures:
A) The layering effect is utilised in evading pursuit by simply changing depth until the U-boat is unable to hear the escort. It is then assumed that the escort will be unable to hear or obtain an echo from the U-boat. Temperature and density measurements are not generally used, although U-boats have conducted thermal surveys in Canadian coastal waters and from Virginia to Maine. Operational U-boats are expected to check the layering conditions from time to time, but [Brauecker] had only a hazy idea about it, and said that he had not intended to carry it out. It would appear that the doctrine regarding layering was fully established by 1942 and has not altered since.
B) The speed of the ship about to be attacked is estimated by counting the RPM of its propellers on hydrophones. The standing war orders contain graphs of speed plotted against propeller RPM for various types of Allied warships and merchants vessels. This procedure appears to have been instituted April 1943.[129]

The interrogation report also contained a section that revealed the Allied intelligence interest in shallow-water operations, particularly in the case of Canadian waters given that the interrogators were Canadian, but also in general. This confirms the fact that the shallow-water operations brought on by the snorkel were being taught in the autumn of 1944 and winter of early 1945 as the reports of successful patrols along the North American coast were distilled at U-boat training schools. One interesting and completely accurate conclusion drawn from years of underwater combat was that the U-boat pressure hull could withstand an immense amount of concussive force before it lost integrity. 'Many depth charges,' a prisoner noted 'had exploded so close above U-boats as to tear away deck structures,' and Brauecker further informed his interrogators that he had seen 'photographs where it was hanging over the sides (like seaweed), but without causing leaks in pressure hull'. This fact was certainly true in the case of *U-853*, where the crew died of blunt-force trauma long before the pressure hull was breached.[130]

Out of 2,199 nautical miles cruised, 1,594 were completed submerged – nearly 75 per cent. *U-889* spent only ninety-three hours surfaced and 711 underwater. It averaged 5.5 knots on snorkel and 1 knot on electric drive. When surfaced, it averaged 6.5 knots.

Two days after *U-889* departed for North American waters, *U-881* (IXC/40) followed under the command of Kapitänleutnant Dr Karl-Heinz Frischke. *U-881* was commissioned in Bremen on 27 March 1944 and was immediately used for experiments. In June that year *U-881* departed Bremen for the Baltic, where it conducted communication tests, probably with the new Kurier system.

U-881 headed eastbound from Swinemünde to Danzig, where it entered port to take on supplies on 29 July. Standard tactical training occurred as part of the Argu-Front from August 1944 until January 1945. In October it suffered collision damage and returned to Kiel, where repairs were made. In January *U-881* received its final overhaul and snorkel installation. *U-881* again departed for the Baltic to complete its anti-aircraft gun training, returning to Kiel by 18 February. After taking on final supplies, *U-881* left Kiel on 3 March for Norway along with *U-546* (IXC/40), *U-218* (VIID), *U-324* (VIIC/41), *U-398* (VIIC) and *U-1109* (VIIC/41).

The channels required for passage closed temporarily due a threat of mines dropped by Allied aircraft so the U-boats had to anchor at Frederikshaven, Denmark, on 14 March for approximately a day. *U-881* reached Horten on 16 March, where it conducted its final snorkel and dive testing before departing on its operational patrol on the 19th. Frischke's U-boat was probably supposed to have been part of *Gruppe Seewolf*, whose boats were departing at the same time, however, technical problems soon delayed *U-881*'s deployment and it did not join them.

U-881 conducted its first snorkel dive off the coast after departing Horten and immediately ran into problems. It sent a wireless message that stated: 'Cylinder liner of Junkers Compressor has split and no spares are onboard.

Query: Can a spare be taken over by Petersen's (U-874) or Kranz's U-boat? Snorkel mast is out of order and cannot be raised. Mile-trail [missing transmission] snorkelling carried out.'[131] Frischke entered Kristiansand for repairs, departing on 21 March for the open ocean. *U-881* reached a point three hours out from Hellesøy (at the entrance to a fjord that led to Bergen) when it reported more snorkel trouble on 30 March. *U-881* arrived at Bergen for repairs and left on its first operational patrol for the third time on 7 April.

When *U-881* departed it was equipped with seven T3A Lut1s, six T5s, and one T3A Fat2.[132] On 19 April Frischke reported his position as AM 4433 (55.27N, 14.35W).[133] This position placed *U-881* just west of Ireland heading south-west. No further communication was heard from Frischke. On 23 April BdU sent the following broadcast:

1. Frischke (U-881), Brauecker (U-889), Marienfelde (U-1228)
Liberty of Action from New York to Hatteras:
If Unfavourable here, also to north up to Gulf of Maine
2. Petersen (U-541)
Occupy as attacking area Naval Grid Square 95 of Large Square East of Green, NH
3. See Para 4 of Ser NR L79 Instruction to Group Sea Wolf[134]

U-881, while not part of *Gruppe Seewolf*, was caught up in the US Naval defensive line established to meet this final deployment of U-boats to the US East Coast. On 6 May the vessel was reportedly sunk by depth charges and hedgehog attack from destroyer escort USS *Farquhar* in the North Atlantic south-east of Newfoundland, near the 200m line in position 43.18N-47.44W. The *Farquhar* was part of the anti-*Gruppe Seewolf* screen and encountered the submerged U-boat by chance. According to the attack report, the only confirmation of the U-boat's demise was several sharp underwater explosions picked up by the sonobuoy. It should be pointed out that no other evidence floated to the surface.

The same day that *U-881* departed for the US East Coast, Kapitänleutnant Kurt Petersen departed Horten for North America on his second patrol in *U-541* on 7 April. His destination was the coast of New Hampshire, as noted in the 23 April transmission from BdU cited above. He sent the requisite passage report on 29 April, citing a position west of Ireland. Once Petersen received the order to surrender transmitted by BdU he headed south and surrendered to the British at Gibraltar on 12 May. Upon arrival half the crew was taken off the boat, while half remained to keep it operational. Peter Fussell served as a petty officer motor mechanic on the escort ship HMS *Kilmington*. As he spoke some German, he was placed onboard *U-541* as a liaison, but with a special mission. He was told to obtain all the information that he could about the snorkel, as Allied intelligence remained intrigued about the device even at the end of the war.[135]

Oberleutnant Marienfelde departed Kristiansand for his second cruise off North America in *U-1228* at 9pm on 13 April. As noted above, *U-1228* received orders on 23 April to operate from New York to Cape Hatteras, with permission to extend its operational area northward to the Gulf of Maine. As Marienfelde passed south of Iceland he manoeuvred through 'many trawlers, fishing vessels, sound buoys' but encountered no Allied aircraft. On 2 May *U-1228* and *U-889* received their 'Guard America' circuit order. By 9 May *U-1228* reported in the clear that it was at point 48.30N-36.20W on course 264 degrees, speed 7 knots. This placed Marienfelde only several hundred kilometres east of the Grand Banks and making good progress towards the North American coast.[136]

After receiving the surrender order from Dönitz, Marienfelde sent a wireless transmission on 11 May to Bernardelli of *U-805* informing the other U-boat commander: 'I am heading for same point as you. Unfortunately, I did not get into OP Area.' On 12 May Marienfelde sent a final message back to Germany that read 'after being picked up by escort on surrender cruise as ordered, we send greetings to our Grand Admiral and our beloved Germany'. Marienfelde then proceeded to Portsmouth, New Hampshire, where he surrendered.[137]

Both *U-1231* (IXC/40), under command of Kapitän zur See Hermann Lessing, and *U-802* (IXC/40), under the command of Kapitänleutnant Rolf Steinhaus, departed Norway for US coastal waters at the end of April. *U-1231* departed Kristiansand on 27 April and *U-802* left Bergen on 3 May. *U-1231* received orders to patrol the Gulf of Maine, while *U-802*'s operational area is less clear.[138] Both surrendered in accordance with Dönitz' orders.[139]

U-boats continued to deploy to the North American coast until the very last days of the war. Starting with *U-869*, more U-boats departed for the US East Coast in the spring of 1945 than at any point since the end of Operation *Paukenschlag*. Among these was *Gruppe Seewolf*.

Gruppe Seewolf, Operation *Teardrop* and the V-Rocket Scare

The United States mainland escaped the destruction unleashed across Europe and Asia during the Second World War. Only the attempted fire bombings of the Pacific Northwest forests in January 1942 by Japanese Pilot Nobu Fujita from the aircraft-carrying *I-25* submarine and the launch of more than 9,000 'fire balloons' in 1944 and 1945, of which some 300 reached the US, came close to resembling an attack on the mainland. By late 1944 the employment of German jet fighters, air-launched missiles and V-rockets brought the spectre of the Nazis deploying a weapon system with the capacity to strike at US cities. The US Navy was caught off guard in 1942 when U-boats devastated shipping along the US East Coast. They did not plan to take the possible return of U-boats equipped with rockets lightly, especially as evidence mounted that such an attack was being planned.

The idea of a rocket attack against the US cities launched from a U-boat germinated slowly within U.S Naval intelligence. When *U-1229* was sunk in September 1944, Oscar Martel, a survivor of the sinking, informed his FBI interrogators that 'a task force of missile-equipped U-boats was being readied for a buzz-bomb attack on the United States'.[140] This was followed by incorrect Tenth Fleet analysis of aerial reconnaissance photos where they determined that wooden tracks used to load torpedoes on U-boats might actually be used as launch rails for rockets. Reports from Supreme Headquarters Allied Expeditionary Force (SHAEF) in Europe reported that U-boats in Norway, specifically in Bergen, were 'designated for a missile strike at New York'.[141] These reports were likewise fuelled by British Admiralty reports that stated that it was possible to equip Type IXCs with a launch mechanism for V1 rockets. All of these assessments were reaffirmed with the capture of two German spies dropped off by a U-boat in December 1944 along the Maine coast.

The snorkel-equipped *U-1230* (IXC/40), under the command of Kapitänleutnant Hans Hilbig, departed Horten on 8 October on a secret mission. *U-1230* was to drop off two secret agents along the coast of Maine. These agents, later captured by the FBI thanks to a tip-off by OP-20-G, subsequently set in motion a near panic along the US East Coast about the possibility of V-rocket launches from U-boats. This episode in the Battle of the Atlantic is relatively unknown to this day.

OP-20-G knew that *U-1230* had special orders and surmised its intent. On 7 January it reported that *U-1230* had landed agents William C Colepaugh, alias 'Willie C Caldwell', and Eric Gimpel, alias 'Edward Green', in Frenchman's Bay, Maine, at the end of November 1944. The clues to this event, as well as the location, were derived from a combination of *U-1230*'s employment of a special cipher that had been used to transmit back the successful mission to BdU, but which had not been broken by OP-20-G, and the 3 December 1944 sinking of the Canadian-flagged steam merchant *Cornwallis* in the Gulf of Maine. Upon notification of the attack, OP-20-G informed the FBI that a U-boat had probably landed agents in the Winter Harbour–Frenchman's Bay area.[142]

Once Hilbig made his way back to open ocean, he began issuing reports in normal cipher that were read by OP-20-G. While these were mainly weather reports, he did make mention of the situation in the Gulf of Maine that gave final confirmation to OP-20-G that it was *U-1230* that had operated there. His intercepted wireless transmission read: 'This U-boat operated only in the Gulf of Maine between Yarmouth and Bar Harbour and found only slight independent coastal traffic but lively fishing activity. A weak patrol was experienced after the *Cornwallis*, a 5,458-ton British MV, was sunk near Mt Desert Rock on 3 December. The "main protection is off the Gulf."'[143] The FBI quickly located and arrested the German agents.

Both were interrogated by the FBI. There was intense interest by the interrogators in the snorkel, its use and the potential employment of rockets. Of the two prisoners, the one named 'Colepaugh' proved both willing to talk and believable to the FBI. He provided extensive commentary on the training and operational employment of the snorkel, and much of his information could be verified through existing Ultra intercepts of OP-20-G, giving him instant credibility. The interrogation now turned to the subject of the U-boat's approach to the US East Coast, the actual insertion of the agents and the overall morale of the crew.

> On about 20 November, the U-boat was over the tip of the bank of Newfoundland. This position was determined by echo sounding. From this point, the U-boat headed due south for deep water and, upon reaching a position 1° South of Sable island, she turned west seeking the Nova Scotia light. The captain was unable to see the light and suddenly realised that he was lost. The boat then surfaced to take radio bearings. Commercial stations of Boston, Portland and Bangor were received. Reception from Boston was the best of the three and on the basis of this D/F thing, it was determined that this boat's position was South of Mt. Desert Rock. The radio operators were vehement in their expressions of joy at hearing American jazz music.[144]

The approach of *U-1230* reaffirms that North America-bound Type IXs cruised along the 200m line before turning west towards their patrol area.

> Shortly thereafter, Mount Desert Rock light was cited and at the same time a liberty ship was seen heading for St John's. She presented a perfect target but no attack was made, much to the disappointment of the crew. It was found that the dampness resulting from condensation which took place during the many days of submerged sailing had caused damage to much of the gear. The echo sounder failed to function, the transformer being almost completely destroyed by dampness …
>
> These repairs lasted for six days. During the daylight hours, the boat

U-858 (IXC/40) after its surrender. Western Allied intelligence services convinced themselves that the six U-boats of *Gruppe Seewolf* were equipped with ballistic rockets destined for Boston, New York and Washington DC. US Intelligence officers believed that the torpedo loading rails seen traversing the port side of the U-boat and forward along its top deck were possible rocket launch rails. *(Author's collection)*

always bottomed, usually in about 100 metres of water. After dark, she proceeded submerged on electric motors except for the normal period immediately after dark before dawn when the snorkel was used for ventilation and charging batteries. The submerged depth was between 30 and 50 m … Occasionally soundings were made even by bottoming the boat … Several times during the six days, fishing boats were heard and once or twice these boats passed directly over the U-boat.

On 29 November, in the afternoon, U-1230 began her passage into Frenchman's Bay. She proceeded submerged on snorkel until about 1900. At 1600, Great Duck Island and Baker Island were cited and a fix was taken. At 1900, the boat collided with the whistling buoy. After this event, the snorkel mast was lowered and the boat proceeded at periscope depth on electric motors. She ran with the tide and the current proved stronger than was anticipated, resulting in the completion of the mission some hours earlier than had been anticipated.

The U-boat, once inside the bay, did not follow the normal channel but proceeded between Porcupine Island and ironbound island. At about 2230, she was a half-mile offshore. A white house on Crabtree Point was sited and the U-boat surfaced with her decks awash and only her conning tower above water.

The U-boat circled around to within a few hundred yards of the shore. The rubber boat was brought up from below and was inflated by a special line which ran through the conning tower hatch and connected with the electric compressor. The inflation was absolutely soundless. Two of our members of the ship's company rowed the two agents ashore and then returned to the U-boat.[145]

During the course of the interrogation Colepaugh made a statement that resonated with OP-20-G and the US Navy's Tenth Fleet more than any other:

> *Colepaugh had heard of the new type of U-boats that were undergoing special training at Stettin. These boats were fitted with a special rocket-firing device and the rumour was that they were to be used against the Eastern coast of the United States. He believed that they were to be used in groups of 10 or more.* [Author's emphasis][146]

The US Navy took the issue seriously. It evaluated this information along with British Admiralty reporting and concluded that, while unlikely, a U-boat could be modified to launch a V-weapon.[147]

Despite the assessment being correct, the possibility nevertheless existed. To provide added context, Allied intelligence had completely failed to recognise the massive German build-up and preparations for Operation *Wacht Am Rhein* launched in mid-December. The Wehrmacht's land offensive in the west shocked the Allies. No one in Allied intelligence circles wanted to be caught off guard again with the war nearing its end. The US Tenth Fleet headquarters viewed the final grouping of U-boats in the North Atlantic known as *Gruppe Seewolf* within the context of this effort to prevent another strategic surprise.

The question to be answered is whether or not U-boats were capable of firing rockets. The answer is a qualified yes. Experiments were conducted as early as 4 June 1942 at Peenemünde, where 30cm short-range artillery rockets were fired from the deck of *U-511*.[148] Six rocket-launching rails were welded to the deck of the U-boat and waterproof cables were run from the rockets to an ignition switch inside the control room. The rockets were made waterproof by sealing their nozzles with candlewax. For the experiment, *U-511* dived to a depth of about 8m and launched the rockets while cruising at a slow speed. All rockets launched from the water successfully and their 275lb warheads accurately reached their intended target some 5 miles away.[149] This was the first time in history that rockets were launched from a submerged submarine.

The Director of the Peenemünde Missile Factory, Generalmajor Walter Dornberger, presented these findings to the Kriegsmarine Weapons Department and contended that a design could be developed that allowed U-boats to attack coastal targets in the United States. The Kriegsmarine rejected the plan, probably at Dönitz's urging, as he remained focused on the resumption of convoy warfare. The rocket rails were subsequently removed from *U-511*.[150] Following the cancellation of these tests a renewed interest in launching V2 rockets from U-boats began in 1944. Klaus Riedel at Peenemünde developed plans under the code name 'Prufstand XII' that intended for a V2 rocket to be towed across the North Sea in a container and launched against targets in Britain. While this project began at the start of 1944, it gained momentum after the launch sites in north-west Europe were lost when the Western Allies broke out of Normandy.[151] The designs for the container mechanism were well thought out. The containers themselves could accommodate eight to ten men, and have bunks, a control room and ballast tanks. This accommodation was originally intended to be occupied for only twenty-four hours, which was the estimated length of time to reach a firing position in the North Sea from the Baltic. The U-boat would control the ballast tanks of the towed containers using hoses. It was believed that a single U-boat could tow three launch containers. Further discussion resulted in the proposal that if the launch crews were kept inside the U-boat itself and ferried over to the containers by an inflatable raft, then the U-boat could possibly make a transatlantic cruise and launch V2s against US cities. The plans were handed over to the Vulcan shipyard in Stettin in August 1944 and three containers were approximately 70 per cent complete by war's end. Dornberger noted that the project had significant promise and only the evacuation of Peenemünde in February 1945 due to the advance of the Red Army put a halt 'to a not unpromising project'.[152]

Perhaps it was the knowledge of Prufstand XII that caused Albert Speer to state in a January 1945 radio broadcast that V-rockets would fall on New York by 1 February. With the advanced state of German rocketry on display with strikes against London, anything was considered possible. According to naval historian Philip Lundeberg, 'the American public, no longer believing in the likelihood of enemy air raids, began to indulge in new apprehensions of war at home. High officials acknowledged that it could happen.'[153]

BdU continually shifted U-boat operations to gain the best advantage it could against Allied shipping during the last twelve months of war. With the

Allies focused on the coasts, BdU, under the direction of Admiral Godt, attempted to form three different *Gruppe* of U-boats in April with the intent to find elusive Allied convoys transiting the Atlantic. Godt rationalised that the Allies had experienced no direct convoy battles in almost eighteen months and were probably unprepared for an attack.

OP-20-G made the following assessment on 20 April about this effort:

> Admiral Dönitz is making a determined effort in three separate sectors to intercept US–UK convoys with small, snort-equipped U-boat Wolfpacks. One group of six 740 tonners (several possibly sunk) is now about 300 miles ESE of Flemish Cap sweeping towards the southern tip of the Grand Banks. Another group of eleven 500-tonners (4 probably sunk) has been ordered to patrol off southern Ireland. The third group of four 500 tonners is patrolling the north-west approaches.[154]

Part of the rationale to employ these groups was probably driven by the desire to slow the Allied advance across western Germany that had been under way since the first week of April. These 'Gruppe', however, were not operating as traditional Wolfpacks. There was not an expectation that these U-boats would be controlled and directed by BdU as in the prior convoy battles of 1942–43.

The two groups operating close to England and Ireland respectively were unnamed, unlike traditional Wolfpacks that operated prior to the spring of 1944. These two groups of U-boats were to remain submerged as directed by BdU. They represented little more than an increased concentration of single U-boats operating in what was expected to be areas dense with inbound Allied shipping. OP-20-G reported on them in their 20 April intelligence assessment. One group of eleven U-boats was assigned to operate along the south-west approaches to the St Georges Channel.[155] Along the north-west approaches four additional U-boats were ordered to operate independently.[156]

The third grouping, known as *Seewolf*, was to locate and attack a convoy in the mid-Atlantic. BdU intended to send a line of Type IX U-boats to 'rake' across the North Atlantic shipping route, termed a *Harke* in German, to intercept a European-bound convoy in a surprise attack. While in theory this line of U-boats called *Gruppe Seewolf* might have attacked in a pack, no U-boat had participated in an actual Wolfpack in more than a year. Few of the commanders involved in this operation had prior experience of a Wolfpack attack. While BdU issued orders that appeared to replicate the heyday of Wolfpack operations where a traditional spotter U-boat sent signals to BdU, who in turn directed other U-boats against the convoy, this was entirely unrealistic. BdU predicated this operation on the idea that there would probably be no Allied aircraft operating from an escort carrier. BdU also conceived this operation as a surprise attack with limited duration. Follow-on orders were intended to redirect all involved U-boats to individual patrol areas along the US East Coast. In essence, this line of U-boats would conduct a one-time attack on the convoy, then continue west towards the North American coast. It was never intended to resume traditional convoy warfare where U-boats would continue to attack the convoy until all torpedoes were expended.

While in theory BdU's proposal was based on tactical surprise, it was at best desperate when viewed against the realities of U-boat operations in April 1945. Surface attacks by U-boats at night were no longer the standard tactic and almost no U-boat commanders had that experience. After a long submerged transit to the mid-Atlantic, many U-boats experienced regular problems, as previously documented. Flak guns were probably unserviceable, offering no means of defence once surfaced. Wireless communications experienced significant failures, prohibiting timely reports or co-ordination. There were the ever-present snorkel problems that could play havoc with any U-boat patrol. In several ways, BdU's effort to organise a group of U-boats was already defeated before it began. The critical factor that doomed BdU's experiment with a snorkel-equipped grouping of U-boats was the same reason that defeated Wolfpack tactics in 1943, which was the need to send frequent command directives by wireless transmission. While still unknown at BdU, most messages transmitted by them to the U-boat force were intercepted through Ultra. As the U-boats that formed *Gruppe Seewolf* began their departures from Norway, the US Navy's Tenth Fleet had organised Operation *Teardrop* in response.

OP-20-G tracked the deployment of five U-boats to the US East Coast in the span of five weeks. These were sent individually. While this deployment represented the greatest concentration of U-boats sent to the area in more than two years, they did not raise significant concern. In mid-March this deployment was supplemented by six additional U-boats that departed for North America in the span of ten days. *U-546* (IXC/40), *U-858* (IXC/40), *U-518* (IXC), *U-880* (IXC/40), *U-805* (IXC/40) and *U-1235* (IXC/40). OP-20-G, and especially the US Tenth Fleet, grew alarmed. Interestingly, there was no reference in OP-20-G's 20 April intelligence assessment of the possibility that this group of U-boats might be carrying V-rockets in an attempt to launch a final wave of terror attacks on US cities. This potential, however, was in fact the driving force behind the organisation of Operation *Teardrop* that now got under way. Perhaps a final, if not alarming, piece of intelligence that raised Allied concerns about the threat of an imminent rocket attack was that among the U-boat commanders operating in *Gruppe Seewolf* was Kapitänleutnant Friedrich Steinhoff of *U-873*. Years earlier, Steinhoff had participated in the early rocket trials while commanding *U-511*. This fact was known to OP-20-G and the US Tenth Fleet.[157]

OP-20-G tracked the movements of *Gruppe Seewolf* through Ultra intercepts and utilised them to co-ordinate the single largest naval defensive line during the war.[158] OP-20-G began to suspect that there was something different about this already unusual deployment of U-boats with the following order to remain silent and send no passage report:

> 0907hrs 2 April 1945
> Contrary to former order, U-boats of Type IXC cruising out at present are to give no passage report.[159]

That evening it became clear to OP-20-G that this group of U-boats was doing something unusual in the North Atlantic by conducting a 'Rake' across the westbound convoy lane, followed by their individual release to assigned attack areas along the US East Coast.[160] The next intercept suggested that these U-boats required to be surfaced for an extended period of time as they were ordered to test radar sets and service their anti-aircraft guns. This could easily have been interpreted as a requirement to be surfaced for a prolonged time in order to prepare and launch a deck-mounted rocket.[161] A total of six separate *Harke* messages were transmitted that gave specific line co-ordinates for the U-boats to approach in an effort to intercept an eastward convoy.[162] The last *Harke* was transmitted at 6.01am on 3 April.[163]

The BdU KTB entry for that day reveals the extent of the plan: 'The next 6 type IXC U-boats proceeding to the North American east coast follow one after another. Interval on average 380 nm. Intention: Execution of a rake of the England–America convoy route … From there independent boat operation in American coastal waters. Detailed instructions concerning behaviour at convoy were transmitted.'[164] This entry confirms that the convoy attack was a limited engagement and not a traditional convoy battle as all U-boats were expected to proceed to the North American coast after the initial attack.

On 9 April at 10.37am these six U-boats were ordered to form *Gruppe Seewolf* by name as BdU assessed that they had all reached their assigned positions. Twelve successive standing lines were ordered in the course of the westerly sweep. The general latitude chosen was in keeping with the main transatlantic convoy lanes. *Gruppe Seewolf* was not going to intercept any convoys as they had already been rerouted out of the area based on the Ultra intercepts. In the place of merchant vessels, this unusual grouping of snorkel-equipped U-boats would now run into a line of US Navy destroyers supported by escort carriers in a never-attempted anti-submarine line intended to stop any U-boat from reaching the US East Coast. This was the first anti-ballistic missile defence screen deployed by the US.

Four US Navy Task Groups (Mission Bay, 22.1; Bogue, 22.3; Core, 22.4; and Croatan, 22.5) plus four destroyer escort groups were sent out to meet *Group Seewolf* under the code name *Teardrop*. Operation *Teardrop* was in fact 'formulated at CINCLANT headquarters in New York early in January 1945' as a direct response to the 'mounting' intelligence that Type IX U-boats in Norway were being equipped with rocket launchers. It should be noted that public concern in New York was aroused by Mayor Fiorello La Guardia himself when he issued a warning on 10 December that a multi-staged V-weapon might be fired across the Atlantic at New York.

Operation *Teardrop* was a reaction to this combined growing threat of U-boat-launched rockets. The plan for *Teardrop* was announced to the New York press on 8 January, probably in part to dampen some of the growing public concern. The announcement recognised the missile threat and 'mandated a full commitment of Eastern, Gulf, and Caribbean Sea Frontier air and surface forces against seaborne missile launchers'.[165] While the defence posture of *Teardrop* was announced, what was kept classified was that there was a multi-pronged offensive as part of the plan. Two major task forces were to deploy as a mid-Atlantic barrier. Each of these two task forces consisted of two escort carriers and twenty or more destroyers. *Teardrop* began with the escort carriers USS *Mission Bay* and USS *Croatan* deployed from Hampton Roads on 25 and 27 March, following the confirmation of the six Atlantic-bound U-boats from Norway. A 120-mile screening line across the mid-Atlantic east of Newfoundland Banks was soon formed.

On 12 April *Gruppe Seewolf* was notified that convoys were in the area. B-Dienst provided the early warning required to prepare to attack, but little did they know that the convoys were being rerouted and an interception line of US Naval destroyers were en route instead.[166] On 16 April TG 22.5 (USS *Croatan*) attacked contacts in vicinity 47°57′N-30°30′W and two U-boats were believed destroyed. These were *U-1235* and *U-880*. The underwater explosion of what was believed to be *U-880* was so violent that it appeared to confirm that perhaps it had been equipped with a rocket.[167] Both *U-1235* and *U-880* were caught on the surface when they were engaged and sunk. Both U-boats were only identified because they were surfaced, and this may well have been due to the extremely foul weather that prevented effective snorkelling.[168] Had either U-boat not been surfaced it is unlikely they would have been found by the task force.

At 11.35pm on 15 April the USS *Stanton* identified a surface contact

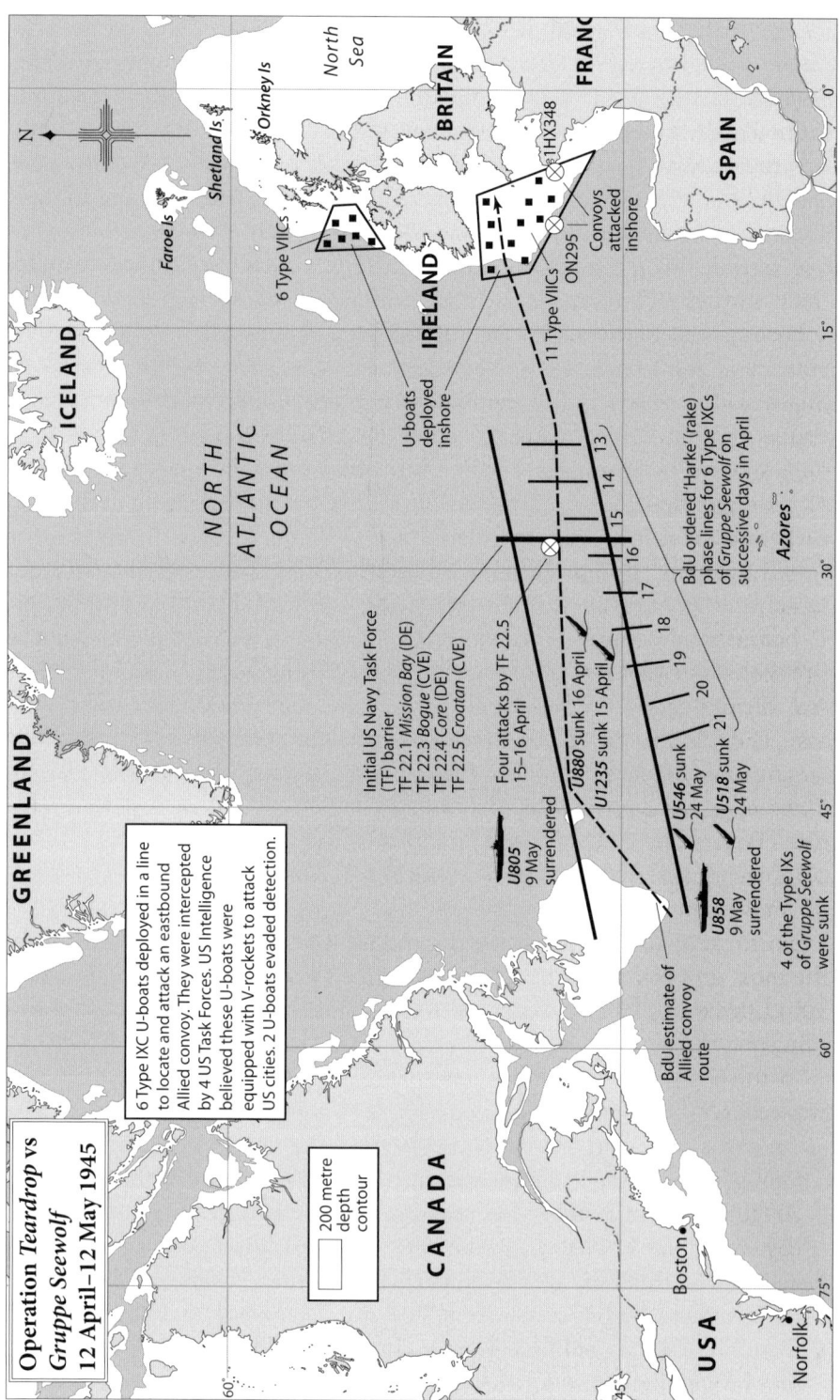

Operation *Teardrop* vs
Gruppe Seewolf
12 April–12 May 1945

6 Type IXC U-boats deployed in a line to locate and attack an eastbound Allied convoy. They were intercepted by 4 US Task Forces. US Intelligence believed these U-boats were equipped with V-rockets to attack US cities. 2 U-boats evaded detection.

200 metre depth contour

CANADA

Boston

Norfolk

USA

GREENLAND

ICELAND

NORTH ATLANTIC OCEAN

N

Shetland Is

Orkney Is

Faroe Is

North Sea

BRITAIN

FRANCE

SPAIN

IRELAND

Azores

6 Type VIICs

11 Type VIICs

U-boats deployed inshore

Convoys attacked inshore

HX348

ON295

BdU estimate of Allied convoy route

Initial US Navy Task Force (TF) barrier
TF 22.1 *Mission Bay* (DE)
TF 22.3 *Bogue* (CVE)
TF 22.4 *Core* (DE)
TF 22.5 *Croatan* (CVE)

Four attacks by TF 22.5
15–16 April

U880 sunk 16 April
U1235 sunk 15 April

U546 sunk
24 May

U518 sunk
24 May

U858
9 May
surrendered

4 of the Type IXs of *Gruppe Seewolf* were sunk

U805
9 May
surrendered

BdU ordered 'Harke' (rake) phase lines for 6 Type IXCs of *Gruppe Seewolf* on successive days in April

13
14
15
16
17
18
19
20
21

approximately 5,000 yards off *Croatan*'s bow, which had slowed to 8 knots due to heavy seas. The USS *Frost* was directed to the contact to assist the *Stanton*. The surface contact submerged and underwater contact was made immediately. *Stanton* 'fired Hedgehog at 2347, making two hits. Contact was regained and held until 2353 when all ship[s] in the area, including CROATAN who was clearing the contact area at 17 knots, were shaken by a terrific explosion. STANTON was shaken so badly she reported that she had been torpedoed and was listing.'[169] The contact continued to move 'very slowly'. Both ships made another attack with hedgehogs, *Stanton* achieving three hits from its third attack at 12.31am on the 16th. Almost an hour later, at 1.14am, 'an extremely violent underwater explosion occurred that was so severe both Frost and Stanton again thought they had been torpedoed. CTG 22.13 ten miles away and CROATAN 12 miles away were both shaken by this detonation.'[170] This was clearly the U-boat imploding as it plummeted into the depths after being mortally wounded from the earlier attack.

At 1.55am in position 47°57N-30°28W the USS *Frost* closed on a surface target that it illuminated with a spotlight and at 600 yards identified as a U-boat with 'a stream-lined conning tower and one gun forward'. It opened fire with available deck guns, though their effect was limited by the heavy seas breaking over the forecastle. The U-boat submerged. All contact was lost. The USS *Huse* and USS *Swasey* joined the search along with *Frost* and *Stanton*. At 3.22am the *Frost* made sonar contact and vectored in the *Stanton*, which made a successful hedgehog attack at 4.03am, scoring four hits. 'Four minutes later a terrific explosion, even more severe than that obtained from the first submarine, was felt by all ships.'[171] The target showed no movement and a large oil slick appeared, followed by several minor explosions. As the report noted: 'The above actions were carried out under the most unfavourable weather conditions – 40–50 knot winds, state 6 seas, 500–1,000-yard visibility and 500 foot ceiling with haze and intermittent rain squalls.'[172]

In the 20 April Intelligence Summary progress against *Gruppe Seewolf* was recorded as follows:

Group Seewolf, originally consist[ing] of six 740 tonners, is presently about 300 miles ESE of Flemish Cap moving south-west-west at about 100 miles a day along the estimated US–UK convoy lane. This group rendezvoused about 600 miles north of Azores and began to move 13 April into daily positions ordered by [BdU], surfaced at night submerged by day. [BdU] told them 'since attack will be a surprise, little or possibly even no air patrolling may be expected and only average surface escorting. Enemy is prepared only for underwater U-boat operations.' ... 'If it is certain that no day air with convoy, attempt to get ahead surfaced, but do not send any further shadower reports, in order to deny to the enemy knowledge of the combined operation which is intended, knowledge of which he would certainly react to with increased use of air during the day. Break off surfaced operation when air appears, and wait for orders.'

Two CVEs and two DE groups established a 120-mile barrier at 30W on 9 April. The night of 15/16 April CROATAN DEs, after several radar contacts, attacked a series of sound contacts during heavy weather and may have sunk several U-boats. Azores-based (Leigh Light) Liberators are supplementing the search to the east and south of the CVE barrier. Two sightings of surfaced U-boats have already been made by these planes. No attacks were made. A relief force of CVEs and DEs will arrive in the area 21 April.[173]

It was on 21 April that the USS *Carter* made sonar contact with *U-518*. The next day, joined by USS *Neal R Scott*, a successful hedgehog attack was launched that resulted in a violent underwater explosion. *U-518* was lost. Half of *Gruppe Seewolf* was now sunk. The same day *Gruppe Seewolf* was dissolved by BdU without any success, as noted through B-Dienst intercepts of Allied convoy traffic.

The southern members of *Gruppe Seewolf,* including the already sunk *U-880* and *U-518*, as well as the still operational *U-858*, were ordered to manoeuvre freely within the Halifax to the Gulf of Maine area. The northern members of *Gruppe Seewolf,* including the already sunk *U-1235* and still operational *U-805* and *U-546*, were ordered to operate from New York south along the US East Coast. The Ultra intercept certainly elevated US Tenth Fleet's concern as the remaining U-boats were now directed to manoeuvre inshore. Under these circumstances, US Tenth Fleet analysts probably interpreted the order by BdU as the V-rocket attack anticipated against Boston, New York, Baltimore or Washington DC.

2154hrs 22 April 1945
To: Group Seewolf
(Offizier M transmission)
1) 'Harke' is ended on 24/4.
2) The 3 southern U-boats may manoeuvre freely in area of Halifax and including Gulf of Maine depending on fuel situation. If because of fog situation is unfavourable you are permitted to move away from shore as far as CB 40 ((38.51N-66.06W 'C')).
3) The 3 northern U-boats may manoeuvre freely from New York to the south. If fuel is low also to the north.

4) Basic rule: Go as close in as possible, even in shallow water. Show your-
selves worthy of the heroic Battle of the Homeland. Move off only if attack
conditions close to shore are unfavourable.[174]

In the early morning haze of 24 April, Oberleutnant Paul Just, commanding
U-546, identified an escort carrier in the distance and was determined to
sink it by penetrating the screening line of destroyers. Just decided to use
the haze and thermal layers to dive under the destroyer screen. However, an
alert sonar operator aboard the USS *Frederick C Davis* notified the watch
officer that he had just identified a moving target. Alarm bells were rung
and a hedgehog attack was readied. Just identified the defensive reaction of
the destroyer and manoeuvred to strike it before he was attacked. He
launched an acoustic torpedo at point-blank range and struck the *Davis*,
amidships sending it down with the loss of 126 of its 192-man crew. During
the next ten hours a classic game of hunter and hunted played out in the
stormy seas of the North Atlantic until a pattern of hedgehogs damaged
U-548 enough that it was forced to surface and was attacked. *U-548* was cat-
astrophically damaged and slipped beneath the waves. Thirty-three of the
German crewmen, including Just, were rescued by the USS *Hayter*, which
had previously rescued the survivors of *Davis*.[175]

OP-20-G recorded the events of *Gruppe Seewolf* as follows in their 19 May
assessment:

Of 6 U-boats (*Gruppe Seewolf*) operating along Atlantic convoy lanes while
en route to US waters 4 probably were sunk by our CVE and DE groups. The
remaining two plus four others were heading for the western Atlantic when
the war ended.
Western Atlantic. *Operation Seewolf*. Admiral Dönitz's last major U-B offensive in the western Atlantic – Seewolf operation – was thoroughly beaten.
Only two of this group of six 740 tonners have surrendered. The remaining
four probably were sunk bur CVE task forces during the third week in April.
One of these, U-546 (Just), was sunk shortly after she had torpedoed and
sank *Frederick C. Davis* (DE 136). Com U-boats had ordered the *Gruppe
Seewolf* to break up on 17 April, the three northernmost U-boats to proceed
to the New York–Hatteras area and the three southernmost to the
Maine–Halifax area.[176]

Indeed, four of the six U-boats that formed *Gruppe Seewolf* were sunk.
U-858 and *U-805* later surrendered off the coast of Cape May, New Jersey,
and Portsmouth, New Hampshire, respectively. The engagement that took
place in this last great mid-Atlantic battle was conducted within an opera-

tional environment that included poor weather, shark-infested waters and near-misses that brought U-boats and Allied escort carriers within visual range of each other. There was certainly a sense of desperation to find and destroy each U-boat. When contact was made, hunter and hunted locked in individual battles for as long as two days. Even when it was understood that almost all of *Gruppe Seewolf's* U-boats had been intercepted and sunk, Ultra reported on 24 April that other westbound U-boats including *U-889*, *U-1228* and *U-881* had been ordered to patrol between New York and Cape Hatteras, fuelling fears of a V-rocket launch until the very last days of the war. This belief probably drove the order for US Navy divers to deploy on the sunken *U-853* and determine if it indeed was equipped with rockets or launch rails.[177]

Operation *Teardrop* was an apparent success as the US Navy deployed their most aggressive anti-submarine defensive screen in its history. Despite this Herculean defensive effort, which was aided by accurate intelligence, two U-boats made it through the screen and an escort carrier came within one vessel's striking range. Farago, as the Tenth Fleet's Chief of OP-16-Z, wrote after the war:

> And, indeed, in broader historical perspective, Operation Seewolf looms up today as a most significant venture with crucial lessons to remember. Despite Ingram's tight barrier defence, despite the most efficient deployment of the protective armada, despite the assemblage of a seemingly foolproof warning system, *two out of seven U-boats still managed to slip through* to reach the East Coast and remain undetected to the bitter end. The fact that these two U-boats succeeded in breaking through the barrier is far more important than the dramatic feat of sinking the other five. [Emphasis in original][178]

The survival of two U-boats represented 30 per cent of the attacking force. This underscores how even under optimal operational conditions, finding and sinking a snorkel-equipped U-boat was extremely difficult. If these two U-boats had been armed with ballistic missiles they might have been able to launch them at US cities. Submarine warfare was changed forever.

Part III:

A CASE STUDY IN U-BOAT HISTORY AND MARITIME ARCHAEOLOGY

Chapter 10

U-869: Catastrophic Snorkel Failure

Few U-boat wrecks have gained as much notoriety in the post-war period as that of *U-869* (IXC/40). The *U-Who?*, as it was formerly known, was discovered on 2 September 1991 by John Chatterton, Richie Kohler and John Yurga. The wreck was made famous by Robert Kurson's book *Shadow Divers* published in 2004. Growing up in New Jersey and having been certified as a scuba diver in 1990, I remember the discovery from when it was first publicised in my hometown paper, *The Bergen Record*. The story of a mysterious wrecked U-boat off the coast immediately captured my attention, as it did many others in the area.

Chatterton solved the main mystery of the U-boat's identity during a daring dive into the wrecked motor electric room in 1997 to recover a spare parts box. Yet, as the Epilogue of *Shadow Divers* correctly opined: 'To this day, mysteries remain.' Kurson asked three questions: Why did *U-869* continue to New York after being rerouted to Gibraltar? How did *U-869* meet her end? How did the crew die?[1] While theories have been posed to answer these questions, none have benefitted from the current archival research into the technical and operational evolution of the U-boat force during the final year of the war. Let us examine each of Kurson's questions and prevailing theories of *U-869*'s demise within the context of Dönitz's 'Total Undersea War'.

Why did U-869 continue to New York after being rerouted to Gibraltar? We now know how problematic communications became with the introduction of the snorkel. U-boats rarely surfaced to transmit signals, let alone to receive any. The deeper a U-boat cruised while submerged, the less likely it was to receive wireless signals from BdU. Constant submergence brought dampness inside the boat that played havoc with wireless gear, if not causing it to fail outright. Atmospherics in the North Atlantic during winter were a known disrupter of low-frequency signals. The documented issues with wireless reception noted in Chapters 2, 6, and 9 should leave no one in doubt that *U-869* simply did not receive the wireless order that redirected it to a new operational area off Gibraltar. A detailed review of all snorkel-equipped Type IXs sent to the North American coast in 1944–45 reveals that every one carried out their initial deployment orders faithfully, only changing locations as directed in BdU guidance – if they received that guidance. As discussed below, even Commander Knowles of OP-20-G was never completely convinced that *U-869* received the change in operational orders and believed that the U-boat probably continued to the Philadelphia approaches that marked its original patrol area. Two Navy Task Groups were directed to search for *U-869* on approach, but never made contact.

How did U-869 *meet her end? How did the crew die?* These two questions are interrelated. Two prevailing theories have been proposed. Chatterton, Kohler and Yurga have argued that a circular-run torpedo sunk *U-869*. The United States Coast Guard rejected this theory and declared in June 2006 that *U-869* was sunk by a surface attack that used a combination of depth charges and hedgehogs from the USS *Howard D Crow* and USS *Koiner* on 11 February 1945. Based on the available evidence at the wreck site, a third plausible theory emerges that *U-869* fell victim to a snorkel failure that resulted in an incapacitating level of carbon monoxide, followed by a build-up of oxyhydrogen battery gas in the control room that generated a catastrophic explosion soon after the boat conducted a routine 'bottoming'.

Before we review the three theories, let us look at how wider knowledge of the snorkel and late-war U-boat operations may have assisted in the identification process of *U-Who?* when it was first discovered. The initial discovery of the U-boat generated a list of questions about whether it was a Type VIIC or a Type IX. A shortlist of U-boat hull numbers was drawn up that included both types. The initial focus of its discoverers was to measure the length of the U-boat or, failing in that effort, to find some piece of evidence that would lead them to the conclusion as to its type. However, finding its snorkel would have instantaneously narrowed the search from a Type VIIC to a Type IX, and placed the time frame for a U-boat to be in that area clearly between February and April 1945 based on the deployment schedule for boats sailing against the US East Coast. No snorkel-equipped U-boat deployed here before January 1945 and only Type IXs were deployed. While several other U-boats were missing at the time, *U-Who?* would have been classified as *U-869*, *U-857* or *U-879* almost immediately. Only one of the U-boats was assigned to the area where it was found on the sea floor, the other two being dispatched to Cape Hatteras. More importantly, U-boats that deployed to the US East Coast in 1945 followed a route along the 200m line before turning west towards their patrol area. In the analysis conducted in the previous chapter we know that U-boats proceeded faithfully to their operational area, until given freedom of manoeuvre. However, this technical and operational data was not available in the published record at the time *U-Who?* was discovered. If it was, it would have left *U-869* as the prime candidate as soon as the snorkel was discovered. This revelation does not take away the accomplishment of Chatterton, Kohler and Yurga in identifying *U-869*. It offers a framework for late-war U-boat wreck analysis in North American waters, as there are other snorkel-equipped Type IXs lying on the sea floor along the US East Coast yet to be discovered and their identities confirmed.

U-869 was commissioned on 26 January 1944 by A G Weser in Bremen under the command of Kapitänleutnant Helmut Neuerburg. *U-869* followed the typical acceptance testing and training regime of almost every U-boat in 1944. UAK occurred in Kiel during the first half of February, followed by assignment to the Argu-Front in the Baltic. *U-869* conducted its final overhaul in Stettin from 20 June until 23 September. During this period its snorkel was retrofitted, a Kurier flash transmission system installed, and a variety of other modifications were made, to include the cutaway hull.[2]

U-869 departed Kiel on 24 November and entered Horten three days later, on the 27th, where it conducted the usual deep dive testing and snorkel training. It departed on 3 December, arriving at Kristiansand the next day where Neuerburg and crew took on fresh provisions and diesel. While how much diesel was taken onboard is not known precisely, what is known is that by December 1944 diesel shortages were common, especially in Norway. Departing U-boats often never received a full allotment. In some cases, chief engineers elected not to completely fill their tanks in order to maintain better trim. It is very likely that when *U-869* departed it was not 'topped off'. On 8 December, *U-869* departed Kristiansand for the western Atlantic and its first operational patrol.

OP-20-G recorded that on 18 December *U-869* departed Kristiansand and was assigned an initial position west of Ireland along with *U-244* (VIIC).[3] Once that point was reached it would receive its final operational patrol area by BdU. *U-244*, however, turned back to Bergen due to trouble with its snorkel and telemeter system.[4] On 29 December *U-869* received orders to head towards the approaches off Philadelphia.[5] During the shift in operations brought on by the snorkel, patrol areas were designated by specific Allied embarkation/debarkation points. A U-boat was expected to maintain its assigned location until the captain determined that no targets were located at the original destination. At that point, BdU authorised independent movement. While on station a U-boat maintained its position by minimising its manoeuvring to a confined area, where it often bottomed the U-boat to wait for passing convoys or unescorted vessels.

The very next day BdU recorded that it 'is worried about *U-869* and *U-1009* (VIIC/41), as neither boat has yet made her passage report despite several requests'.[6] *U-869* was making its way through the Iceland Passage, also known as the Faroe Islands Passage. This area claimed a number of outbound snorkel-equipped U-boats. On 3 January 1945 BdU recorded that:

> With submarine losses as low as they are, it is striking how many seem to be Type IXC submarines while still outward bound in the Iceland Passage (U-1226, U-877. There is considerable anxiety about U-869). Losses were most probably caused by snorkel breakdowns. As however it is likely that patrols will be increased, U-1233 was warned and ordered not to take any risks during her passage.[7]

Commander Knowles recorded in the 3 January U-boat Intelligence Summary that: 'U-869 now estimated in the central [North Atlantic] has been ordered to head for a point about 70 miles south-east of New York approaches. During November this U-boat was used in Kurier tests (radio flash transmissions) in the Skagerrak.' It was noted that: 'This is the first U-boat in the western Atlantic to be sent south of the Gulf of Maine since U-518 operated off Hatteras in September.'[8] This fact caught the attention of OP-20-G and they spent considerable energy trying to understand *U-869*'s location, which grew confusing in the coming days.

U-869 was the first U-boat directed against this area of the US East Coast in years. While it might have been only a few months since *U-518* self-deployed against the area around Hatteras, that U-boat never once saw the coast, staying in deep water between Bermuda and the 200m line. *U-869*'s order was different. It was heading into the shallows off the Delaware Bay.

On 6 January BdU requested Neuerburg to report *U-869*'s position 'at once'.[9] Neuerburg responded that same day. His transmission was not intercepted through Ultra, possibly because he used the short-burst Kurier system that was unreadable by Allied intelligence. BdU recorded the message as follows in their KTB:

> U-869 reported from AK63, in answer to a request for position. There was some concern about the submarine as she should have been considerably further south-west, if she had proceeded along the normal route through the Iceland Passage. According to our calculations (taking an average day's run

of 55 miles) the boat must have gone through the Straits of Denmark. The
boat is to report her fuel reserves tonight, so that a decision can be taken as
to allocation of operational area.[10]

The assertion by BdU that *U-869* entered the Atlantic through the
Denmark Strait to the north of Iceland is not a proven fact. This entry also
runs counter to the fact that BdU originally believed the boat to be about
225 miles south-west of AK63 on the 6th, which was not an unreasonable
delta in distance. It is unlikely that the Denmark Strait was traversed by
Neuerburg given how far south along the Norwegian coast his deployment
began. The slow progress can easily be explained by a more conservative
employment of the snorkel. For example, in looking at the captured documents of *U-190*, we know that a Type IX running the snorkel on full diesels
for ten hours and electric motor for fourteen hours in a twenty-four-hour
period can average 102 miles a day. However, this rate of speed was only
utilised by *U-190* (and other boats) on the outward/return journey in the
mid-Atlantic between Iceland and Greenland. Poor surface conditions,
Allied air activity, or snorkel problems caused a U-boat to limit snorkel use
to as few as two hours a day while running the electric motor the rest of the
time. If the snorkel wasn't working at all, the U-boat would turn back for
repairs, as *U-1233* did twice after its initial departure towards the North
American coast on 11 December. Limited use of the snorkel resulted in a
U-boat cruising about 38 miles in a day. BdU's average mile calculation was
itself an assumption. The fact that *U-869* reported from a position
500 miles due south, and only slightly west, of Iceland appears to confirm
a normal transit through the Faroe Islands passage. As we will see below,
the diesel consumption rate for *U-869* also casts doubt on a passage north
of Iceland.

On 7 January BdU sent a message to Neuerburg that stated: 'Continue
southward cruise. Report fuel tonight. Circuit is Ireland.'[11] BdU recorded on
8 January that: 'No report was received from *U-869* as to the state of her
fuel, in spite of continuous inquiries. The boat was allocated an operational
area off Gibraltar. Sea area to the west of CG 9592, but not within the Straits
of Gibraltar. To proceed snorkelling when entering CG.'[12] It is not clear if
BdU transmitted the new operational area that day, or simply noted the
impending change in their war diary. OP-20-G intercepted BdU's order on
9 January that stated: 'U-869 ((Neuerburg)): Attack area is sea area west of
concentration point SQCG 9592 ((35.57 N, 05.42 W – Straits of Gibraltar)).
Approach submerged by day, surfaced by night. From CG approach
submerged, snorkelling.[13]

U-869 was redirected to Gibraltar primarily due to the reported success

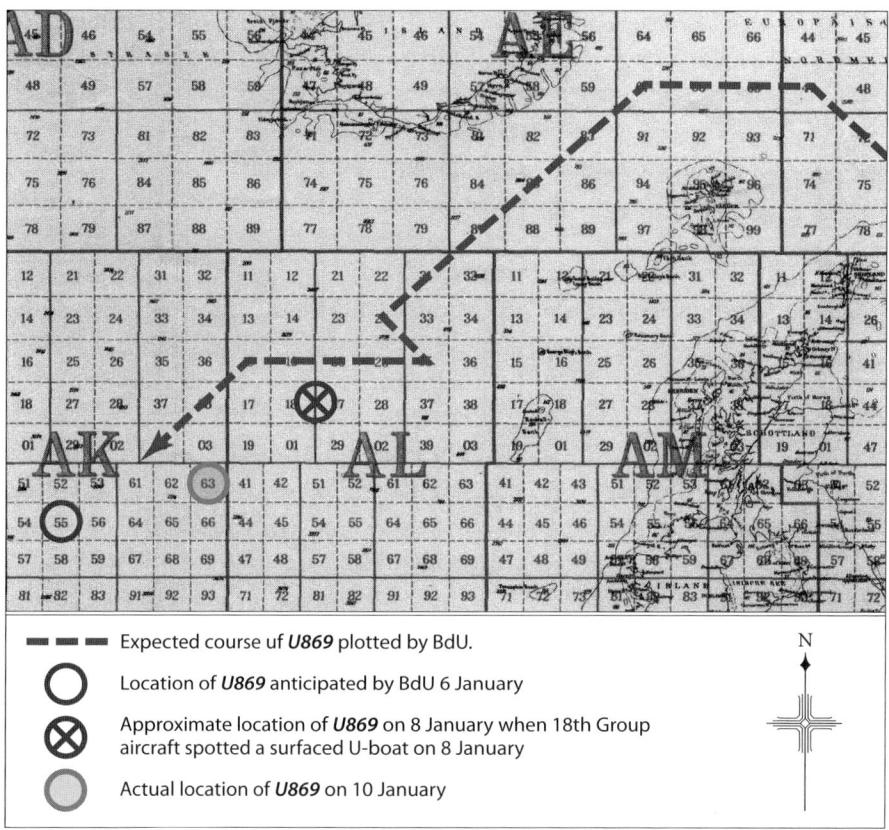

━ ━ ━ Expected course uf *U869* plotted by BdU.

○ Location of *U869* anticipated by BdU 6 January

⊗ Approximate location of *U869* on 8 January when 18th Group aircraft spotted a surfaced U-boat on 8 January

○ Actual location of *U869* on 10 January

N

that *U-870* achieved there. From BdU's perspective, they were looking to take advantage of the favourable tactical situation in that area and believed that *U-869* should move there rapidly.

A response was finally received from Neuerburg on 10 January to BdU's question about his diesel reserves requested four days earlier. He responded, 'Still have 179 CBM fuel remaining.'[14] *U-869* had been outward bound for just over a month. Its reported remaining diesel was consistent with other U-boats that proceeded through the normal Faroe Islands passage south of Iceland. If we look at *U-190*'s diesel consumption, we see that it began its final patrol with 228,930 litres. Exactly one month later it recorded having 167,940 litres on hand. This suggests that *U-869*'s diesel consumption was appropriate for a passage south of Iceland, especially as we do not know the exact level of fuel when it departed. We know through the interrogation of *U-190*'s commander that he proceeded into the Atlantic through the normal Faroe Islands passage between 62° and 63° North. He sent his obligatory passage report once he crossed over the 'Rosengarten' minefield. In thirty days *U-190* cruised approximately 2,700 miles at an average rate of 90 miles per day. *U-190*'s commander employed the snorkel on full diesels for an average of six hours per day when crossing through the Faroe Islands.[15] This aggressive use of the snorkel is clear by *U-190*'s high rate of diesel consumption compared with that of *U-869*. Had *U-869* travelled north around Iceland, as assumed by BdU, then *U-869* would have used far more diesel as that route was approximately 500 miles longer. *U-869* was clearly transiting at a slower speed given its lower consumption of diesel, relying more on its electric motors.

OP-20-G pinpointed *U-869*'s wireless signal through direction finding as being sent from 56.45N-26.00W.[16] This position, when coupled with a comparison of diesel expenditure, reinforces the assessment that *U-869* travelled through the Faroe Islands passage. It should also be added that not a single snorkel-equipped Type IX that was ordered to the North American coast has been identified as entering the North Atlantic from north of Iceland.

While *U-869*'s seemingly slow progress might be attributed to caution on Neuerburg's part, as this was his first operational deployment with the snorkel (whereas Commander Reith of *U-190* was on his second snorkel patrol), it equally might have represented snorkel problems that forced him to slow his transit. While Neuerburg reported his diesel status, this may have been solely on the basis of prior guidance to issue a passage report, and not to a specific request from BdU. This explains why he did not acknowledge the new operational area radioed on the 9th. He probably never received the message.

BdU's KTB reveals an entry of relevance to this story. On 8 January B-Dienst intercepted a U-boat sighting, probably from No. 162 Squadron Royal Canadian Airforce operating out of Iceland. The report stated that at 4.30pm an aircraft 'made a location on a suspected submarine, prepared to attack, in an unidentified position (U-1233?)'.[17] Again the staff at BdU assumed the boat's identity. *U-1233* departed for the North American coast the third time on 24 December. This was sixteen days after *U-869* departed. However, *U-1233* started farther north along the Norwegian coast when it departed Bergen. It is possible that *U-1233* might have reached a point south of Iceland and was the U-boat spotted, if it averaged an unlikely 71 miles a day surfaced. There is no KTB for *U-1233* and only one wireless transmission was intercepted from this boat through Ultra on 4 March during its return transit. We cannot rule out the possibility that this was indeed *U-869* caught on the surface two days earlier trying to transmit a passage report.

On 11 January the daily situation report of *Oberkommando der Marine Seekriegsleitung* [OKM SKL] recorded that: 'U-869 is in transit to Gibraltar operations area.'[18] This is the third assumption recorded by BdU staff. Perhaps the staff officer assigned was new to U-boat operations, but it appears odd that *U-869*'s change in direction was recorded with such finality without a wireless confirmation.

U-869 continued towards its original deployment area near the Philadelphia approaches. Neuerburg simply did not receive the messages to redirect his boat to Gibraltar due to the well-documented issues in wireless transmission.

OP-20-G's 17 January U-boat Intelligence Summary assessed that: 'The U-boat heading for the New York approaches, U-869 (Neuerburg), is presently estimated about 180 miles SSE of Flemish Cap.' She reported her position in about 56N 27W on 6 January and was told to "continue southward cruise". She is expected to arrive in the New York area at the beginning of February'.[19] OP-20-G interpreted 'southward cruise' as meaning towards the US East Coast. Two days later, OP-20-G recorded an intercept that read: 'To: Neuerburg (869). We expect your arrival in OP Area on about 1/2. Hechler (U-870) is there, but is probably on return cruise.'[20] Commander Knowles recorded that no response from Neuerburg was received.

Almost three weeks later, on 18 February, it was recorded in the daily OKM SKL that: 'From B-Dienst report 1100 hours off Gibraltar a ship was torpedoed (U-869).'[21] BdU clearly believed Neuerburg had proceeded to the new operational area. This is confirmed by another Ultra intercept on 19 February that recorded a transmission to *U-1279*, *U-869* and *U-300* that read 'Guard America'. This was a request to change wireless radio circuits. Both *U-1279* (VIIC/41) and *U-300* (VIIC/41) were operating off Gibraltar, and clearly BdU believed *U-869* was as well.

Commander Knowles did not believe so. Given his access to Ultra, he knew more about U-boat operations than anyone in the US Navy or Coast Guard at that time. He also knew the problems with U-boat wireless communication brought on by the snorkel and North Atlantic atmospherics, apparently better than the staff at BdU. His 25 January assessment recorded:

The intentions and location of U-869 (Neuerburg) who was ordered to the New York area 29 December are obscure since Control sent her a conflicting message 19 January saying that she was expected to arrive in U-870's area, off Gibraltar, about 1 February. Based on the signals she received it appears likely that U-869 is continuing towards her original heading off New York. On the other hand a reply to Control's message of 19 January (referred to above) would seem to be in order unless U-869 shifted radio watch without orders and missed this signal. (The *CORE* will begin sweeping for this

U-boat shortly prior to proceeding against the U-boats reporting weather in the [North Atlantic]).[22]

Knowles was on the right track in his thinking that *U-869* did not receive the new order and was en route to its assigned patrol area. On 3 February he recorded:

> The western Atlantic situation remains confused because of conflicting dispatches sent to U-869 and the unknown heading given U-1233. One of these U-boats probably is approaching either New York or Halifax and it may well be that both are in western Atlantic waters. U-1233 (Kuhn), who was sent three messages in special cipher shortly after sailing about 24 December, was reminded of 'ordered reports' 17 January and then asked for a position report five times between 19 and 22 January. She has not been heard from since sailing. On 26 January Control assumed that this U-boat had been responsible for the torpedoing of a ship whose distress traffic had been rebroadcast by Bermuda. She was then told to occupy at her discretion either the area given in heading orders or that of U-1232, off Halifax. Nothing further has developed in connection with U-869 (Neuerburg) since 19 January when Control assumed she was heading for the Gibraltar approaches although in accordance with prior orders she should have been heading for the New York approaches.
> Note. The source of the message rebroadcast by Bermuda has not been determined but may have been a drill message. The *CROATAN* and TG 22.9 (4 DE) are now sweeping for U-869 estimated approaching New York. The *CORE* also made a sweep for this U-boat while en route to the North Atlantic. No contacts were reported from any of the groups.[23]

U-1233 (IXC/40) followed *U-869* out to the North Atlantic, but suffered from extensive snorkel problems and returned to Norway. On 16 February Knowles assessed:

> The situation in the western Atlantic has not yet been clarified. Two U-boats are estimated on patrol, one in the New York approaches, the other off Halifax, but there have been no incidents other than somewhat doubtful sound and radar contacts to confirm their presence. Both have sufficient endurance to remain on patrol for several weeks longer.[24]

An interesting event appeared in the OKM SKL that has gone overlooked in the story of *U-869*. On 17 February an entry was added that read: 'By B-Dienst report U-boat sighted by American steamer in CA 5640

(U-1233?).'[25] BdU did not know that *U-1233* turned back to Norway with snorkel problems. They assumed that since *U-869* deployed to Gibraltar, this sighting could only be *U-1233*.

If this was indeed a U-boat, it could only be *U-869*. However, once again, the staff at BdU convinced themselves incorrectly that Neuerburg received his new deployment orders. There was no other U-boat in the area at the time of the reported sighting. This report could certainly have been a misidentification by an Allied vessel. Yet, B-Dienst seemed confident enough to relay the report to BdU, who often used intercepted Allied merchant reports to confirm U-boat locations in the last year of the war. The location of the sighting was near the 200m line, due east of Cape May/Point Peasant, New Jersey, where U-869 was expected to be located on approach to its deployment area. We know that U-boats used this underwater feature as a navigation aid when transiting along the North American coast.

BdU continued to believe Neuerburg was operating near Gibraltar. On 16 March the OKM SKL noted that: 'From B-Dienst report 14 and 15 March U-boat located and repeated tactical Radio Messages in the Gibraltar area (U-869 possible).'[26]

Based on Ultra intercepts Commander Knowles recorded the following on 5 March: [27]

> The two long un-located U-boats estimated off Halifax and New York are now probably homebound. The orders of U-869 (Neuerburg), originally given New York approaches as a heading, may have been countermanded in an 'Ursula' dispatch which sent her to Gibraltar approaches instead. In either event this U-boat should now be homebound.[28]

Knowles never assessed that *U-869* had been sunk by any Allied air or surface vessel attack. He only alluded to *U-869*'s fate in his final U-boat fleet assessment:

> … 2) U-869 was estimated to have arrived in Gibraltar area about 1 February. She made no reports and operating area and was presumed lost by BdU (commander U-boats) on 20 February.
> Comment: Since U-869 departed Kristiansand South on 8 December 1944, she had been at sea 75 days on 20 February and could have remained in the operational area until at least 1 March. BdU apparently chose 20 February for her loss without any other basis than the fact that U-869 made no reports while in her operational area and the date therefore would have to be an arbitrary one.

It is noted that there were no attacks made on shipping in the Gibraltar area while U-869 was there, other than the aforementioned attacks by U-300 on 17 February.

There were several attacks during February which could have resulted in the loss of U-869, namely:

1) USS Atherton attack at 1651Z/18 February,
2) USS O'Toole attack at 0120Z/26 February,
3) USS Fowler and F.S. L'Indiscret attacks at 0648 and 1500Z/28 February,
Of these attacks, (3) above appears the most promising, particularly the resulting debris where depth of water was 1265 fathoms.
Recommendation:
1) Reassesses (3) above from G to B — Probably sunk.
2) In event none of the above attacks is acceptable to the committee, it follows that loss of U-869 must be attributed to 'Cause Unknown'.
K.A. Knowles[29]

U-869 ultimately came to rest on the sea floor in position 39.33N, 73.02W off the coast of Cape May, New Jersey, in the same grid square location where a merchantman spotted a U-boat on 17 February.

When *U-869* was discovered, two areas of damage were identified. In an article authored by Chatterton, Kohler and Yurga for *Wreck Diving* magazine in 2009 they stated:

There was an area in the foreword most section of the aft torpedo room where the pressure hull had been compromised, and the thick steel of the pressure hull pushed inward. This was severe damage, and typical of depth charge damage we had seen on other U-boat wrecks, like the U-853.

However, in the area around the control room, the damage was far more severe and markedly different. The damage was focused on the port side of the control room, where the pressure hull was completely blown away, virtually from bulkhead to bulkhead, and, from as far down as the sand, going up and across the top of the starboard side. The conning tower was displaced and lying on the port side of the wreck, adjacent to the main body of the wreckage. The remaining pressure hull on the starboard side of the control room was also fractured. In addition, there were large jagged cracks in the top of the pressure hull, running both forward into the officers' quarters, and aft into the diesel engine room.

All of the external hatches were blown open, or completely off their hinges. The only way we can suggest for this to happen is from a reverse differential pressure wave inside the U-boat, creating more pressure inside the submarine than outside. This not only indicates a powerful explosion, but also that the sub was filled with air at the time of the event.[30]

We will now re-evaluate the two prominent theories for the reason why *U-869* sunk.

Theory #1: Circular-Run Torpedo

Chatterton, Kohler and Yurga first proposed the hypothesis in 1998 that *U-869* fired a T5 acoustic torpedo that malfunctioned and turned on the U-boat, sinking it in what is known as a circular run. This hypothesis asserted that a T5 torpedo shot detonated at or near the port side of the hull near the control room and caused a catastrophic explosion that resulted in *U-869*'s sinking.

Chatterton, Kohler and Yurga cited the possibility of a circular-run torpedo by pointing to a BdU order issued on 1 January 1944 that stated: 'On crash-diving after firing an acoustic torpedo from the bow tube, the boat must submerge to a depth of 30m – not in sixty seconds, but as quickly as possible.'[31] This suggested that if a U-boat did not immediately submerge it ran the risk of the torpedo hitting the U-boat if the guidance mechanism failed. This order was issued at a time when the T5 was still new. More importantly, it was issued when no U-boat was retrofitted with a snorkel and tactical procedures had not shifted to submerged operations.

After the introduction of the snorkel, new torpedo launch procedures were adopted. U-boats were no longer cruising surfaced looking for a target, then launching a torpedo while maintaining the same bearing as they might have done in the early years of the war. In 1944–45 they often fired a torpedo from a position of depth. This meant that a torpedo proceeded on its own to a higher point in the water column to reach its target. In most cases a U-boat left the area quickly while simultaneously changing its position in the water column.

Experience Message No. 152 issued on 14 November 1944 ordered that: 'behaviour after firing torpedoes, especially in the vicinity of the coast: move away from the place of firing and then, but not until then, lie on the bottom in order to escape direction-finding and hydrophone pursuit' (Chapter 6). From a tactical perspective, the intent was to fire a torpedo from depth and get out of the area as quick as possible. It was acknowledged in Current Order No. 67, also issued in November 1944 (see Chapter 6), that U-boats should be prepared to fire torpedoes by sound alone. Such torpedo launches should be conducted at a depth no greater than 20m. Immediately after firing, the U-boat 'must dive to a greater depth (at least 50m), in order to avoid the possibility of torpedoes passing overhead, when travelling to a higher level. (When firing Zaunkönig torpedoes [T5], speed should not exceed 3 knots).' This suggests that under the new guidance a U-boat was likely to be: a) already submerged at a depth no deeper than 20m when it fired a torpedo and that once it did fire one, it would conduct an evasive manoeuvre that probably placed it at a different, typically lower point in the vertical water column. While this does not rule out a circular-run hit on *U-869* completely, it makes its chances far less likely in February 1945 than it did in January 1944 given the typical submerged firing position a U-boat now found itself in. Out of all the snorkel-equipped U-boats studied for this work only *U-806* (see Chapter 9) heard one torpedo it fired from a fan of three pass by its conning tower while submerged, followed by an explosion some nine minutes later without damage. Circular-run torpedo misses were *exceedingly rare* in the last twelve months of the war.

If a circular-run torpedo detonated at a point amidships on *U-869* and caused a catastrophic explosion it certainly would have occurred at a point within 30m or less of the surface. Such a catastrophic explosion would have been heard on Allied hydrophones or even with the naked ear. Recall the report of the *Frost* in Chapter 9 after its hedgehogs had contacted the submerged U-boat on 15 April. The resulting explosion was so massive that two destroyers and an escort carrier miles away from the detonation and travelling at 17 knots felt the concussion wave. One of the destroyers thought it had been struck by a torpedo and was listing as a result. If the explosion occurred during daylight hours in fair weather, then the explosion might have been seen as a churning sea with debris. Long-run torpedoes that exploded or premature detonations were recorded in similar situations by escort vessels and merchantmen alike, as discussed in previous chapters. Yet no Allied report has been identified to date for such an explosion. If *U-869* was struck by its own torpedo fired at an Allied vessel in range, there can be no doubt that a detonation report would have been made. OP-20-G used such reports to help identify the possible locations of snorkel-equipped U-boats, but no such report made its way to them from the US Navy's Tenth Fleet.

A catastrophic detonation at 20 or even 50m would have caused *U-869* to descend another 50 or 20m respectfully to the ocean floor. The U-boat would have quickly lost trim as the air rushed out and water flooded in, probably rolling the U-boat to starboard and thus causing debris to empty and spread across the ocean floor. But that did not happen. *U-869* is resting almost peacefully in an upright position with no impact damage to the stern or bow. Most of its contents were intact when the U-boat was discovered. This is strong evidence that the boat was on the bottom when it met its demise.

The fact that the conning tower was lying so close to the U-boat confirms that the vessel did not make a lengthy or violent descent to the bottom. The conning tower appears to have been lifted off its bolts and placed on the sand to the portside. An examination of other U-boat wrecks, as noted below, confirms the oddity of *U-869*'s position in the sand. Perhaps most important is the fact that the damage around the control room clearly demonstrates an internal and not an external explosion of the type that might have been caused by a torpedo exploding outside the hull.

Theory #2: Sunk by Depth Charge and Hedgehog Attack

In 2006 the US Coast Guard Historical Center recorded the fate of *U-869* as being explicitly as the result of surface action. The following account is described by Harold Moyers on the United States Coast Guard website:

Early evening February 11, 1945 was overcast and unseasonably warm in the mid forty degree range. The sea was calm with a slight swell from the east. Lt. John Nixon commanded the Crow. The anti-submarine warfare officer was Ensign I. G. 'George' King, who at 24 was just a few years older than some of the men under him. At 4.39 PM the sonar operator, Howard Denson, yelled out a strong contact. The contact was from sonar, a machine that produced a pinging noise and then analysed a return echo. A good operator could distinguish a steel object from a hard sea bottom or a school of fish. Denson was a good operator, he was an original member or 'plank owner' of the Crow's crew. He was well trained on his sonar equipment, as were most operators, the increasingly lopsided Battle of the Atlantic testified to that. His contact was so strong that ASW (Anti-Submarine Warfare) officer King ordered preparations for an immediate hedgehog attack without waiting for the captain's orders. A 'hedgehog' was a special anti-submarine weapon mounted on the forward deck of the destroyer. It fired 24 missiles forward of the speeding vessel. The grouped missiles resembled a porcupine, or as the English say, 'hedgehog'. Each missile contained a 38 lb. warhead that only detonated on contact with a hard surface. The missiles landed on the water in an elongated elliptical pattern and rapidly sank until making contact, striking a sand bottom wouldn't set them off.

The destroyer approached the submerged contact at 4.53 PM, fourteen minutes after making contact and firing her hedgehogs. Carpenter's Mate Robert Quigley was below deck in the stem of the Crow. He knew nothing of the attack until the hedgehogs went off. At least one had detonated and the violence of the explosion was so great that he thought a torpedo had struck his own ship. He ran on deck only to witness an emerging oil slick on the water's surface. 'What the hell's going on?' he asked gunner's mate Ted

Sieviec. Sieviec was his bunkmate and had also fired the hedgehogs. 'We are attacking a submarine,' he replied.

The Crow instantly called for help in the attack. The USS Koiner answered the call and turned north-west and headed the fifteen miles to the Crow at flank speed. A request also went out to CINCLANT (Commander in Chief Atlantic) for a hunter killer group to pick up the attack. Hunter killer groups were specialists; they usually patrolled with a light aircraft carrier and contained several high-speed destroyers. Once they picked up the scent, they would stay on a target for hours, even days. The Crow and the Koiner requested the hunter group because they needed to rejoin the convoy as rapidly as possible. Their absence left the convoy vulnerable to attack from any other submarine that may be lurking nearby.

The Crow continued her attack as she waited for relief. At 5.17pm four depth charges were dropped on the slowly moving contact. This resulted in air bubbles and more oil coming to the surface. Twenty-five minutes later three more depth charges were dropped. Again, air bubbles and oil came to the surface. At 6pm the Koiner arrived and investigated the sonar contact, which was now stationary on the bottom. As the Crow stood off, Lieutenant Commander Judson of the Koiner ordered an attack. In all, Judson ordered three attacks on the stationary target, each attack brought oil to the surface but no movement. He lowered a small boat over the side and Chief Ring investigated the dark water over the attack site. Ring soaked up oil on a rag and returned to the Koiner. Lieutenant Commander Judson ordered both vessels to return to convoy CU 58 and take up station. At 7.26 they were under way. Judson classified the contact non-sub. CINCLANT was notified that the hunter killer group was no longer needed. The men of the Howard D. Crow were disappointed, errant depth charge attacks don't bring air bubbles and oil to the surface. They really felt they got one. In the escort report for CU 58 the event was written off as an attack on a wreck 'submarine or otherwise' as the report stated. The attack occurred at an inexact point in the ocean roughly 39.30 North, 72.58 West. Sixty years after the attack, 92-year-old Charles Judson still recalls the night. 'I thought I was attacking a wreck, it never moved the whole time I attacked it.' Convoy CU 58 successfully crossed the Atlantic, with no losses.[32]

As Moyers concluded:

The known location of the U-869 is 4.5 miles from the reported position of the Crow and Koiner attack. Navigation of that era was an inexact science, 4.5 miles is remarkably close. If after the war assessors had known a German U-boat was in that area in February '45 they most certainly would have taken a closer look at the destroyers' attack. The most interesting thing about the Crow/Koiner attack is the date, February 11, 1945. The U-boat had reported its position January 6, 1945 at 56.21 North, 26.45 West. At this point she had travelled 2070 miles from Norway, or 69 miles per day. German U-boat command expected her to arrive in her Gibraltar operation area on February 1, 1945. This was a distance of 1770 miles. This also equalled 69 miles per day. The U-boat, however, never headed to Gibraltar, she headed to a point off New Jersey; this distance was 2430 miles. If she averaged 69 miles per day it would have taken 35 days to reach the location in which she sank. That date would have been February 11, 1945; the exact date of the Crow/Koiner attack.[33]

Unfortunately, much of Moyers' online article that represents the US Coast Guard's official report of *U-869*'s sinking is assumptive at best on all of its points about *U-869*'s demise. Moyers conducted no original research and incorporated nothing about changing U-boat tactical procedures during 1944–45. His calculation for time/distance that placed *U-869* in the area on 11 February is based on BdU's own incorrect assertion of *U-869*'s path. He used a presumed distance of 2,000 miles based on a route north of Iceland. *U-869* could have made the distance of 69 miles per day, but only if it cruised while predominately surfaced, and that did not happen. This time/distance analysis is an important fact in debunking Moyers' account.

The likely course of *U-869* through the normal Faroe Islands passage represented a shorter 1,500-mile trip. That distance divided by thirty days provides a rate of 50 miles per day, suggesting a slower than normal, but not too abnormal, passage. If *U-869* followed a normal route along the 200m line to its operational area, and it was indeed spotted on 17 February according to B-Dienst, then Neuerburg made the 2,500-mile journey in thirty-eight days for an average of 65 miles per day. Compare that to Moyers' assertion that *U-869* was attacked and sunk on the 11th. That means that *U-869* travelled an approximate 2,600 miles in six fewer days. That calculation results in an average of 81 miles a day. This is extremely unlikely as it required *U-869* to travel at almost twice the normal speed to reach its operational area when compared with *U-190*. This could only be accomplished by travelling surfaced. Not even running the diesel engines on snorkel for ten hours a day could attain this speed. Analysing the procedures and actual patrols of every U-boat that saw action off the North American coast in 1944–45 demonstrates that only *U-1229* cruised surfaced before it reached the 200m line against standard operating procedures. It was located and sunk accordingly in the mid-Atlantic. In 1945, no U-boat could cruise the six to ten hours per day surfaced required to support Moyers' time/distance assertion without being located long before it reached the point on the map where *U-869* met its demise.

Recall that two entire US Navy Task Groups were pursuing *U-869*. Had this U-boat travelled surfaced for any amount of time, it would have been easily sunk before it ever reached the 200m line east of Cape May. Even BdU understood tactical realities when they broadcast to *U-869* on 7 January to approach Gibraltar 'submerged by day, surfaced by night. *From CG approach submerged, snorkelling.*' [Author's emphasis] The time/distance analysis offers a compelling counter-argument to the assertion that *U-869* was sunk on 11 February. Finally, the diesel consumption rate of *U-869* does not support Moyers' calculations at all.

Even if we assume that *U-869* was identified at a depth of 70m and attacked, the amount of damage caused by the brief surface action resulted in an amazing catastrophic explosion that should have sent a tremendous pressure wave, air bubbles and debris into the water column that ultimately would have been heard by hydrophone operators onboard the US Coast Guard escort vessels, as well as felt and seen by those on deck. None of this was recorded by the crews of either the USS *Howard D Crow* or USS *Koiner*. As Moyers noted in his article, even the crew suspected they had attacked a wreck because the target never moved and the debris was inconclusive. Today we have the benefit of a growing maritime archeological record of what late-war depth charge and hedgehog damage achieved on a German U-boat to compare against that of *U-869*.

Both theories are strongly countered by decades of surveys conducted on U-boat wreck sites. British maritime archaeologist Innes McCartney surveyed scores of First and Second World War German U-boats sunk around the British Isles at depths and conditions like *U-869*. In surveying fourteen wrecks of snorkel-equipped U-boats that fell victim to either depth charges, hedgehog, or a combination of both, none suffered any damage like that of *U-869*'s control room area. More importantly, all settled on the sea floor at a list, almost all at greater than 45°, whether destroyed by depth charge, hedgehog, or deep sea mine at or near the sea floor, as in the case of *U-480*. All surveyed wrecks were Type VIICs. This suggests that the damage they suffered should perhaps be more extensive than that of the larger Type IX. Yet, none show any damage as catastrophic as that suffered by *U-869*. In at least three of the attacks, German survivors were pulled from the water, suggesting that the crew was moving through the boat and actively trying to escape once they realised their boat's hull integrity was compromised.

In US waters we also have the wreck of the *U-853* to compare with *U-869* as Chatterton, Koehler and Yurga did in their effort to determine how it sank. This author also dived the *U-853* and assessed the damage for himself.

It should be noted that the damage to *U-853* is consistent to the findings of U-boats surveyed by McCartney, with the exception that it sits upright like *U-869*. This, however, is accounted for by the fact that *U-853* was 'bottomed' when first identified by its pursuers, then it tried to creep away close to the bottom in order to hide its acoustic signature.[34] *U-853* was tracked and attacked for five straight hours while operating at a depth of about 100ft, which is 120ft shallower than *U-869*. The attack on *U-853* was far more intense and extensive that that of the two US Coast Guard escorts against their supposed submerged target of *U-869*, yet the damage to *U-869* was paradoxically more catastrophic. *U-853* suffered its main damage just forward of the control room on the upper deck while the boat was at or already on the bottom. This may have contributed significantly to its upright position. It was noted that on *U-853* the crew attempted to escape and died of blunt-force trauma before the water entered the boat through a cracked pressure hull and flooded the U-boat. As the crew's remains were located in and around the normal exit points of the U-boat, this is a strong indication that the commander gave the order to 'bottom' and abandon the U-boat, leaving *U-853* resting in the upright position. A very different picture of *U-869* emerges when compared with the location of its crew's remains, as discussed in Theory #3 below.

Theory #3. Catastrophic snorkel failure
Nearly a dozen snorkel-equipped Type IX U-boats mysteriously disappeared during the war. Their cause of loss is unknown but attributed by BdU to a snorkel failure. As none of these U-boats have been previously located, we have no maritime archaeological survey to determine what a U-boat that met such a fate looks like on the sea floor. In previous chapters it was revealed how several U-boats almost succumbed to carbon monoxide poisoning. In such a case the crew narrowly averted being incapacitated and the U-boat careening off into the depths to settle on the bottom as if nothing had happened, or if in deep enough water, to erupt from the external water pressure causing a catastrophic hull implosion. As previously documented in Chapter 2, there was another form of failure that could be caused by snorkelling. A dangerous build-up of noxious and explosive oxyhydrogen gas from the batteries could occur after the completion of a snorkel run. If the gas was not properly vented it could result in a catastrophic explosion from within the U-boat, according to period documents.

U-boats could snorkel at any time to recharge batteries or even run their diesels to transit more quickly while remaining submerged. This latter use of the snorkel was carried out primarily to get to/from the operational area, though it could be used shortly after an attack to get away quickly. In the

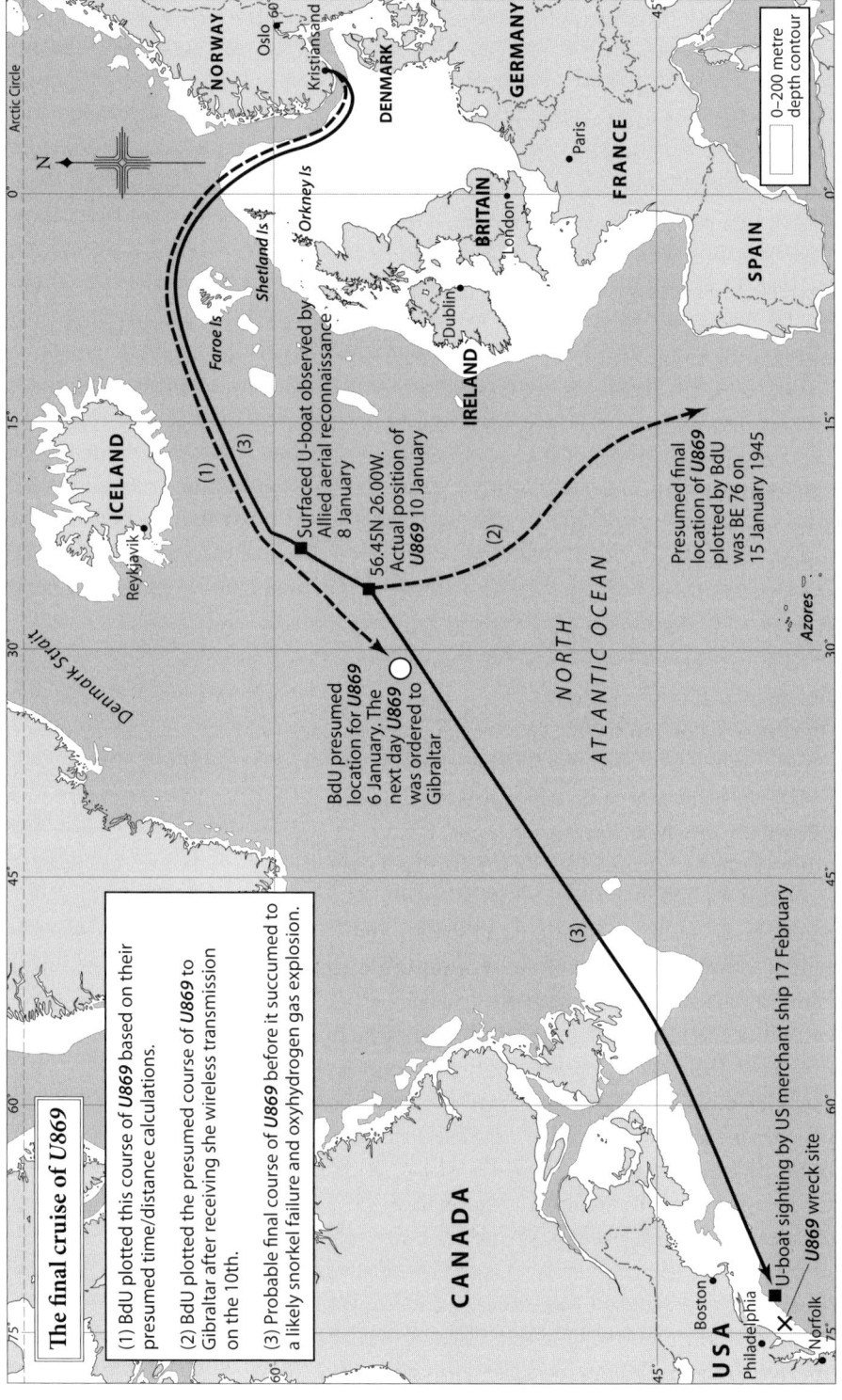

The final cruise of U869

(1) BdU plotted this course of *U869* based on their presumed time/distance calculations.

(2) BdU plotted the presumed course of *U869* to Gibraltar after receiving she wireless transmission on the 10th.

(3) Probable final course of *U869* before it succumbed to a likely snorkel failure and oxyhydrogen gas explosion.

case of *U-869*, it appears that Neuerburg was probably using his snorkel to charge his batteries given his location near the coast. U-boats that remained submerged for long periods adopted the tactic of 'bottoming', which could be effective in a tactical situation where the U-boat needed to hide below a thermocline to avoid detection from Allied ASDIC. It was also used to rest the crew and conserve oxygen and battery power while on an extended patrol in a coastal operational area. This procedure was established by BdU based on the experience of snorkel-equipped U-boats and broadcast out as Experience Message 113 titled 'Silent Trim' sent on 1 July 1944 (see Chapter 6). In the experience message it was noted how *U-397* remained on the bottom for fourteen days at a depth of 25m waiting for a sound contact to pass overhead instead of actively searching for a target. When *U-397* ran low on battery power or oxygen it would raise off the bottom, snorkel, then bottom again and wait.

The final actions *of U-869* can be developed within the context of the known actions followed by almost every Type IX that operated off the North America coast in 1945 and available tactical procedures developed for snorkel boats. Neuerburg traversed the 'Rosengarten' south of Iceland submerged, then proceeded mainly on the surface from a point south of Iceland to the Flemish Cap. He then submerged and cruised south. After nearly two months at sea Neuerburg reached a point on the 200m line east of Cape May, along the general north–south convoy route between Philadelphia and New York where he was directed by BdU.

His designated area of operations was the entrance to the Delaware Bay, between Cape May, New Jersey and Delaware Capes, which represented the embarkation/debarkation point for the Port of Philadelphia. Unlike the days of Operation *Paukenschlag* where U-boats simply cruised surfaced at night back and forth along the coast for hundreds of miles looking for Allied shipping, the snorkel-equipped U-boat stayed submerged in a limited patrol area until released by BdU or the U-boat's commander determined the specific area no longer had opportunities for attack.

On 17 February, Neuerburg briefly surfaced his U-boat. There are any number of reasons why *U-869* might have briefly surfaced at this point in its patrol along the 200m line. Based on a survey of hundreds of snorkel-equipped U-boat KTBs, the main reasons were to take a brief astronomical fix to confirm a navigation course, attempt to send/receive an emergency wireless transmission, or to conduct emergency repairs on a snorkel. Other reasons most certainly exist but are not as prevalent in the historical record given what we know of late-war tactical procedures. Whatever the reason, some portion of *U-869* (snorkel head, periscope, or its conning tower) was spotted by a merchant vessel, who quickly reported the U-boat sighting.

This report was intercepted by B-Dienst and recorded in BdU's KTB, as previously noted. Neuerburg either spotted the merchant vessel himself or picked up the radio warning of *U-869*'s presence. He decided in response to move closer to the coast in his directed operational area and bottom to avoid any potential anti-submarine warfare group that might conduct a search for him.

Even if the actual sighting of *U-869* did not occur as recorded by the B-Dienst intercept, Neuerburg was familiar enough with BdU's guidance to move close to the coast and bottom his U-boat. From this position he would wait for the sounds of a convoy to pass overhead and attack.

Neuerburg probably conducted a final snorkel run to recharge the batteries and refresh the air in the boat before he settled on the ocean floor in 70m of water. As per normal snorkelling procedure, battery charging could last several hours. The battery gas was then vented. He issued the order to lower the snorkel, followed by another to bottom *U-869*. U-boats grew adept at using undersea terrain features to mask themselves while bottomed. It is probably no coincidence that *U-869* came to rest in a natural depression that is about 30ft deeper than the surrounding sea floor.

As *U-869* landed upon the soft sand to rest in an upright position, the crew retired to their bunks and berths in the forward and aft torpedo rooms as well as the NCO quarters. They rested to conserve oxygen as per standard procedure, and a mere skeleton crew stayed at their stations. The lights were probably turned out to discourage conversations. The hydrophone remained manned in order to listen for approaching surface ships. Even Neuerburg probably retired to his captain's bunk for a brief rest.

Perhaps an hour later, one by one, each crewman, most of whom were already sleeping, succumbed to carbon monoxide poisoning without even knowing what was happening, as in the case of *U-1228* (see Chapter 9). As detailed in Chapter 7, the longer a snorkel-equipped U-boat was on patrol, the more CO gases bonded with haemoglobin, accelerating its deadly effect. A catastrophic leak of CO gases from the snorkel exhaust trunking was not needed to generate the condition required for what occurred next – an explosive oxyhydrogen scenario. All it took was the crew to simply be operating at a reduced mental capacity, which in turn led to mistakes that could result in catastrophe.

Those crewmen still awake began to nod off and finally fell into eternal sleep. Perhaps the exhaust piping on the port side of the U-boat leading from the diesel engine room to the boot heel of the snorkel mast had malfunctioned. As the diesels ran and the batteries charged, little of the carbon monoxide produced by the diesel engines was vented. Instead, it built up inside the boat. Alternatively, the snorkel float valve malfunctioned, and not enough fresh air was brought into the boat. In either case, while the crew members succumbed to hypoxia, explosive oxyhydrogen gas built up in the battery tanks and leached out into the boat, where it expanded within the open space of the control room.

There were many reasons that the unvented oxyhydrogen could build up, most notably due to improper venting or overcharging. BdU issued Current Order No. 2 in November 1944 that contained very specific guidance under Section E.(4) 'The most careful venting of batteries' so that such a dangerous situation could be avoided (see Chapter 4). Explosive oxyhydrogen built from a normal operating range of 0.5–1 per cent to a catastrophic 4–5 per cent. Numerous ignition triggers of the gas were possible with an incapacitated crew. All that was needed was a short in a wire or circuit – any electrical charge – and the result was a massive explosion, far larger than what occurred in the ex-German submarine *U-3017* while operating with a British crew (see Chapter 2). The internal explosion ruptured the port-side hull, blew out all the hatches, and unseated the conning tower. Water rushed into the boat. The crew remained where they went to rest and at their final stations after bottoming. Carbon monoxide poisoning ensured no one was alive to try to escape the stricken vessel.

We know such an event was possible based on period documents and eyewitness accounts. Evidence from the wreck site supports this theory.

Evidence #1. The U-boat sits upright. This is highly unusual for any U-boat that would have succumbed to a circular torpedo run, depth charge, or hedgehog attack at midwater column based on almost thirty known U-boat wreck surveys. Even those U-boats that succumbed to an external explosion from a deep mine around the English coast lie at 45° to 90° angles on the bottom, and in almost every case these were explosions that occurred at or near the sea floor. The position of *U-869* strongly suggests a controlled landing on the bottom, guided and maintained through active trim monitoring by the crew from inside the control room. The catastrophic damage to the port side simply could not have occurred at any point when the U-boat was higher in the water column without the boat listing when it settled.

Evidence #2. The main damage to the U-boat is a catastrophic *internal* explosion at the port side of the control room, where the exhaust snorkel trunking ran from the diesel engines to the snorkel boot heel. We know that crews were warned that a build-up of explosive gas could occur inside the U-boat when the batteries were not properly vented. It is logical that the oxyhydrogen build-up occurred in the control room/conning tower area as

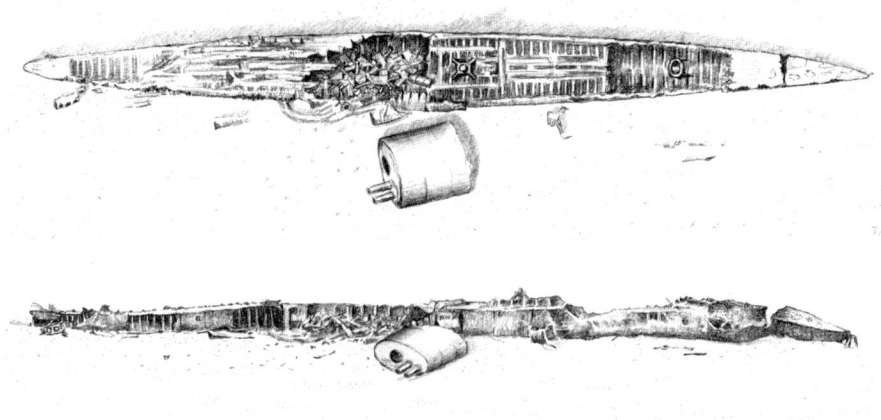

A top and port-side view of the wreck of *U-869*, c.2015. The bow is to the left and stern to the right. *U-869* sits upright, as it was likely 'bottomed' with its crew in their bunks at rest, as per tactical guidance of the time, and supported by the location of the human remains on the wreck site. There is no debris field, and its conning tower appears to be lifted off the hull and placed intact on the sand next to it. As detailed in the text, no torpedo or depth charge attack could cause such resulting damage. *U-869*'s likely demise was an internal explosion caused by a build-up of oxyhydrogen gas from faulty snorkel exhaust trunking. The crew probably succumbed to carbon monoxide poisoning before the explosion. *(Author's collection)*

this was the largest compartment in the boat. The gas expanded outward and upward into the largest cavity of the U-boat through the normal process of physics.

Evidence #3. Lack of a debris field. Given the extent of the explosion and resulting damage, one should expect to locate objects over a wider area if the internal detonation had occurred higher in the water column. The explosion appears to have occurred while *U-869* was at rest on the bottom, as evidenced by the location of the conning tower and other debris being with 10ft of the wreck. There is no evidence of wire dragging.[35] As previously mentioned, *U-869* sits in a natural depression that suggests it was chosen specifically as a location to bottom.

Evidence #4. The location of the crew's remains is absolutely telling. Chatterton revealed to the author that: 'Remains of the crew were found in several concentrated areas, all inside the sub, and away from exposure to the open ocean. The aft torpedo, NCO quarters and forward torpedo rooms were the main concentrations.'[36] These are the precise locations the crew retired while at rest when the U-boat was bottomed after a snorkel run. If the U-boat was under attack while the crew was at normal stations, then the remains could be expected to be more distributed and not concentrated as they are. If the U-boat was stricken, the crew might have attempted to escape, but there appears to be no sign of this as in the case of *U-853*.

There is the fact that the aft hull is compromised in a single location that approximates the potential damage from a depth charge or hedgehog. This can readily be explained by other causes besides the reported attack on 11 February. While it is plausible that *U-869* had already succumbed to a catastrophic internal explosion caused by a snorkel failure before the USS *Crow* and USS *Koiner* made contact with the wreck of *U-869*, it is also as likely that some other US Coast Guard or Navy vessel identified a submerged contact and dropped a depth charge or hedgehog, but never made a report after the 17th, realising it was simply a wreck. It should be noted that no unexploded ordnance has yet been found around *U-869*. Hedgehogs that did not contact a U-boat did not explode. They can readily be found near their intended sunken victim. To date none have been located around *U-869*. An example of this can be seen with the sunken *U-275* (VIIC) that lies in 56m of water off Beachy Head in the English Channel. It succumbed to an underwater mine and came to rest at 45° to starboard. However, two unexploded 'squids' were located around the wreck site. These were clearly dropped after the U-boat was initially sunk. In this case Allied surface vessels made a contact with an anomaly not marked on their charts as an existing wreck and launched an attack as per standing procedure.[37]

Given the evidence derived from period archival documents, the probability that *U-869* succumbed to a snorkel exhaust trunking failure that resulted in a catastrophic oxyhydrogen explosion must be considered as the primary reason for its destruction. The condition of the wreck site supports this conclusion, from the position of the U-boat on the sand, the evidence of an internal explosion, and the final resting places of the crew. If it can be confirmed that *U-869* succumbed to an internal oxyhydrogen explosion through metallurgical testing, then this will make this U-boat the first one identified as a victim of a likely snorkel failure. The wreck site deserves further maritime archaeological study.

Conclusion

Post-war Historiography

Histories of the Battle of the Atlantic universally fail to appreciate the impact that the introduction of the snorkel had on the evolutionary shift in U-boat operations at the end of the war. German U-boat histories of the Second World War are dominated by the period 1940–43 and written by, or about, veterans that never saw a single operational patrol in a snorkel-equipped U-boat. Out of the top twenty-five U-boat aces of the war, only one – Heinrich Lehmann-Willenbrock – commanded an operational snorkel-equipped U-boat. However, he did not take part in the inshore campaign during this cruise. Well-known U-boat commanders including Kretschmer, Lüth, Topp, Merten, Prien, Schepke, Witt and Lemp never experienced a patrol on a snorkel-equipped U-boat nor had any understanding of its potential.

Lothar-Günther Buchheim, author of the popular anti-war book *Das Boot*, never sailed on a snorkel-equipped U-boat. Yet he disparaged the device in his follow-on 1976 book *Der U-Boot Krieg*, even though he admitted 'it was a life saver'. The U-boat force was given an 'orthopedic contraption', Buchheim stated colourfully, by leadership that called it an 'epoch-making invention'.[1] While Dönitz gave the snorkel device due credit in his post-war memoir, he also had no practical experience with the snorkel and spent only about twenty pages covering the period of the U-boat war from 1944–45.[2] He longed only for the day his 'wolves' could return to the heyday of convoy warfare.

The problem in German U-boat veteran historiography is that no one grasped how the snorkel fundamentally altered the nature of submarine warfare. The potential resumption of anti-convoy operations remained paramount in the minds of Dönitz and his U-boat men because it recalled the heyday of success and brought meaning to the force's sacrifices. However, there was never going to be a resumption of such operations because the challenge of submerged communications was never overcome during the war. Not even the introduction of the Type XXI 'wonder weapon' was going to change that fact. There was never a post-war survey by German naval historians of the impact of the snorkel within the U-boat fleet, leaving the broader understanding of the Battle of the Atlantic over-whelmingly distorted towards the earlier period of convoy battles.

Most British and American authors remain content to view the Battle of the Atlantic through the narrow optic of convoy warfare, and within that limited view argue that the U-boat as a weapon system was defeated in May 1943. Many opine that continued resistance by the U-boat force after May 1943 was folly, despite any wartime technical developments.

As an example, Ed Offley's 2011 work, *Turning the Tide: How a Small Band of Allied Sailors Defeated the U-Boats and Won the Battle of the Atlantic*, argues the well-worn thesis that the U-boat was defeated in May 1943 and forced to withdraw from the Atlantic. His view of the U-boat's continued deployment during the following two years was that they served little purpose beyond 'cannon fodder'.[3] While he briefly discusses Dönitz's actions to restore the U-boat force, he cites only the future development of the high-speed Electro-boats and Walter turbines, never once mentioning the snorkel. Offley, like many authors, is content to interpret the remaining years of the Battle of the Atlantic through the balance sheet of tonnage sunk versus U-boats destroyed.[4] It is a victor's perspective that offers little historical value.

Arguably, one of the most audacious attempts at solidifying the victor's perspective of the Battle of the Atlantic came from former Second World War US Submarine veteran Clay Blair, who took a direct attack in his assessment of both the U-boat and its technology. He was determined to counter what he believed was a growing U-boat 'mythos' in the late 1980s and early '90s, fuelled in popular literature by scores of U-boat veteran memoirs and movies such as *Das Boot* that found eager audiences in Great Britain and the United States. Blair published his two-volume history *Hitler's U-Boat War* starting with *Volume 1* in 1996 and continuing with *Volume 2* in 1998. His scope was the U-boat itself and not just the convoy battles of the mid-Atlantic. In the foreword of his first volume he set a con-trary tone regarding wartime technological advances in the U-boat force by dismissing any evolutionary value of the Type XXI offhandedly, despite the known benefits of its hull form and internal mechanics widely copied after the war by all major navies. He specifically dissected its snorkel apparatus into 'imperfect', 'hazardous' and 'nightmarish'.[5] In his second volume he addressed the introduction of the snorkel across the U-boat diesel force in counterfactual terms. He stated that the snorkel was 'technically primitive';

only employed for one to four hours a day; a snorkelling U-boat was completely 'deaf' and could not use its radio receivers or hydrophones; a U-boat that snorkelled could not use its periscope; snorkels were prone to emit exhaust smoke; snorkels leaked carbon monoxide into the pressure hull; a snorkelling U-boat had no way to get rid of its waste; and arguably the most erroneous statement that 'almost without exception, U-boat crews distrusted snorts and hated to use them'.[6] All of Blair's statements are gross exaggerations or counterfactual when compared against period primary documents. In Blair's desire to diminish the evolutionary contribution to modern submarine development made by German wartime engineers, he asserted that the US Navy advanced into the nuclear-powered submarine age with such sophistication as to leave behind all 'hopelessly archaic' German technical innovations, like the snorkel.[7] His amateurish historical assertions are contradicted by official US Navy technical assessments.[8]

In the earliest published work on the last year of the Battle of the Atlantic, British naval historian V E Tarrant, writing in his 1994 book *The Last Year of the Kriegsmarine, May 1944–May 1945*, stated that the snorkel 'was never welcomed by the majority of the U-boat crews'.[9] His work on this critical, transformative period of the Battle of the Atlantic only focused on the building programmes related to the new Electro-boats and ignored the evolution of tactics and operations brought on by the snorkel. While American authors might be excused from understanding the snorkel's impact, as snorkel-equipped U-boats only made an appearance off the US East Coast in the waning months of the war, the British, and to a lesser extent the Canadians, dealt with them for an entire year during the inshore campaign.

The point of view that the diesel U-boat was defeated in May 1943 as a weapon system and that the snorkel, unwelcome by U-boat crews, had little or no impact during the war is not corroborated by wartime or post-war primary documents. The diesel U-boat as a weapon system was not defeated in May 1943, only the surface-based Wolfpack tactics it employed against mid-Atlantic convoys. The U-boat survived, and even thrived with the introduction of the snorkel, as the Western Allies struggled to overcome the resurgent menace it had once thought defeated. While it is true that defeating the Wolfpack alleviated the single greatest threat to Great Britain's survival and thus the Allied war effort, the introduction of the snorkel and shallow-water tactics diminished Ultra's impact and continued to strain Allied resources. The idea of snorkel-equipped Type XXIs returning to the mid-Atlantic to reignite convoy warfare certainly was a threat that the Allies remained concerned about until the end of the war, but the reality was that BdU planned to send them individually to the coasts of North America and the United Kingdom to operate continually submerged close to Allied ports and within narrow channels and waterways. Surface-based Wolfpack tactics were gone forever.

Canadian maritime historian and former Wilfrid Laurier University professor Roger Sarty is one of the very few historians of the period who viewed the last twelve months of the Battle of the Atlantic through the filter of the snorkel's impact. He wrote in his 1997 article 'The Limits of Ultra: The Schnorchel U-boat Offensive Against North America, November 1944–January 1945' that the:

> Schnorchel caused profound difficulties for the Allied anti-submarine forces because of the change in U-boat tactics that the new equipment made possible. Submarines that neither signalled nor surfaced were safe from the radar-equipped aircraft that had long been the basis of the successful, economical defence of coastal waters … It soon became clear that protection of shipping against a single schnorchel boat well-situated in coastal waters required fully as many warships and even more aircraft than an active defence of a large convoy at mid-ocean against dozen of submarines.[10]

Sarty was closer to historical reality than most authors writing of this period.

Wartime View

No Allied power endured the struggle against the German U-boat in the mid-Atlantic and along their coast more than Great Britain. In November 1944 Royal Navy Captain Clarence Howard-Johnson, who served as the Royal Navy's Director of the Anti-U-boat Division, declared during the resurgent U-boat's inshore campaign that:

> The snorkel has had such far-reaching results that the whole character of the U-boat war has been altered in the enemy's favour. Frequently he has managed to penetrate to and remain on our convoy routes in focal areas with impunity in spite of intensive air and surface patrols. With more experience in training and with the confidence engendered by his present immunity from air, and often from surface attack, he is likely, in the future, to do us more real harm than he has up to the present.[11]

This was a sentiment echoed by Royal Navy Admiral Submarines Sir George Creasy, who directed British submarines to adopt the snorkel during the war on a limited trial basis in order to understand this innovation and how to counter the emerging threat. He soon recognised that there was no longer a future for the surface-bound submersible as the age of the true submarine was within technological sight.[12]

The performance of the snorkel in the latter half of 1944 was so successful that the Ministry of Propaganda decided to capitalise on the technical innovation. The following radio broadcast aired on 22 March 1945 in conjunction with the release of *Die Deutsche Wochenschau*, which showed newsreel footage of the new snorkel-equipped U-boats. The snorkel was considered a 'secret' development for nearly a year and was now unveiled to the German public for the first time. It is a surprisingly accurate account of the Battle of the Atlantic:

The German public has learned about the new technical development of U-boat warfare for the first time from the report concerning the air mast of the U-boat, which appeared in the High Command communiqué. The facts now published were apparent already in the news of the past few weeks. When a number of U-boat commanders were decorated with the Knight's Cross of the Iron Cross it was emphasised that they had won it in particularly difficult areas and on their first operational trip. Furthermore, on recommendation of Grand Admiral Dönitz, the Führer awarded the Knight's Cross with Swords to Prof. Hellmuth Walter for his special merits in the technical development of the German U-boats. Lastly, the monthly declarations of Roosevelt and Churchill on the U-boat campaign as well as the speeches of Canadian and North American ministers of which we have given reports in our service, showed the enemy's considerable anxiety about this steady increase of German U-boat successes …

It has been emphasised in the German reports that the latest successes were achieved not by an entirely new type of U-boat, but by boats of the type which have proved efficient during the period of 1941–1943, and which were fitted with the air mast to enable them to proceed continuously submerged …

Now also the U-boat crews, in spite of being severely strained physically by long months of submerged travelling, are effectively using their new technical equipment, above all in the most dangerous areas close to the enemy ports. In the shallow waters a U-boat, once discovered by the enemy, finds himself in a most difficult situation. But the men of the U-boats take upon themselves these dangers and losses because of the better chances of successes as at this stage every sinking of an enemy ship is particularly important. It is by no means intended to speak now prematurely of a 'new large-scale U-boat offensive'. The reports on the air mast show, however, that important technical inventions have been made, with which we again overtake the enemy's U-boat defence.[13]

Compare the above propaganda broadcast to the actual Top Secret intelligence assessment by OP-20-G released just one month later on 20 April 1945 that stated plainly: 'The last 46 days has seen a marked increase of U-boat pressure against allied shipping, despite the desperate situation in the Homeland and in the Baltic …'[14] This intelligence assessment issued just weeks before the end of the war in Europe is a clear testament to the fact that the U-boat was not a defeated weapon system. It had survived the 'Black May' of 1943 and remained a tactical, if not strategic, concern for the Allies.

Enigma ciphers were ordered changed as concern grew in BdU of their possible compromise. While some Enigma ciphers required days to break, significantly diminishing their value, others still had to be broken. Kurier – the new flash transmission system that could not be read by Allied cryptologists – was being increasingly employed.

Operational U-boat deployments increased to the highest level in more than a year. Allied ship sinkings were up and there was continued concern about the potential deployment of the Type XXIs. The largest concentration of U-boats in nearly three years arrived off the North American coast despite the knowledge of their movement through Ultra and the deployment of the single greatest anti-submarine screen employed by the US Navy in its history. What hampered the U-boat's success continued to be the ability, though reduced, of Allied cryptologists to ascertain U-boat deployments and re-route convoys.

The final situation update of the U-boat force was written by OP-20-G's Navy Reserve Lieutenant W V Quine on 2 May, just days before the end of the war. He noted that there were 192 U-boats in the Atlantic and Arctic, with 118 at sea and seventy-four in port. This was an increase of seven over the previous week. He assessed that:

> As yet there is no sign of any serious break-up in the German naval organisation in the Baltic. The situation is still quite confused because of the continual transferring of [U-boats] out of the enemy's reach in the rush to get [U-boats] finished for frontline operations. Orders, however, seem to be carried out effectively and the loss of [U-boats] appears to be relatively small.

Quine's final assessment contained one of the last Ultra intercepts of the war that noted the singular importance of the snorkel. On 24 April a wireless message was intercepted that read 'complete repairs, including installation of snorkel, in Rostock on 6 Type XXIII and in Wismar on 3 Type XXIII was assured'.[15] With the Soviet Army surrounding Berlin, the US Army on the Elbe River and the British advancing on the main U-boat production facilities in north-west Germany, the U-boat force remained potent and organised. The installation of the snorkel remained one of the highest priorities for BdU, even in the last days of the war.

What a snorkel-equipped U-boat demonstrated during the war, too often lost on period historians, was that a submarine that didn't surface and didn't transmit by radio was almost impossible to track, find and destroy. It was a situation that foreshadowed the future of 'Total Undersea Warfare' in the atomic and nuclear age.

The Legacy

In the post-war period the United States, Great Britain and Soviet Union exploited the significant lead in technology enjoyed by wartime Germany. Not all technology was exploited universally, as it depended greatly on the country's strategic priority. Among the most sought-after technology was German designs for rockets, avionics and U-boats. It is a known fact that the final drive against north-west Germany by General Sir Bernard Montgomery's 21st Army Group was designed to prevent the Soviet Union from reaching Denmark and German ports in that area. The objective was to halt the Soviet advance at Wismar on the Baltic coast, which had the benefit of limiting their access to advanced German U-boat technology, specifically the Walter turbine.

Among the Western Allies it was the United Kingdom that took the lead in the exploitation of U-boats. Under the terms of Operation *Eclipse*, British forces occupied northern Germany to include all the U-boat production facilities and ports. They quickly gained access to engineers, captains and crewmen. Most of all surrendering U-boats fell into the hands of the Royal Navy, who initiated an immediate post-war testing programme. Among the main technological innovations studied and exploited was the snorkel. Their results were passed on to the United States Navy's Bureau of Ships, who also evaluated the wartime German innovation with great interest.

The US Navy's post-war assessment of the snorkel was clear. It had to be adopted, even though the Navy's two-cycle diesel engines could not be retrofitted with the device outright, and that improvements had to be made based on German wartime experiences:

Engine must be designed for snorkelling upfront. Do not implement exhaust drive superchargers. Extensible mast as designed was technically not viable. Folding mast was better. Designs should be made to prevent periscope vibration at high snorkelling speeds. Power-operated head valve for the induction system was required. Design should minimise resistance in the raised and housed position of the snorkel mast. Apply anti-radar coverings to the snorkel head. Remove the maximum amount of moisture from the air intake.

Automatic depth control was not necessary but useful to avoid crew strain during long underwater patrols.[16]

It was the snorkel that was the prerequisite for the modern submarine, as former defence analyst and submarine historian Dr Norman Friedman wrote in his book *US Submarines since 1945*.[17]

The first US submarine that tested the snorkel was the *Irex* (SS-482). Within eighteen months of the end of the war the US Navy had completed designs for the modern telescoping snorkel. The *Irex* was ordered to Portsmouth, New Hampshire, for a retrofit in December 1946, followed by operational testing of the device. The *Irex* conducted snorkel testing from July 1947 until February 1948. After a successful evaluation, the *Irex* joined Submarine Squadron 8 at New London as the US Navy's first operational snorkel submarine.

The US Navy did in fact adopt a telescoping snorkel despite its own recommendation to pursue a folding mast design. Initially the US Navy installed two separate masts, one for induction and one for exhaust. The induction mast led into a moisture separator and then into the main engine induction valve via a 22in pipe. Each diesel engine exhaust led directly into an uptake, exiting the submarine either through a car-type muffler or the snorkel exhaust trunk. Later, the US Navy reverted to the original German snorkel design and combined induction and exhaust pipes into a single mast when they began to retrofit their own submarine fleet through the 'Greater Underwater Propulsion Program', otherwise known as the 'GUPPY'. The GUPPY was the first US submarine that operated with a snorkel.

The US Navy's 1961 edition of its submarine technical training manual known as NAVPERS 16160-B *The Submarine*, issued to all crew members of the new GUPPY modified submarines, offered unusually high praise to their former German enemy nearly twenty years after the end of the war with the following commentary on the snorkel. The Introduction to Chapter 15's 'The Snorkel System' reads:

> The theory of the snorkel had been known for several years; but, it was not until 1943 that the German Navy converted such theory into practical operation … the German Navy *perfected snorkel designs* and incorporated the device in their submarines. *This move increased the efficiency and success of German underseas craft immeasurably*.' (Emphasis added)[18]

Contrary to almost all post-war histories of the German U-boat force and the Battle of the Atlantic, the US Navy understood the snorkel's impact during the war and its evolutionary role in submarine warfare. The US Navy ensured their own submariners knew this as well.

The snorkel began to transform US Navy submarine operations in the Cold War era. Intelligence gathering became a new, if not critical, component to its mission. In 1949 the snorkel-retrofitted Fleet Submarines *Cochino* (*SS-345*) and *Tusk* (*SS-426*) entered the Barents Sea. *Cochino* was also equipped with a version of the GHG Balkon passive sonar. Its goal was to conduct the first intelligence-gathering mission close to the coast of Russia; a task that could only be accomplished by a snorkel-equipped submarine. Unfortunately, *Cochino* experienced a snorkel defect like some of its German U-boat counterparts did during the war. In rough seas the submarine was unable to maintain trim while snorkelling and the snorkel valve failed to close when it was submerged. Water rushed in and a series of unfortunate events unfolded that resulted in a build-up of toxic gas and a battery explosion. While the crew was rescued after a fourteen-hour fight to save the sub, the *Cochino* was lost. It sunk on 26 August 1949, some five years after the first German snorkel-equipped U-boat entered the English Channel.[19]

The snorkel remained a key component of post-war submarine design even into the nuclear age (despite the counterfactual claims of Blair). The first nuclear-powered submarine, USS *Nautilus*, also included a snorkel as a back-up to get the submarine home without surfacing in the case the nuclear reactor failed.[20] In the modern submarine age surfacing meant the loss of the submarine's most critical asset – invisibility. Once a submarine breached the surface it lost the element of surprise, but a snorkel provided the ability to remain submerged even in a crisis onboard the boat. The future of submarine warfare meant never operating on the surface. This was the embodiment of Walter's *Ortungskampf* (battle of location concept) he championed during the war.

The Royal Navy adopted the snorkel during the end of the war, as they saw its potential to alter the course of the U-boat campaign. They needed to understand it, and how it functioned, both technically and tactically. Before the end of the war the Admiralty ordered that one U, S, T, and A Class submarine be equipped with a snorkel. Experiments continued by the Royal Navy well into the post-war period.

The Admiralty already had an eye towards the potential Soviet threat, and they were quick to exploit German naval technology and scientists. The Royal Navy had two main exploitation priorities regarding U-boats. Like the US Navy, they were the snorkel and Type XXI design. Unlike the US Navy, which already had an eye towards nuclear power, the Royal Navy's third priority was Walter's hydrogen peroxide closed propulsion system.

The Royal Navy's secret intelligence unit, the 30 Assault Group, entered

Kiel and immediately located Dr Walter at his home next to his factory and design offices. Along with Walter came some 50,000 pages of microfilm recordings in six boxes that he had buried in a secret location on the north coast. The original documents had been burned. These documents covered the entire technical development of German U-boats through the war. Along with the British came US Navy Captain Albert Mumma, originally of the Alsos Mission (looking for German nuclear, chemical and biological weapons research), and in the last days of the war part of the US Navy's Technical Mission Europe. He was one of the seventy-five-man task force that captured Kiel.[21]

Walter was interrogated extensively after the war. He informed his interrogators that he saw no future for a submarine that operated on the surface and that all design functions must be subordinated to that purpose. It was a vision he himself set on this course with the introduction of the snorkel, the Type XXI and the Walter Prototype. The Royal Navy adopted Walter's design.

The Admiralty moved quickly to locate and raise the *U-1407* hydrogen peroxide-equipped Type XVII to keep it from the Soviets. Testing was carried out in Kiel between August and September 1945 of the Walter turbine U-boats by Walter and his staff of engineers under the watchful eyes of the Royal and U.S Naval officers. After the successful trial in Kiel harbour the British offered Walter and a small group of his trusted engineers' contracts to go and work for them in England.[22] *U-1406* was provided to the US Navy, but they did not operate that U-boat after quickly deciding to pursue nuclear propulsion instead of the Walter turbine. The *U-1407* was refitted by Vickers under the guidance of Walter himself in 1947. In 1948, *U-1407* was commissioned into the Royal Navy as HMS *Meteorite* and went through extensive operational testing off the coast of Scotland.[23]

The Royal Navy concluded that while the *Meteorite* was unstable on the surface, it was 'outstanding' underwater and that its high speed, which came at a high cost in fuel, was best employed in escape underwater as originally envisioned by Walter during the war. The Royal Navy went on to commission HMS *Explorer* and HMS *Excalibur* to conduct underwater speed trials based on the principles of the Type XXVI. These hydrogen peroxide submarines achieved the underwater speeds of 25 knots that Walter had theorised was possible during the war. The Royal Navy concluded on their own that the diesel submarine fleet had reached its limits of endurance and speed. Walter's ideas had been vindicated by the very Royal Navy his designs had hoped to defeat. Admiral Creasy stated of Walter's design that 'we stand on the threshold of very considerable technical development …'[24]

Despite the efforts of the British to keep the most advanced U-boat technology out of Soviet hands, they failed. The Red Army had seized two unfinished Type XXIs, *U-3528* and *U-3542*, at Schichau on the Baltic coast, Walter's central design office for the Type XVIIB and XXVI at Blankenburg, and the Bruchner-Kanis factory that produced the Walter turbines in Dresden and at Weinrieb in Chemnitz. It was assessed by the Western Allies that one turbine of 2,500 shaft horsepower and one of 7,500shp were acquired by the Soviets.[25] Beyond the new U-boat designs, the Soviets captured plans for advanced German torpedoes, internal electronics, the GHG passive sonar array and German technical experts themselves. This was cause for alarm at the highest levels in the US Navy.[26]

Under the code name Medusa, two Soviet research institutes, Andreev and Krylov, adopted the German U-boat research and begin to pursue it at an accelerated rate in 1947–48. The Soviets soon adopted the advanced German designs and specifically the snorkel apparatus in their ocean-going Whiskey and coastal Malyutka-class submarines.[27] The Whiskey class had already been designed before the end of the war as an improvement to the existing 'S' class, but German U-boat technology was quickly retrofitted. The Whiskey class was produced in more numbers than any other submarine in history, surpassing even the German Type VIIC.

The Soviets went on to develop the S 99 (Project 617) in 1951, known in NATO circles as Whale, which was a near exact copy of the German U-boat Type XXVI. With the help of captured German engineers, the Leningrad-Shuvalovo shipyard developed the first 7,500hp hydrogen peroxide engine for the Soviet Navy. The first operational tests began in June 1952. It was later commissioned into the Soviet Navy in 1956 and achieved an underwater speed of 20 knots, making it the fastest submarine in the Soviet fleet at that time. An explosion on the high-pressure line ended its brief career and it was decommissioned as the Soviet Navy shifted from hydrogen peroxide to nuclear power. However, the hull form and underwater principles it derived from building Walter's Type XXVI were all carried forward into the next generation of Soviet submarines.

The Soviet Navy took an immediate interest in adopting Alberich and furthering the concepts of acoustic camouflage. While the US and, specifically the Royal Navy, were keen to understand Alberich from the perspective of countering its capability, the technical problems of adhesive turned both western naval powers off from further pursuit.[28] The Soviets applied their version of a rubberised coating to both their Whiskey and smaller Malyutka-class submarines.[29] The coatings were initially applied to the exterior hull, however, the Soviets began to pursue the German innovation of applying it on internal surfaces, to include their double hull, in order to reduce the transmission of sound.

Every navy in the world copied the German snorkel configuration. It remains a critical feature even on nuclear submarines today. In this 1948 press photo the ex-*U-2513* is pictured with a fully extended snorkel mast compared with the retrofitted snorkel installed under the US Navy's GUPPY programme on the *SS-347* (Cubera). The US Navy lauded the German-engineered design, giving the Kriegsmarine full credit for operationalising the snorkel device under wartime conditions. *(Author's collection)*

Starting with the first Soviet nuclear submarines of the Project 627/November Class, almost all Soviet combat submarines were coated with what modern naval architects call anechoic tiles. Shock absorbers were also installed to reduce engine vibrations.[30] While acoustic dampening was not a priority, creating an atmosphere capable of supporting a crew for fifty

An unidentified Royal Navy Amphion-class submarine showing a retrofitted snorkel mast in the post-war period. The mast and snorkel head show significant similarities with the wartime German Type II mast. *(Author's collection)*

days without surfacing was.[31] It was an endurance objective that mirrored the submerged U-boat operations in the last year of the war achieved through the snorkel.

Soviet investment in submarine technology continued at an extraordinary rate through the 1980s. A 1988 *Naval Proceedings* article argued that, based on developmental trends, the Soviets would all but overtake the US in advanced designs by 2000.[32] The fact that the Soviets had mastered the process of acoustic camouflage introduced by the Germans became evident in the recovery operations of the downed *Kursk* (K-141) in 2000.

On 12 August 2000 the Russian Navy's Oscar-II class nuclear-powered cruise-missile submarine suffered a catastrophic explosion from a hydrogen peroxide-fuelled Type 65 practice torpedo. Hydrogen peroxide, it should be noted, was the key component of Walter's closed-circuit turbine engines. Its cost and highly volatile nature when exposed to an accelerant such as oxygen were among the main reasons that both the US and Royal Navies abandoned it after 1950.[33] The explosion collapsed the first three compartments of the submarine, sending it to the bottom in 108m of water in the Barents Sea.

British and Norwegian undersea salvage experts led the search team looking for the stricken *Kursk*. They were given its precise co-ordinates by the Russian Navy. At 4.26am on Sunday, 20 August an ROV was lowered down from the *Seaway Eagle* to 300ft, just 75ft off the seabed, and its active sonar turned on. As the ROV's sonar began to sweep for the stricken Russian submarine the British operators could not find the *Kursk*. It wasn't there. According to the ROV operator 'the sonar received absolutely no signal. The *Kursk* had apparently vanished.' Confusion reigned onboard the search vessel. Numerous search passes were made over the location of the *Kursk* until finally a faint 'ping' was returned. The seven-bladed massive twin bronze propellers, standing high off the seabed, were the only physical component of the submarine that gave away the *Kursk*'s location. According to the ROV operator, 'confusion turned to amazement as the men realised that the acoustic tiles on the outer hull of the *Kursk* were so effective that they had been absorbing the ROV's active sonar signals'.[34]

The Soviet Navy enjoyed a thirty-year lead in the operational employment of Alberich, known today as 'anechoic tiles'. The US and Royal Navies did not start applying such tiles until the 1980s. The first US submarine coated was the USS *Batfish* in 1980, but the US Navy did not systematically adopt the technology until 1988. Even today the US Navy faces ongoing struggles with adhesive properties, as evinced in the recent reports about the Virginia Class 'mould-in-place' urethane coating.[35]

Walter's concepts continued in the post-war Federal German Navy. The introduction of the German Type 212 class submarine in 2003 ushered in the most advanced non-nuclear submarine in operation today. This highly advanced design developed by Howaldtswerke-Deutsche Werft AG (HDW) features both diesel propulsion and an air-independent propulsion (AIP) system using Siemens proton exchange membrane (PEM) compressed hydrogen fuel cells. The Type 212A can operate at high speed on diesel power or switch to the AIP system for silent slow cruising, staying submerged for up to three weeks without surfacing or using its snorkel. According to Doug Thomes, writing in the *Canadian Naval Review*:

> The second of class U-32 set a record in April 2006 when it conducted an uninterrupted dived transit from the Baltic to Rota Spain, a distance of 1,500 nautical miles in two weeks. These vessels are very stealthy by virtue of their lack of a need to snorkel and are much more habitable than their predecessors: the accommodation improvements have enabled the abandonment of the German practice of hot bunking for the first time and there are now dining and working spaces separated from the sleeping quarters.[36]

The Type 212A hull design and composite material make it one of their quietest and hardest to detect submarines in the world. The X-shape stern design allows it to operate in coastal water as shallow as 17m. A direct line can be drawn to the Type 212 and subsequent 214 and 216s from the effective wartime performance of the Type XXIIIs in shallow water.

It remains a testament to German wartime innovation and engineering that almost all modern submarines, whether diesel or nuclear powered, are equipped with a version of the snorkel, and some with anechoic tiles. All strive to remain unseen and undetected in Walter's vision of 'Total Undersea War' ushered in after the introduction of the snorkel into the U-boat fleet at the end of 1943.

Appendices

List of Diesel Snorkel U-boats

Below is a list of 353 diesel U-boats that had a snorkel installed. This represents the most accurate list published anywhere to date. It was derived from an exacting review of all available KTBs, surviving photos and available U-Bootbläter (U-Boat information sheets located at the Deutsches U-Boot Museum).

A small number of U-boats are suspected of having received a snorkel

U-Boat	Type	Snorkel Installed	Order Num	Built By	Pulley	Piston	Type I	Type
92	VIIC	Y						
107	IXB	Y					x	
143	IID	?						
145	IID	?						
149	IID	?						
150	IID	?						
154	IXC	Y					x	
155	IXC	Y					x	
168	IXC/40	Y						
170	IXC/40	Y					x	
180	IXD1	Y						
181	IXD2	Y						
183	IXC/40	Y						
190	IXC/40	Y				x	x	
195	IXD1	Y						
212	VIIC	Y						
214	VIID	Y						
218	VIID	Y					x	
219	XB	Y						
228	VIIC	Y						
234	XB	Y				x		x
235	VIIC	Y	S76	Germaniawerft Kiel	x		x	
236	VIIC	Y	G72					
237	VIIC	Y	S192	Germaniawerft Kiel				
239	VIIC	Y	G41	Howaldtswerke-Deutsche Werft Kiel				
241	VIIC	Y				x	x	

installation but are not confirmed. The list includes the snorkel order number when available, the type of snorkel mast (Type I flange or Type II non-flange), the lifting mechanism used (pulley or piston), what snorkel head valve was installed (ball, ring or pneumatic float) and if the snorkel head was coated with anti-radar protection. In addition, other relevant modifications are noted that include: Alberich coating; the type of sonar array installed (GHG Balkon or Zwiebel; and for the Type IX if it had a cut-away bow.

Parentheses () in the table denote where a U-boat was upgraded from a Type I to a Type II mast or a ball float to a ring float during its service. A '?' indicates the possibility that the specific feature existed, but is not confirmed. *U-539*'s '*' notes that its cutaway bow was longer than those of other Type IXs.

ball float	Ring Float	Pneumatic Float	Anti-radar Coated	Alberich	GHG Balkon	Zwiebel	Cut Away Hull
							X
					X		
							X
					X		
					X		
	X		X				
	X		X				
	X		X				

U-Boat	Type	Snorkel Installed	Order Num	Built By	Pulley	Piston	Type I	Type
242	VIIC	Y	S122	Holmwerft Danzig				
243	VIIC	Y				x	x	
244	VIIC	Y						
245	VIIC	Y						
246	VIIC	Y						
247	VIIC	Y						
248	VIIC	Y						
249	VIIC	Y	G53	Germaniawerft Kiel		x		x
251	VIIC	Y	S188	KMW Betrieb Hamburg				
255	VIIC	Y						
256	VIIC	Y						
260	VIIC	Y					x	
262	VIIC	Y						
264	VIIC	Y						
267	VIIC	Y	S144	Deutsche Werft Kiel				
269	VIIC	Y			x			
275	VIIC	Y			x		x	
278	VIIC	Y	G49	D-heim		x		x
281	VIIC	Y				x	x	
285	VIIC	Y						
286	VIIC	Y						
287	VIIC	Y	S77	Howaldtswerke-Deutsche Werft Hamburg				
291	VIIC	Y	G57	KMH TRU				
293	VIIC/41	Y			x		x	
294	VIIC/41	Y				x		x
295	VIIC/41	Y				x		x
296	VIIC/41	Y						
297	VIIC/41	Y	S57	Danziger Werft				
300	VIIC/41	Y						
307	VIIC	Y						
309	VIIC	Y					x	
310	VIIC	Y						
312	VIIC	Y						
313	VIIC	Y				x		x
315	VIIC	Y						
316	VIIC	Y	G76					
318	VIIC/41	Y						
320	VIIC/41	Y	G69	Lübecker Flender-Werke				
321	VIIC/41	Y	S146	Lübecker Flender-Werke				
322	VIIC/41	Y	G22			x		?
324	VIIC/41	Y	S148	Lübecker Flender-Werke				

all oat	Ring Float	Pneumatic Float	Anti-radar Coated	Alberich	GHG Balkon	Zwiebel	Cut Away Hull
	X						
	X		X				
	X		X				
	X		X				
	X						
			X				
	X		X				
	X		X				
	X						
	X		X				
	X		X				
	X		X				
	X		X				

U-Boat	Type	Snorkel Installed	Order Num	Built By	Pulley	Piston	Type I	Typ
325	VIIC/41	Y	S110	Lübecker Flender-Werke		x		x
326	VIIC/41	Y	S143	Lübecker Flender-Werke				
327	VIIC/41	Y	S138	Lübecker Flender-Werke				
328	VIIC/41	?						
333	VIIC	Y						
348	VIIC	Y	S132	Schichau Konigsberg				
349	VIIC	Y	S193	KMW Betrieb Hamburg				
350	VIIC	Y	S163	Deutsche Werft Finkenwerke				
363	VIIC	Y						
368	VIIC	Y	G70					
369	VIIC	Y	S185	Deutsche Werft Hamburg		x		x
382	VIIC	Y						
385	VIIC	Y						
390	VIIC	Y						
393	VIIC	Y	G82	Howaldtswerke-Deutsche Werft Kiel				
396	VIIC	Y						
397	VIIC	Y	G78					
398	VIIC	Y						
399	VIIC	Y	S133	Howaldtswerke-Deutsche Werft Kiel				
400	VIIC	Y	G50	Howaldtswerke-Deutsche Werft Kiel			x	x
407	VIIC	Y						
413	VIIC	Y						
423	VIIC	Y						
427	VIIC	Y						
428	VIIC	Y	S191	KMW Betrieb Hamburg				
429	VIIC	Y	S194	KMW Betrieb Hamburg				
430	VIIC	Y	G74					
437	VIIC	Y						
441	VIIC	Y			x		x	
474	VIIC	Y	S80	Deutsche Werft				
475	VIIC	Y	S126, S176	Holmwerft Danzig / Kiel				
477	VIIC	Y						
478	VIIC	Y						
479	VIIC	Y	S120	Schichau Konigsberg				
480	VIIC	Y				x	x	(x)
481	VIIC	Y	S155	Deutsche Werft		x		
482	VIIC	Y						

...all oat	Ring Float	Pneumatic Float	Anti-radar Coated	Alberich	GHG Balkon	Zwiebel	Cut Away Hull
	X		X				
	X		X				
	X		X				
	X						
	X		X				
	X		X				
	X		X				
	X		X				
	X		X				
	X		X				
	X						
	X						
	X		X				
	X		X				
	X		X				
	X						
				X			
		X					

U-Boat	Type	Snorkel Installed	Order Num	Built By	Pulley	Piston	Type I	Typ
483	VIIC	Y						
484	VIIC	Y	G35	Deutsche Werft				
485	VIIC	Y	S40/ G40	Deutsche Werft Gotenhafen				
486	VIIC	Y	S97	Deutsche Werft W. Gotenhafen				
490	XIV	Y				?	x	
516	IXC	Y					x	(x)
518	IXC	Y					x	
530	IXC/40	Y					x	
534	IXC/40	Y					x	(x)
539	IXC/40	Y				x		x
541	IXC/40	Y						
543	IXC/40	Y					x	
546	IXC/40	Y					x	
547	IXC/40	Y					x	
548	IXC/40	Y					x	
549	IXC/40	Y					x	
554	VIIC	Y	G83	KMW Wilhelmshaven				
560	VIIC	Y	S197	Nordseewerke Emden				
565	VIIC	Y						
575	VIIC	Y						
579	VIIC	Y						
596	VIIC	Y						
621	VIIC	Y						
636	VIIC	Y						
637	VIIC	Y	G56	Deutsche Werft Kiel				
642	VIIC	Y						
650	VIIC	Y					x	
667	VIIC	Y						
668	VIIC	Y						
671	VIIC	Y						
672	VIIC	Y						
673	VIIC	Y						
677	VIIC	Y	S199	Deutsche Werft Hamburg				
678	VIIC	Y						
680	VIIC	Y						
681	VIIC	Y						
682	VIIC	Y	S83	Howaldtswerke-Deutsche Werft Hamburg				
683	VIIC	Y	S134	Howaldtswerke-Deutsche Werft Hamburg				

Ball Float	Ring Float	Pneumatic Float	Anti-radar Coated	Alberich	GHG Balkon	Zwiebel	Cut Away Hull
	(x)			X			
	X		X	X			
							X
							?
			X				X
	(x)						
					X		x(*)
	X						
	X						?
	X		X				
	X		X				
			X				
	X		X				
	X		X				
	(x)				X		
	X		X				

U-Boat	Type	Snorkel Installed	Order Num	Built By	Pulley	Piston	Type I	Typ
708	VIIC	Y	G86	Nordseewerke Emden				
711	VIIC	Y						
712	VIIC	Y	G58, S195	KMH TRU / Deutsche Werft Hamburg				
714	VIIC	Y						
715	VIIC	Y						
716	VIIC	Y						
717	VIIC	Y	S123	Deutsche Werft Gotenhafen				
719	VIIC	Y						
720	VIIC	Y	G71					
722	VIIC	Y	G29	Howaldtswerke-Deutsche Werft Kiel				
733	VIIC	Y	G74					
735	VIIC	Y	S117	Flensburger Schiff.				
736	VIIC	Y						
737	VIIC	Y						
739	VIIC	Y	G48	D-heim				
741	VIIC	Y					x	
743	VIIC	Y						
745	VIIC	Y	S127	Holmwerft Danzig				
746	VIIC	Y	G59, S196	KMH Kiel / Howaldts-werke Hamburg				
748	VIIC	Y	G92	Deutsche Werft Hamburg				
749	VIIC	Y	G85	Germaniawerft Kiel				
750	VIIC	Y	S167	Flensburger Schiff.				
758	VIIC	Y						
763	VIIC	Y						
764	VIIC	Y					x	
767	VIIC	Y						
772	VIIC	Y			x		x	
773	VIIC	Y						
774	VIIC	Y						
775	VIIC	Y	S67	KMW Wilhelmshaven				
776	VIIC	Y	S129	Howaldtswerke-Deutsche Werft Hamburg	x		x	
777	VIIC	Y	S111	KMW Wilhelmshaven				
778	VIIC	Y					x	
779	VIIC	?						
802	IXC/40	Y					x	
803	IXC/40	?					x	
804	IXC/40	Y					x	

all loat	Ring Float	Pneumatic Float	Anti-radar Coated	Alberich	GHG Balkon	Zwiebel	Cut Away Hull
	X		X				
	X		X				
	X						
					X		
	X		X				
	X		X				
	X		X				
	X		X				
	X		X				
	X		X				
	X		X				
	X		X				
	X						
							X

U-Boat	Type	Snorkel Installed	Order Num	Built By	Pulley	Piston	Type I	Typ
805	IXC/40	Y					x	
806	IXC/40	Y					x	
822	VIIC	Y						
825	VIIC	Y					x	
826	VIIC	Y	S58	Deutsche Werft Gotenhafen		x	x	
827	VIIC	Y	G52	Schichau Konigsberg				
828	VIIC/41	Y	G81	Bremen Vulkon				
853	IXC/40	Y				x	x	
855	IXC/40	Y					x	
857	IXC/40	Y					x	(x)
858	IXC/40	Y				x	x	
859	IXD2	Y						
862	IXD2	Y						
863	IXD2	Y						
864	IXD2	Y						
865	IXC/40	Y					x	
866	IXC/40	Y					x	
867	IXC/40	Y					x	
868	IXC/40	Y					x	
869	IXC/40	Y				x	x	
870	IXC/40	Y					x	
871	IXD2	Y						
872	IXD2	Y						
873	IXD2	Y				x	x	
874	IXD2	Y				x	x	
875	IXD2	?						
876	IXD2	Y						
877	IXC/40	Y					x	
878	IXC/40	Y						(?)
879	IXC/40	Y						(?)
880	IXC/40	Y						(?)
881	IXC/40	Y						(?)
883	IXD2	Y						
889	IXC/40	Y				x	x	
901	VIIC	Y	S151	Holmwerft Danzig		x		x
903	VIIC	Y	G77					
905	VIIC	Y	S65	Germaniawerft Kiel				
907	VIIC	Y	G34	Howaldtswerke-Deutsche Werft Kiel				
923	VIIC	Y	G80	KMW Wilhelmshaven				
925	VIIC	Y						

Ball Float	Ring Float	Pneumatic Float	Anti-radar Coated	Alberich	GHG Balkon	Zwiebel	Cut Away Hull
							X
			X				
	X						
	X		X				
	(x)						?
							X
							X
							X
							X
							X
	X						
					X		
	(?)						?
	(?)						?
	(?)						?
	(?)				X		?
					X	X	
	X		X				
	X		X				
			X				
	X		X				

U-Boat	Type	Snorkel Installed	Order Num	Built By	Pulley	Piston	Type I	Typ
926	VIIC	Y	S149	Howaldtswerke-Deutsche Werft Kiel				
927	VIIC	Y	S135	Deutsche Werft Kiel				
928	VIIC	Y	S139	Neptun Rostock				
929	VIIC/41	Y				x		x
930	VIIC/41	Y	S90	Neptun Rostock				
953	VIIC	Y	S137	Lubecker Flenderweke	x			
956	VIIC	Y						
958	VIIC	Y	G47, S153	Ö/Deutsche Werft Gottenhafen				
963	VIIC	Y						
965	VIIC	Y						
968	VIIC	Y						
971	VIIC	Y						
975	VIIC	Y	G84	Howaldtswerke-Deutsche Werft Hamburg				
977	VIIC	Y	S170	Howaldtswerke-Deutsche Werft Hamburg		x		x
978	VIIC	Y				x	x	
979	VIIC	Y						
982	VIIC	Y	G87	Howaldtswerke-Deutsche Werft Hamburg				
984	VIIC	Y			x		x	
985	VIIC	Y						
988	VIIC	Y				x		x
989	VIIC	Y						
991	VIIC	Y	S49	Schichau Konigsberg				
992	VIIC	Y						
993	VIIC	Y				x		x
994	VIIC	?						
995	VIIC/41	Y				x		x
997	VIIC/41	Y	S69	Germaniawerft Drontheim				
998	VIIC/41	?						
999	VIIC/41	Y	G93	KMW Wilhelmshaven				
1001	VIIC/41	Y	S131	Schichau Konigsberg				
1002	VIIC/41	Y	S136	Bu Vulkan Hamburg				
1003	VIIC/41	Y	S50			x	x	
1004	VIIC/41	Y						
1005	VIIC/41	Y	S140	KMW Wilhelmshaven				
1006	VIIC/41	Y						
1007	VIIC/41	Y						

Ball Float	Ring Float	Pneumatic Float	Anti-radar Coated	Alberich	GHG Balkon	Zwiebel	Cut Away Hull
	X		X				
	X		X				
	X						
	X		X				
	X		X				
			X				
	X		(s)				
	X		X				
	X		X				
	X		X				
	X						
	X						
	X						
	X		X		X		
	X		X				

U-Boat	Type	Snorkel Installed	Order Num	Built By	Pulley	Piston	Type I	Typ∢
1008	VIIC/41	Y						
1009	VIIC/41	Y				x	x	
1010	VIIC/41	Y	S147	Howaldtswerke-Deutsche Werft Hamburg				
1014	VIIC/41	Y						
1016	VIIC/41	Y	S157	Holmwerft Danzig				
1017	VIIC/41	Y	S79	Schichau Konigsberg				
1018	VIIC/41	Y						
1019	VIIC/41	Y	S84	Howaldtswerke-Deutsche Werft Kiel				
1020	VIIC/41	Y						
1021	VIIC/41	Y				x	x	
1022	VIIC/41	Y					x	
1023	VIIC/41	Y					x	
1024	VIIC/41	Y						
1025	VIIC/41	Y	S72	Flensburger Schiff.				
1026	VIIC(?)	Y	S158	Flensburger Schiff.				
1028	VIIC(?)	Y	S160	Flensburger Schiff.				
1029	VIIC(?)	Y	S166	Flensburger Schiff.				
1030	VIIC(?)	Y	S162	Germaniawerft Kiel				
1051	VIIC	Y						
1053	VIIC	Y						
1054	VIIC	Y				x	x	
1055	VIIC	Y	S66	Germaniawerft Kiel				
1056	VIIC	Y	S161	Germaniawerft Kiel				
1057	VIIC	Y	S156	Germaniawerft Kiel				
1058	VIIC	Y	S70	Germaniawerft Kiel			x	
1060	VIIF	Y	G45	Germaniawerft				
1061	VIIF	Y	G39	Germaniawerft		x		
1063	VIIC/41	Y						
1064	VIIC/41	Y						
1065	VIIC/41	Y						
1101	VIIC	Y	S164	Deutsche Werft Finkenwerke				
1103	VIIC	Y	S59, S165	KMW Wilhelmshaven / Finkenwerke				
1104	VIIC	Y	S68	Nordseewerke Emden				
1105	VIIC	Y				x	x	
1106	VIIC	Y						
1107	VIIC/41	Y	G89	Flensburger Schiff.				
1108	VIIC/41	Y	S86	Nordswerke Emden			x	
1109	VIIC/41	Y				x		x

…all Float	Ring Float	Pneumatic Float	Anti-radar Coated	Alberich	GHG Balkon	Zwiebel	Cut Away Hull
	X		X				
			X				
	X		X				
	X						
			X				
					X		
	X						
			X				
	X		X				
	X		X				
	X		X				
	X		X				
			X				
	X		X				
	X		X				
			X				
	X		X				
	X		X				
				X	X		
				X			
	X		X	X			

U-Boat	Type	Snorkel Installed	Order Num	Built By	Pulley	Piston	Type I	Typ
1131	VIIC	Y	S150	Howaldtswerke-Deutsche Werft Kiel				
1161	VIIC	Y	G79					
1162	VIIC	Y	S168	Howaldtswerke-Deutsche Werft Kiel				
1164	VIIC/41	Y	G28	Howaldtswerke-Deutsche Werft Kiel				
1165	VIIC/41	Y	G55	Deutsche Werft Kiel		x		x
1167	VIIC/41	Y	S186	Deutsche Werft Hamburg				
1168	VIIC/41	Y	S173	Deutsche Werft Gotenhafen				
1169	VIIC/41	Y	S71	Schichau Konigsberg				
1171	VIIC/41	Y	S152	Holmwerft Danzig		x		x
1172	VIIC/41	Y	S50					
1191	VIIC	Y						
1192	VIIC	Y	G94	KMW Wilhelmshaven				
1193	VIIC	Y	G90	Germaniawerft Kiel				
1194	VIIC	Y	S187	Deutsche Werft Hamburg		x		x
1195	VIIC	Y	G51	Deutsche Werft Kiel				
1197	VIIC	Y	S198	Deschimag, Vremen				
1198	VIIC	Y	G75			x		x
1199	VIIC	Y						
1200	VIIC	Y						
1201	VIIC	Y	S171	Howaldtswerke-Deutsche Werft Hamburg				
1202	VIIC	Y				x	x	
1203	VIIC	Y	S91	Holmwerft Danzig				
1204	VIIC	Y	G95, G97					
1205	VIIC	Y	G96, G98					
1206	VIIC	Y	S128	Howaldtswerke-Deutsche Werft Hamburg				
1207	VIIC	Y	G88	Deutsche Werft Hamburg				
1208	VIIC	Y	S92	Holmwerft Danzig		x		x
1209	VIIC	Y	S81	Schichau Konigsberg				
1210	VIIC	Y	S177	Germaniawerft				
1221	IXC/40	Y					x	
1222	IXC/40	N					x	
1223	IXC/40	Y					x	
1225	IXC/40	Y					x	
1226	IXC/40	Y					x	

Ball Float	Ring Float	Pneumatic Float	Anti-radar Coated	Alberich	GHG Balkon	Zwiebel	Cut Away Hull
	X		X				
	X		X				
	X		X				
	X		X				
	X		X				
	X		X				
X			X				
	X		X				
	X				X		
	X		X				
	X		X				
	X		X				
	X		X				
	X		X				
	X		X				
	X		X				
	X		X				
	X		X				
	X		X				
							X

U-Boat	Type	Snorkel Installed	Order Num	Built By	Pulley	Piston	Type I	Type
1227	IXC/40	Y					x	
1228	IXC/40	Y	S82	Schichau Konigsberg		x	x	
1229	IXC/40	Y				x	x	
1230	IXC/40	Y					x	
1231	IXC/40	Y					x	
1232	IXC/40	Y					x	
1233	IXC/40	Y				x		x
1234	IXC/40	?				x		
1235	IXC/40	Y					x	
1271	VIIC/41	Y	S169	Flensburger Schiff.				
1272	VIIC/41	Y	S141	Schichau Konigsberg				
1273	VIIC/41	Y	S119	Holmwerft Danzig				
1274	VIIC/41	Y	S78	Schichau Konigsberg				
1275	VIIC/41	Y	S142	Deutsche Werft Gotenhafen				
1276	VIIC/41	Y						
1277	VIIC/41	Y						
1278	VIIC/41	Y						
1279	VIIC/41	Y	S121	Holmwerft Danzig		x		x
1301	VIIC/41	Y	G54	Flensburger Schiff.				
1302	VIIC/41	Y	S118	Flensburger Schiff.				
1303	VIIC/41	Y	S159	Flensburger Schiff.				
1304	VIIC/41	Y				x		x
1305	VIIC/41	Y	S145	Flensberger Schiff		x		x
1306	VIIC/41	Y						
1307	VIIC/41	Y	S108	Flensberger Schiff		x		x
1308	VIIC/41	Y	S109	Flensberger Schiff				

Ball Float	Ring Float	Pneumatic Float	Anti-radar Coated	Alberich	GHG Balkon	Zwiebel	Cut Away Hull
X							
X	X						
X							
X							
X			X				
X							X
X							?
X							?
X							?
	X		X				
	X		X				
	X		X				
	X		X				
	X						
	X		X				
	X		X				
	X		X				
				X			
	X		X				
					X		
	X				X		
	X				X		

Appendix B

List of Acoustically Camouflaged U-boats

This table lists the thirteen U-boats that received an Alberich coating. Note that two did not have a snorkel installation, and that another three are Type XXIIIs. The rest of the data is the same as in Appendix A.

U-Boat	Type	Snorkel Installed	Order NO.	Built By	Pulley	Piston	Type I
67*	IXC	N					
470	VIIC	N					
480	VIIC	Y					
485	VIIC	Y	S40/G40	Deutsche Werft Gotenhafen			
486	VIIC	Y	S97	Deutsche Werft Gotenhafen			
1105	VIIC	Y				x	x
1106	VIIC	Y					
1107	VIIC/41	Y	G89	Flensburger Schiff.			
1304	VIIC/41	Y				x	
1306	VIIC/41	Y					
4704	XXIII	Y					
4708	XXIII	Y					
4709	XXIII	Y					

*Alberich was removed before final patrol.

Type II	Ball Float	Ring Float	Telescoping	Anti-radar Coated
X	X			
	X	(x)		
		X		X
	X			
		X		X
X				
			X	
			X	X
			X	X

Appendix C

Snorkel-Equipped U-boats off the North American Coast

This table provides data on the thirty-eight snorkel-equipped U-boats that patrolled along the North America coast in 1944–45. It excludes the few snorkel-equipped U-boats that were sent to the Caribbean, Gulf of Mexico or South America.

U-Boat	Type	Departure Date	Initial Ordered Operational Area	BdU Redirected Operational Area	Final known Operational Area
107	IXB	10-May-44	US/Cape Hatteras	CA/Halifax	CA/Halifax
154	IXC	20-Jun-44	US/Cape Hatteras	–	–
"Sunk 3-Jul-44, NW of Madeira, Portugal by USS *Inch* and USS *Frost*. No survivors. 34000N/19030W."					
518	IXC	15-Jul-44	Panama	–	US/Cape Hatteras - Berr
802	IXC/40	16-Jul-44	CA/St Lawrence River	–	CA/St Lawrence River
1229	IXC/40	26-Jul-44	Canadian Coast to drop off Agents	–	
"Sunk 20-Aug-44, SE of Newfoundland by TBF Avengers of VC-42, USN CVE USS *Bogue*, 41 survivors lo					
541	IXC/40	06-Aug-44	CA/St Lawrence River	–	CA/St Lawrence River
1221	IXC/40	20-Aug-44	CA/Halifax	–	CA/Halifax
1223	IXC/40	28-Aug-44	CA/St Lawrence River	–	CA/St Lawrence River
865	IXC/40	08-Sep-44	CA/Newfoundland	–	CA/Newfoundland
Reported snorkel problems. Likely disappeared in the Norwegian Sea.					
1226	IXC/40	30-Sep-44	Canadian Coast	Weather Boat	–
Reported snorkel problems. Likely disappeared between Iceland and the Canadian coast.					
867	IXC/40	09-Sep-44	CA/Labrador	Back to Port	
"Lost diesel engines, attacked by air after Ultra intercept of distress call, then scuttled off the coast of Nc					
1230	IXC/40	08-Oct-44	US/Gulf of Maine to drop off agents	–	
1228	IXC/40	12-Oct-44	CA/St Lawrence River	–	CA/St Lawrence River
1231	IXC/40	18-Oct-44	CA/St Lawrence River	–	CA/St Lawrence River
806	IXC/40	30-Oct-44	CA/Halifax	–	CA/Halifax
1232	IXC/40	10-Nov-44	CA/Halifax	–	CA/Halifax
869	IXC/40	08-Dec-44	US/Philadelphia	Gibraltar	US/Philadelphia
Likely snorkel failure that resulted in a catastrophic internal explosion of oxyhydrogen gas.					
1233	IXC/40	24-Dec-44	Unk	US/Cape Hatteras	US/South of Long Island
857	IXC/40	06-Feb-45	US/Cape Hatteras	Freedom of manoeuvre along the coast	
"Likely sunk on 30-Apr-45, NE of Cape Hatteras by USS *Natchez*, USS *Coffman*, USS *Bostwick*, USS *Thom*					

Due to the changing operational situation in the Atlantic, U-boats were often redirected on their outbound patrol. However, many U-boats never received their new instructions and continued on to their original destination, which is why this table includes that data where available.

Additionally, this table includes information about each U-boat's fate as there are several sunken wrecks yet to be located along the North American coast. At least four of these lost U-boats may have suffered a snorkel failure and, like *U-869*, await an accidental discovery at a diveable depth.

Final Disposition of Patrol	Sunk by Air/Surface	Likely Sunk by Snorkel Failure	Ultra Derived Sinking
Returned	–	–	–
Sunk	Surface	–	Y
Returned	–	–	–
Returned	–	–	–
–	Sunk	Air	N
U-219. 42020N/51039W. Cruised surfaced and did not follow standing snorkel guidance."			
Returned	–	–	–
Returned	–	–	–
Returned	–	–	–
Unk	–	Y	N
Unk	–	Y	N
Scuttled	Air Assist	–	Partial
US/Gulf of Maine	Returned	–	–
Returned	–	–	–
Returned	–	–	–
Returned	–	–	–
Returned	–	–	–
Unk	–	Y	N
Returned	–	–	–
Likely US/Cape Hatteras Likely Sunk	Surface		N
)34N/74000W. Not confirmed. "			

U-Boat	Type	Departure Date	Initial Ordered Operational Area	BdU Redirected Operational Area	Final known Operational Area
866	IXC/40	06-Feb-45	CA/Halifax	Freedom of manoeuvre along the coast	
"Sunk on 18-Mar-45, SE of Halifax by USS *Lowe*, USS *Menges*, USS *Pride*, USS *Mosley*. 43018N/61008W					
879	IXD2	11-Feb-45	US/Initial course heading toward Cape Cod	US/Cape Hatteras	
Reported snorkel problems.					
190	IXC/40	19-Feb-45	CA/Halifax	–	CA/Halifax
853	IXC/40	23-Feb-45	US/Gulf of Maine	Freedom of manoeuvre to CA/Halifax or US/New	
"Sunk on 6-May-45, NE of Block Island by USS *Atherton*, USS *Moberly*. 41013N/71027W. "					
530	IXC/40	03-Mar-45	US/New York	–	US/New York
Arrived in Argentina on 10 July					
548	IXC/40	07-Mar-45	US/Gulf of Maine	–	–
"Sunk on 19-Apr-45, SE of Halifax by USS *Buckley*, USS *Reuben James*. 42019N/61045W. "					
546	IXC/40	11-Mar-45	Seewolf	US/New York south to Cape Hatteras	
"Sunk on 24-Apr-45, NW of Azores by USS *Flaherty*, USS *Neunzer*, USS *Chatelain*, USS *Varian*, USS *Janss*					
858	IXC/40	11-Mar-45	Seewolf	US/Gulf of Maine to CA/Halifax	
518	IXC	12-Mar-45	Seewolf	US/Gulf of Maine to CA/Halifax	
"Sunk on 22-Apr-45, NW of Azores by USS *Carter*, USS *Neal A. Scott*. 43026N/38023W. "					
880	IXC/40	14-Mar-45	Seewolf	US/Gulf of Maine to CA/Halifax	
"Sunk on 16-Apr-45, North Atlantic by USS *Frost* USS *Stanton*. 47053N/30026W. "					
805	IXC/40	17-Mar-45	Seewolf	US/New York south to Cape Hatteras	
1235	IXC/40	19-Mar-45	Seewolf	US/New York south to Cape Hatteras	
"Sunk on 15-Apr-45, North Atlantic by USS *Frost* USS *Stanton*. 47054N/30025W. "					
873	IXD2	30-Mar-45	Far East	Caribbean	–
889	IXC/40	05-Apr-45	US/New York to Cape Hatteras	–	
881	IXC/40	07-Apr-45	US/New York to Cape Hatteras	–	
"Sunk on 6-May-45, SE of Newfoundland by USS *Fanquhar*. 43018N/47044W. "					
541	IXC/40	07-Apr-45	US East Coast	–	US
1228	IXC/40	14-Apr-45	US/New York to Cape Hatteras		Freedom of manoeuvre
1231	IXC/40	27-Apr-45	US/Gulf of Maine	–	US
802	IXC/40	28-Apr-45	US/East Coast	–	US

Final Disposition of Patrol	Sunk by Air/Surface	Likely Sunk by Snorkel Failure	Ultra Derived Sinking	
CA/Halifax	Likely Sunk	Surface	Y	
Unk	Unk	–	N	–
Surrendered	–	–	–	
East of Block Island	Sunk	Surface	N	
Surrendered	–	–	–	
Sunk	Surface	–	Y	
US	Sunk	Surface	Y	
Joseph C. Hubbard, USS *Pillsbury*, USS *Keith*. 43053N/40047W. "				
US	Surrendered	–	–	
US	Sunk	Surface	Y	
US	Sunk	Surface	Y	
US	Surrendered	–	–	
US	Sunk	Surface	Y	
Surrendered	–	–	–	
	Surrendered	–	–	
US	Sunk	Surface	Y	
Surrendered	–	–	–	at Gib on 29 Apr
of Maine	US	Surrendered	–	
Surrendered	–	–	–	
Surrendered	–	–	–	

Kriegsmarine Communication Guidance for Snorkel U-boats

Below is an undated German wartime document that provides guidance on communication by snorkel-equipped U-boats. It was probably produced in early spring 1945. The document has a post-war reference of PG 31752 NID (3900). Two aspects stand out. The first is that it appears that the Kurier flash transmission system was more widely employed in late-war U-boats than previously acknowledged. Second, is the confirmation that the communication to/from a snorkel-equipped U-boat was very difficult under the best of circumstances. This fact must be incorporated in analysing the tactical behaviour of snorkel-equipped U-boats. However, if effective submerged communication between snorkel-equipped U-boats through Kurier had been achieved before war's end, there would have been a substantial negative impact on Allied land operations in Europe through effective coordination of attacks against sea ports.

The communication of U-boats with each other on operational switch will remain as before without significant restrictions. However, the maximum distance of U-boats between each other will be no more than 100 nautical miles.

Transmission by Kurier
Kurier signals can only be received in the home country. Because rod antennas are probably less effective than the current net deflectors, the same restrictions apply to receipt of Kurier signals in the home country as to [illegible] telegraphy.
Kurier signals are not receivable at all times in all parts of the ocean. Therefore, there is no assurance of silent reporting for boats in every case! Other boats do not get Kurier signals until they are sent by land-based radio stations through recoding. If the set-up on land is appropriate, one can count on a time delay of 10 minutes until repeat on longwave and shortwave.
Direction finding: The boat cannot conduct direction finding on shortwave.

High-frequency, ultra-high frequency
  Receiving: Secure with direction-finding equipment without restrictions
  in all parts of the ocean.
  Transmission: No capability of transmission using high-frequency and
  ultra high-frequency.
  Direction finding: High-frequency and ultra-high-frequency without
  restriction, but not when direction finding is done on medium frequency.

Medium Frequency
  Receiving: No limitations.
  Transmission: No transmission capability.
  Ultra-high-frequency
  Receiving and transmission:
  Ultra-high-frequency communication only between boats (only up to
  15 nautical miles); primarily for communication between U-boats and air-
  craft. No limitation of range when compared to before. Range 200
  nautical miles.
  Direction finding: by [Allied] boat, no; through an aircraft, yes!

New communication for 'snorkelling boats'
Ancillary antenna
Shortwave
  There is only one antenna (Ölasta) [hydraulic extensible rod antenna used
  at periscope depth] available for sending and receiving. There is an additional reception capability through one of the snorkel round dipoles. (The
  quality of the reception on the round dipole is still being tested.)
  The boat can send on shortwave while travelling with snorkel and simultaneously receive (to a limited extent)! The snorkelling boat can be guided from land using shortwave with no limitation as to space or time of day!

Transmission using Kurier
  For release of Kurier signals, the same applies as above.
  The 'snorkelling boat' can report using Kurier without making noise, but
  with limitations as to space and time due to the (probably) lower capability of the Ölasta!
  Shortwave direction finding is interrupted only for a short time by sending using Kurier! So that it can't be found by direction finding.

High-frequency and ultra-high-frequency
  High-frequency: limited reception on Ölasta. No direction-finding
  capability.

Ultra-high-frequency: Reception only if direction finder is extended, so there is limitation of travel!

The boat has clear reception and transmission on shortwave when travelling with snorkel. Therefore, use ultra-high-frequency only if high-frequency reception is impeded. Generally therefore there is no travel restriction!

Direction-finding capability on ultra-high-frequency with sensing.

At present, the capability of putting ultra-high-frequency receivers on the head of a snorkel, which would make ultra-high-frequency reception possible without travel restriction, is being tested.

Medium frequency

Only reception for observation. No direction finding capability! If a direction-finding [illegible] on the snorkel head is possible, then so is direction finding.

Ultra-high frequency

Transmission and reception as when surfaced. However, do not send on shortwave at the same time.

Appendix E

Allied Vessels and Tonnage Sunk () by Snorkel U-boats June 1944–May 1945

	Jan	Feb	Mar	Apr	May	Jun
1944						"12 (58,3
1945	"14 (68,492)"	"18 (77,129)"	"15 (66,959)"	"12 (66,584)"	"4 (10,894)"	
	Total Allied Vesels Sunk 120					
	"Total Tonnage Sunk (636,697)"					

New communication for the 'submerged boat'
Only ultra-high-frequency reception and direction finding without sensing, but the capabilities have not yet been entirely clarified.
Tests are in progress. Maximum depth for reception is 20 to 22 metres with the strongest ultra-high-frequency transmitters and good reception conditions.
The depths will be less as the distance increases!
In the north Atlantic, one can count on a depth of about 18 to 20 metres!
Reduction of travel during reception of ultra-high frequency!

Underwater telegraphy
Capability of use is low because the enemy takes bearings immediately.
Range under favourable conditions is 30 nautical miles.

Jul	Aug	Sep	Oct	Nov	Dec
"14 (62,380)"	"17 (92,922)"	"8 (51,605)"	"4 (1,685)"	"5 (25,597)"	"11 (54,123)"

Bibliography

Sources cited in the endnotes and directly relevant to the topics contained in the text are listed below. However, far more material was consulted as background research. I have not cited every U-boat KTB, Allied Task Force after action report or individual vessel report reviewed, as this expanded the bibliography unnecessarily. More than 350 individual U-boats were researched. Their KTBs, Ultra intercepts, *Bootbläter*, interrogation reports and available period photographs were identified and reviewed for the period covered in this text. Every BdU and S.K.L. entry from May 1943 until May 1945 was evaluated for related information.

Germany
Bundesarchiv-Militärarchiv, Freiberg
RM 6 Oberbefehlshaber der Kriegsmarine
RMD 6 Amtsdrucksachen Marine.- Bau-, Betriebs- und Bedienungs-
   vorschriften
RM 7 Seekriegsleitung der Kriegsmarine
RM 20 Marinekommandoamt der Reichsmarine und Kriegsmarine
RM 25 Hauptamt Kriegsschiffbau
RM 87 Befehlshaber der Unterseeboote der Kriegsmarine
RM 98 Unterseeboote der Kriegsmarine
W-04 Kartei Technische Pläne

German U-boot Archiv, Cuxhaven
Bootbläter (assorted U-Boat hull numbers)
Schnorchel Technische Daten (3 Binders)

Zentrales Institut des Sanitätsdienstes der Bundeswehr Kiel-Kronshagen
   und Schifffahrtmedizinisches Institut der Marine, Kiel
SchiffMedInstM. Dok. Nr. 10975
Malorny, Lecturer Dr med. habil. Gunther. *Carbon Monoxide on
   Submarines*. Translation prepared by: US Fleet, US Naval Forces,
   Germany. Technical Section (Medical).

Uffenorde, Lecturer Dr med. habil. Hellmut. *Otological Experience with Snorkel-Equipped U-Boats*. Translation prepared by: US Fleet, US Naval Forces, Germany. Technical Section (Medical).

Great Britain
Public Records Office, Kew
Admiralty (ADM) Papers of Secretariat and Operational Records
ADM 1/17549. Schnorchel/Snorkel.
ADM 1/17601. Operational Experience against U-boats fitted with Snorkel.
ADM 1/17667. Reich and Europe/Technical Development of U-boat War.
ADM 1/18557. Trials of captured German U-boats.
ADM 116-5571. TNC UK Inspection Reports.
ADM 116/5571a. U-boat Testing.
ADM 116/5571b. U-boat Testing.
ADM 204/1610. Detection of Snorkel exhaust by Thermal Radiation.
ADM 204/2982. Detection of Snorkel by Hydrophone.
ADM 213/868. Submarine Acoustic Camouflage.
ADM 259/434. Signals from Rubber Covered and non-Rubber Covered U-boats.
ADM 259/633. Signals from Rubber Covered and non-Rubber Covered U-boats.
ADM 281/143. Prisoner of war statements from *U-1209*, *U-877*, *U-671*.
ADM 334/53. Attacks on snorkel masts.

Air Ministry
AIR 15/058. Practical Experience against U-boats fitted with Snorkel.
AIR 20/1504. Snorkel and ASV MK XVII.

GCCS Naval Section: Naval Decrypts
HW 18/288. Schnorchel/Snorkel, 1944 OCT–1945 APR 22.
HW 18/290. Baltic Operations (Ostsee), 1944 NOV 20–1945 MAR 16 and Alberich (reducing radar return), 1944 SEP 11–1945 MAR 18.
HW 18/293. Morale, fighting spirit, 1945 JAN 31–1945 MAY 2.
HW 18/401. *U-38*, *U-139*, *U-246*, *U-326*, *U-621*, *U-739*, *U-825*, *U-827*, *U-857*, *U-881*, *U-1056*, *U-1105*; 1944 JUN 1–1945 APR 30.

Ministry of Defence
Hessler, Günter, *The U-Boat War in the Atlantic 1939–1945*. Ministry of Defence, HMSO. London, 1992.

Royal Navy Submarine Archive, Gosport
ADM 1990/197. Relating to the Trials to compare Rubber-coated and non-Rubber-coated Type VIIC U-boats *U-1105* and *U-1171* respectively.
ADM 1/16169. Alberich, 'Rubber Covering of U-boat Hulls'.

United States
US National Archives Records Administration (NARA)
Record Group 38. Records of the Office of the Chief of Naval Operations.
Intercepted Enemy Radio Traffic and Related Documentation 1940–1946. Assorted U-boat hull numbers as cited.

German Archives, Tambach
Office of Naval Intelligence, Special Activities Branch, OP-16-Z, Interrogations and Documents from U-boats and Raiders 1943–1945. Assorted U-boat hull numbers as cited.

Record Group 242
T1022. Records of the German Navy, 1850–1945. Kriegstagebücher (KTB) & Stehender Kriegsbefehl Des Führers/Befehlshaber der Unterseeboote (F.d.U./BdU.).
Assorted dates and U-boats hull numbers, as cited.

Record Group 457
SRMN-030. Bi-Weekly Messages on U-boat Trends 1 September 1942–1 May 1945, 1 May 1945.
SRMN-037. U-Boat Intelligence Summaries 1943–May 1945, 16 March 1945.
SRMN-048. OP-20-GI Report of U-boat Disposition and Status, December 1942–2 May 1945.
SRMN-054. (Part 2). OP-20-GI Special Studies Relating to U-boat Activity 1943–1945, Nature of Kurier Transmissions, dated 18 December 1944.
U.S Naval Technical Mission in Europe Technical Report No. 287-45, Tactical Planning for High Speed U-boats, 11 September 1945, p. 4, hereafter cited as NARA/NTME/287-45.
U.S Naval Technical Mission Europe. Technical Report No. 312-45. German Submarine Design 1935–45. (July 1945).
U.S Naval Technical Mission Europe, Technical Report No. 517-45, 'The German Schnorchel', 27 October 1945.
US Navy Technical Mission in Europe Report No. 352-45, Rubber Covering of German Submarines Anti-Asdic (German Code Name 'Alberich') dated 20 September 1945.

U.S Naval Technical Mission in Europe Report No. 403-45 The Influence of High Submerged Speed on German Submarine Hulls, August 1945, p. 1, hereafter cited as NARA/NTME/403-45.

Sound Absorption and Sound Absorbers in Water (Dynamic Properties of Rubber and Rubberlike Substances in the Acoustic Frequency Region) by Walter Kuhl, Erwin Meyer, Hermann Oberst, Eugen Skudrzyk, and Konrad Tamm, collected by Erwin Meyer and translated by Charles E. Morgan, Jr. (Bureau of Ships: Washington, DC, June 1947).

Online Source for Primary Documents
www.dutchsubmarines.com/boats/boat_o19.htm
www.history.navy.mil
http://historisches-marinearchiv.de
www.ibiblio.org/hyperwar
https://uboat.net
www.Uboatarchiv.net

Secondary Sources
Books
Blair, Clay, *Hitler's U-Boat War: The Hunted, 1942–1945*. Modern Library. New York, 1998.

_____, *Hitler's U-Boat War: The Hunters, 1939–1942*. Modern Library. New York, 1996.

Boyd, Carl and Akihiko Yoshida, *The Japanese Submarine Force and World War II*. Naval Institute Press. Annapolis, 1995.

Cremer, Peter, *U-Boat Commander: A Periscope View of the Battle of the Atlantic*. Naval Institute Press. Annapolis, 1985.

Delize, Jean, *U-Boat Crews: The day-to-day life aboard Hitler's submarines*. Histoire & Collections. Paris, France, 2007.

Dönitz, Karl, *My Ten Years and Twenty Days*. Naval Institute Press. Annapolis, 1990.

Easton, A. *50 North*. The Ryerson Press. Toronto, 1963.

Farago, Ladislas, *The Tenth Fleet, The Story of the Submarine and Survival*. Ivan Obolensky, Inc. New York, 1962.

Franks, Norman and Eric Zimmerman, *U-Boat versus Aircraft*. Grub Street. London, 1988.

Friedman, Norman, *US Submarines Since 1945: An Illustrated Design History*. Naval Institute Press, Annapolis, 1994.

Gannon, Robert, *Hellions of the Deep: The Development of American Torpedoes in World War II*. Penn State University Press. New York, 2009.

Guske, Heinze F K, *The War Diaries of U764, Fact or Fiction*. Thomas Publications. Gettysburg, PA, 1992.

Hamilton, Aaron, *German Submarine U-1105 'Black Panther': The Naval Archaeology of a U-Boat*. Ospey Publishing. New York. 2019.

Hennessy, Peter and James Jinks, *The Silent Deep: The Royal Navy Submarine Service since 1945*. Penguin Books. Great Britain, 2016.

Hickam, Homer H Hickam, *Torpedo Junction. U-Boat War off America's East Coast*. Naval Institute Press. Annapolis, 1989.

Köhl, Fritz and Axel Niestlé, *Vom Original zum Modell: Uboottyp VIIC: Eine Bild-und Plandokumentation*. Bernadr & Graefe Verlag. Bonn, Germany, 2006.

_____, *Vom Original zum Modell: Uboottyp IXC: Eine Bild-und Plandokumentation*. Bernadr & Graefe Verlag: Bonn, Germany, 1990.

Kurson, Robert, *Shadow Divers*. Random House. New York, 2004.

Lundeberg, Phillip K, 'Operation Teardrop Revisited,' in *To Die Gallantly*. Ed by Timothy J Runyan and Jan M Copes, Westview Press. Oxford, 1994.

McCartney, Innes, *The Maritime Archaeology of a Modern Conflict. Comparing the Archaeology of German Submarine Wrecks to the Historical Text*. New York. Routledge Studies in Archaeology, 2015.

Moore, Robert, *A Time to Die: The Untold Story of the Kursk Tragedy*. Crown Publishers. New York. 2002.

Offley, Ed, *Turning the Tide: How a Small Band of Allied Sailors Defeated the U-Boats and Won the Battle of the Atlantic*. Basic Books. New York, 2011.

Palmer, Bill, *The Last Battle of the Atlantic: The Sinking of the U-853*. Thunderfish Video and Publications. China, 2012.

Peffer, Randall, *Where Divers Dare: The Hunt for the Last U-Boat*. Berkley Caliber. New York, 2016.

Polmar, Norman and K J Moore, *Cold War Submarines: The Design and Construction of US and Soviet Submarines*. Potomac Books Inc. Washington DC, 2004.

_____ and Jurrien Noot, *Submarines of the Russian and Soviet Naves, 1718–1990*. Naval Institute Press. Annapolis, 1991.

Rössler, Eberhard, *U-Boottyp XXI*. Bernard & Graefe in der Mönch Verlagsgesellschaft mbH. Bonn, Germany, 2013.

_____, *Die Sonaranlagen der deutschen Unterseeboote*. Bernard & Graefe Verlag. Bonn, Germany, 2006.

_____, *The U-Boat. The evolution and technical history of German submarines*. Arms and Armor Press. New York, 2001.

_____, *U-Boot Schnorchel: Entwicklung und Einsatz, 1943–1944*. Verlagshaus M&M. Martenshagen, Germany.

Sakaida, Henry, Gary Nila and Koji Takaki, *I-400: Japan's Secret Aircraft-Carrying Strike Submarine, Objective Panama Canal*. Crécy. Hong Kong, 2010.

Sontag, Sherry and Christopher Drew with Annette Lawrence Drew, *Blind Man's Bluff: The Untold Story of American Submarine Espionage*. Public Affairs: New York, 1998.

Tarrant, V E, *The Last Year of the Kriegsmarine: May 1944–May 1945*. Naval Institute Press. Annapolis, Maryland, 1994.

Technikmuseum U-Boot Wilhelm Bauer, 1999.

Urbanke, Axel, *Suppliers of the Grey Wolves: The Story of the German Submarine Tankers 1941–44*. Luftfahrtverlag Start. Bad Zwischenhahn, 2013.

Werner, Herbert A, *Iron Coffins: A personal account of the German U-Boat battles of World War II*. Holt, Rinehardt and Winston. New York, 1969.

Wetzel, Eckard, *U-995*. Motorbuch Verlag. Stutgart, Germany, 2004.

Wiggins, Melanie, *U-Boat Adventures*. Naval Institute Press. Annapolis, 1999.

Wynn, Kenneth. *U-Boat Operations of the Second World War, Vol. 2: Career Histories, U511–UIT25*. Chatham Publishing. UK, 1998.

_____, *U-Boat Operations of the Second World War, Vol. 1: Career Histories, U1–U510*. Chatham Publishing. UK, 1997.

Articles

Barge, F A, 'NRL Memorandum Report 2146: Underwater Acoustic Absorption Characteristics of Composites of Wood, Rubber, and Steel.' Technical Memorandum File No. TM 78-52 May 1978. The Pennsylvania Status University Applied Research Laboratory.

Bauer, Arthur O, 'Some hardly known aspects of the GHG, the U-Boat's group listening apparatus.' Published Online.

Beesly, Patrick, 'Ultra and the Battle of the Atlantic, The British View.'

Chatterton, John, Richie Kohler, and John Yurga, 'The Fate of U-869 Reexamined, Part III: The Loss of the German Submarine.' *Wreck Diving Magazine*, Issue 19, 2009.

Cole, William, 'Navy subs still show issue with Stealth coating.' *Honolulu Star-Advertiser*, 5 March 2017.

Holler, Richard A, 'The evolution of the Sonobuoy from World War II to the Cold War.' *US Journal of Underwater Acoustics*, January 2014.

Jones, Mark C, 'Give Credit Where Credit is Due: The Dutch Role in the Development of the Schnorkel.' *The Journal of Military History*, Vol. 69, No. 4, October 2005.

Knowles, Kenneth, 'Ultra and the Battle of the Atlantic, The American View'. Naval Symposium at the US Naval Academy in Annapolis. 28 October 1977.

Lastinger, J L and G A Sabin, 'Underwater Sound Absorbers: A Review of Published Research with an Annotated Bibliography'. Methods and Systems Branch, Underwater Sound Reference Division, 5 August 1970. Naval Research Laboratory.

McLean, Douglas M, 'Confronting Technological and Tactical Change: Allied Anti-Submarine Warfare in the Last Year of the Battle of the Atlantic'. *Canadian Military History*, Vol. 7, No. 3, Summer 1998.

Niestlé, Axel, 'The 'Atlas' Survey Zone: Deep-sea Archaeology & U-Boat loss Reassessments'. Odyssey Papers 12. 2010.

Tollaksen, D M Ensign, USN, 'Last Chapter for U-853'. US Naval Institute Proceedings. December 1960.

PHD Dissertations, Unpublished Manuscripts, and Assorted Papers

Bechtold, Hans crewmember of U-235, Letter dated 10 November 1989.

Brümmer-Patzig, Helmut. 'Baubelehrung fur UD.4, 11.04, von Königsberg zur Rotterdam' (Undated article).

Krebs, Dipl.-Ing. Harry, Former chief engineer of U-236 and retired Oberstleutnant (Ing.), Letter dated Bonn 1 February 1985.

Llewellyn-Jones, Malcolm. The Royal Navy on the Threshold of Modern Anti-Submarine Warfare, 1944–1949, PHD Dissertation. Department of War Studies, King's College London, 2004.

Waller, Derek, 'U-1105 in the US Navy – 1945 to 1949'. Undated.

Notes

Introduction

[1] *Schnorchel* is a German word defined as a vulgar term for a crooked or large nose. Across primary documents from four countries there proved to be no consistency in the term *Schnorchel*. German documents used the term *Schnorchel*, while British and Canadians used Snort or *Schnorkel*, and US documents employed a combination of all three with the addition of snorkel. I have adopted the use of snorkel universally in order to make it easier for the reader. The snorkel became one of the most tested and evaluated U-boat innovations in the post-war period.

[2] This initiative, the first of its kind, was the basis for post-war stealth technology, whereby aircraft were encased in a rubberised coating designed to absorb radar signals. This very concept was already theorised and being tested by the Luftwaffe before the end of the war.

[3] *Alberich* was named for a dwarf king who had a hat of invisibility.

[4] *Schornsteinfeger* was applied to almost all outbound U-boats after November 1944, though specific records often do not exist to document when the coating was applied.

[5] National Archives Records Administration (NARA) T-1022/Roll 3900 (hereafter cited as NARA/T3022/3900) Oberkommando der Kriegsmarine (*OKM*) 1.Seekriegsleitung (*SKL*) daily situation report for February 24, 1945 (hereafter cited as *OKM/1.SKL*).

[6] This fear was not fantasy and is discussed in detail in the *Gruppe Seewolf* section of Chapter 9.

[7] This was the first time in history that humans remained underwater, without natural light, with limited oxygen content, for these lengths of time.

[8] '*Ultra and the Battle of the Atlantic*', *The British View* by Patrick Beesly, p. 8.

[9] Ibid., *The American View* by Kenneth Knowles, p. 15.

[10] See for example, V E Tarrant, *The Last Year of the Kriegsmarine: May 1944–May 1945* (Naval Institute Press: Annapolis, Maryland, 1994), p. 207.

[11] For a detailed discussion of *U-1105*, see the author's *German Submarine U-1105 'Black Panther': The Naval Archaeology of a U-Boat* (Osprey Publishing: New York, NY, 2019).

[12] Two excellent works that utilise the snorkel as important discriminators in maritime archaeological surveys of U-boats are Innes McCartney's Doctoral Thesis, *The Maritime Archaeology of a Modern Conflict. Comparing the Archaeology of German Submarine Wrecks to the Historical Text* (New York: Routledge Studies in Archaeology, 2015) and Axel Niestlé, 'The 'Atlas' Survey Zone: Deep-sea Archaeology & U-Boat loss Reassessments' (Odyssey Papers 12, 2010).

Chapter 1

[1] The German cryptologic service known as B-Dienst had broken the Allied merchant signals code and provided BdU with accurate Allied convoy movements. In addition, BdU's efforts were aided by *Luftwaffe* long-range reconnaissance based in north-west France in the form of FW-200 Condors from *I./KG.40*.

[2] Günter Hessler, *The U-Boat War in the Atlantic 1939–1945* (Ministry of Defence, HMSO: London, 1992), Section 48–49, p. 27. This work was written by Dönitz's son-in-law, who served as his staff officer in the Operations section of the BdU staff during the war. After the

war, while in captivity, he was granted access to a large amount of captured German documents, though not everything that might have been available, and wrote this history that
amounts to the official German version of the U-boat war. While dated, and incomplete, it still
remains the best source of German operational and tactical U-boat practices during the war.

3   Eberhard Rössler, *The U-Boat. The Evolution and technical history of German submarines*
(Arms and Armor Press: New York, 2001), pp. 145–46.
4   Rössler, pp. 155–56.
5   Ibid., p. 157.
6   National Archives Records Administration, *U.S Naval Technical Mission Europe. Technical
Report 312-45. German Submarine Design 1935–45.* (July 1945) hereafter cited as NTME
TR-312-45.
7   Hessler, Section 200, p. 20.
8   NARA T1022/4065. BdU KTB entry for 24.6.1944.
9   Hessler, Section 200, p. 20.
10   Rössler, p. 157.
11   Ibid., pp. 157–59.
12   Public Records Office, Admiralty Records 281/143. *Report of Second Visit to Germany
Re Submarine Construction. July–August, 1945.* Hereafter cited as PRO/ADM 281/43.
13   Hessler, Section 352.
14   Bundesarchiv-Militärarchiv. RM7/189. I.SKL Teil C VII. Uberleugen Des Chefs Der SKL und
Niederschriften über Vorträge und Besprechungen beim Führer. Vom: Januar 1943.
Bis: December 1944. Hereafter cited as BAMA RM7/189.
15   Ibid.
16   Jean Delize, *U-Boat Crews: The day-t-day life aboard Hitler's submarines* (Histoire &
Collections: Paris, France: 2007), p. 50.
17   Hessler, Section 348.

Chapter 2

1   Public Records Office, Admiralty 1-17549, 'OP-16-Z Special Report 1-45 Schnorchel,
Scientific Research and Experiment Department Admiralty', 15 February 1945, hereafter cited
as PRO/ADM1-17549.
2   National Archives Records Administration U.S Naval Technical Mission Europe, Technical
Report 517-45, 'The German Schnorchel', 27 October 1945, hereafter cited as NARA
NTME/TR 517-45.
3   Rössler, pp. 168, 175–178, 198.
4   U.S Patent No. 803.177, Serial 246,157 and 246,158 February, 1905.
5   Mark C Jones, 'Give Credit Where Credit is Due: The Dutch Role in the Development of the
Schnorkel' in *The Journal of Military History*, Vol. 69, No. 4 (October 2005) pp. 994–95.
6   Ibid., p. 997.
7   Ibid.
8   www.dutchsubmarines.com/boats/boat_o19.htm.
9   Jones, p. 997.
10   Ibid., pp. 1001–02.
11   Ibid., p. 1006.
12   Helmut Brümmer-Patzig 'Baubelehrung UD.4, 11.40, von Königsberg nach Rotterdam'
(Undated article).
13   Ibid. According to a February 1945 British Naval Intelligence report, trials were conducted in
the Baltic Sea at the end of 1942. The report identified *U-448* as the first Type VIIC to be fitted
with a rigid air mast during its time with the 8th U-boat Flotilla at some time in November or
December 1942. The report claimed that *U-448* was fitted temporarily with a non-extensible
'H'-shaped air mast with separate air induction and diesel exhaust tubes in Danzig. This
installation probably did not seem to have any form of automatic shut-off valve for the air

intake at the origination point in the mast. It was noted that 'success with the arrangement was moderate, the gear was removed and further trials temporarily abandoned'. (PRO/ADM1-17549). A careful review of German archival records has produced no evidence that *U-448* ever received an 'H'-configuration air mast. This British intelligence report was probably produced from false statements made by the crew. In February 1945 the British were eager to understand the snorkel's development and probably prodded *U-448*'s crew on the topic, receiving a made-up story as a result.

14 Public Records Office Admiralty 1-17667 'Letter from Prof. Walter to Admiral Doenitz on Necessity for fast U-boat and Schnorkel' dated 1 August 1945, hereafter cited as PRO/ADM 1-17667 and Admiralty, Office of the Director of Naval Construction, 281-143 'Report of Second Visit to Germany re Submarine Construction. July–August, 1945' hereafter cited as PRO/ADM 281-143.

15 PRO/ADM 281-143, Hessler, Section 347, Karl Dönitz, *My Ten Years and Twenty Days* (Naval Institute Press: Annapolis, 1990) p. 354.

16 Brümmer-Patzig.

17 Jones, p. 1007.

18 NARA/NTME/TR 517-45.

19 Rössler, p. 199.

20 Dipl.-Ing. Harry Kerbs, Former chief engineer of *U-236* and retired Oberstleutnant (Ing.), Letter dated Bonn 1 February 1985.

21 Dipl.-Ing. Harry Kerbs, Former chief engineer of *U-236* and retired Oberstleutnant (Ing.), Letter dated Bonn February 1, 1985.

22 Hans Bechtold, crewmember of *U-235*, Letter dated 10 November 1989.

23 Ibid.

24 *Entstehungsgsheschichte vom Deutschen 'Schnorchel', Kapitel 3.* (unpublished and undated), Snorkel Technical Documents, U-boot Archive, Cuxhaven, Germany.

25 Hessler, Section 420.

26 I have used the wartime term of 'folding' as translated from the German word for the device, however, the 'folding' snorkel is best described as a 'hinged' device given the fact that it does not fold onto itself.

27 NARA/NTME/TR 517-45.

28 Hessler, Section 420.

29 Exceptions, of course exist. For example when looking at commissioning photographs of some of the last diesel U-boats to be commissioned, *U-1307* (VIIC/42), commissioned on 17 November 1944, is identified through a photograph showing a snorkel bracket affixed to its conning tower. This was very rare. Its sister U-boat, *U-1305* (VIIC/41), commissioned on 13 September 1944, does not. Reviews of all other commissioning photographs by the author have revealed no other U-boat at the time of commissioning with a snorkel installation at that time.

30 *Entstehungsgsheschichte vom Deutschen 'Schnorchel'.*

31 There may be others, possibly as many as a dozen more, but probably only photographs will confirm them.

32 Rössler, p. 200.

33 PRO/ADM 281-143.

34 Bundesarchiv-Militärarchiv, RM 98-735, hereafter BAMA/RM98-735.

35 *Schnorchel Technische Daten*, U-boot Archiv, Cuxhaven, Germany.

36 Sangerhausen was the Kriegsmarine supply depot for Gruppe Mitte.

37 Bundesarchiv-Militärarchiv, RM 98-768, hereafter BAMA/RM98-768.

38 National Archives Records Administration, Records of the German Navy, 1850–1945 (242), T1022 Roll 2980, U-534 KTB, hereafter cited as NARA/RG242/T1022/Rxxx/U-xxx

39 Norman Franks & Eric Zimmerman, *U-Boat Versus Aircraft* (Grub Street: London, 1988) pp. 178–79.

40 Hessler, Section 420.

41 See Chapter 9, reference to *U-190* (IXC/40).

42 Hessler, Section 420.

43 PRO/ADM 1-17549 and *Besondere Schnorchelerfahrungen Nr. 3* by Thedsen, U-Bbot Archiv, Cuxhaven, Germany.

44 Hessler, Section 420.

45 BAMA/RM98-760.

46 Axel Urbanke, *Suppliers of the Grey Wolves: The Story of the German Submarine Tankers 1941–44* (Bad Zwischenhahn: Luftfahrtverlag Start, 2013), p. 326.

47 NARA/RG38/ONI Interrogation Reports/Box 40, *U-1229*.

48 Gosport Archives, A1990/197. Relating to the trials to compare rubber-coated and non-rubber-coated Type VIIC U-boats *U-1105* and *U-1171* respectively. Report on the explosion onboard *U-3017*.

49 Ibid.

50 Ibid. Handwritten letter from Captain s/m Loch Ryan to Admiral (Submarines), Northways, London. No: 201/2529. 2 September 1945.

51 According to an OSS report submitted in 1944, agents confirmed that Horten was the main snorkel training base. PRO/ADM 1-17549.

52 Detail of the *Huascaran* was provided by U-boat veteran Fritz Deters that was supplied during an interview conducted by Arthur O Bauer in 2014.

53 Report on the Interrogation of Survivors (not in the C.B. 04051 series) (Combined report *U-413*, *U-1209*, *U-877* and *U-1199*) and C.B. 04051 (99) 'U-406, U-386, and U-264' Interrogation of Survivors May 1944. Available online: www.uboatarchive.net.

54 Melanie Wiggins, *U-Boat Adventures* (Naval Institute Press: Annapolis, 1999) pp. 176–77.

55 PRO/ADM 1-17549.

56 This information was provided by the commanding officers of *U-871* and *U-672*. See NID 1P/W/REP/6/44. C.B. 04051 (99) 'U-406, U-386, and U-264' Interrogation of Survivors May 1944. Available online: www.uboatarchive.net.

57 Rössler, p. 200 and McCartney, p. 189.

58 Vorläufige Beschreibung und Betriebsvorschrift der U-boot Schnorchel Anlage, Tiel 3, U-boot Archiv, Cuxhaven, Germany, hereafter cited as U-boot Boot Schnorchel Anlage, Tiel 3.

59 PRO/ADM 1-17549.

60 Fritz Köhl and Axel Niestlé, *Vom Original zum Modell: Uboottyp IXC: Eine Bild-und Plandokumentation* (Bernadr & Graefe Verlag: Bonn, 1990), p. 30.

61 Ibid.

62 Ibid.

63 NARA RG38 UD-09D 22, German Archives Tambach, Box T94, 'Schnorchel', hereafter cited as RG38/UD-09 22/Tambach/Box T94.

64 Ibid.

65 NARA/NTME/TR 517-45.

66 U-boot Boot Schnorchel Anlage, Tiel 3.

67 A detailed discussion can be found in Chapter 7 of the issues identified with Type VIIC GW motors and the snorkel.

68 PRO/ADM 1-17549.

69 U-boot Boot Schnorchel Anlage, Tiel 3.

70 NARA/NTME/TR 517-45.

71 Ibid.

72 PRO/ADM 281-143.

73 Ibid.

74 PRO/HW/18-288, 1413/31/3/45.

75 PRO/ADM/281-143.

76 See sketches in NARA/NTME/TR 517-45.

77 U-boot-Archiv, Cuxhaven, Letter from Wolfgang Giebel.
78 PRO/ADM 281-143.
79 Ibid and NARA/NTME/TR 517-45.
80 See for example, Rössler, pp. 352–53, Fritz Köhl and Axel Niestlé, *Vom Original zum Modell: Uboottyp VIIC: Eine Bild-und Plandokumentation* (Bernadr & Graefe Verlag: Bonn, 2006), p. 59, or Revell of Germany's 1/144 and 1/72 U-boat Type VIIC/41 'Atlantic Version'. It must be stated that there was never an 'Atlantic Version' of the Type VIIC/41. This is a complete misnomer. Both model kits were based on *U-995* and have incorrectly been moulded to have no starboard side external snorkel trunking. In addition, Revell has produced no U-boat model kits to date with a Type I snorkel mast.
81 Eckard Wetzel, *U-995* (Motorbuch Verlag: Stutgart, 2004), pp. 145, 146–47.
8   The author's online article 'Carbon Monoxide Poisoning and the forgotten Exhaust Shutoff Valve on the Type VIIC' published by the Deutsches U-boot Museum in 2018, sparked the Bundesmarine to consider adding this piping back to *U-995* in the next restoration process.
83 This photograph sample was graciously supplied by Axel Niestlé.
84 PRO/ADM/18-288, 0805/21/3/45.
85 PRO/ADM/281-143. Prisoner of war statements from *U-1209*, *U-877*, *U-671*.
86 Ibid. Prisoner of war statements from *U-1229*, *U-1006*, *U-877*.
87 PRO/ADM/18-288, 1515/3/4/45, National Archives Records Administration, Special Research History (SRH), Battle of the Atlantic, Vol. IV (025) .Technical Intelligence from Allied C.I., 1941–1945', hereafter cited as NARA/SRH/025 and National Archives Records Administration, Special Research History (SRH), Battle of the Atlantic, Vol. I (009) 'Allied Communications Intelligence, December 1942–May 1945', hereafter cited as NARA/SRH/009. Available online at www.ibiblio.org/hyperwar/ETO/Ultra
88 While U-boat Command never realised that their Enigma cipher was broken, U-boat commanders instinctively learned that they were being located on the surface and attacked.
89 This guidance was specific to Type XXIs but based on the last thirty days of initial snorkel-equipped diesel boat operation. See 'Considerations for the Employment of the Type XXI' dated 10 July 1944, p. 42. NARA/RG242/T1012/R3900.
90 NARA/RG242/T1022/R3673/U-427.
91 Stephen Puleo, *Due to Enemy Action: The True World War II Story of the USS Eagle 56* (The Lyons Press: Guilford, CT, 2005), p. 146.
92 Ursula was reconstructed on the basis of information correlated from the normal radio traffic to and from the U-boats; the special ciphers that were read were broken by the mistakes made and revealed in the normal traffic. National Archives Records Administration, Special Research History (SRH), Battle of the Atlantic, Vol. II (008) 'U-boat Operations – December 1942 to May 1945', p. 162, hereafter cited as NARA/SRH/008. Available online at www. ibiblio.org/hyperwar/ETO/Ultra.
93 TICOM I-9 Notes on 'Kurier' Communication System (11 June 1945), U.S Naval Technical Mission Europe: 'Notes on the 'Kurier' System of U-boat Communication (7 July 1945), and 'Memorandum: The Kurier Problem' dated 26 November 1947 available at www. ticomarchive.com/iv-case-studies/kurier.
94 National Archives Records Administration, Record Group 457 SRMN-054 (Part 2), OP-20-GI Special Studies Relating to U-boat Activity 1943–1945, *Nature of Kurier Transmissions*, dated 18 December 1944, hereafter cited as NARA/RG457/SRMN-054.
95 PRO/ADM/281-143.
96 Hessler, Section 446.
97 'Elektra' was an updated version of the beam-based Low-Frequency Radio Range (LFR) employed by the United States during the 1930s. Elektra was further modified to create 'Sonne' ('sun' in German) by electronically rotating the signal to create a series of beams that sweep across the sky. Using simple timing of the signal, an aeroplane navigator could determine the angle to the station. Two such measurements could then provide a radio fix.

Accuracy and range were excellent, with fixes around ¼ of a degree being possible at 1,000 miles range. Elektra-Sonne was employed extensively by the Luftwaffe during the war. Sonne was so useful that it found widespread use by United Kingdom forces as well, and they took over operation after the war. The system was used for long-range navigation under the 'Consol' name. New stations were constructed around the world over the next twenty years. The system remained in partial use into the 1990s, with the last transmitter in Norway turned off in 1991 after the fall of the Soviet Union.

98 NARA/RG457/SRMN-054, *U-Boat Communications, January 1944*, dated 15 February 1944.

99 NARA/SRH/008, p. 162, 1653/22 March 1944.

100 Ibid., 1850/31 March 1944.

101 NARA/RG242/T1022/R4186. Item 7991, 1917/6 November 1944. 'Folder on wireless messages or telegrams on tactical problems.'

102 NARA/SRH/025, 2040/16 November 1944.

103 Ibid., 1819/31 January 1945.

104 NARA/RG457/SRMN-054, *U-Boat Communications, January 1944*.

105 NARA/SRH/025, 2005/3 November 1944.

106 Ibid., 1156/1443/24 December 1944.

107 NARA/RG242/T1022/R3072/U-480 and R2936/U-155 KTB. See also NARA/SRH/025, 2239/2 November 1944.

108 Arthur O Bauer 'Some hardly known aspects of the GHG, the U-boat's group listening apparatus.' pp. 15–16 and Eberhard Rössler, *Die Sonaranlagen der deutsche Unterseeboote* (Bernard & Graefe Verlag: Bonn, 2006), pp. 67–74.

109 NARA/RG242/T1022/R3673/U-1305 KTB.

110 PRO/ADM/281-143.

111 Ibid.

112 Ibid.

113 Ibid.

114 Ibid.

115 Rössler, p. 200.

116 NARA/RG242/T1022/R4065/FdU-BdU KTB, 16–29 February 1944. Available online: www.uboatarchive.net.

117 Report on the Interrogation of Survivors – C.B. 04051 (99) (Combined report *U-406*, *U-386* and *U-264*), May 1944. Available online: www.uboatarchive.net.

118 NARA/RG242/T1022/R4065/FdU-BdU KTB, 1–15 March 1944.

119 NARA/RG242/T1022/R4065/FdU-BdU KTB, 15–31 May 1944.

120 National Archives Records Administration, Record Group 38, Office of Naval Intelligence, Special Activities Branch, OP-16-Z, Interrogations and Documents from U-boats and Raiders 1943–1945, Box 19, U-490, hereafter cited as NARA/RG38/Interrogation Reports/Box XX/ U-xxx.

121 NARA/RG242/T1022/R4065/FdU-BdU KTB, 16–31 March and 11 March 1944.

122 NARA/RG457/SRMN 030/1 June 1944.

123 Hessler, Section 437.

124 NARA/NTME/TR 517-45.

125 Ibid.

Chapter 3

1 Unless otherwise cited, the information in the chapter is derived from National Archives Records Administration, Combined Intelligence Objectives Sub-Committee G-2 Division, SHAEF (Rear), APO 413, The Schornsteinfeger Project, Target Number 1/549 Radar, Reported by Sqn Ldr G G Macfarlane, undated, hereafter cited as NARA/CIOS/RXXVI-24. This extremely interesting document was based on interviews with German engineers and technicians directly involved in the anti-radar coating utilised on German U-boats. It is a

highly technical document.

2   Neither Kühnhold nor Kupfmüller were interrogated by the Allied authorities.

3   PRO/ADM/281-143, Appendix No. 17, Provisional Instructions of Pasting of Snorkels with 'Wesch' Mats, October 1944.

4   This estimate corresponded to what was learned of the manufacturing details at IG Oppau and Weinheim according to MacFarlane, the author of CIOS/RXXVI-24.

5   PRO/HW/18-288, 0829/0850/0856/0916/1/12/44.

6   NARA/CIOS/RXXVI-24.

7   PRO/HW/18-288, 2250/28/11/44.

8   Ibid., 0428/22/4/45.

9   NARA/NTME/TR 517-45 and Report on the Interrogation of Survivors (not in the C.B. 04051 series) (Combined report *U-413*, *U-1209*, *U-877* and *U-1199*) and C.B. 04051 (99) 'U-406, U-386, and U-264' Interrogation of Survivors May 1944. Available online: www.uboatarchive.net. It was noted that: 'In one account, U-1209 received a wood covering in Kiel around the top metre of the snorkel to avoid radar detection. This is likely the only known case and was possibly a trial.'

10   Ibid., 1127/1120/3/4/45.

11   NARA/NTME/TR 517-45.

12   Ibid.

Chapter 4

1   The US Navy showed little interest in the rubber coatings of U-boats after the war. Not until the 1980s when Soviet submarines were identified utilising the technique, as revealed in the conclusion of this book, did the US Navy focus on the subject.

2   Sound Absorption and Sound Absorbers in Water (Dynamic Properties of Rubber and Rubberlike Substances in the Acoustic Frequency Region) by Walter Kuhl, Erwin Meyer, Hermann Oberst, Eugen Skudrzyk, and Konrad Tamm, collected by Erwin Meyer and translated by Charles E Morgan, Jr. (Bureau of Ships: Washington DC, June 1947), p. v; hereafter cited as Meyer, et al.

3   Meyer, et al., p. vii.

4   Ibid.

5   Ibid.

6   Ibid., p. 289.

7   PRO/ADM/213-868 Submarine Acoustic Camouflage. Summary of Meyer and Oberst's accounts of the Laboratory Development and the Full Scale trials of the German project 'Alberich' (Department of Physical Research, Admiralty) June 1948. This document cited a further thirteen studies on the topic of acoustic camouflage, only two of which were located by this author in either the NARA or PRO.

8   NARA US Navy Technical Mission in Europe Report No. 352-45, Rubber Covering of German Submarines Anti-Asdic (German Code Name 'Alberich') dated 20 September 1945 hereafter cited ad NARA/NTME/352-45.

9   J L Lastinger and G A Sabin, 'Underwater Sound Absorbers: A Review of Published Research with an Annotated Bibliography' Methods and Systems Branch, Underwater Sound Reference Division, 5 August 1970. Naval Research Laboratory. p. 7.

10   Rössler, pp. 145–46.

11   Lastinger and Sabin. P. 7.

12   F A Barge, 'NRL Memorandum Report 2146: Underwater Acoustic Absorption Characteristics of Composites of Wood, Rubber, and Steel.' Technical Memorandum File No. TM 78-52 May 1978. The Pennsylvania Status University Applied Research Laboratory. p. 2.

13   PRO/ADM/213-868, p. 17.

14   Ibid., p. 6. 'Later the change in U-boat tactics required camouflage effective at 40 metres …'. The US Navy's report is clear: 'The chemical design of Alberich has been a matter of finding

by experiment a material with high viscus dampening. For the composition chosen the complex molecules of elasticity has a base angle whose tangent is from 0.5 to 0.7 at the depth of 40 metres.' NARA/NTME/352-45, p. 5.

[15]   NARA/NTME/352-45, p. 20.

[16]   PRO/ADM/281-143, p. 42.

[17]   Ibid.

[18]   Rössler, p. 146.

[19]   Ibid.

[20]   O.N.I. 250 – G/Serial 16 'Report on the Interrogation of Survivors from U-67 sunk on 16 July 1943' (www.uboatarchive.net/U-67A/U-67INT.htm) and Kenneth Wynn, *U-Boat Operations of the Second World War, Vol. 1: Career Histories, U1–U510* (Chatham Publishing: UK, 1997), p. 48.

[21]   Rössler, p. 146.

[22]   Ibid., p. 157. The belief at BdU was that a thicker hull would allow the benefit of: shielding of ASDIC by a greater depth; forcing the enemy to expend more depth charges in their attempt to sink a U-boat; and better protection of the crew through reducing the possibility of a pressure hull rupture.

[23]   U-470 KTB and Wynn, p. 312.

[24]   Naval Intelligence Division (NID) S.W.1. 08408/43. C.B. 04051 (90) 'U-470', 'U-533' Interrogation of Survivors, December 1943, available at www.uboatarchive.net; hereafter cited as NID/SW1/08408/43/CB 04051 (90)/Interrogation of Survivors.

[25]   Hessler, Section 246. Hessler states that while a suitable adhesive material had been found by 1943 '… the fitting of boats was costly and lengthy, the plan was dropped, although our scientists could suggest no other method of countering ASDICs.'

[26]   Rössler, p. 146.

[27]   NARA/NTME/352-45, p. 7.

[28]   Rössler, p. 146.

[29]   NID.I/PW/TEC/9/45.

[30]   Royal Navy Archives, Admiralty 1-16169 'Rubber Covering of U-Boat Hulls', p. 2; hereafter cited as RNA/ADM/1-16169.

[31]   Operation *Regenbogen* was the code name for the mass scuttling of the German U-boat fleet at the end of the war. The order to scuttle the fleet was issued at some point at the start of May, then countermanded by Dönitz himself. The total number of U-boats scuttled was about 195, though perhaps as many as half of them were scuttled by their crews before the actual order was given.

[32]   Rössler, p. 146.

[33]   NARA/NTME/352-45, p. 4

[34]   The earliest reference appears to be 7 February 1945. Rössler, p. 263.

[35]   NARA/T-1022/RG242/R3072/U-485 KTB.

[36]   'Subject: Interrogation of Survivors from "U 541", "U 485" and "U 963"' dated 3 June 1945, available at www.U-Boatarchive.net.

[37]   NARA/NTME/352-45, pp. 20–21.

Chapter 5

[1]   See design drawings in Rössler, pp. 180–81, and note the dates associated with each. Note also that the snorkel was introduced at the end of the Walter design process that ran parallel to the DWK designs that had no snorkel. It does not appear that the final design dated with only the date of '1943' included the proposed snorkel.

[2]   Ibid., p. 208.

[3]   Ibid, pp. 208–9.

[4]   The undated design of Type XIII located in NARA/NTRE 312-45 is devoid of a snorkel.

[5]   PRO/ADM 281-143, p. 21.

6   Snorkel Masts: Development, desirable improvements, and requirements for new concepts, Kriegsmarine Document dated 17 April 1945, Author's collection.

7   NARA/NTME/TR 517-45.

8   See Schnorchelmasten, Tiel 4, U-Boot Archiv, Cuxhaven and Snorkel Masts: Development, desirable improvements, and requirements for new concepts, Kriegsmarine Document dated 17 April 1945.

9   Eberhard Rössler, *U-Boottyp XXI* (Bernard & Graefe in der Mönch Verlagsgesellschaft mbH: Bonn, 2013), p. 166.

10 The technical history of the only existing Type XXI, the Wilhelm Bauer in Bremerhaven, notes this fact: 'Although the tests did not start until August 1943 and were viewed with great scepticism, in particular from the front, an *extensible snorkel was incorporated into the existing Type XXI design*.' (Author's emphasis). Technikmuseum U-Boot Wilhelm Bauer (1999), p. 78.

11 NARA/NTME/TR 517-45.

12 Ibid.

13 Ibid.

14 ATM is a technical measure of atmosphere equal to 98.0665 kilograms force per square centimetre.

15 Reports of Snorkel and periscope oscillations on *U-2505* on 10 January 1945 and Snorkel and periscope fluctuations on *U-3517* on 6 January 1945. Author's collection.

16 National Archives Records Administration RG 457 SRMN-048 OP-20-GI Report of U-Boat Disposition and Status, December 1942–2 May 1945, hereafter cited as NARA/RG457/SRMN-048.

17 PRO/ADM/18-288, 1042/23/4/45.

18 National Archives Records Administration, Record Group 38 Ultra Intercepts, U-2511, hereafter cited as NARA/RG38/U-xxxx. The 4 April 1945 Ultra intercept for *U-2511* reads: 'Loudness, type of tone, and duration of these noises were clearly recognised as signs of the beginning of permanent distortion or destruction and were evaluated as such.'

19 NARA/NTME/TR 517-45. Marinebaudirektor Oelfken's patent for a combined periscope/snorkel bracket stated clearly the problem his design solved: 'The submarine's speed when using the snorkel is limited by the vibration of the snorkel mast and also of the periscope which is raised during this operation.' PRO/ADM/281-143, Appendix No. 22, Combined Schnorkel/Periscope Support.

20 NARA/NTME/TR 517-45.

21 National Archives Records Administration, Record Group 457, SRMN 037 U-Boat Intelligence Summaries 1943–May 1945, 16 March 1945, hereafter cited as NARA/RG457/SRMN 037/ xxxx. These were Top Secret intelligence summaries circulated among a select group within the US Navy.

22 BAMA/RM7-192, 17.2.1945.

23 NARA/RG457/SRMN 037/3 April 1945.

24 Peter Cremer, *U-Boat Commander: A Periscope View of the Battle of the Atlantic* (Naval Institute Press: Annapolis, 1985), p. 202.

25 See online article, www.u-boot-archiv-cuxhaven.de/lang1/u_2511.html.

26 Ibid. Bredow remarks how Lawrence Paterson, who is a diver and not a historian, continued to perpetuate the myth of the Type XXI simulated attack in his own books in 2009 that contained no original research. Paterson's works generally do not contain original archival research.

27 NARAT1012/R3900 PG31752NID.

28 Ibid., p. 235.

29 Ibid.

30 Ibid., p. 238.

31 NARA/NTME/TR 517-45.

32 NARA U.S Naval Technical Mission in Europe Technical Report No. 287-45, *Tactical Planning*

for High Speed U-Boats, 11 September 1945, p. 4, hereafter cited as NARA/NTME/287-45.

33 NARA/NTME/TR 403-45. The Influence of High Submerged Speed on German Submarine Hull, 31 August 1945.

Chapter 6

1   Hessler, Section 432.
2   Ibid., Section 439.
3   NARA/RG457/SRMN 037, 3 June 1944.
4   Hessler, Section 434.
5   Ibid., Section 435.
6   National Archives Records Administration Record Group 242/T-1022/Roll 4065/BdU Kriegstagebücher (KTB) War Diary, 1–15 June 1944, hereafter cited as NARA/T1022/R4065/BdU KTB.
7   Ibid., 11 June 1944.
8   Ibid., 15 June 1944.
9   Ibid., 30 September 1944.
10 Ibid., 20 June 1944.
11 Hessler, Section 442.
12 Ibid., Section 442.
13 NARA/RG457/SRMN 030, 1 July 1944.
14 Hessler, Section 439.
15 NARA/T1022/R465/BdU KTB, 16–30 June 1944.
16 NARA/RG457/SRMN 037, 22 June 1944.
17 Ibid., 30 June 1944.
18 Ibid., 1 July 1944.
19 NARA/T1022/R465/BdU KTB, 6 July 1944.
20 Ibid., 13 July 1944.
21 Ibid., 15 July 1944 and NARA/RG457/SRMN 037, 20 July 1944.
22 NARA/RG457/SRMN 037, 13 July 1944.
23 NARA/RG457/SRMN 030, 29 July 1944.
24 NARA/T1022/R3390, U-763 KTB.
25 NARA/RG457/SRMN 030, 29 July 1944.
26 Ibid.
27 Herbert A Werner wrote *Iron Coffins: A personal account of the German U-Boat battles of World War II* (Holt, Rinehardt and Winston: New York, 1969). There are aspects of his published account, however, that do not correspond to his wartime KTB. He also used his book to criticise BdU, probably because he was passed over to command a new Type XXI.
28 NARA/T1022/R465/BdU KTB, 22 July 1944.
29 Ibid., 30 September 1944, 'Final Summary of Channel Operations'.
30 NARA/RG457/SRMN 037, 13 July 1944.
31 Ibid.
32 NARA/RG457/SRMN 030, 15 July 1944.
33 Ibid., 29 July 1944.
34 NARA/SRH/008, p. 133.
35 NARA/RG457/SRMN 037, 20 July and 29 July 1944.
36 Technology transfers occurred on a number of occasions with the Japanese. See Carl Boyd and Akihiko Yoshida, *The Japanese Submarine Force and World War II* (Naval Institute Press: Annapolis, 1995), p. 108 and Henry Sakaida, Gary Nila and Koji Takaki, I-400: Japan's Secret Aircraft-Carrying Strike Submarine, Objective Panama Canal (Crécy, Hong Kong, 2010), p. 94 for an image of the anechoic coating applied to the hull based on the *Alberich* design, p. 98 for the snorkel configuration that had a separate snorkel intake and exhaust mounted on different pipes and p. 99 for the German-manufactured periscopes installed.

37 NARA/T1022/R465/BdU KTB, 7 August 1944.

38 Ibid., 7 August 1944.

39 Hessler, Section 456.

40 NARA/T1022/R465/BdU KTB, 10 October 1944.

41 NARA/RG38/Box 160/U-1229.

42 NARA/T1022/R465/BdU KTB, see entries for 3, 4, 7, 10, and 14 August 1944.

43 NARA/R457/SRMN 037, 4 August 1944.

44 NARA/T1022/R465/BdU KTB, 7 August 1944.

45 NARA/R457/SRMN 037, 9 August 1944. See messages (2058/7) and (1301/8).

46 Ibid., 29 August 1944.

47 Ibid.

48 NARA/T1022/R465/BdU KTB 8 August 1944 and HMSO Section 454.

49 Hessler, Section 454.

50 Captured documents from the surrendered *U-249* show the evolution of tactics and procedures in November and December 1944. Current Order No. 23 available online: www.uboatarchive.net/BDU/BDUOrder23.htm.

51 NARA/R457/SRMN 037, 9 August 1944.

52 Hessler, Section 456.

53 NARA/R457/SRMN 037, 12 September 1944.

54 NARA/T1022/R465/BdU KTB, 30 September 1944, 'Final Summary of Channel Operations'.

55 NARA/RG457/SRMN 030, 1 September 1944.

56 NARA/T1022/R465/BdU, 10 September 1944 and NARA/R457/SRMN 037, 12 September 1944.

57 NARA/R457/SRMN 037, 23 September 1944.

58 NARA/RG457/SRMN 030, 15 September 1944.

59 NARA/RG242/T1022/R3072, U-482 KTB.

60 NARA/R457/SRMN 037, 12 September and 10 October 1944.

61 NARA/T1022/R465/BdU KTB, see entries for 1–15 September 1944.

62 NARA/R457/SRMN 037, 12 September 1944.

63 NARA/RG242/T1022/R3402, U-985 KTB.

64 NARA/R457/SRMN 037, 12 September 1944.

65 NARA/T1022/R465/BdU KTB, Appendix 1 to diary of 26 September 1944.

66 NARA/R457/SRMN 037, 23 September 1944.

67 NARA/RG457/SRMN 030, 30 September 1944.

68 NARA/T1022/R4186 Item 7991. Ultra Intercept (1104/5).

69 NARA/RG457/SRMN 030, 30 September 1944.

70 Ibid. and NARA/R457/SRMN 037 10 and 27 October 1944.

71 NARA/T1022/R4186 Item 7991.

72 Ibid.

73 NARA/R457/SRMN 037, 10 and 27 October 1944.

74 Ibid., 10 October 1944.

75 NARA/RG242/T1022/R3047, U-281 KTB.

76 Public Records Office, GCCS Naval Section: Decrypts, HW 18-293 'Morale, Fighting Spirit, 1945 Jan 31–May 2nd', 1941/19/10/45, hereafter cited as PRO/GCCS Decrypts/HW18-293.

77 PRO/GCCS Decrypts/HW18-293, 1546/22/10/45.

78 Hessler, Section 474.

79 Ibid., Section 473.

80 NARA/T1022/R4066/BdU KTB, 22 October 1944.

81 NARA/R457/SRMN 037, 10 October and 27 October 1944.

82 Ibid., 4 December 1944.

83 Ibid., 1 November 1944.

84 Ibid., 17 December 1944.

85 NARA/T1022/R4066/BdU KTB, 1–15 November.

86 NARA/R457/SRMN 037, 15 November 1944.

87 NARA/T1022/R3900/BdU KTB, 2 December.

88 NARA T1012/R3900/PG31752NID, p. 8.

89 NARA/T1022/R4066/BdU KTB, 1–15 November.

90 Public Records Office, GCCS Naval Section: HW 18-288, Schnorchel, 1944 Oct–1945 April 22, 0948/23/11/44, hereafter cited as PRO/GCCS Schnorchel/HW18-288 and NARA/T1022/R4186 item 7991.

91 Captured documents from *U-249* show the evolution of tactics and procedures in November and December 1944. Appendix I. www.uboatarchive.net/BDUKTB.htm.

92 Captured documents from the surrendered *U-249* show the evolution of tactics and procedures in November and December 1944. Current Order No. 1 available online: www.uboatarchive.net/BDUKTB.htm.

93 Captured documents from the surrendered *U-249* show the evolution of tactics and procedures in November and December 1944. Current Order No. 67 available online: www.uboatarchive.net/BDUKTB.htm.

94 Captured documents from the surrendered *U-249* show the evolution of tactics and procedures in November and December 1944. Current Order No. 80 available online: www.uboatarchive.net/BDUKTB.htm.

95 NARA/R457/SRMN 037, 15 November 1944.

96 NARA/R457/SRMN 030, 15 November 1944.

97 NARA/RG242/T1022/R3072, U-483 KTB.

98 Ibid.

99 NARA/T1022/R465/BdU KTB, 22 November 1944.

100 Overfall is a nautical term that means a turbulent section of a body of water caused by strong passing currents.

101 NARA/R457/SRMN 037, 4 December 1944.

102 Ibid. See also NARA/T1022/R465/BdU KTB, 17 November 1944.

103 PRO/GCCS Schnorchel/HW18-288, 1827/1627/19/11/44.

104 NARA/R457/SRMN 037, 4 December 1944.

105 NARA T1012/R3900/PG31752NID, p. 11.

106 NARA/RG242/T1022/R3764, U-1003 KTB.

107 NARA/RG457/SRMN 030, 15 December 1944.

108 NARA/R457/SRMN 037, 17 December 1944 and PRO HW 18-288 1030/15/12/44.

109 Captured documents from the surrendered *U-249* show the evolution of tactics and procedures in November and December 1944. Current Order No. 4 available online: www.uboatarchive.net/BDUKTB.htm. See also NARA/R457/SRMN 037, 17 December 1944.

110 Ibid.

111 NARA/RG38/Box 159/U-1232.

112 NARA/SRH/008, p. 165.

113 NARA/RG242/T1022/R3763, U-978 KTB.

114 NARA/T1022/R1725/OKM-1.SKL, 7 January 1945.

115 NARA/R457/SRMN 037, 17 December 1944.

116 NARA/T1022/R3900/OKM-1.SKL, 22 December 1944.

117 Ibid., 30 December 1944.

118 NARA/T1022/R465/BdU KTB, 30 December 1944 and PRO/GCCS//HW18-288 2120/30/12/44 and NARA/T1022/R4186 Item 7991.

119 NARA/T1022/R4066/BdU KTB, 14 January 1945 'Appendix 3 to War Diary 1.1.1945'.

120 Hessler, Section 471 and Dönitz, p. 424.

121 NARA/RG457/SRMN 030, 1 January 1945.

122 BAMA/RM7-192, 17.2.1945.

123 BAMA RM 7-88-92. FC. pp. 329, 420, 447, 455.

[124] NARA/RG457/SRMN 051A/OP-20-GI Memoranda to COMINCH F-21 on German U-Boat Activities October 1943–May1945, PPB 88/8 Jan.

[125] NARA/R457/SRMN 037, 3 February 1945.

[126] NARA/RG457/SRMN-051A/OP-20-GI Memoranda to COMINCH F-21 on German U-Boat Activities October 1943–May 1945, 16 January 1945.

[127] NARA/R457/SRMN 037, 3 January 1945.

[128] NARA/T1022/R1725/OKM-1.SKL, 3 January 1945.

[129] NARA/T1022/R3900/PG31752NID, p. 15.

[130] NARA/SRH/008, p. 164.

[131] NARA/R457/SRMN 037, 16 March 1945.

[132] U-668 Bootbläter, U-Boot-Archiv, Cuxhaven.

[133] NARA/R457/SRMN 037, 3 February 1945.

[134] NARA/T1022/R3900/OKM-1.SKL, 10 January 1945.

[135] NARA/T1022/R4186 7991.

[136] NARA/R457/SRMN 037, 16 January 1945.

[137] Ibid., 25 January 1945.

[138] Ibid., 3 January 1945.

[139] Ibid., 17 January 1945.

[140] Ibid., 3 February 1945.

[141] Ibid.

[142] NARA/T1022/R4186 Item 7991.

[143] NARA/R457/SRMN 037, 3 February 1945.

[144] NARA/SRH/008, p. 164.

[145] PRO/GCCS Decrypts/HW 18-293, 0232/0339/0400/0500/19/2/45 and NARA/T1022/R4186 Item 7991.

[146] NARA/R457/SRMN 037, 16 March 1945.

[147] Ibid.

[148] NARA/T1022/R4186 Item 7991.

Chapter 7

[1] *Die Entstehungsgeschichte vom Deutschen Schnorchel.*

[2] Dr Guenther Malorny, 'Carbon Monoxide on U-Boats' (1994).

[3] Admittedly, no document states this explicitly. This determination of the exhaust trunking was based on Malorny's comments, and a careful study of the exhaust trunking configuration.

[4] Malorny.

[5] Ibid., and Dr Hellmut Uffenorde 'Otological Experience with Snorkel-Equipped U-Boats' (?).

[6] Malorny.

[7] Uffenorde.

[8] Ibid.

[9] Ibid.

[10] PRO/GCCS/HW18-288 1542/10/4/45.

[11] NARA/T1022/R4065/BdU KTB, 5 July 1944 and NARA/RG242/T1022/R3402, U-984 KTB.

[12] Hessler, Section 444.

[13] Ibid.

[14] Ibid.

[15] Ibid., Section 445.

[16] Ibid., Section 457.

[17] NARA/T1022/R4066/BdU KTB, 19 September 1944.

[18] The fate of *U-869* is discussed in detail in Chapter 11.

[19] Hessler, Section 445.

[20] NARA/T1022/R4186 Item 7991.

[21] NARA/RG457/SRMN 037, 15 November 1944.

22 PRO/GCCS/HW18-288, Ultra/SIP/SJA/1039 RP/73 sent from Naval Attaché Berlin to Tokyo, 6 October 1944 at 1500.

Chapter 8

1 NID 04045/44. Intelligence Division, Admiralty, S.W.I. *Interrogation of U-Boat Survivors, Cumulative Edition, June 1944.* Available online at www.uboatarchive.net/Cumulative Edition.htm.

2 RG38/UD-09 22/Tambach/Box T94.

3 NARA/RG457 SRMN 051A U-Boat Activity 43-45 OP-20-GI Memoranda to COMINCH F-21 on German U-Boats, Memorandum for Captain Wenger, 'Review of Current Situation U-Boats, January 1945' 16 January 1945.

4 Ladislas Farago, *The Tenth Fleet, The Story of the Submarine and Survival* (Ivan Obolensky, Inc.: New York, 1962), p. 282.

5 Ibid., p. 283.

6 Ibid., p. 284.

7 PRO/AIR 15-058 'Operational Experience against U-Boats Fitted with Schnorchel', ORS/OC Report No. 325.

8 NARA/RG457/SRMN 037, 5 March 1945.

9 'Report on Development in A/S Tactics in the United Kingdom, June 1944', AWM 54, 81/4/81, p. 12 as cited in Malcolm Llewellyn-Jones, *The Royal Navy on the Threshold of Modern Anti-Submarine Warfare, 1944–1949*, PHD Dissertation (Department of War Studies, King's College London: 2004) p. 88. See Richard A Holler's 'The evolution of the Sonobuoy from World War II to the Cold War' published in the *US Journal of Underwater Acoustics*, January 2014, for a description of how the tactic was employed.

10 Captain C D Howard-Johnston, DAUD, and Captain N A Prichard, DASW, Ref. D. 559 (Draft), 5 August 1945, ADM 1/17653 as cited in Llewellyn-Jones, p. 88.

11 PRO/AIR 20-1504, 'Schnorchel and ASV MKXVII', meeting minutes.

12 Ibid.

13 PRO/GCCS Schnorchel/HW18-288, 1450/1600/3/3/45.

14 Ibid., 1940/10/3/45 and 2306/16/3/45.

15 Hessler, Sections 91 and 119.

16 CB 04050/44 entitled 'Inshore Operations by U-boats' dated 30 March 1944, NAC, RG24, 83-84/167, Vol.2616, File 16121-5, Vol.1 as cited in Douglas M McLean, 'Confronting Technological and Tactical Change: Allied Anti-Submarine Warfare in the Last Year of the Battle of the Atlantic', published in Canadian Military History, Vol. 7, No. 3, Summer 1998, p. 25.

17 Directorate of History and Heritage, Canadian Department of National Defence (DHH) ADM 223/20, November 1944, as cited in McLean, p. 36.

18 A Easton, *50 North* (Toronto: The Ryerson Press, 1963), pp. 251–53.

19 Ibid., pp. 254–56.

20 NARA/T1012/R4065, BdU KTB, 10 June 1944.

21 NARA/T1012/R3402, U-984 KTB.

22 Ibid.

23 Easton, p. 256.

24 Ibid., p. 258.

25 Ibid., pp. 258–59.

26 'Note on the Deployment of A/S Forces Against U-boats Operating in British Inshore Waters' by Professor E J Williams, Assistant Director of Naval Operational Research in the Admiralty, 26 December 1944, NAC RG 24, 11752, MS 369-2 as cited in Mclean, p. 30.

27 'Notes on Two U-boat Cruises in the English Channel', DDIC, DAUD, DNOR, OIC/SI/1021, 24 July 1944, ADM 223/261 as cited in Llewellyn-Jones, p. 88.

28 'U-boat Situation, Week Ending 28 August 1944', 1 Captain Rodger Winn, RNVR, OIC/SI.

1062, n. d., ADM 223/172, as cited in Llewellyn-Jones, p. 89.

29 Message from Commander-in-Chief, Western Approaches to General Distribution, 131845Z September 1945. This message amended slightly a previous one sent out on 9 September, placing more emphasis on the likelihood that a *U-boat* would bottom. NAC RG 24, 83-84/167, Vol. 2616, File 16121-5 Vol. 2, as cited in McLean, p. 28.

30 Admiralty Message C A/S O Number 6, to wide distribution 271816Z October 1944, NAC RG 24, 83-84/167, Vol. 2616, File 16121-5 Vol. 2. 'Curly' torpedoes was the generic British term applied to German-pattern running torpedoes. These were standard torpedoes equipped with either 'Lut' or 'Fat' devices that caused them to begin alternately turning first one direction and then another so as to repeatedly comb the intended area where a convoy was expected to pass. 'Gnat' was the British term for the German Type V acoustic homing torpedo. Details of Admiralty knowledge of German torpedoes can be found in the Admiralty Monthly Anti-Submarine Report for February 1945. DHH Library, D780M66, 1945, as cited in Mclean, p. 29.

31 Admiralty Message to AIG #2 359AZ, Repeated to Commander 12th Fleet, 26 August 1944, Folder CNA 7-6-1, Vol. 11022, RG 24, NAC as cited in Llewellyn-Jones, p. 95.

32 NARA/RG457/SRMN 037, 17 January 1945.

33 'Inshore Campaign against U-Boat Operations, 1945, Survey of A/U Operations …', ADM 1/17653, as cited in Appendix 4 in Llewellyn-Jones, pp. 268–69.

34 DNOR Report 'Survey of A/ U Operations in U.K. Coastal waters July 1944–May 1945' dated 13 July 1945, DHH ADM 205/44 as cited in McClean.

35 'Survey of A/U Operations in UK Coastal Waters, July 1944–May 1945.' [W H McCrea], DNOR, 13 July 1945', ADM 1/17653, p. 7 as cited in Llewellyn-Jones, p. 101.

36 'Interrogation of Survivors From "U.541", "U.485" and "U.963"', 3 June 1945, from Staff Officer (Intelligence), Gibraltar, available online at www.uboatarchive.net/U-485-541-963INT.htm.

37 Royal Navy Archives, Gosport/ADM 1-16169 Alberich, 'Rubber Covering of U-Boat Hulls, Submarine Protection Against Underwater Explosion, 23 November 1944.

38 PRO/ADM 281-143, p. 109.

Chapter 9

1 Calculated based on the U-boat deployment statistics provided by Hickam in his appendix. See Homer H Hickam, *Torpedo Junction. U-Boat War off America's East Coast* (Naval Institute Press: Annapolis, 1989), pp. 296–305.

2 I have carefully evaluated every surviving U-boat KTB, interrogation report and Ultra intercept for each snorkel boat that deployed to the North American coast. With the understanding that not every U-boat's documents survived the war, I have identified not a single snorkel-equipped U-boat that sailed to the North Atlantic from Norway north of Iceland. Every one evaluated for this chapter transited to the North Atlantic south over the 'Rosengarten'.

3 NARA/RG242/T1022/R4066/BdU KTB, 30 December 1944.

4 NARA/R457/SRMN 037, 22 June 1944.

5 NARA/RG242/T1022/R3034-35, U-107 KTB.

6 NARA/RG457/SRMN 037, 29 July 1944.

7 NARA/Report of anti-submarine action of USS *FROST* (DE-144), 4 July 1944.

8 Ibid.

9 NARA/RG457/SRMN 037, 29 July 1944.

10 No U-boat KTB, crewmember account or experience report reviewed in the course of research for this book has revealed any discomfort caused by continuous submerged operations in warm climates.

11 NARA/RG457/SRMN 037, 19 August 1944.

12 Ibid., 23 September 1944.

13 Ibid., 27 October 1944.

14 NARA/SRH/008, p. 169.

15   NARA/RG457/SRMN 030, 15 February 1945.
16   Ibid.
17   PRO/GCCS Decrypts/HW18-293, 2115/2129/2142/2210/31/1/45.
18   NARA/T1012/R4065, BdU KTB, 20 July 1944.
19   NARA/RG242/T1022/R3463, U-802 KTB.
20   NARA/RG457/SRMN 037, 9 August 1944.
21   NARA/RG242/T1022/R3463, U-802 KTB.
22   Ibid.
23   Ibid.
24   NARA/RG38/Box 159/U-1229.
25   Ibid.
26   NARA/RG457/SRMN 037, 15 November 1944.
27   NARA/RG242/T1012/R3900/PG31752NID.
28   NARA/RG242/T1022/R4066/BdU KTB, 12 September 1944.
29   NARA/RG38/Box 159/U-1223.
30   Ibid.
31   Ibid.
32   Ibid.
33   Ibid.
34   Ibid., NARA/RG242/T1022/R4066/BdU KTB, 26 November 1944 and 24 December 1944 and NARA/RG38/Box 159/U-1223.
35   NARA/RG242/T1022/R4066/BdU KTB, 7 October 1944.
36   NARA/RG457/SRMN 037, 15 November 1944.
37   NARA/RG457/SRMN 037, 27 October 1944.
38   Ibid.
39   NARA/RG242/T1022/R3900, OKM 1.SKL, 2 December 1944.
40   NARA/RG457/SRMN 037, 15 November 1944.
41   NARA/RG242/T1022/R3764, U-1228 KTB.
42   NARA/RG242/T1022/R4066/BdU KTB, 20 September 1944, and ADM199-1786.
43   NARA/RG457/SRMN 037, 15 November 1945.
44   NARA/RG242/T1022/R3764, U-1228 KTB.
45   Ibid.
46   NARA/RG457/SRMN 037, 17 December 1944.
47   NARA/RG38/Ultra/Box 159/U-1231.
48   NARA/RG457/SRMN 037, 17 December 1944.
49   Circular shots due to a torpedo malfunction were rare late in the war. I have identified only two reported instances in the last twelve months of the war when such an event occurred, though more cannot be ruled out. Even less likely was a U-boat being hit by one during this time frame. This is because, based on new tactical procedures, U-boats conducted immediate evasive manoeuvres after firing, changing depth and direction and making a self-detonation by a circular-run torpedo very unlikely.
50   NARA/RG457/SRMN 037, 31 December 1944.
51   NARA/RG38/Ultra/Box 159/U-1232.
52   Ibid.
53   NARA/RG242/T1012/R3900/PG31752NID.
54   NARA/RG38/Ultra/Box 159/U-1232.
55   Ibid.
56   NARA/RG457/SRMN 037, 25 January 1945.
57   Ibid.
58   NARA/SRH/008, p. 169.
59   Ibid.
60   NARA/RG457/SRMN 037, 25 January 1945.

61 NARA/RG457/SRMN 037, 5 March 1945.
62 T1022/RG242/R4186 Item 7991, 21 March 1945.
63 Ibid.
64 Ibid.
65 NARA/RG242/T1022/R3900, OKM 1.SKL, 9 March 1945.
66 NARA/RG38/Ultra/Box 152, U-866.
67 *U-866* was 872 nautical miles distance from the sinking point on 5 March, and *U-857* was 1,200 nautical miles away on 6 March. *U-866* was an average of 67 nautical miles per day away from these co-ordinates, while *U-857* was 85 nautical miles per day distant. Either U-boat could have been in position when comparing the average distance completed by *U-190* while employing the snorkel (see *U-190*'s interrogation report).
68 NARA/RG38, Office of Naval Intelligence, Special Activities Branch, OP-16-Z, Interrogations and Documents from U-Boats and Raiders 1943–1945, Box 9, U-190. Hereafter cited as NARA/RG38/ONI Interrogation Reports.
69 NARA/RG38/ONI Interrogation Reports/Box 9, U-190.
70 Ibid.
71 NARA/RG457/SRMN 037, 20 April 1945.
72 Ibid., 29 July 1944. *U-539* sank 14,413 (GRT) during this patrol while under the command of Kapitänleutnant Hans-Jürgen Lauterbach-Emden.
73 NARA/RG457/SRMN 037, 9 August 1944.
74 Ibid., 29 August 1944.
75 NARA/RG242/T1022/R3068, U-518 KTB.
76 Ibid.
77 NARA/RG242/T1022/R4066/BDU KTB, 12 January.
78 NARA/RG457/SRMN 037, 3 February 1945.
79 NARA/RG38/Ultra/Box 159/U-1233.
80 NARA/RG242/T1022/R4066/BdU KTB, 12 January 1945.
81 NARA/RG457/SRMN 037, 3 February 1945.
82 NARA/RG38/Ultra/Box 159/U-1233.
83 NARA/RG242/T1022/R3900/OKM-1.SKL, 4 March 1945.
84 NARA/RG38/Ultra/Box 159/U-1233.
85 NARA/RG38/Ultra/Box 151/U-857.
86 The 'America' radio circuit consisted of three separate circuits as follows: America 1, A&B for the eastern North Atlantic; America 2, C&D for the western Atlantic north of a line that ran from Key West to the Azores; and America 3, E&F for the mid-Atlantic, Caribbean, and South American coastal areas. These circuits were used to optimise communication frequencies in a specific area.
87 NARA/RG38/Ultra/Box 151/U-857.
88 NARA/RG242/T1022/R3900/OKM-1.SKL, 9 March 1945.
89 NARA/RG38/Ultra/Box 151/U-857.
90 NARA/RG38/Ultra/Box 153/U-879.
91 Ibid.
92 Ibid.
93 Ibid.
94 Ibid.
95 Ibid.
96 Ibid.
97 Ibid.
98 Ibid.
99 Ibid.
100 Ibid.
101 Ibid.

102 Ibid. On 15 March *U-907* completed a seventy-one-day patrol off of Reykjavik and weather reporting and weather duties in the north Atlantic.

103 Ibid.

104 Ibid.

105 NARA/RG38/Ultra/Box 153/U-879.

106 NARA/RG242/T1022/R3900/OKM-1.SKL, 18 March 1945.

107 NARA/RG457/SRMN 037, 20 April 1945.

108 Puelo, p. 126. In answering the US Navy Court of Inquiry question about the surfaced 'submarine' he saw after the sinking of USS *Eagle 56*, Seaman 1st Class Daniel E Jaronik stated: 'I looked at it for a couple of seconds ... It was all black and I could see red and yellow markings on it.' *U-853*'s conning tower was adorned with a red and yellow trotting horse and shield.

109 Ensign D M Tollaksen, USN 'Last Chapter for U-853' published in US Naval Institute Proceedings (December 1960), p. 89.

110 NARA/RG38/Ultra/Box 129/U-480.

111 NARA/RG38/Ultra/Box 133/U-530.

112 NARA/RG38/ONI Interrogation Reports/Box 23, U-530.

113 NARA/RG457/SRMN 037, 19 May 1945.

114 The website www.Uboatarchive.net contains two reports produced by OP-16-Z and the Office of The Naval Inspector General regarding looting and other abuses perpetrated by some members of US Navy boarding parties and workers at the Portsmouth Naval Yard in New Hampshire where a number of surrendered German U-boats were berthed. German documents and other items of intelligence value were removed by ratings without permission. Personal effects of German sailors were also removed and the interrogations of some prisoners exceeded normal protocols. All these actions were conducted against standing orders. The incidents were investigated thoroughly and disciplinary action taken.

115 NARA/RG38/ONI Interrogation Reports/Box 37, U-889.

116 Ibid.

117 Ibid.

118 Ibid.

119 Ibid.

120 Ibid.

121 On 12 September 1942 *U-156* torpedoed the *Laconia*, a large British liner carrying refugees and Italian prisoners of war in the South Atlantic, bound for England. The U-boat commander was surprised by the Italian voices, and Italy being an allied nation, decided to attempt to assist the struggling passengers. Kapitänleutnant Werner Hartenstein, the commander of *U-156*, radioed in the clear that he was attempting to rescue struggling passengers and requested a cease fire. *U-156* rescued some 400 survivors, about half onboard and half in life boats that were being towed. Three days later two other German and one Italian submarines arrived to assist in the rescue effort. However, the Allies did not oblige the request for a cease fire. On 16 September an American B-24 Liberator operating from Ascension Island flew over the scene and identified the life rafts marked with a red cross under tow. The U-boats cut the tow lines and submerged, taking the rescued passengers with them onboard below the surface. This incident resulted in Dönitz issuing the Laconia Order that read:

1. Every attempt to save survivors of sunken ships, also the fishing up of swimming men and putting them onboard lifeboats, the set-up right of overturned lifeboats, the handing over of food and water have to be discontinued. These rescues contradict the primitive demands of warfare esp. the destruction of enemy ships and their crews.
2. The orders concerning the bringing in of skippers and chief engineers stay in effect.
3. Survivors are only to be rescued if their statements are important for the U-boat.
4. Stay hard. Don't forget that the enemy didn't take any women and children into regard when bombing German towns.

The Laconia Order was interpreted by the Allies as meaning that U-boats were ordered to kill survivors. This was not the case, although it clearly could be interpreted that way. The intent was to dissuade U-boat commanders from putting their own craft at risk during wartime. Moehle was sentenced to five years' imprisonment after the war for proactively passing on this order.

[122] NARA/RG38/ONI Interrogation Reports/Box 37, U-889.

[123] NARA/RG38/Ultra/Box 153/U-881.

[124] NARA/RG38/ONI Interrogation Reports/Box 37, U-889.

[125] Ibid.

[126] Ibid.

[127] Ibid.

[128] Ibid.

[129] Ibid.

[130] See NARA COMSUBLANT/Box 14-5, Diver's Examination of U-Boat. 9 May 1945, and Captain Bill Palmer, *The Last Battle of the Atlantic: The Sinking of the U-853* (Thunderfish Video and Publications: China, 2012), p. 66.

[131] PRO/GCCS Decrypts/HW 18-401, 1051/19/3/45.

[132] PRO/GCCS Decrypts/HW 18-293, 0314/8/4/45.

[133] NARA/RG38/Ultra/Box 153/U-881.

[134] NARA/RG38/Ultra/Box 153/U-881 and PRO/GCCS Decrypts/HW 18-401, 0219/23/4/45.

[135] Peter Fussell, 'The Surrender of U-541', U-541 *Bootblätter*, U-Boot Archive, Cuxhaven.

[136] NARA/RG38/Ultra/Box 159/U-1228.

[137] Ibid.

[138] NARA/RG38/Ultra/Box 159/U-1231, 1157/25/Y.

[139] http://uboatarchive.net/Admiralty/AdmiraltyMessage1945-APR-Frame.htm. *U-802*'s specific orders have not been identified in primary documents. The 11th U-Flotilla sent a wireless transmission on 4 May intercepted by Ultra that read: 'The following left Bergen at 2330B/3/5: U-802 – Schmoeckel for 4th War Cruise, and U-1005 – Lauth for 2nd cruise against the enemy.' U-802 reported her position at the time of surrender heading due west towards the Faroe Islands passage. NARA/RG38/Ultra/Box 149/U-802.

[140] Phillip K Lundeberg, 'Operation Teardrop Revisited', *To Die Gallantly*, p. 214.

[141] Ibid., p. 215.

[142] NARA/RG457/SRMN 037, 7 January 1945.

[143] NARA/RG457/SRMN 037, 17 January 1945.

[144] NARA/RG38/ONI Interrogation Reports/Box 159, U-1230.

[145] Ibid.

[146] Ibid.

[147] NARA/RG457/SRMN 037, 16 February 1945.

[148] Lundeberg, p. 212.

[149] Norman Polmar and K J Moore, *Cold War Submarines: The Design and Construction of US and Soviet Submarines* (Potomac Books Inc.: Washington DC, 2004), p. 85 and 'Raketen-Unterwasserschiessversuche von U-511' from Schiffsmodel-Illustrierte 'Marine' Nr. 1, (October, 1979).

[150] Ibid.

[151] Ibid., p. 103.

[152] Ibid., p. 104.

[153] Lundeberg, p. 212.

[154] NARA/RG457/SRMN 037, 20 April 1945.

[155] Ibid.

[156] Ibid.

[157] Lundeberg, p. 219.

[158] Ultra intercepts for *Seewolf* are derived from NARA/RG38/Ultra/Box 131/U-518, Box 134/ U-146, Box 150/U-805, Box 151/U-858, Box 153/U-880, U-881, and Box 160/U-1235.

159 Ibid.
160 Ibid.
161 Ibid.
162 Ibid.
163 Ibid.
164 Ibid.
165 Lundeberg, p. 216.
166 Ultra intercepts for *Seewolf* are derived from NARA/RG38/Ultra/Box 131/U-518, Box 134/ U-146, Box 150/U-805, Box 151/U-858, Box 153/U-880, U-881, and Box 160/U-1235.
167 Lundeberg, p. 218 and Farago, pp. 16–19.
168 Farago, pp. 16–17.
169 NARA/Croatan TG 22.5. Report of Operations – Task Group 22.5, 24 March–14 May 1945. Dated 14 May 1945.
170 Ibid.
171 Ibid.
172 Ibid.
173 NARA/RG457/SRMN 037, 20 April 1945.
174 Ultra intercepts for *Seewolf* are derived from NARA/RG38/Ultra/Box 131/U-518, Box 134/ U-146, Box 150/U-805, Box 151/U-858, Box 153/U-880, U-881, and Box 160/U-1235.
175 Lundeberg, p. 222.
176 NARA/RG457/SRMN 037, 19 May 1945.
177 The US Tenth Fleet sent divers down to examine *U-853* who reported seeing 'tracks' running fore and aft that could be used for 'robot bombs', but these were torpedo-loading rails for 'launch rails'. The fact that the divers were making these observations is a strong indication they were asked to look for launch mechanisms on *U-853*. NARA COMSUBLANT/Box 14-5, Diver's Examination of U-boat. 9 May 1945.
178 Farago, pp. 22–23.

Chapter 10

1 Robert Kurson, *Shadow Divers* (Random House: New York, 2004), p. 324.
2 See Richie Koehler's online history of *U-869*: www.u869.com/en/history)
3 NARA/RG38/Box 152/U-869.
4 SKL 15-31 December PG30361.
5 NARA/T1022/R4066/BdU KTB, 29 December 1944.
6 Ibid. *U-1009* was ordered to the North Channel, where it conducted several unsuccessful attacks, then it proceeded to the North Atlantic on BdU orders to act as a weather boat. It returned to Trondheim after a sixty-day patrol.
7 NARA/T1022/R4066/BdU KTB, 3 January 1945.
8 NARA/R457/SRMN 037, 3 January 1945.
9 NARA/RG38/Box 152/U-869.
10 NARA/T1022/R4066/BdU KTB, 6 January 1945.
11 NARA/RG38/Box 152/U-869.
12 NARA/T1022/R4066/BdU KTB, 7 January 1945.
13 NARA/RG38/Box 152/U-869.
14 NARA/RG38/Box 152/U-869.
15 NARA/RG38/ONI Interrogation Reports/Box 9, U-190.
16 NARA/RG38/Box 152/U-869.
17 NARA/T1022/R4066/BdU KTB, 8 January 1945.
18 NARA/T1022/R1725/OKM-1.SKL, 11 January 1945.
19 NARA/R457/SRMN 037, 17 January 1945.
20 NARA/RG38/Box 152/U-869.
21 NARA/T1022/R3900/OKM-1.SKL, 18 February 1945.

22   NARA/R457/SRMN 037, 25 January 1945.
23   NARA/R457/SRMN 037, 3 February 1945.
24   NARA/R457/SRMN 037, 16 February 1945.
25   NARA/T1022/R3900/OKM-1.SKL, 17 February 1945.
26   NARA/T1022/R3900/OKM-1.SKL, 16 March 1945.
27   NARA/RG38/Box 152/U-869.
28   NARA/R457/SRMN 037, 5 March 1945.
29   NARA/RG457/SRMN 040/Assessment of U-Boat Fleet at End of World War II, June–October
     1945.
30   *Wreck Diving Magazine*, Issue 19 (2009) 'The Fate of U-869 Reexamined, Part III: The Loss of
     the German Submarine', by John Chatterton, Richie Kohler, and John Yurga, p. 35.
31   Ibid.
32   See the US Coast Guards official account: www.uscg.mil/history/WEBCUTTERS/
     U869_Crow_Koiner.asp.
33   Ibid.
34   Ensign D M Tollaksen, USN 'Last Chapter for U-853' published in U.S Naval Institute
     Proceedings (December 1960), pp. 85–87. *U-853* was the first U-boat that the US Navy
     encountered that attempted to use the tactic of 'bottoming' to avoid detection.
35   Interview with John Chatterton, November 2016.
36   Ibid.
37   McCartney, p. 168.

Conclusion

1   Lothar-Günther Buchheim, *The U-Boar War* (Alfred A Knopf Inc.: New York, 1978), section
     'Snorkels instead of miracles.'
2   Grand Admiral Dönitz, *Memoirs: Ten Years and Twenty Days*, translated by R H Stevens
     (Naval Institute Press: Annapolis, 1990), pp. 406–429.
3   Ed Offley, *Turning the Tide: How a Small Band of Allied Sailors Defeated the U-Boats and Won
     the Battle of the Atlantic* (Basic Books: New York, 2011), p. 368.
4   Ibid., p. 381.
5   Clay Blair, *Hitler's U-Boat War: The Hunters, 1939–1942* (Modern Library: New York, 1996),
     pp. x–xi. Blair's broad-brush history of the Battle of the Atlantic are replete with factual errors
     when compared against primary documents. His personal desire to diminish the U-boat's
     technical and operational role in submarine development dulled his historical insight.
6   Clay Blair, *The Hunted, 1942–1945* (Modern Library: New York, 1998), p. 572.
7   Blair, *Hitler's U-Boat War*, p. xi.
8   Despite some of its inherent snorkel problems, the US Navy concluded that the Type XXI
     presented 'a weapon of more advanced design, for the medium it works in, than any hereforth
     developed'. US Navy Board of Inspection Survey of ex-U2513, U-873, and U-858, 16 April
     1946. Author's archive.
9   V E Tarrant, *The Last Year of the Kriegsmarine, May 1944–May 1945* (Naval Institute Press:
     Annapolis, 1994), p. 30.
10   Roger Sarty, 'The Limits of Ultra: The Schnorchel U-Boat Offensive Against North America,
     November 1944–January 1945', published in *Intelligence and National Security*, Vol. 12. No. 2
     (Frank Cass: London, 1997), p. 62.
11   TNA/ADM/1/16396, Director of Anti-Submarine Division, 29 November 1944.
12   Peter Hennessy and James Jinks, *The Silent Deep: The Royal Navy Submarine Service since 1945*
     (Great Britain: Penguin Books, 2016) p. 47.
13   PRO/ADM/1-17667.
14   NARA/RG457/SRMN-048, OP-20-GI Report of U-Boat Disposition and Status, December
     1942–2 May 1945.
15   Ibid.

16 NARA NTME/TR 517-45.

17 Norman Friedman, *US Submarines Since 1945: An Illustrated Design History* (Annapolis: Naval Institute Press, 1994), p. 11.

18 NAVPERS 1616-B, *The Submarine* (ComSubLant, Standards and Curriculum Division, Training, Bureau of Naval Personnel: 1961), p. 183. Reprint edition. (PerriscioeFilm.com: 2008)

19 Sherry Sontag and Christopher Drew with Annette Lawrence Drew, *Blind Man's Bluff: The Untold Story of American Submarine Espionage* (Public Affairs: New York, 1998), pp. 6–12.

20 Norman Polmar and K J Moore, *Cold War Submarines: The Design and Construction of US and Soviet Submarines* (Potomac Books Inc.: Washington, DC, 2004), p. 57.

21 Albert G Mumma was later promoted to rear admiral in 1954 and assumed command of the Bureau of Ships where he oversaw the US Navy's nuclear submarine development and championed the adoption of the teardrop hull design as proposed by Walter.

22 Eberhard Rössler, *Die schnellen Unterseeboote von Hellmuth Walter* (Bernard & Graefe in der Mönch Verlagsgesellschaft mbH: Bonn, 2010), p. 125.

23 Hennessy and Jinks, pp. 47–53.

24 Ibid., p. 51.

25 Norman Polmar and Jurrien Noot, *Submarines of the Russian and Soviet Navies, 1718–1990* (Naval Institute Press: Annapolis, 1991), p. 137.

26 Ibid., p. 138.

27 Polmar and Moore, p. 24 and Friedman, p. 63.

28 Polmar and Moore, p. 24.

29 Ibid., pp. 44–45.

30 Ibid., p. 75.

31 Ibid.

32 Polmar and Noot, p. 215.

33 Hennessy and Jinks, p. 58.

34 Robert Moore, *A Time to Die: The Untold Story of the Kursk Tragedy* (Crown Publishers: New York, 2002), pp. 189–90.

35 William Cole, 'Navy subs still show issue with Stealth coating', *Honolulu Star-Advertiser*, 5 March 2017.

36 Doug Thomas, 'Submarine Developments: Air-Independent Propulsion' Canadian Naval Review, Vol 3, Number 4 (Winter 2008), pp. 35–36.

Index